STO

3·14·77

A COMPANION TO THE OPERA

A COMPANION TO THE OPERA

by **ROBIN MAY**, *pseud.*

Robert Stephen May

HIPPOCRENE
BOOKS, INC.

HIPPOCRENE BOOKS, INC.
NEW YORK, N.Y.

First published 1977

To
ANTHONY BATE
who managed to make me
a perfect Wagnerite

and
in memory of
JOAN
who grew to love Verdi and Puccini
and never complained that
I went to everything else
as well

HIPPOCRENE BOOKS, INC.
171 Madison Avenue
New York, N.Y. 10016

Library of Congress Catalog Card Number 76–52790

ISBN 3 88254 439 X

Printed in Great Britain

Contents

Illustrations

Programme Notes and Acknowledgements

The shape of this book roughly follows the guidelines laid down in Roy Pickard's *A Companion to the Movies*. It is likely to cause ferocious arguments, but, it may be hoped, enjoyable ones. Most chapters have an explanatory introduction, but a word about the first one, *Composers: Some Famous Operas*, may be in order. The featured operas are representative of the development of the art and include several that for historical reasons could not be left out, e.g. *Der Freischütz*. Of the five composers who dominate the repertoire—Mozart, Verdi, Wagner, Strauss and Puccini—only the last is confined to a single entry, because he can be represented by one opera: the others cannot. To prevent reprisals, it should be stated that I write as a hardline Puccinian.

I have usually given the original title of a work, except when faced with Slavonic operas. It is not elitist to do this, especially in a reference book, though, like my friends, I do not refer to *Barbiere* or *Holländer* in private conversation. Like other compilers, I do not pretend to be totally consistent.

The time span of the book is 1597 to 1975, though there are a few late insertions for 1976, a year when inflation continues to threaten the very existence of opera, which, ironically, is growing steadily more popular across the world. To pinpoint the date of these notes, they are being written on March 14, 1976, the day after the exchange visits between La Scala and Covent Garden have ended. Even the Royal Opera House's warmest admirers had been worried about the choice of repertoire for Milan, to their shame; for Colin Davis and his colleagues have enjoyed triumphs in what had seemed the unlikely trio of *Benvenuto Cellini*, *Peter Grimes* and *La Clemenza di Tito*. As for La Scala, if *Simon Boccanegra* was the pinnacle of a hugely successful, rapturously welcomed, stay in London, the most emotional moment of all came after the end of the last *La Cenerentola* when the great Chorus sang that most moving, evocative and stirring of unofficial national anthems, Verdi's 'Va, pensiero' from *Nabucco*. For once, the old theatrical tag, 'not a dry eye in the house', was literally true.

* * * * *

A book like this could never be written without constant use of the back numbers of *Opera* magazine, admirably edited for many years by Harold Rosenthal, who succeeded its founder, Lord Harewood. The former's and John Warrack's *The Concise Oxford Dictionary of Opera* is an invaluable *A* to *Z* on the subject, while Lord Harewood's edition of *Kobbé's Complete Opera Guide* is also a compiler's friend. Other books that have been useful are to be found listed in the bibliography.

I am grateful to William Mann and Philip Hope-Wallace for friendly advice, based on their deep knowledge of opera and their unending love of it; also for information sent to me by the distinguished critic Giorgio Gualerzi via my dear Italian-based friend, Liz Bowker, news of whose death in her twenties reached me during the writing of this book. I would also like to thank other friends for stimulating operatic conversations and arguments down the years, especially Alicia Gains, Frank Seton, Jane Graining, Mary Jobson, Freeman Southwell, Hugh Whitemore, Stephen Mead, David Billyeald, Peter Golds, Sheila Colvin, Thomson Smillie of Scottish Opera and Wexford, John Hardy and Peter Orr.

R.M., Wimbledon, 1976

Illustrations

The author and publishers would like to thank the following for the photographs used between pages 152 and 153:

(1) *Donald Southern:* Boris Christoff as Boris Godunov; Domingo and Tinsley in *Cavalleria Rusticana*; Jon Vickers and Heather Harper in *Peter Grimes*; Marie Collier in *The Makropoulos Case*; (2) *Anthony Crickmay:* Alberto Remedios and Clifford Grant in *The Twilight of the Gods*; (3) *Reg Wilson:* Ludmila Dvorakova and Jess Thomas in *Tristan und Isolde*; (4) *Camera Press Ltd:* Callas as Tosca; Shirley Verrett as Carmen (photo by Jane Brown); (5) *Houston Rogers:* Callas and Gobbi in *Tosca*; (6) *Decca Record Co.:* Sutherland as Lucia; Leontyne Price; Georg Solti; (7) *RCA:* Toscanini.

Sherrill Milnes (photo by Clive Barda); (8) *C.B.S. Records:* Bruno Walter; (9) *E.M.I. Ltd:* Beverly Sills; (10) *G. Mac-dominic:* Giulini; (11) *Scottish Opera: Così fan tutte*; (12) *Welsh National Opera & Drama Co. Ltd, Jenufa*; (13) *Aldeburgh Festival:* Benjamin Britten and Peter Pears (photo by Clive Strutt).

All other illustrations are from the Robin May Collection.

The author would like to thank the Press Officers and their staffs of all the companies listed above for their friendly co-operation in selecting photographs, also Avon Moore of the Royal Opera House and Helen Salomon of the English National Opera and their staffs.

COMPOSERS

Some Famous Operas

LA FAVOLA D'ORFEO   1607

1607 was a vintage year, for that most operatic of supreme
dramas, *Antony and Cleopatra*, was almost certainly produced
then, and so was *Orfeo*: *favola* means 'fable'. It was just a
decade since the Florentine Camerata (see page 328), who had
'invented' opera, were able to enjoy the very first one, Peri's
Dafne. They believed that they were recapturing the true
essence of Greek drama which was intoned to music, not sung
as they thought. So they opted for musical declamation, the
dramatic recitative which Monteverdi was to raise to sublime
heights, and which was to be a particular glory of Italian
opera down to the age of Verdi. But Monteverdi and his most
gifted contemporaries made their recitative into endless
melody centuries before Wagner coined the phrase. *Orfeo* is
replete with it, along with songs and dances. It was Monteverdi's first opera, but he was already 40, famous and a genius,
great enough to show that genius early in the opera. The blissful
atmosphere of Act I, with Orpheus and his Euridice still
united, inspired him to the superb paen of praise to married
happiness, 'Rosa del ciel' (Rose of Heaven), sung by Orpheus.
Yet soon the joy is shattered by the coming of a messenger
bringing news of his wife's death, a wonderful, tragic scene
from which springs Orpheus's lamentation, 'Tu se' morta,
se' morta ma vita'. The opera continues on the same exalted
level.

We know what instruments Monteverdi had, and he indi-
cated the combinations he wanted for dramatic colouring, but
the exact and rich tapestry of sound—how dazzling it must
have been—is unknown to us. The controversial job of recon-
struction is left to 'realizers'.

Composer	Claudio Monteverdi
Librettist	Alessandro Striggio
Time and place	Legendary Ancient Greece

First produced at the Accademia degl' Invaghiti, Mantua, in February 1607 in a private performance, with Giovanni Gualberto as Orfeo, then publicly on February 24 at the Court Theatre, Mantua.

The opera's rediscovery began in 1904 in Paris, realized by Vincent d'Indy. Sadly, the chance to make it as popular in Britain as *Poppea* was lost by Sadler's Wells Opera (1965) when Raymond Leppard, everyone's Monteverdian hero except the stern unbending purist's, elected to give the work in Italian. His reasons for doing this—to achieve a unique link between words and music—were honourable but wrong, and unfortunately lost many potential converts.

ALCESTE   1767

It is Gluck's misfortune to be only slightly better known in performance today than those operatic composers he discredited, but that does not lessen his crucial importance. Having abandoned over-elaborate vocalization in his *Orfeo* and cut the number of characters in that opera to three, so concentrating totally on the main drama, he created in *Alceste* a true music drama. He wiped out the concert-in-costume, the zombie-like art, of *opera seria*, where the music, however fine, had not been enough to save dead text and deader form.

Alceste is music drama of the 'beautiful simplicity' to which Gluck aspired. Even the overture, he wrote in his foreword, 'should prepare the spectator for the plot and, as it were, its contents'. It does. The story of how Alceste offers to die in place of her husband, Admetus, but is reclaimed from Hades by Hercules, became truly dramatic in the hands of Gluck and his librettist and fellow reformer, Calzabigi. Space forbids reproduction of the foreword in full—it may be found in Kobbé—but Gluck wrote of his aim to keep the music of *Alceste* free from the abuses which had crept into Italian opera via singers' vanity and complaisant composers, thus making the most splendid and beautiful of all arts the most ludicrous and boring. He demanded that musicians return to the real task of serving poetry by intensifying expressed emotion and the potential of every situation, without interruption of the action or weakening it by too much ornamentation. He also abandoned the use of the castrato.

Composer	Christoph Willibald Gluck
Librettist	Ranieri da Calzabigi
Time and place	Legendary Thessaly

First produced at the Burgtheater, Vienna, on December 26, 1767, with Antonia Bernasconi as Alceste and Giuseppe Tibaldi as Admetus. A revised version, sung in French, was given in Paris in 1776.

Modern productions of the opera use the best of both versions. The best-known aria is Alceste's stirring and powerful 'Divinités du Styx', and there are magnificent moments of dramatic recitative and splendid scenes for the chorus.

IDOMENEO   1781

This passionate work was almost totally neglected in the 19th century, and not until the Glyndebourne revival of 1951 under Busch did it achieve real recognition. Now it is fairly well known, but few older operagoers will have forgotten the shock of delight when they discovered that this *opera seria* was not a dutifully youthful Mozartian bow to an earlier, almost moribund form, bearing little relation to the glories to come, but a noble, deeply moving work of genius. Even the legendary story becomes stirring when mantled in such conviction and fire. Originally Mozart wrote the part of Idamante, son of Idomeneo, King of Crete, for a male soprano, but it is now—as it was on occasion in Mozart's day—given to a tenor. The tragic, central situation is set in motion when the anguished King, who has rashly vowed to sacrifice the first living thing that he sees to the sea god in return for Neptune's quelling of a storm, sees his own son, Idamante. Other major roles are Electra and Ilia, both of whom love Idamante, but Idomeneo's is the greatest creation in the opera, greater even than the frantic Electra.

Composer	Wolfgang Amadeus Mozart
Librettist	G. B. Varesco, after an earlier text by Campra
Time and place	After the Trojan War in legendary Crete

First produced at Munich on January 29, 1781, with Anton Raaff as Idomeneo, dal Prato as Idamante, Dorothea and Elisabeth Wendling as Ilia and Electra, and Panzacchi as Arbace, Idomeneo's confidant.

The opera had a number of performances in Germany and Austria between the wars, including revised editions by Strauss and Wolf-Ferrari. Glasgow saw the first British performance in 1934, Glyndebourne's in 1951 being the first professional performance in Britain.

LE NOZZE DI FIGARO   1786

Faced with the daunting prospect of selecting one representative opera from Mozart's four supreme masterpieces, the compiler can save his sanity by opting for perfection in every department, which means choosing that jewel of Western civilization and most entertaining of comedy operas, *Figaro*. For three acts we are treated to matchless music drama, da Ponte's superb essence of Beaumarchais's play being transfigured by Mozart from biting satire to warmth and boundless humanity without any loss of humour. The characters are as much our friends as are the cast of *Twelfth Night*, while the plot is carried forward with astonishing speed, depth and clarity. Only in the last act does the pace slacken into stretches of sublime self-indulgence, but, with arias of such quality, who could complain? And what atmosphere they create! Figaro's 'Aprite un po' (Yes, fools you are) combines jealousy, heartache and comedy all at once; Susanna's 'Deh vieni non tardar' (Then come my heart's delight) is at once double-edged and sublime; the Count is forgiven by the Countess in a masterstroke of noble grace hard on the heels of farce.

Only the very greatest masters can create the deepest emotion in a comedy, especially a broad one, without wounding the genre, and Mozart continually proves himself such a master in *Figaro*; and what emotion it is, from the uncertain ecstasy of young love that the page Cherubino expresses in 'Non so più' when he wonders if pain or pleasure fills him, to the depths of the Countess's first restrained anguish for lost love, 'Porgi amor' (God of Love).

Except in festival conditions, this opera should always be given in the language of the audience, when it becomes a mass celebration of communal and intimate joy. When sung in Italian at Covent Garden, the silence of the audience at *Figaro* is often deafening enough for *Parsifal*. For those who know the opera by heart this does not matter, but this divine comedy was not written for an élite.

Composer	Wolfgang Amadeus Mozart
Librettist	Lorenzo da Ponte after Beaumarchais
Time and place	The 18th century, at the Count's chateau near Seville

First produced at the Burgtheater, Vienna, on May 1, 1786, with Mme Laschi as the Countess, Nancy Storace as Susanna, Mandini as Count Almaviva and Francesco Benucci as Figaro.

In his Kobbé entry on *Figaro*, Lord Harewood speaks of the fault of piling on superlatives when describing Mozart's operas, and proceeds to do so. I am glad to join him in sin.

FIDELIO   1805, 1806, 1814

Beethoven's only opera is about freedom, justice and married love, a highly moral work as befitted one who found the theme of *Don Giovanni* repugnant. Its admirers fall into three categories: the first wait for memorable and sublime moments in Act I but only become totally gripped by the opera in Act II; the second are spellbound from the beginning; the third are convinced that it is the greatest and noblest of all operas.

The story of the brave and loving wife, Leonore, who disguises herself as an aptly named man, Fidelio, works in the prison where Florestan, her husband, lies in a dungeon for a political crime, and rescues him in the most melodramatic circumstances, is said to be based on fact. The opera starts quietly as a *Singspiel*, the German version of *opéra comique*, but, from the famous quartet onwards, the atmosphere is heightened. The wicked prison governor is a stagey villain, but effectively symbolic of darkness, a darkness from which his prisoners are briefly released by Fidelio's kindly employer, Rocco, while she scans them hoping to see Florestan. The chorus of freedom which the men sing, even more than Leonore's great scene of hate and love, 'Abscheulicher!' (Foul murderer!), is the supreme moment of the act, and it means even more to mid-20th-century audiences than it did in Beethoven's day.

So the stage is set for the Dungeon Scene, melodrama raised by the composer to matchless heights, which make the 'in-the-nick-of-time' ending totally believable. After Pizarro has been foiled by Fidelio's pistol, and a trumpet call announces the coming of the good Don Fernando, there follows a reunion which, after a few broken words between husband and wife, the most poignant spoken words in opera, is musically over-whelming. The words in English are: 'O, my Leonore, what have you done for me?' 'Nothing, nothing, my Florestan!', divine economy and in context overwhelming. Assuming the temperature is right and some vain conductor does not hold up the proceedings by forcing the *Leonora No. 3* overture on us, as even the great ones often do, the final rejoicings are overwhelming also. Light, in the person of the visiting minister, Don Fernando, triumphs, the prisoners are released, and Leonore takes the chains from her Florestan.

Composer	Ludwig van Beethoven
Librettist	Josef Sonnleithner from an earlier French drama by Bouilly
Time and place	18th-century Spain

First produced at the Theater an der Wien, Vienna, on Novem-ber 20, 1805, in three acts with Anna Mildner as Leonore. A second version was given in March 1806, in two acts, the third and final version in Vienna in 1814.

Of the four overtures to the opera, the *Leonora No. 3* is the finest. *Fidelio*, the one usually used, is the most fitting for the opening of the work. The opera's real popularity dated from 1823 when the greatest of all Leonores, Schröder-Devrient, sang it in Vienna in the presence of the stone-deaf composer.

IL BARBIERE DI SIVIGLIA   1816

Since the mid-1950s, Londoners at least have been able to enjoy an astonishing number of operas by Rossini, but *The Barber* remains the only work firmly in the standard repertoire, while once it was the sole survivor of the slump in Rossini's fortunes. No less than seven composers set Beaumarchais's play to music before Rossini sent even the best version, by Paisiello, into near oblivion. Comparisons between *Figaro* and *The Barber* are unnecessary. If Rossini had attempted the former, he could not have attained the depth of the emotion his idol achieved, but *The Barber* is set earlier, when the Count was courting his Rosina, not betraying her. So we have a fast, funny, tuneful work of heady zest and brilliance, one of the greatest of all comic operas, a combination of bewitching and

exhilarating music, superb theatre, and memorable characterizations, not least the two bass roles, Dr Bartolo and
Don Basilio. Rosina's 'Una voce poco fa' is known well beyond
the opera house, while Figaro's 'Largo al factotum' must be
one of the four or five arias that almost everyone has heard.

Composer	Gioacchino Rossini
Librettist	Cesare Sterbini, after Beaumarchais
Time and place	18th century Seville

First produced at the Teatro Argentina, Rome, on February
20, 1816, with Giorgi-Righetti as Rosina, Manuel Garcia as
Count Almaviva and Luigi Zamboni as Figaro.

The first Rosina was a coloratura-mezzo, but sopranos sing
the role more often than not today. Her lesson-scene aria,
'Contro un cor', is frequently replaced by a showpiece. I once
heard: 'Lo, hear the gentle lark'. The first performance was a
notorious flop, with supporters of Paisiello crowding into the
theatre and, with unexpected disasters on stage, things went
from bad to worse. While Garcia was tuning his guitar, a
string broke to the joy of all, and the entire first act was ruined
by 'all the whistlers in Italy'. That Don Basilio fell through a
trap door and a cat wandered across the stage at one point
only increased the joyful sadism, while Rossini was hissed and
the second act was hardly audible at all. The composer stayed
at home in bed for the second performance, which, as it
happened, went well.

DER FREISCHÜTZ 1821

This opera, constantly adored in Germany and irregularly
given elsewhere, is of colossal historical importance, a daunting
claim for a jolly, tuneful, fresh, romantic masterpiece whose
main character, according to Pfitzner, is the German forest.
With it, Weber founded and inspired the German romantic
school, paving the way for Wagner, who worshipped him.
We are in grown-up fairy-tale land in *Freischütz*, a fantastical,
supernatural land, but with no Wagnerian complexities. We
believe in Agathe, Max, Aennchen and Kaspar, especially the
first two who are given magnificent music, but we do not need
to discuss them. The famous Wolf's Glen scene, where magic
bullets are made by the wicked Kaspar for the less-than-
spotless hero, Max, was stirring melodrama in the 1820s, but

tame, enjoyable stuff today. Yet Weber, in full romantic flood, provided such beautifully orchestrated, evocative and melodic music for his woodland tale that the opera creates a sense of well-being at least in a non-German audience. As for Weber's countrymen, it occupies a place in their affections which is hard for Britons to comprehend, for there is no equivalent work in our musical or dramatic history.

Composer	Carl Maria von Weber
Librettist	Friedrich Kind after a story by Johann Apel and Friedrich Laun
Time and place	Mid-18th-century Bohemia

First produced at the Schauspielhaus, Berlin, on June 18, 1821, with Carl Stümer as Max and Caroline Seidler as Agathe.

The opera enjoyed a success, first in Berlin, then elsewhere in Germany, which has no parallel in German operatic history. It stirred a people for more than musical reasons, as some of Verdi's operas were later to do in Italy. Its title cannot be Anglicized, though literally it means 'The Freeshooter'. Such a marksman beats his rivals by using 'free', extra effective, bullets which have been made with the Devil's help.

NORMA 1831

Otto Klemperer once stalked out of a Covent Garden performance of Bellini's *La Sonnambula*, finding its gruel far too thin for his magisterial taste. Later, on television, *Norma* was mentioned in the insulted titan's presence. The granite face cracked. 'Ah, *Norma!*' he breathed.

Ah, *Norma*, indeed. Even those not ensnared by Bellini's lotus land of long, sighing melodies salute his masterpiece, the one occasion when the languid Sicilian created a great lyric drama with a climax of exalted tragedy in its final scene. And nowhere did his gift for dramatic recitative, in the very best traditions of the earliest operatic masters, shine more brightly. Audiences who know no Italian can only glimpse the splendour of the introduction to that ultimate Bellinian melody, 'Casta diva'. The setting is Ancient Gaul and Norma, the only-too-human high priestess of the chaste goddess, has had two children by Pollione, one of the Roman enemy. The Roman has left her for a younger priestess, her friend, Adalgisa, and Norma, in her despair, almost kills her children. Finally, having declared her guilt to the Druids, she mounts her funeral pyre with her faithless lover, Pollione, in a scene of lyric and dramatic glory. Not the least part of her greatness is that she is a positive heroine, a woman of action, and for this the admirable librettist, Romani, must share some of the credit.

Does this pinnacle of *bel canto* opera lose its tension because of the unending flights of Bellinian melody, such as the duets for Norma and Adalgisa which have been driving audiences into panic exaltation for nearly 150 years? The answer is simple: never, if the singers are right. The conductor is crucially important, too, and the producer must be admirable. But Bellini depends on his interpreters. Even genius is not enough if they are unworthy.

Composer	Vincenzo Bellini
Librettist	Felice Romani after Soumet's play
Time and place	*c*. 50 B.C., in Gaul

First produced at La Scala, Milan, on December 26, 1831, with Pasta, Grisi, Donzelli and Negrini (as Oroveso, Norma's father).

Malibran was Pasta's most famous contemporary rival in the part of Norma, while in modern times the supreme Normas have been Rosa Ponselle and Callas.

DON PASQUALE 1843

This is Donizetti's comic masterpiece, a melodic soufflé which uses the stock comic plot of the old fool who loves a young girl, and how he is outwitted by all and sundry. If it were merely funny, romantic and tuneful—and it is all three in abundance—it would not justify an appearance in this select list. But, in *Don Pasquale*, Donizetti discovered the very spirit of melodic invention, in comedy and, in the last act, in sheer enchantment. The delicious Serenade is followed by 'Tornami a dir', a love duet, steeped in romantic charm and a peak of the golden age of *bel canto*. Bellini (in *I Puritani*) wished to make his listeners die with singing. The less homicidal Donizetti was capable, too, of such moments.

Composer	Gaetano Donizetti
Librettists	The composer and Giovanni Ruffini after Angelo Anelli's *Ser Marc' Antonio*
Time and place	Early 19th century Rome

First produced at the Théâtre des Italiens, Paris, on January 3, 1843, with Giulia Grisi as Norina, Giovanni Mario as Ernesto, Antonio Tamburini as Dr Malatesta and Luigi Lablache as Don Pasquale.

The opera was the only work by Donizetti to survive the slump in his fortunes for much of this century in many countries outside Italy and America.

RIGOLETTO 1851

After Verdi's morning glory, the rapid professional routine shot through with continuous signs of genius during his 'galley years', came the first three masterpieces, *Rigoletto*, *Trovatore* and *Traviata*. Perhaps today the third of them is the most loved, or so it would seem by assessing delighted comment, but it was *Rigoletto*, sturdy melodrama transformed by melody, musical characterization and total commitment into a blazing work of art, which announced that the composer had reached maturity. And it was art which the least experienced listener could comprehend. From the doom-laden prelude and the dangerous gaiety of the opening court scene to the luridly theatrical and totally successful last act, the tension is sustained, the menace is never obliterated by the succession of stunning tunes.

Piave deserves credit for his libretto, based on Hugo's *Le Roi s'amuse*. The king became a duke because, in the political climate after the revolutions of 1848, stage monarchs were not welcomed by Authority. Hugo himself was originally hostile to the opera, but recanted to the point of admitting that the duet between Sparafucile and Rigoletto and the great last act quartet improved on his play. The conflicting emotions of the quartet provide one of the ultimate justifications, for opera-lovers at least, for claiming opera as the supreme art, and even the less bold can at least understand the claim.

Composer	Giuseppe Verdi
Librettist	Francesco Maria Piave
Time and place	15th-century Mantua

First performed at the Teatro la Fenice in Venice on March 11, 1851, with Teresa Brambilla at Gilda, Felice Varesi as Rigoletto and Raffaele Mirate as the Duke.

The popularity of the opera has never waned with the public even when Verdi was patronized or condemned by so-sensitive

critics and arbiters of taste. That Verdi was anxious not to let
'La donna e mobile' reach the streets before the first perform-
ance is a reminder of a happier age when opera was pop. *The
Times* of London (in 1853) considered that *Rigoletto* was
Verdi's feeblest opera, except for *Luisa Miller*. Rossini said:
'In this music I at last recognize Verdi's genius.'

LES TROYENS   1863, 1890, 1957
'Hector Berlioz thought big,' proclaimed *The Times* after the
greatest night in the composer's controversial history, June 6,
1957. On that glorious occasion, at Covent Garden, *The
Trojans* was given more or less complete and on a single evening
for the first time, thus vindicating Berlioz's gigantic vision.
Only the second half of the opera, *Les Troyens à Carthage*, was
given—with heavy cuts—in his lifetime (1863), while the first
complete performance, including the opening, *La Prise de
Troie* (The Fall of Troy), was given over two nights at Karlsruhe
in 1890.

Since 1957 there have been greater performances, better
conducted ones, better sung (as a whole) and better directed,
also more complete ones, but the performances of the 1957
production were the turning point and, for many operagoers,
some of the supreme hours of their entire theatrical life. It is
this production, not the 1863 one, whose details are listed below.

It was found that the opera was totally viable, that the
Gluckian, yet utterly Berliozian, *Fall of Troy* and the warm,
romantic, and finally tragic, *The Trojans at Carthage* combined
to make an epic of epics, even, for those for whom Virgil,
Berlioz's inspiration, and words like 'Troy' and 'Carthage'
have no magic. Before that night of nights, only the 'Trojan
March' and, especially, 'The Royal Hunt and Storm', were
known.

Today, though the opera still has its detractors, and despite
the cost of mounting it, it has become quite widely known in
Europe and America, and has been fully recorded. There are
too many felicities to mention where in a score where even the
ballet music is superb, and where a scene for Hector's widow
and son, both silent, would melt a heart of granite; but towards
the opera's end, climax after climax occurs like range upon
range of foothills and mountains. After an ecstatic love duet in
Act IV, Act V begins with the song of Hylas the sailor, a song

of yearning for his homeland in which the surge of the sea steals and breaks through the accompaniment. Soon Aeneas abandons Dido for his duty and departs in a flourish of glorious vocal rhetoric, leaving the queen to her despair and final epic death by her own hand, after a vision of Hannibal has been succeeded by one of the brazen might of Rome.

Composer	Hector Berlioz
Librettist	The composer, after Virgil's Aeneid Book IV
Time and place	Troy and Carthage during and after the Trojan War

First produced on one evening at Covent Garden, June 6, 1957, with Jon Vickers as Aeneas, Blanche Thebom as Dido and Amy Shuard as Cassandra, conducted by Rafael Kubelik and produced by Sir John Gielgud.

The finest Aeneas has been Jon Vickers, especially in 1957, the finest Dido, Janet Baker, for Scottish Opera and at Covent Garden, where Colin Davis, the greatest living Berliozian, conducted.

TRISTAN UND ISOLDE   1865
This is the most intense love story in all drama, musical or otherwise, a superbly constructed tragedy which is almost totally devoted to love and sexual passion. It is often said that modern music dates from the chord which follows the first four notes of the prelude to Act I, and only the very inexperienced can fail to grasp that this is Wagner's first great music drama, complete with symphonic texture, the composer's 'endless melody', leading motives and no set pieces—not even Isolde's *Liebestod* (love death), for the entire work has built up to it. The old legend has Tristan and Isolde fall in love after drinking the love potion, but Wagner has them frustratedly loving each other from the start, the potion being a tension breaker of cataclysmic power. We may note the transition from yearning to ecstasy and finally to death and fulfilment in death; we may admire the burning singleness of purpose of the work, the restless harmonies; yet fundamentally, this music drama was the high point of German romanticism as well as the explosive birth of a new era.

Once *Tristan* has got in the very bones of listeners, they are never quite the same after a great performance of it. At first, perhaps, the highspots alone will conquer them: the greatest of all love duets, the *Liebestod*, or those endless, breathless moments at the end of Act I when the spellbound lovers stand stupefied as the world suddenly surges around them. Yet soon the drama becomes a whole, a long evening which is all too short. The other characters are not ciphers, Brangäne and Kurwenal being particularly well drawn, but as in *Antony and Cleopatra*, which also has a *Liebestod*, only the lovers ultimately count. *Tristan* is a miracle to be experienced. Those to whom it means nothing are unblessed.

Composer	Richard Wagner
Librettist	The composer, from the Cornish legend
Time and place	The sea, Cornwall and Brittany in legendary times

First produced at the Court Theatre, Munich, on June 10, 1865, with Malvina and Ludwig Schnorr von Carolsfeld as Tristan and Isolde, conducted by Hans von Bülow.

On the day of the first orchestral rehearsal, Cosima von Bülow, already Wagner's mistress, bore her third daughter, who was christened Isolde. She was Wagner's child. There was a death as well as a birth associated with Tristan, for the unfortunate Schnorr von Carolsfeld died of rheumatic fever and heart failure on July 21, aged only 29.

DIE MEISTERSINGER VON NÜRNBERG   1868

This is the opera about which Perfect Wagnerites and outsiders usually agree, for its mellow warmth and rich humanity are irresistible to the fortunate, despite the work's great length. The devout find the opera too short, but Wagner cannot have been unaware of the risk of alienation. His last act is longer than the whole of *Falstaff*, but its last scene, brilliantly set in the open air, contains marches and dances, a chorus in honour of Hans Sachs which is of surpassing nobility, the comedy of Beckmesser's botched prize song, the real thing by Walther, and such rousing acclamations that the audience is sent home totally satisfied.

Before these revels, we have experienced an intensely interesting first act where, amongst other happenings, Wagner/ Walther shakes up the pedants and critics. The second act, dominated by Hans Sachs, has a riot at its climax of midsummer madness, followed by one of the best small parts outside Shakespeare, patron saint of small part players. Wagner's is the night-watchman and his music is simple, tuneful and sublime. There follows the first scene of Act III, preceded by a grave prelude where we first hear in the orchestra the noble tune we shall later hear sung, 'Awake, draws nigh the break of day', words of the real Hans Sachs. Then comes the making of the Prize Song, Beckmesser's attempt to steal it, and, later, the quintet for Sachs and the pairs of lovers, Walther and Eva, David and Magdalena. Finally we go into the open beside a river, into Elysian fields.

This is a singers' opera, rich in characters, melody and straightforward orchestration. It is greatly loved.

Composer	Richard Wagner
Librettist	The composer
Time and place	Mid-16th-century Nuremberg

First produced at the Royal Court Theatre, Munich, on June 21, 1868, with Mathilde Mallinger as Eva, Franz Betz as Hans Sachs and Franz Nachbaur as Walther, conducted by Hans von Bülow.

In the third draft of the text, Wagner called Walther's chief critic, the town clerk Beckmesser, 'Hanslich', an open insult to his most important critical enemy, Eduard Hanslick.

BORIS GODUNOV   1874

'Not the best of Russian operas, but unquestionably the greatest,' wrote Stephen Williams in *Come to the Opera*, which sums up the status of *Boris* admirably. For it is a work of genius worthy of comparison with Shakespeare and Michelangelo at their grandest, yet which nobody knows for certain how to perform. The original version, in seven scenes, without love interest and ending with the death of Boris, was turned down by the St Petersburg Opera in 1870, but the revised and expanded 1874 version has caused controversy enough. Banned after twenty-five performances, it was revived in 1896 (Mussorgsky's short, pathetic life having ended in 1881) with the score re-orchestrated by Rimsky-Korsakov. That he softened the composer's splendidly stark sound is undeniable and a perpetual irritant to purists, yet it was this version which made the opera world-famous, especially after the great Chaliapin made the title-role his own.

Mussorgsky ended his 1874 revised version with a thrilling scene in Kromy Forest, with the co-heroes, the Russian people, dominating the proceedings. But when star singers play Boris, in the West, at least, the death of Boris usually ends the opera. Yet whichever permutation is used, *Boris* always retains its sledgehammer impact and emotional power. The part of the guilt-ridden Tsar who has murdered his way to the throne, is one of the supreme roles in all opera, a veritable Russian Macbeth. It is also one of the shortest great roles in opera but, such is the composer's genius, it still dominates it. The part requires a dark-voiced bass with the range of a baritone, tremendous presence and at least good acting, though Chaliapin and his finest successors have led audiences to expect great acting. Mussorgsky created a teeming world of vivid characters in *Boris*, but none more vivid than the crowd. His masterly reproduction of Russian speech-rhythms, and equally masterly use of actual and invented folk tunes, add to the opera's towering stature: there is no greater Russian music than this. That the composer of the coronation scene, the scene in the roadside inn, Boris's soliloquy, 'I have attained the highest power', his death scene and other wonders, so mismanaged his life is saddening, but his artistic achievement was staggering.

Composer	Modest Mussorgsky
Librettist	The composer, after Pushkin
Time and place	Russia and Poland, 1598–1605

First produced in St Petersburg on February 8, 1874, with Melnikov as Boris.

The Rimsky-Korsakov version was first given in St Petersburg (1896), Chaliapin first singing the role of Boris in 1899. The original version was first staged abroad at Sadler's Wells in 1935.

CARMEN 1875
Bizet's masterpiece is unfailingly popular, its combination of magnificent, easy-to-grasp tunes and strong story compensating for the difficulty of casting the heroine and hero, and the fact that it is frequently badly acted by principals and chorus

alike. To find a good Carmen vocally, dramatically and physically is challenging enough (and Carmen of all operatic parts must have allure), while her distraught lover, Don José presents equal problems. It is significant that the role was the only tenor one which Chaliapin wished to play because, unlike Carmen, the operatic *femme fatale*, Don José disintegrates during the course of the action.

Bizet had trouble with the ladies of the Opéra-Comique, who resolutely refused to become cigarette girls. Now their successors are only too willing to act, but they and their admirers, unless a strong producer is in charge, tend to stray into the world of Romberg and Friml and the local amateur operatic society. And when spoken dialogue is (correctly) used in place of recitatives, bad speech in a multiplicity of accents is the order of the day.

Yet *Carmen* lives, even though too often in the theatre it becomes a series of highlights and longueurs. Given reasonably good casts, Acts II and IV are usually the most successful, but Act I can be a series of dramatic fits and starts, and Act III, potentially so exciting, and with a tender interlude of sheer sweet glory for poor Micaela, Don José's abandoned and loving sweetheart, often misfires.

Not a word of this is directed at Bizet or his librettists. They set up what has been called the 'perfect opera', the first and best musical. It is our fault if we cannot perform it perfectly.

Composer	Georges Bizet
Librettists	Henri Meilhac and Ludovic Halévy, after Mérimée's novel
Time and place	*c* 1820, Spain

First produced at the Opéra-Comique, Paris, on March 3, 1875, with Galli-Marié as Carmen, Paul Lhérie as Don José, Jacques Bouhy as Escamillo and Marguerite Chapuy as Micaela, conducted by M. Deloffre.

Bizet's opera is essentially very French, coloured by some Spanish rhythms and a patina of Spanish 'sound'. This is, of course, no criticism of the work. Much so-called national sound is a myth: what matters is the musical and dramatic quality, which in *Carmen* is staggering. Typical is the marvel of a sequence in Act II, when Carmen dances for Don José, the retreat sounds in the background, he starts to return to barracks, she furiously turns on him and he responds with the Flower Song, one of the greatest, most poignant, love songs ever written. Yet Carmen's first audience was not impressed by these and other triumphs. The night was not the fiasco of legend, indeed Act I was well received, but the last act played to an almost empty auditorium and the critics were venomous. Bizet died in June, four months before the opera triumphed in Vienna. Parisians, who had been so stunned and outraged by the realistic happenings on stage, the bourgeois allegedly being greatly shocked, had to wait until 1883 to see the opera and make amends, for it had been dropped by 1876. Now it is so great a symbol of musical France that the de Gaulle regime, wrongly but understandably, felt able to remove this greatest of *opéras comiques* to the Opéra.

EUGENE ONEGIN   1879
This series of lyrical scenes sometimes disappoints newcomers to it who expect Tchaikovsky, the master of very theatrical concert hall works, to bring the same extrovert drama into the opera house. Yet it is rare to meet a regular operagoer who has not succumbed to the elegiac charms of the work. Even Stalin adored the opera, whatever that proves. Though the composer could hardly change a title of Pushkin's, whose poem inspired the opera, it should really be called Tatiana, for Tchaikovsky gave his heart to the heroine and Onegin's music is mainly unmemorable. Tatiana pours her own tender heart out in a letter to the Byronic Onegin only to be coldly rejected by him, yet years later, when she has matured into a great lady, he finds himself rejected by her. The Letter Scene is Tchaikovsky's greatest single operatic achievement, a whole night compressed into a long and rapturous declaration of first love, as she passionately puts her thoughts on paper. The warmly drawn Lensky, who is shot in a duel by Onegin, is a fine creation, as is Tatiana's uncomplicated sister, Olga. Typical of Tchaikovsky's mastery are his contrasted dance sequences. For the ball in honour of Tatiana's birthday, a ball which ends so tragically, he provides a no-nonsense, tuneful middle-class waltz of great charm, but at Prince Gremin's palace in St Petersburg the polonaise is superbly aristocratic. Only in the last scene of all does the composer falter, by leaving his two principals in a short tense scene lacking in memorable music,

let alone melody. If the pair are not good actors, anti-climax is likely to occur.

Composer	Peter Ilyich Tchaikovsky
Librettists	The composer and K. S. Shilovsky after Pushkin
Time and place	Early 19th-century Russia

First produced at the Imperial College of Music, Moscow, on March 29, 1879, then professionally at the Bolshoi, Moscow, on April 23, 1881.

The opera became even more popular after the Revolution. It had reached London in 1892 and was first given in New York (with Muzio and De Luca) at the Met in 1920.

OTELLO   1887

This is the perfect tragic opera and, *pace* the critics, because tragedy is greater than comedy, Verdi's supreme masterpiece, even if musically *Falstaff* is a greater miracle. The public has never had any doubts. *Falstaff* is respected, is now a house-filler with the right cast, is loved for many of its magical moments, but over the last quarter of a century, *Otello* has become a major popular favourite and every visit to a performance of it is a notable occasion in an operagoer's life.

Boito produced the perfect libretto for Verdi, his much-acclaimed compression of the play only being fully appreciated by those who know their Shakespeare. His decision to start the opera with the landing in Cyprus gave Verdi the opportunity to create the most electrifying opening in all opera. Some operagoers claim that Verdi surpasses Shakespeare, but to equal him is surely triumph enough. In one particular he surpassed him, though, for his Desdemona is a more vital creation than Shakespeare's even before her long Willow Song in the last act with its overwhelming climax, Desdemona's cry of 'Ah, Emilia, Emilia, addio'.

The central scene of the play is the second half of Act III, Scene iii, from 'Farewell the tranquil mind' to the stupendous Oath duet, climaxed by Iago's sublimely sinful, 'I am your own for ever'. That Verdi could match this scene, including Iago's description of Cassio's alleged dream, 'Era la notte', a suggestive masterpiece, is one of the chief wonders of this marvel of a score.

Verdi's Iago is less complex than Shakespeare's much discussed creation because Boito, in a rare addition to the play, wrote the famous 'Credo' for him, with Iago believing in a cruel God, who has fashioned him in his own image. As for Otello, he is totally Shakespearean, though the actor of Shakespeare's Othello has nothing as terrifying as Otello's short opening scene, the trumpet blast of rejoicing beginning with the stupendous call, 'Esultate' (Hear glad tidings.).

Composer	Giuseppe Verdi
Librettist	Arrigo Boito after Shakespeare
Time and place	15th-century Cyprus

First produced at La Scala, Milan, on February 5, 1887, with Pantaleoni as Desdemona, Tamagno as Otello, Maurel as Iago, and Faccio as conductor.

After the initial excitement and enthusiasm, the opera became respected and greatly admired rather than loved, but, as we have seen, passionately loved it now is.

LA BOHÈME   1896

Though often cursed with shoddy or non-existent production, by stout, ageing, apparently perpetual students, and by a cynical lack of orchestral rehearsal, *Bohème* remains unsinkable. It is the one Puccini opera which even those lost souls who do not love the composer manage to enjoy, and it contains the most appealing music he ever wrote. *Bohème* is adored by the young and the remembering old alike.

The opera is short and masterly: the high spirits and sentiment of the first act, with its unfailingly magical ending; the kaleidoscopic gaiety and romance of the Café Momus scene; the passionate lyricism of the third act when the days of wine and roses are already over; the last act, melancholy, then exuberant, and suddenly, when Musetta breaks the scene to tell the four Bohemians that Mimi is desperately ill, eternally moving. That sudden entrance of Musetta is only one among many theatrical coups in the opera, a scalpel cut which destroys the over-frenzied atmosphere in a moment.

William Ashbrook, author of *The Operas of Puccini*, has noted the unifying idea of cold that runs through the whole opera, and hunger and poverty are there, too. Yet this is more than balanced by loving warmth and youthful exuberance.

There is even a sequence in which the whole art of opera is justified, the quartet in Act III when Marcello and Musetta are quarrelling violently and Rodolfo and Mimi are lost in rapturous remembrance of happier days. In *The Joy of Music*, Leonard Bernstein, first on television and then in book form, showed how this was a classic example of the advantage that opera has over all other theatrical arts.

Each role in the opera is good, while Rodolfo, Mimi, Musetta and Marcello are answers to the (right) singers' prayers. Puccini tapped his freshest melodic vein in *Bohème*, and clothed his inspirations in dazzling orchestration.

Composer	Giacomo Puccini
Librettists	Giuseppe Giacosa and Luigi Illica, after Henri Murger's *Scènes de la vie de Bohème*
Time and place	Paris, *c* 1830

First produced at the Teatro Regio, Turin, on February 1, 1896, with Cesira-Ferrani as Mimi and Gorga as Rodolfo, conducted by Toscanini.

The opera was not a success at first, especially with most of the critics, though the public was soon enthusiastic, selling the house out twenty-four times that February. But *Bohème*'s unending popularity dates from the Palermo performances in April, 1896.

PELLÉAS ET MÉLISANDE
Like a single giant outcrop of rock on a vast plain, Debussy's masterpiece stands in isolation from the great ranges of the operatic repertoire. One of the many exciting things about exploring that repertoire is the discovery of how, say, Verdi's predecessors anticipated him and how his early works look forward to later glories; but the muted, twilight world of *Pelléas* is unique. It is not easily entered and many never find its secret. Debussy, though he admired Wagner as a genius, had no sympathy with the 'arch-poisoner' and his symphonic methods and *leitmotivs*. The libretto is taken from Maeterlinck's famous play, but whereas Wagner would have left nothing unsaid on such a subject (which shares with *Tristan* the theme of a fatalistic love), playwright and musician, as Stephen Williams wrote, 'say just enough to set our imagination

dreaming'. The music, notably in the interludes, has moments of great emotion, but, like the symbolistic and sometimes somnambulistic drama, is unexaggerated and precise. The most famous example of this—notorious, perhaps—is the climax of the love duet where Pelléas simply admits: 'Je t'aime' and Mélisande replies: 'Je t'aime aussi', as different from Wagner as a Nicholas Hilliard miniature is from the roof of the Sistine Chapel. There is room, of course, for both.

Composer	Claude Debussy
Librettist	The composer, from Maurice Maeter-linck's play of the same name
Time and place	Medieval European legend

First produced at the Opéra-Comique, Paris, on April 30, 1902, with Mary Garden as Mélisande and Jean Périer as Pelléas, conducted by Messager.

Maeterlinck, having first agreed to an opera of his work, was so furious that his wife was not chosen as the heroine that he publicly damned the project. Carré, the Director of the theatre, had chosen the Aberdonian, Mary Garden, whose Anglo-Saxon accent at the famous moment, 'Je ne suis pas heureuse', had the audience laughing, but she and her fellow Briton, Maggie Teyte, remain the most famous interpreters of the role. As for the opera, after initial hostility, it was soon recognized as a masterpiece. Its text is of crucial importance and there is a strong case for its being sung in the language of the audience.

JENUFA   1904
The fight to win an audience for Janáček in western Europe and America is not yet won, indeed at times it seems as if it never will be. If the breakthrough comes it will almost certainly be through this lyric masterpiece. Those who find some of the composer's subjects unappealing can surely respond to this story of Jenufa, an unhappy girl, jilted and pregnant, whose well-meaning monster of a stepmother kills Jenufa's child. There is even a movingly optimistic ending when she finally discovers the worth of a young man she has despised, who once even slashed her face with a knife in his anguish. A genuine love duet ends the opera, and there is nothing to alarm any disciple of Puccini or Richard Strauss.

It must be admitted that Janáček's use of words, partly

because of his fascination with Czech speech rhythms, makes translation difficult and adds to the problems of non-native singers, but his use of (invented) folk melodies, his keen dramatic sense, characterization and stark but totally satisfying orchestration, add up to unique musico-dramatic experiences. Critics who berate the public and inform them that *Jenufa* and his other works are the finest operas of the century do Janáček a disservice. Such overpraise is nearly always counter-productive and house-emptying. But this beautiful opera was written in the same year as *Madama Butterfly*, and its second act—to take but one example—begins with a tensely melodic prelude, gives us in a scene between Jenufa and her stepmother some of the most affecting music ever written about mother love, broken by menacing overtones of the tragedy to come, and has Jenufa bidding her stepmother goodnight to radiantly moving melody. Then comes stark tragedy. This is Czech *verismo*. But perhaps only a cast of superstars will convince the public at large that the opera is for everyone.

Composer	Leoš Janáček
Librettist	The composer, after Gabriella Preissová's 1840 drama
Time and place	19th-century Moravia

First produced at Brno on January 21, 1904, with Marie Kabelacova as Jenufa and Leopolda Svobodova as the Kostelnička.

The opera is always known in Czechoslovakia as *Její Pastorkyňa*, 'Her Foster-daughter'. The stepmother's title comes from the fact that she is sextoness of the church.

ELEKTRA   1909
'The work is a masterpiece of brutality,' wrote Neville Cardus in the *Guardian* after Rosa Pauly's electrifying performance as Elektra at Covent Garden in 1938, adding that 'the orchestra pursues the singers like a fury crowned with snakes'. The Covent Garden orchestra today is said to enjoy playing Strauss above all other composers, hardly surprising as his professional wizardry gives every department such opportunities. *Elektra* is here chosen rather than his first major opera, *Salome*. The former is perfectly representative of one side of his genius, because in it he first collaborated with Hugo von Hofmannsthal,

and because it outstrips *Salome* in every department, reaching greatness. The characterization is far more developed and, despite most violent tactics, true tragedy is achieved. It helps, of course, that the theme is tragic, not morbid to the point of sickness like *Salome*. We are lifted to the grandeur of tragedy at the very outset, the theme of the already murdered Agamemnon having a gut impact proclaiming total mastery.

Hofmannsthal originally wrote *Elektra* as a one-act verse drama freely based on Sophocles's play, and it was this that inspired Strauss to write his opera and begin his long collaboration with the poet. Kenneth McKee has said of Hofmannsthal's Elektra that 'her life is one long, tortuous swing of the death-dealing axe', and, indeed, she has come close to the animal, especially outwardly, in her frenzy for revenge of her murdered father. Almost as rewarding a role for a great actress-singer is Klytemnestra, the tormented, debauched mother of Elektra and murderer, with her lover Aegisthus, of Agamemnon. The less complex Chysothemis completes this trio of marvellous parts. The recognition scene between Elektra and her brother Orestes is the moving emotional climax of the opera whose one much-criticized section is Elektra's dance of triumph after Orestes has killed their mother and her lover. The right artist can overcome the musical scruples of those who find it a monstrous café waltz. Others swallow it whole. 1964525

Composer	Richard Strauss
Librettist	Hugo von Hofmannsthal, from his own play after Sophocles
Time and place	The Royal Palace at Mycenae in legendary times

First produced at Dresden on January 25, 1909, with Anny Krull as Elektra, Margarethe Siems as Chrysothemis, Schumann-Heink as Klytemnestra, and Karl Perron as Orestes, conducted by Ernst von Schuch.

Elektra now seems to have found real popularity, though the stellar nature of casts at Covent Garden at least, and conductors of the calibre of Kleiber, Kempe and Solti, have influenced the size of houses. Probably the quality of recorded sound over the last decades has been decisive, for this is a daunting score at first hearing, one which repays homework with dividends.

DER ROSENKAVALIER 1913

Proof of this opera's enormous popularity is the fact that Covent Garden audiences, mainly non-German speaking, are prepared to sit through acres of words, words, words, many of them uttered by the libidinous country gentleman, Baron Ochs. This popularity is due to many factors: its 'plethora of waltz rhythms' (Kobbé); the heart-stopping rapture of the presentation of the rose by Octavian to Sophie; the final sublime trio and divinely simple duet, the trio in particular having layers of emotion and recognition far beyond music. It is private emotion and public, for this *fin de siècle* opera was written just before the First World War and even now can stir hearts with a vision of a lost world. It is also loved for its characters, Sophie, the matchless 'juvenile', the passionate Octavian, Ochs, who is worthy of Fielding, and, above all, the Marschallin, who, because of the genius of Strauss and Hofmannsthal, is one of the most vivid creations in all opera. Though much older than Octavian, she is still a beauty, and her famous monologue at the end of Act I is the autumnal reverie of a beautiful woman who resents a single crowsfoot, not someone who is past attracting the opposite sex. As William Mann, writing of the end of the opera in a Covent Garden programme, has put it, 'Is Sophie . . . strong enough to hold Octavian from the arms of (the Marschallin)? *Der Rosenkavalier* ends high-spiritedly, but with a question mark in its wake.'

Octavian is the greatest 'breeches role' in opera and, as such, upsets those occasional operagoers who cannot accept a woman playing a man, a highly sexed knight of the rose who is demonstrably incapable, yet who in the prelude to the opera has been indulging in the most explicit love-making in all music, *Tristan* included. It is foolish to argue with objectors, simply hope they will succumb, which they probably will with the right casts.

The ensembles of the opera are scintillating, the comedy is often riotous, but it lives because we believe in the world fashioned by composer (using a huge orchestra) and librettist. Above all, it lives by the erotic sheen, the sensuous appeal of its music which is sheer delight.

Composer	Richard Strauss
Librettist	Hugo von Hofmannsthal
Time and place	18th-century Vienna

First produced at the Hofoper, Dresden, on January 26, 1911, with Margarethe Siems as the Marschallin, Minnie Nast as Sophie, Eva von der Osten as Octavian and Carl Perron as Ochs, conducted by Ernst von Schuch, and anonymously but brilliantly directed by Max Reinhardt.

Perfection is rare in opera by its very nature, but in the 1920s this opera was blessed with a cast which constituted a 20th-century legend, comparable to similar galaxies in the 1830s and 1840s: Lotte Lehmann as the Marschallin, Elisabeth Schumann as Sophie, Delia Reinhardt as Octavian and Richard Mayr as Ochs, conducted by Bruno Walter. This world of wonder first sang at Covent Garden in 1924.

WOZZECK   1925

Berg's masterpiece of musical theatre is one of the few operas of the last half-century to have gained a real public. It is based on Büchner's superb play, *Woyzeck*, the playwright being a genius who also wrote *Danton's Death* and who died in 1837, aged only 23, a unique disaster in dramatic history. Berg's opera does him justice, though critics and musicians fail usually to acknowledge just how difficult this score is for the public even today. Phrases like 'imperishable beauty' do not ring true to those trying to grapple with the music.

Fortunately, Berg's dramatic flair is evident from the start, even to the most inexperienced. The story is of an ordinary soldier, simple to the point of dumbness, badly treated by all authority, and betrayed by his woman, yet capable, like her, of inspiring our pity. Lurid drama, then a masterstroke climaxes the opera, with Wozzeck murdering his Marie, then drowning when he goes to recover the knife. At the end, their child cannot understand when he is told that his mother is dead and goes on playing with his hobby-horse. The tremendous interlude between the final scenes is the emotional climax of *Wozzeck* and, according to Erwin Stein, 'the change of accent is striking and its sincerity makes us realize why we love Berg's music'. 'Love among the highbrows', grimaced a friend of mine when he read that after a performance. But *Wozzeck* is not for highbrows; indeed, many very irregular operagoers respond to it, for it is music drama which speaks to all.

Composer	Alban Berg
Librettist	The composer after Büchner's play
Time and place	An early 19th-century German town

First produced at the Berlin Staatsoper on December 14, 1925, with Leo Schützendorf as Wozzeck and Sigrid Johannsen as Marie, conducted by Eric Kleiber.

The opera reached America (Philadelphia) by 1931, but not Britain until 1952 when Eric Kleiber gave a series of unforgotten, often sadly attended, always greatly welcomed, performances.

PETER GRIMES   1945

Thirty years ago this masterly first opera seemed to herald the dawn of a golden age of English music drama with Britten as its Marlowe. But the very problem of writing modern opera has made a golden age out of the question, so *Grimes*, which looked like being as influential as *Tamburlaine*, has proved chiefly a magnificent prelude to a personal age of glory.

By the standards of modern opera, *Peter Grimes* is widely loved. It is excellently constructed, though there are moments when the text becomes too 'literary', and is memorably characterized musically and dramatically, and scored excitingly, movingly, hauntingly and with superb assurance. Britten and his librettist Montague Slater, using Crabbe's poem *The Borough*, created a world on stage as vivid as a Mussorgsky creation. There are many moments of deep emotion and there is some real humour, and, glory be, there are highspots to be cherished as we cherish such passages in Shakespeare or Verdi: stirring, beautiful meaningful choruses; superb interludes, especially the Moonlight prelude to Act III; Ellen Orford's majestically reproachful, 'Let her among you without fault cast the first stone'; Grimes's mystic, introspective reverie, 'Now the Great Bear and the Pleiades', in the pub scene, an astonishing evocation of a world elsewhere; the women singing 'Do we smile or do we weep'; and many others, not forgetting one of the greatest pauses in opera, and certainly one of the tensest, between shouts of 'Peter Grimes ... Peter Grimes', as the townspeople-turned-mob bay for Grimes's blood.

Only those who must have love duets and conventional stories are unlikely to reach the heart of *Peter Grimes*. True, the anti-hero, though a more sympathetic outsider than Crabbe's, is bound to no one's heart with hoops of steel, but this brilliant and totally professional opera comes straight from the heart and those who cannot grapple it to their own are to be pitied.

Composer	Benjamin Britten
Librettist	Montague Slater after Crabbe's *The Borough*
Time and place	The Borough, towards 1830

First produced at Sadler's Wells Theatre, London, on June 7, 1945, with Peter Pears as Peter Grimes and Joan Cross as Ellen Orford, conductor, Reginald Goodall.

Grimes has been the most successful of British operas at home and abroad. The most remarkable and convincing actor-singer of the title-role has been Jon Vickers.

MOSES UND ARON   post-1957
Schoenberg finished Acts I and II of his masterpiece, but completed only the text of Act III. Considered by its first (and so far, last) British producer, Peter Hall, 'the only great tragedy this century has produced' (O'Casey? O'Neill?), it is about communication between God and Man. Moses receives the truth direct from God but leaves it to the more articulate Aron to present it to the people in terms they can understand, in the process of which Aron inevitably distorts the truth.

This sober-sounding theme does not prevent music of great power and expressiveness being heard, and a musically and dramatically sensational orgy being staged in honour of the Golden Calf while Moses is on Mount Sinai. His is a spoken part, or rather is speech-song, half-way between speech and song, a speciality of the composer and of Berg, while Aron is given suitably exuberant ornamental music to sing.

Schoenberg wanted listeners to forget that he had used 12-note composition technique, indeed he said: 'My works are 12-note *compositions*, not *12-note* compositions'. It is impossible at present to know if *Moses und Aron* will ever be truly popular. It is a very serious, often exciting, work of art by a deeply religious, questing composer, whose stature grows with the years. It is also very expensive to stage. Schoenberg took a calculated risk casting his Moses as a non-singer. The last words of the opera as we have it are 'O Word, Word that I lack!' after which Moses sinks in despair to the ground, an astonishing unoperatic end to an astonishing work.

Composer   Arnold Schoenberg
Librettist   The composer, from the Bible

First produced at Zurich on June 6, 1957, with H. H. Fiedler as Moses and Helmut Merchert as Aron, conducted by Hans Rosbaud.

It had previously been given a concert performance under Rosbaud on the radio in 1954. The famous Solti/Hall production at Covent Garden in 1965 was preceded by a barrage of publicity, even in the tabloids, greater than the combined pre-performance puffs for Callas nights, Sutherland nights and the première of *The Trojans* put together, much being made of naked virgins and sensational orgies. Packed houses resulted and total strangers to opera were seen in the Garden, how many no one will ever know. But the cheers were genuine and great—how much for the opera, how much for a titanic achievement, again we shall never know.

Selected Composers

ADAM, ADOLPHE (1803–56). French composer who, under Boïeldieu's influence at the Conservatoire, began to write *opéras comiques*, the most long-lasting being *Le Postillon de Longjumeau* (1836) and *Si j'étais roi* (1852).

ALBERT, EUGEN D' (1864–1932). German composer and pianist, born in Glasgow of French descent. After his light one-acter, *Die Abreise* (1898), he switched to a German form of *verismo* with his best-known work, *Tiefland* (1903), suitably full of passion and murder. Of his eighteen other operas, only *Die toten Augen* ('The Dead Eyes', 1916) had a major success.

ALFANO, FRANCO (1876–1954). Italian. Best known for his worthy attempt to finish *Turandot* after Puccini's death in 1924, a very difficult assignment which most opera-lovers think he handled reasonably well. He wrote a number of operas himself, gradually breaking away from *verismo*, the best known being *Risurrezione* (1904).

AUBER, DANIEL FRANÇOIS ESPRIT (1782–1871). French. With the librettist Scribe, he composed many comic and serious operas of considerable charm. Anyone who has experienced *Fra Diavolo* (1830) in the theatre must wonder why, in these days of early 19th-century Italian revivals, Auber is so neglected. His other works include *Le Domino Noir* (1837) and an opera which had an even greater effect than Verdi's *La Battaglia di Legnano* (see p. 97). Auber's moment of history came in Brussels in 1830 when his two-year-old opera, *La Muette de Portici* (The Dumb Girl of Portici), also known by its hero's name, *Masaniello*, actually triggered off the Belgian Revolution against the Dutch. The audience, inspired by the revolutionary story in which the people are treated heroically for the first time in opera, along with their hopes and fears, rushed into the streets, fired the populace and set off a train of events which led to independence. The tuneful, virile music is Auber's greatest achievement, the composer revealing emotional depths and originality in this story, based on an actual rising by the Neapolitans against the Spaniards in 1647, which he never attained elsewhere.

BALFE, MICHAEL (1808–70). Irish composer and singer whose romantic career embraced the first Papageno in English and *The Bohemian Girl* (1843). The popularity of this pleasant opera in the British Isles lasted almost a century, its most famous number being 'I dreamt that I dwelt in marble halls', and none of his other twenty-eight operas rivalled it.

BARBER, SAMUEL (1910–). American. *Vanessa* (1958), with a libretto by Menotti, was successful in the U.S.A., while his less admired *Antony and Cleopatra* (1966) opened the new Metropolitan Opera House in the Lincoln Center.

BARTÓK, BÉLA (1881–1945). Hungarian. His only opera was an early one-acter, *Duke Bluebeard's Castle* (1918), full of the most striking and melodious music, though the work is too static for some tastes.

BEETHOVEN, LUDWIG VAN (1770–1827). German. His only completed opera, *Fidelio*, is for many one of the greatest, if not the greatest, of all operas, this despite revisions and debatable structure. *Fidelio* is discussed on page 17.

BELLINI, VINCENZO (1801–35). Italian. His masterpiece, *Norma*, is discussed on page 20. Outside Italy, most of his operas, *Norma* always excepted, remain controversial, passion-ately adored by those intoxicated by his long, intensely lyrical melodies, and criticized by detractors for such lack of dramatic force that some still regard them as naïve museum pieces, mere showcases for singers and therapy for canary-fanciers. Even the new age of *bel canto* ushered in by Callas in the 1950s has not entirely evaporated these criticisms, partly because the composer brings out the Puritan in some un-self-indulgent listeners, partly because there is an element of truth in them.

Born in Catania, Sicily, Bellini studied in Naples, his first opera being *Adelson e Salvina* (1825). There followed *Bianca e Fernando* (1826) and *Il Pirata* (1827), his first reasonably well-known opera today, and one which saw his partnership with the very fine librettist Romani begin. Which is a good moment to quote Wagner, who not only liked Bellini because 'his music is strongly felt' but also because it is 'intimately bound up with the words'. Too many Anglo-American listeners underrate the composer because they do not appreciate the splendour of his dramatic recitative.

In 1829 came *La Straniera* and *Zaira*, then, in 1830, *I Capuletti ed i Montecchi*, a most beautiful work. Two masterpieces followed in 1831, *La Sonnambula*, too milk-and-water for unbelievers, and *Norma*. *Il fù ed il sarà* (1832) and *Beatrice di Tenda* (1833), the latter full of glorious melodies and anticipations of Verdi, were to be surpassed by Bellini's final work, *I Puritani di Scozia* (1835), whose weak libretto by Pepoli cannot dampen a melodic flood torrential even by Bellinian standards. The Mad Scene, 'Qui la voce', ranks with 'Casta diva' as an ultimate peak of Romantic art, and the opera as a whole saw Bellini's orchestration, always utterly effective if too simple for gourmets, becoming more adventurous. His early death must be considered a major disaster.

BENEDICT, (SIR) JULIUS (1804–85). German composer and conductor, naturalized English. His best-known opera is the once adored *The Lily of Killarney* (1862).

BENJAMIN, ARTHUR (1893–1960). Australian. His four operas are *The Devil Take Her* (1931), a farcical piece; the *opera buffa*, *Prima Donna* (1933); the rousing *A Tale of Two Cities* (1949); and *Tartuffe*, whose vocal score was finished when he died.

BENNETT, RICHARD RODNEY (1936–). English. His operas include *A Penny for a Song*, *Victory* and, most notably, the earlier *The Mines of Sulphur* (1965). His admirers long for the melody at his command to emerge.

BERG, ALBAN (1885–1935). Austrian composer, much influenced by his teacher, Schoenberg, to whom he dedicated *Lulu*. His great *Wozzeck* is discussed on page 37. His unfinished *Lulu*, first produced in 1937, is a dodecaphonic (12-note) opera in three acts, musically even finer than *Wozzeck*, though not, perhaps, so moving for audiences. Berg provided his own libretto from Wedekind's *Erdgeist* and *Die Büchse der Pandora*. Lulu's sexual and other adventures culminate in her being murdered by Jack the Ripper. She has destroyed those who loved her and become a London prostitute before meeting a suitably lurid end. It was first performed at Zürich, and achieves a remarkable effect, not least because every character, serious and comic, is strongly surrounded by atmospheric music.

BERKELEY, (SIR) LENNOX (1903–). English. His first opera, *Nelson* (1953), was fascinating, but not a success, partly because of its structure. He has also written the entertaining *A Dinner Engagement* (1954), a one-act comedy (libretto by Paul Dehn), and *Ruth* (1956), also in one act (libretto by Eric Crozier), and *The Castaway* (1967).

BERLIOZ, HECTOR (1803–69). French. The greatest operatic genius of his nation, or a flawed genius, according to taste. A century after his death he remains as controversial as ever (though not to his devotees, this author included), but at least his works are often now heard almost as he intended, most notably *Les Troyens* (1856–8), discussed on page 23. The failure of *Benvenuto Cellini* (1838) turned him away from opera, yet this youthful work is packed with melody, incident, fire and enchantment, even if its plot is not ideal, and comedy and the heroic do not always blend happily. The most famous scene is the Roman Carnival and, from the first, the opera had admirers. His dramatic legend, *La Damnation de Faust*, musically superb, is drama personified and therefore is sometimes staged, to the satisfaction of many and the raised eyebrows of many more. Lord Harewood has called *Faust* too dramatic for the concert hall, insufficiently stageworthy for the opera house, yet modern staging techniques have reached a point that, given a truly musical director, there is every chance of major success. Parts of Michael Geliot's production for Sadler's Wells Opera (1969) showed what can be achieved, though barring a hot line to Valhalla, it is impossible to know for certain if Berlioz would approve. What is certain is that if the operatic climate in his France had been healthier, he would have written more operas. Unfortunately, the French wanted talent, not genius.

Béatrice et Bénédict (1862) is based on *Much Ado About Nothing*, Berlioz extracting the lovers' 'merry war' and leaving out the serio-sinister plot of Shakespeare's play. No greater tribute can be paid to Berlioz than to say that much of the music is worthy of the enchanted original, especially the duet, 'L'amour est un flambeau', which ends the opera, and, earlier, a Nocturne for Ursula and Hero and a trio for Hero, Beatrice and Ursula. Unfortunately for Anglo-Saxon audiences, there is an alarming amount of spoken dialogue for the average singer to maul. Liszt championed the opera as he had *Benvenuto*. Berlioz said that he wrote it as a rest after his exertions on *Les Troyens*, as well as a tribute to his adored Shakespeare. Until *Otello* and *Falstaff*, it remained the only opera which did not diminish the greatest of all dramatists.

BERNSTEIN, LEONARD (1918–). American composer and conductor, whose only opera, *Trouble in Tahiti* (1952), is less distinguished than his fine score for *West Side Story* (1957) and his masterly, and often very operatic, one for the delightful *Candide* (1956). Also see page 223.

BISHOP, (SIR) HENRY (1786–1855). English composer, the first to be knighted (1842), and best remembered now for one immortal song, 'Home, Sweet Home' from one of his sixty operas, *Clari, The Maid of Milan* (1823), and one still popular showpiece, 'Lo, Hear the Gentle Lark'. In his own day he busily butchered masterpieces, *Don Giovanni, Figaro, Fidelio* and *Il Barbiere* being among those 'improved'—improvements which included gems of his own.

BIZET, GEORGES (1838–75). French. His *Carmen*, one of the half-dozen most popular operas ever composed, is discussed on page 27. Like Berlioz, he suffered greatly from being an original and a genius in the most traditionalist of operatic countries of the 19th century. His operas before *Carmen* were mostly cursed by poor books, though all are shot through with melodic perfection and sheer delight. His earliest include *Docteur Miracle* (composed 1856 or 1857), a one-act operetta of promise if not much originality, and *Don Procopio* (composed 1858–9). Then came *Les Pêcheurs de Perles* (The Pearl Fishers, 1863), an improbable tale, Carré and Cormon providing a setting in ancient Ceylon. Bizet could not make a music drama of it, but it is a most enjoyable opera. Two highspots in the opera show him at his finest: the tenor aria, 'Je crois entendre' (I hear as in a dream), and the glorious tenor-baritone duet, 'Au fond du temple saint' (In the depths

of the temple). The theme of friendship recurs—perhaps too much—throughout the opera.

Less-known works include: *Ivan IV* (composed 1862–3); *La Jolie Fille de Perth* (1867) with its enchanting Serenade; the unfinished *La Coupe du Roi de Thule*, and other operas and *opéras comiques*, the best being the opera *Djamileh*, first given in 1872. None of these achieved the perfection of his incidental music to Daudet's *L'Arlésienne*, but most of them show signs of the glory to come in *Carmen*. Bizet's early death was a musical catastrophe.

BLACHER, BORIS (1903–75). German. Born in China of Russian parents and one of the most original operatic talents of the century. His six operas include *Die Flut* (The Tide, 1947), a dramatic one-acter, the comic *Preussisches Marchen* (Prussian Fairy Tale, 1952), the abstract *Abstrakte Oper No. 1* (Abstract Opera No. 1, 1953), and *Rosamunde Floris* (1960) in which the orchestra plays a minor role. Also a librettist of two operas by Einem (see page 53).

BLITZSTEIN, MARC (1905–64). American. He abandoned experimental music to get his political feelings across; indeed, his *The Cradle Will Rock* (1937), a fiery anti-capitalist opera, produced by Orson Welles, was hailed by Brooks Atkinson as the 'most

versatile triumph of the politically insurgent theatre'. It ran
into trouble with authority.

BOÏELDIEU, ADRIEN (1775–1834).
French. His work, one or two
overtures apart, is rarely heard
outside France. The most
obscure Rossini and Donizetti
works are happily being ex-
humed these days, yet two
world famous works, *Le Calife
de Bagdad* (1800) and *La Dame
Blanche* (1825—one of the
most successful *opéras comiques*
ever written), are treated in
many countries as musical
lepers.

BOITO, ARRIGO (1842–1918).
Italian composer and librettist
(his texts are considered on
p. 269). This Italo–Pole, col-
laborator with and friend of
Verdi, and lover of Duse, wrote
two operas, *Mefistofele* (1868)
and *Nerone* (posthumously
given, 1924). The first failed at
La Scala, but is fairly frequently performed, though
opinions about it vary enormously. It uses the first part of
Goethe's play, as does Gounod,
but also strays into the second
part and, as Kobbé says, 'the
main thread of the action
suddenly seems broken'. The
Marguerite story belongs to
Part One. The philosophical
Part Two is not very fertile
ground for opera. Yet the
opera abounds in the most
beautiful music and any
performance, too often in the
concert hall, should be eagerly

sought out; its Prologue in
Heaven is worthy of Michelangelo. *Nerone* aims even higher
than *Mefistofele*, but is far less
successful. Boito's lyric power
had diminished, though page
after page is full of beauty. The
word 'worthy' can be applied
to the work, but worthiness
has never been enough or
operas far more modern than
Nerone would be popular.

BORODIN, ALEXANDER (1833–
87). Russian. Best known outside Russia for his orchestral
music. He only completed one
opera, *The Bogatirs* (1867);
Mlada (1872) only exists as an
Act IV. However, his *Prince
Igor* (1869–87), completed by
the master finisher, Rimsky-
Korsakov, is a splendid epic,
even if nothing in it matches the
—what other description will
do?—barbaric splendour of the
Polovtsian Dances.

BOUGHTON, RUTLAND (1878–
1960). English. His ambition,
as an English Wagnerian, was
to make Glastonbury into a
British Bayreuth. His operas,
with one exception—*The Immortal Hour* (1922) which had
a colossal success in the 1920s—
have already been forgotten.

BRITTEN, BENJAMIN (1913–76).
English. By far the most
successful operatic composer
ever to appear in Britain, and
one of the few in the last half-
century to be truly popular, not
in the widest Verdi–Puccini

sense, but with many thousands in his own country and abroad. His career has been a reproach to those who despairingly regard opera today as solely a museum art.

Britten wrote an operetta, *Paul Bunyan* (1941), which he later withdrew. In 1945, his *Peter Grimes*, featured on page 38, proclaimed the arrival of a masterly operatic talent. Financial aid for the Arts being in its infancy in Britain, the composer formed the English Opera Group (see page 315) and composed the chamber opera, *The Rape of Lucretia* (1946), a strikingly successful work for a 12-piece orchestra. There followed *Albert Herring* (1947), a delightful Suffolk comedy based on a Maupassant story, as full of local types as *Grimes*, and technically and theatrically an advance on the earlier operas, if naturally less charged with emotion. Next came Britten's version of *The Beggar's Opera* (1948), typically inventive, yet, like every other version, not the final solution, and the delightful *Let's Make An Opera* (1949). In this, the first part has children, adults and audience rehearsing—in play form—for an opera, *The Little Sweep*. It was first given at the Aldeburgh Festival, founded in 1948 by Britten, Eric Crozier (librettist of *Albert Herring*) and Peter Pears (see page 181).

The year 1951 was an important one, with Britten's realiza-tion of Purcell's *Dido and Aeneas*, and first performances of *Billy Budd*, libretto by E. M. Forster from the story by Melville. Set on a man-o'-war and therefore sea-haunted like *Grimes*, it marked another advance (and has since been slightly revised) and, more importantly, is powerful and very moving. If its construction and text are not faultless, its second half (in the new, two-act version) has an emotional impact which, for many, is unique in modern opera. Billy, the Good Sailor, is a total success, so is his sensitive captain, 'Starry' Vere, only the villainous Claggart being some-what stagey. There followed *Gloriana* (1953), the Corona-tion opera misunderstood by many (though not all) of its first audiences and shamefully by many critics, and abused for its subject matter at such a time. It is now loved by thousands, despite a certain weakness of characterization, Elizabeth and Essex excepted, and despite allegedly debilitating scenes of pageantry. The portrait of Elizabeth, musically and dra-matically (William Plomer) is masterly.

In *The Turn of the Screw* (1954) from Henry James's novel, he returned superbly to chamber opera, after a break with *Gloriana*, exploring the world of innocence corrupted. The opera is thematically even more integrated than *Billy Budd*. *Noyes Fludde* (1958), based on one of the Chester Cycle of Mysteries, is quite simply the best work for children since *Hansel and Gretel*. (Many feel its divine simplicity, inventiveness, charm and use of children makes it the supreme children's music drama.) *A Midsummer Night's Dream* (1960) is in two versions, chamber and full-scale opera. It uses half the original words and ranks as a wonderful realization of the play in music. The three worlds of fairies, mechanicals and lovers, plus the lesser world of the nobility, are superbly differentiated, and when at last the lovers were perfectly played (Covent Garden, 1973) the one weak link in the music no longer seemed weak. Purists resent the Pyramus and Thisbe scene being chiefly a Donizettian pastiche, but audiences rightly take no notice of them.

Britten next turned to Parables for Church Performance, *Curlew River* (1964) and *The Burning Fiery Furnace* (1966), both highly imaginative. The opera *Owen Wingrave* (1971), based on a story by Henry James about a young army-cadet-turned-pacifist from a military family, and first given on television, saw a rare misjudgement on Britten's part, in that he made all Wingrave's opponents unbearable. As a pacifist himself, the attitude is understandable, but artistically it flaws a work whose main character is beautifully drawn

and whose music reaches new heights. There followed *Death in Venice* (1973) from Mann's novel and far truer to the book than the famous film. The fine libretto is by Myfanwy Piper. Its structure has divided opinion deeply, but musically it is beautiful, often thrilling and always theatrically effective. The present author, prevented from hearing the work until 1975, can state with total honesty that no modern opera has so gripped and moved him at first hearing, not even others of Britten's, and that structurally not even the much argued-over ballet seemed anything but right. To be overwhelmed by an opera written in the 1970s is as startling as it is deeply gratifying. Only ill-health can surely prevent Britten producing more—why be shy of the word?—masterpieces.

BUSH, ALAN (1900–). English. His Marxist sympathies are reflected in his and his librettist-wife Nancy's choice of subjects: *The Press-Gang* (1946), an operetta for children; *Wat Tyler* (1950); *The Spell* (1953), an operetta; and *The Men of Blackmoor* (1955).

BUSONI, FERRUCIO (1866–1924). Italian composer and pianist, whose four operas have been more honoured in Germany than in Italy. They are *Die Brautwahl* (The Chosen Bride, 1912); *Turandot* (1917); *Arlecchino* (1917) and *Doktor Faust* (completed by Jarnach, his pupil, and first given in 1925). Of German-Italian origin, his musical outlook was more Germanic than Italian, and he was an innovator, attempting his own new classicism. Busoni's masterpiece is *Doktor Faust* whose admirers find it full of strength, grandeur and nobility, as well as beauty, but this reworking of an old puppet play is too austere for many tastes.

CATALANI, ALFREDO (1854–93). Italian. Greatly admired by Toscanini, his best-known work is *La Wally* (1892), a beautiful opera, popular in Italy still, but unaccountably neglected elsewhere. The finest of his other four operas is *Loreley* (1890). Influenced by German romanticism, his music is yet typically Italian, and his over-shadowing by the *verismo* school has been unjustified, unless one accepts Mosco Carner's dictum, 'noble yet rather anaemic music'.

CAVALLI, PIER FRANCESCO (1602–76). Italian. An 'Interesting Historical Monument' until the late 1960s, though in his day he was the leading operatic composer after Monteverdi, writing forty-two works. The best known in his own time was *Giasone* (1649), but now, thanks to Raymond Leppard and Glyndebourne, two others have been performed and greatly enjoyed, *L'Ormindo* in

1968 and *La Calisto* in 1970. Some experts may—and do—challenge Leppard's realizations of these baroque masterpieces, but he has made them artistically valid. Cavalli is revealed as a master of fast-moving, melodic, emotional, brilliant, theatrical and entertaining operas—which live, not least because, for all their fantastical plots, they are concerned with human hopes, fears and desires.

CESTI, PIETRO ANTONIO (1623–69). Italian. A contemporary of Cavalli, but not yet re-discovered, despite his genius for writing good tunes. His best-known opera was *Il Pomo d'Oro* (The Golden Apple, 1666).

CHABRIER, EMMANUEL (1841–94). French composer and Wagnerite. His *Gwendoline* was too Wagnerian for Paris, being given in Brussels in 1886, but more successful than this and other works is his comic opera, *Le Roi Malgré Lui* (1887).

CHARPENTIER, GUSTAVE (1860–1956). French. His most successful work is *Louise* (1900), full of musical charm and advanced thinking about the lot of working girls. Its enormous appeal to the French has never ceased, but it is all too rarely heard outside France. Paris is the heroine as well as Louise. A sequel, *Julien* (1913), failed.

CHERUBINI, LUIGI (1760–1842). Italian. He turned to the French school, writing some thirty operas, including one masterpiece, *Médée* (1797), and two great successes, *Lodoiska* (1791) and *Les Deux Journées* (The Two Days, 1800, also known as 'The Water Carrier'). A disciple of Gluck and a musician admired by Beethoven, he helped found romantic opera, though he considered his own work somewhat severe. *Médée* is a work of classic grandeur, rediscovered in modern times thanks to Callas.

CILEA, FRANCESCO (1866–1950). Italian. His most famous work is *Adriana Lecouvreur* (1902). This attractive opera, based on the famous semi-historical drama by Scribe and Legouvé about the celebrated 18th-century actress and her love for Maréchal de Saxe, is still widely performed in Italy. It is enjoyed by singers and audiences—when they are allowed to hear it. Other operas include *L'Arlesiana* (1897), full of charming music, and *Gloria* (1907).

CIMAROSA, DOMENICO (1749–1801). Italian composer of some sixty operas, the most famous being the scintillating *Il Matrimonio Segreto* (The Secret Marriage, 1792). Its first performance before Emperor Leopold II of Vienna was such a success that he gave the cast supper and had them sing the opera again.

COPLAND, AARON (1900–). American. *The Second Hurricane* (1937) is a 'play opera' for high schools and is influenced by jazz; *The Tender Land* (1954) is a mid-Western Depression drama in the same haunting vein as much of his regional American music.

CORNELIUS, PETER (1824–74). German. His *Der Barbier von Bagdad* (1858) lives on for its lyric charm, humour, characterization and entertainment value.

CROSSE, GORDON (1937–). English. His operas include the gripping *Purgatory* and *The Story of Vasco* (1974).

CUI, CÉSAR ANTONOVICH (1835–1918). Russian. He founded the nationalistic 'Mighty Handful' of composers with Balakirev. (The rest were Borodin, Mussorgsky and Rimsky-Korsakov.) Cui wrote six operas, but is best remembered operatically for his completion of Mussorgsky's *Sorochinsky Fair*.

DALLAPICCOLA, LUIGI (1904–75). Italian. His use of dodecaphony has not subdued his native love of voice and song, both usually at a discount with 12-note composers. His *Volo di Notte* (Night Flight, 1940), examines the sacrifices demanded by an all-important air operation, while *Il Prigioniero* (The Prisoner, 1950) is a tense, shatteringly absorbing work set in the time of the Spanish Inquisition in the Netherlands.

DARGOMIZHSKY, ALEXANDER (1813–69). Russian. He was gradually influenced by the principles of the 'Mighty Handful' (see CUI above), but without the talent to continue the reforms of the Handful's mentor, Glinka, or the will to stand aside from contemporary tastes. His *Esmeralda* (1839) is based on Hugo's *Notre-Dame de Paris* and is French in style. *Russalka* (1856), a failure at first, showed a growing feeling for melodic recitative. His posthumously produced *The Stone Guest* (1872) has the (Don Juan) characters singing 'mezzo-recitative' with a natural and very influential setting of word-rhythms.

DAVIES, PETER MAXWELL (1934–). English composer of *Taverner* (1972), thrilling music-theatre, though the score divided opinion.

DEBUSSY, CLAUDE (1862–1918). French. His only opera, *Pelléas et Mélisande* (1902), is discussed on page 32.

DELIBES, LÉO (1836–91). French. He wrote three works for the Opéra-Comique: *Le Roi l'a Dit* (The King Has Commanded It, 1873), *Jean de Nivelle* (1880) and *Lakmé* (1883). This last, about the love of an English officer and a Brahmin priest's daughter, has always been

hugely popular in France. It is tuneful, delightfully scored and suitably mock-oriental, has had the advantage of a Sutherland recording, has one of the most sure-fire operatic hits in the 'Bell Song', yet is signally neglected in most countries.

DELIUS, FREDERICK (1862–1934). English. His operas owe what recognition they have had to the constant belief in them by Beecham. *A Village Romeo and Juliet* (1900, produced 1907) is the only one to achieve something like minor popularity. *Irmelin* (1890) was given by Beecham at Oxford in 1953, and *Koanga* (1895, produced 1904) revived by him at Covent Garden in 1935. Of his other works, only *Fennimore and Gerda* (1908) has been produced.

D'INDY, VINCENT (1851–1931). French. His six operas and operettas, several reflecting his devotion to Wagner, are mere names today. His most significant work is *Fervaal* (1897).

DONIZETTI, GAETANO (1797–1848). Italian. He wrote some seventy-five works for the stage, more and more of which are being resurrected for the melodic plunder within them. A master craftsman geared to the needs of an age of great singers, by 1950 he had almost vanished from the repertoire outside Italy, only his comic masterpiece *Don Pasquale* (1843) totally surviving the sneers and ignorance bred from sheer lack of performance. Since then, partly because of changing public tastes, partly—the two are linked—because of the championship of Callas and Sutherland, his music is again widely loved and singers have appeared who can do it justice.

Trained in Bergamo, his birthplace, and Bologna, his first success was *Enrico di Borgogna* (1818). Few pre-1830 works can be heard today. British audiences cannot yet whistle the main tunes of *Emilia di Liverpool* (1824), the first Donizetti work to be heard in Vienna, but these earlier works were given all over Italy. From 1830, with Bellini's star in the ascendant, he raised his standards, *Anna Bolena* (1830), with a fine libretto by Romani and a stellar original cast, sweeping Europe. Modern revivals have proved its power, only those who cannot forgive Donizetti for failing to be born with Verdi's instinct for drama failing to acknowledge the strength of its finest scenes. Its final scene is a triumph even without the supreme advocacy of Callas.

Notable later works include the enchanting comedy, *L' Elisir d'Amore* (1832), abused by British guardians of taste as late as the 1950s; *Lucrezia Borgia* (1833), riddled with melody even by Donizettian standards; *Maria Stuarda*

(1834), famous for its (unhistorical) confrontation between Mary and Elizabeth I; *Marino Faliero* (1835), which has many champions, and *Lucia di Lammermoor* (1835) which even in the dark days was held to have great moments: The Sextet, the Mad Scene. Callas, Sutherland and others have almost restored it to its 19th-century fame, when for many, it was a touchstone of Romantic art.

Later works include *Roberto Devereux* (1836); *Poliuto* (1839); *La Fille du Régiment* (1840) to a French libretto, once again in favour; *La Favorite* (1840), never out of favour amongst the discerning, and better known as *La Favorita*; *Linda di Chamounix* (1842); *Don Pasquale* (1843), described on page 21; *Maria di Rohan* (1843) and *Don Sebastiano* (1843). His last work was *Caterina Cornaro* (1844) and several operas were produced posthumously.

This composer of so much happy music died insane of syphilis. His critics abhor a lack of profundity in his many serious works, even his most famous, and, indeed, only in its finest moments is a Donizetti tragic opera able to shake off a certain jauntiness and become a major work of art. But no opera-lover should be shy of publicly rejoicing in enjoying Donizetti's serious works, just as he should not imagine that a single one of them, even *Lucia*, is artistically as perfect as *Don Pasquale*.

DUKAS, PAUL (1865–1935). French. His one opera is *Ariane et Barbe-bleue* (1907) influenced by *Pelléas* and with a text adapted from Maeterlinck's play.

DVORÁK, ANTONIN (1841–1904). Czech. His ten operas, unlike his enormously popular orchestral favourites, are rarely heard outside his homeland. The only exception is *Rusalka* (1901), a fairy tale piece with one famous aria, 'O Silver Moon'. Adored in Czechoslovakia, the opera is sometimes given elsewhere, while the other ones most regularly revived by the Czechs are *The Jacobin, The Pig-Headed Peasants, The Peasant Rogue, The Devil and Kate* and *Dimitrij*, a sequel to the Boris Godunov story. The first of these and the last two have been very occasionally exported. Despite delightful moments, none are truly successful operas.

EGK, WERNER (1901–). German. He has become genuinely popular in his native country, if not much outside it. His first, very assured, stage work was *Die Zaubergeige* (The Magic Violin, 1935), an amusing work full of folk tunes. *Peer Gynt* (1938) followed, and then came a revised radio work, *Columbus* (1942), an opera-oratorio influenced by Stravin-

sky and Honneger; *Irische Legende* (1954) from Yeats' *The Countess Cathleen*, full of impressive music rather than dramatic conviction; and *Der Revisor* (The Government Inspector, 1957), an entertaining version of Gogol's famous play.

EINEM, GOTTFRIED VON (1918–). Austrian composer and pupil of Blacher. His best-known operas, both strikingly theatrical, are from famous sources: *Dantons Tod* (Danton's Death, 1947) from Büchner's magnificent play, and *Der Prozess* (The Trial, 1953), from Kafka'a enigmatic novel. Blacher provided him with librettos for both. His *The Visit of the Old Lady* is from Dürrenmatt's play *The Visit*, with a libretto by the dramatist.

ERKEL, FERENC (1810–93). Hungarian composer and nationalist, whose *Bátori Mária* (1840) saw the start of a national school of opera. *Hunyadi Lázló* (1844) electrified audiences for patriotic as well as musical reasons, while *Bánk Bán*, produced in 1861 became and remains a national operatic anthem.

FALLA, MANUEL DE (1876–1946). Spanish. His *La Vida Breve* (The Short Life, 1905) is splendidly atmospheric and haunting, though the plot promises more than it achieves. The tragic heroine Salud and the vigorous popular scenes are on two different, though effective levels; indeed, the work has been performed as an opera-ballet. *El Retablo de Maeso Pedro* (1923) from *Don Quixote* is more maturely Spanish but less popular.

FIBICH, ZDENĚK (1850–1900). Czech. His seven operas are little known outside Czechoslovakia. His finest is *Sarka* (1897), a very effective version of a Czech legend.

FLOTOW, FRIEDRICH VON (1812–83). German. He is remembered for one utterly delightful opera, *Martha* (1847), a charming love story set in Queen Anne's reign, with moments of forceful writing for the unhappy hero, several excellent tunes, cunningly moving use of the old Irish air, 'The Last Rose of Summer', and one major aria, 'M'appari'. The opera's popularity has usually distressed the austere.

FORTNER, WOLFGANG (1907–). German. He came to opera late, apart from a piece for schools. His two well-known operas, drawn from plays by Lorca, keep much of the drama intact, the words often being left without music. They are *Bluthochzeit* (Blood Wedding, 1957) and *In seinem Garten liebt Don Perlimplin Belisa* (The Love of Don Perlimplin and Belisa in the Garden, 1962). He uses serial and other techniques.

GAGLIANO, MARCO DA (*c.* 1575–1642). Italian. A founding father of opera, whose *La Flora* (1628) survives, but whose admired version of *Dafne* (1607) is lost. The preface to the latter demands an end of singers' abuses and the need for dramatic realism exactly 150 years before Gluck was demanding the same thing in the preface to *Alceste*.

GALUPPI, BALDASSARE (1706–85). Italian. He wrote some 100 operas, his finest being comedies, most notably *Il Filosofo di Campagna* (1754).

GERSHWIN, GEORGE (1898–1937). American. He wrote two operas. The first, *Blue Monday* (1923), later renamed *135th Street*, is in one act and has popular songs linked by jazz recitatives. *Porgy and Bess* (1935), though more a success with drama than music critics when it opened, has gradually become the American national opera, especially after the book was tightened and the recitatives (out of place in the work) were pared down in 1942. This Black jazz/folk/serious score lives by its melodies, characterization and vitality of its music and drama. Since the famous 1953 revival with Leontyne Price and William Warfield, which was seen at home and abroad, it has been established as a classic.

GERSTER, OTTMAR (1897–1969). German. Two of his operas

have been very successful: his folk-opera *Enoch Arden* (1936), based on Tennyson's poem and full of tunes and sea sounds, and *Die Hexe von Passau* (The Witch of Passau, 1941).

GIANNINI, VITTORIO (1903–66). American composer, brother of the soprano, Dusolina Giannini, and son of Ferruccio (see page 148). His operas include *Lucidia* (1934), *The Scarlet Letter* (1938), produced in Hamburg with his sister in the lead, and *The Taming of the Shrew* (1954).

GIORDANO, UMBERTO (1867–1948). Italian. He wrote ten operas, one of which is still enormously popular in Italy and—when the public is allowed to hear it—much enjoyed elsewhere. It is *Andrea Chénier* (1896), about the French poet executed in the Revolution, a stirring piece of *verismo*. With fine singers, its effect is magnificent, concealing the fact that inspiration sags somewhat between pages of sheer glory, most notably Chénier's stunning 'Improviso', one of the most fervent revolutionary outbursts in all opera. Giordano's other remembered work is *Fedora* (1898), based on Sardou's play set in Tsarist Russia. It is rarely given outside Italy.

GLINKA, MIKHAIL IVANOVICH (1804–57). Russian. Said Stravinsky of the 'father of Russian

music': 'Poor Glinka, who was only a kind of Russian Rossini, has been Beethovenized, and nationally monumented'; though elsewhere he said of him: 'His music is minor, of course, but he is not; all music in Russia stems from him'. Glinka was not the first to use folk songs in opera, but his predecessors, Italian- French- and German-orientated, could not be described as nationalist in the way Glinka is because of two works, *A Life for the Tsar* (1834–6) and *Russlan and Ludmilla* (1838–41). The first, originally and now known as *Ivan Susanin*, is truly Russian, for all its Italian and French grand opera overtones, especially in its magnificent choral scenes. Old Susanin, the hero, is utterly Russian and the first of a line of Russian bass heroes the most famous of whom is Boris Godunov.

Russlan and Ludmilla, less successful but even more Russian, taps the other great native operatic treasure trove, the fairy tale. The colourful score and equally colourful plot is hardly a unified whole, and the opera had less success than *Susanin*.

GLUCK, CHRISTOPH WILLIBALD (1714–87). German, possibly of Bohemian origin, whose importance in operatic history is immense, even though none of his operas are regularly performed. And his reputation as a major reformer is not helped by the fact that the works against which he rebelled are largely forgotten. Added to this, even the finest of his operas—for all their sublime moments and championship by musicologists, critics and a minority of operagoers—are perhaps too formal for the average operagoer because they lack obvious melodic appeal. This would seem a good moment to mention that he apparently achieved some of his greatest moments when seated at a piano in the middle of a field, with a bottle of champagne on each side of him. By the standards of any age, this has style.

He began by accepting the musical conventions of his day: *da capo* arias (see page 330), *recitativo secco* (harpsichord chords used as 'punctuation'), a wealth of ornamentation provided by the singers, whether apt or not, and the use of castrati (see page 329). His first opera, with a libretto by Metastasio, the high priest of the genre, was *Artaserse* (1741), and not until *Orfeo ed Euridice* (1762), which had a libretto by Calzabigi, a poet as devoted to reform as he was, did he begin to achieve his ends. Accompanied recitative, deep human emotions, the exploitation of singers and chorus, and the limitation of the power of singers, together with a restoration of the original concept of opera—a classical linking of drama and music—combined to produce a masterpiece. The

lead was written for a castrato male alto, which raises insoluble problems today, though a contralto is the usual solution. In 1774, Gluck rewrote the part for a tenor for the Parisian production. *Alceste* (1767), featured on page 14, took the reforms still further, not least in an historic preface which was a call to purity in opera, by curbing singers, having music serve the poetry and by striving for simplicity. There followed *Paride ed Elena* (1770), then—Gluck's first French opera—*Iphigénie en Aulide* (1773), which led to Gluck's much publicized rivalry with Piccinni. (If only there could be public operatic rivalry today!) *Armide* (1777) was less successful, though, ironically, Piccinni began to follow Gluckian principles; however, *Iphigénie en Tauride* (1779) was a great success and, for many, is Gluck's finest score. Two stories about it must be told in even the shortest account of the composer. The first concerns the Abbé Arnaud. When someone remarked on the many fine moments in the opera, he said there was only one. 'Which?' he was asked. 'The entire work!' More significant is the reaction of the orchestra to a passage where Oreste was singing, 'Le calme rentre dans mon coeur' (The calm returns to my soul). The players said they did not understand the agitated orchestral accompaniment at that point. 'Go on all the same,' called Gluck. 'He lies. He has killed his mother!'

This was Gluck's last major achievement. Less technically assured than many less influential masters, he ranks as the re-founder of opera after it had lost its way in the mid-17th century, despite the glorious musico-dramatic examples of Monteverdi and Cavalli.

GOEHR, ALEXANDER (1932–). English. Born in Germany, his opera, *Arden Must Die*, has made a mark.

GOLDMARK, CARL (1830–1915). Austro-Hungarian. The most successful of his operas was his first, *Die Königin von Saba* (The Queen of Sheba, 1875), a tuneful work which was very popular at home and abroad.

GOTOVAC, JAKOV (1895–). Yugoslav. Best known for his *Ero the Joker* (1935), a folk-opera, influenced by Italian models.

GOUNOD, CHARLES (1818–93). French. His *Faust* (1859) was once the most popular of all operas. It is rightly called *Marguerite* in Germany, for it inhabits a different world to Goethe's masterpiece. It is none the worse for that, for the score abounds in beautiful music, though Gounod was seduced into thinking he was a master of the grand and the epic, whereas he was essentially a master of the emotions of ordinary and domestic virtues. Perhaps the success of his Mephistopheles went to his head. His other operas include *Sapho* (1851), *Le Médicin Malgré Lui* (1858); *La Reine de Saba* (1862); *Mireille* (1864) and *Roméo et Juliette* (1867). These last two can be seen in France, and *Roméo* was once frequently performed abroad, still appearing from time to time, especially in America.

GRAENER, PAUL (1872–1944). German composer of eight operas, most of them tragic. His best known are *Don Juans letzte Abenteuer* (Don Juan's Last Adventure, 1914) and *Friedemann Bach* (1931).

GRANADOS, ENRIQUE (1867–1916). Spanish composer of a number of operas which are truly native despite European influence. The finest and best known is *Goyescas* (1914).

GRÉTRY, ANDRÉ (1741–1813). French. Of Walloon descent, he was a master of *opéra comique* and the musical father of Boïeldieu, Auber, Adam, etc. His best-known works today are *Richard Coeur-de-Lion* (1784) and *Zémire et Azor* (1771).

HALÉVY, FROMENTAL (1799–1862). French composer of Jewish origin, whose most famous opera is *La Juive* (The Jewess, 1835), once very popular and still occasionally revived, mainly because he could write superb parts for singers. Eleazar was the role which Caruso was singing when his career came to an abrupt end on stage, while Rachel has been sung by Pauline Viardot, Ponselle, etc.

HAMILTON, IAIN (1922–). Scottish composer of the effective music drama, *The Catiline Conspiracy* (1974).

HANDEL, GEORGE FRIDERIC (1685–1759). German, naturalized English composer, whose operas, once considered museum pieces full of exceptionally beautiful tunes, attract a growing band of devotees. However, it is hard to believe that the stage works of a musician whose greatness is unquestioned will ever become part of the general repertoire for, whatever his ardent champions say, they lack sustained drama of the sort minor Italian composers have provided. He worked within the stultifying conventions of his day and, despite threats to throw a singer out of the window, these included all-powerful singers (their *da capo* arias with a first part, second part and first part repeated with ornaments, all too often negating characterization and situation), and also the convention of singers leaving the stage after singing their arias. Trios and quartets were very rare—the libretti, good or bad, would hardly shine in such circumstances—and the entire operation, as never before or since in operatic history, was geared to the needs of the star performers plus their adoring canary-fanciers. Somehow, before turning to the (ironically) greater dramatic triumphs of his oratorios, he managed to produce a body of work which, given fine singers, can still exalt, if hardly satisfy, the average operagoer with wide tastes. True Handelian opera-lovers will, of course, have none of these reservations. For them his operas are Olympian.

His first operas were produced in 1705, though both of them, *Almira* and *Nero*, are lost; but it was in London that he found his own German-Italian voice, arriving in the capital in 1710 and giving his *opera seria*, *Rinaldo* (1711). Notable works include *Radamisto* (1720), a mature, personally involved opera and, after several lesser pieces with appalling librettos, *Giulio Cesare* (1724), the greatest Roman of them all being sung by a castrato. Orchestrally, this is full of thrilling moments, like *Tamerlano* (1724), which also has fine accompanied recitative and a splendidly powerful death scene. *Rodelinda* (1725), like *Tamerlano*, has a tenor in a main part, a rarity in its time. It was another success.

The flood of operas that followed included *Admeto* (1727); *Riccardo Primo* (1727); *Orlando* (1733), one of his finest operas; *Alcina* (1735), full of ravishing music; *Serse* (1738), which begins with that operatic-turned-(fatuously) religious pop, 'Ombra mai fu'—Handel's Largo—and *Deidamia* (1741), his last opera. A number of his oratorios and other vocal works are staged from time to time, including *Belshazzar*, *Samson*, *Jephtha*, *Hercules* and *Semele*, this last containing captivating music. The pastoral *Acis and Galatea* is also staged, indeed was so performed in Handel's day, and quite frequently since. The oratorios saw the chorus playing a greater part than before. The switch to oratorio was mainly due to intrigues against him, to the opposition of singers and other composers and also to the huge success of *The Beggar's Opera*. Handel's melodies, operatic and otherwise, were greatly loved by the British people of his day, being heard far beyond the opera house and concert hall. He was that rarity, a hugely popular composer of genius.

HAYDN, JOSEPH (1732–1809). Austrian. His fifteen surviving operas cannot, even by devotees, be considered in the same league as his major orchestral, instrumental and choral works. However, there is a wealth of fine music in them, for all the normal weakness of the libretti, and one work, *Il Mondo della Luna* (1777), edited by Robbins-Landon, the leading Haydn expert, has been widely given.

It is from a Goldoni play and the score is delightful and witty. Before this re-discovery, the best-known work was *Lo Speziale* (The Chemist, 1768), again from a Goldoni text. Inheriting the conventions of *opera seria* and *opera buffa*, Haydn increased the role of the orchestra in opera and towards the end of his career began to feel his way towards music drama, though not enough of a revolutionary to achieve one. Gradually music and drama became welded together along the lines laid down by Gluck until in *L'Anima del Filosofo* (1791), Haydn almost created a Gluckian *opera seria*, including fine use of the chorus to heighten the drama.

HENZE, HANS WERNER (1926–). German. One of the small handful of major writers of operas since the war. His first success was a version of the Manon Lescaut story, *Boulevard Solitude* (1952), in which ballet plays an important part. In this and later works he showed himself a lyrically inclined disciple of Schoenberg—not a contradiction in terms—his next opera being *Das Ende einer Welt* (The End of a World, 1953) for radio, a satire that first showed the composer's fascination with the problem of the artist in society. In 1953 he moved to Italy, which increased his feeling for the lyrical. *König Hirsch* (King Stag, produced 1956) is a vast work after Gozzi about a king's duty, an impressive, less severely 12-tone conscious, lyrical work, which was later shortened by the composer. *Der Prinz von Homburg* (1960), from Kleist's play, ranges musically wider than before and is theatrically very skilful. *Elegy for Young Lovers* (1961), to a W. H. Auden–Chester Kallman text has a poet using and destroying his friends for his Art. It is 12-tonal yet full of melody, including mad scenes plus coloratura and flute. *The Bassarids* (1966) has the same librettists and is drawn from the *Bacchae* of Euripides, though using contemporary and universal terms of reference. Shaped like a giant symphony in one act, it has been criticized for Henze's 'inability to write economically, and to jettison ruthlessly the musical dross' (Harold Rosenthal in *Opera*, 1966), though praised by Rosenthal for its vocal, instrumental and choral writing and hailed by others as a 20th-century masterpiece. *We come to the River*, Covent Garden, 1976.

HERBERT, VICTOR (1859–1924). Irish-American. He is best remembered for his Broadway shows and songs, but wrote two operas, *Natoma* (1911) and *Madeleine* (1914).

HÉROLD, FERDINAND (1791–1833). French. He absorbed German and Italian ideas and produced one colossal success, *Zampa ou La Fiancée de Marbre* (Zampa or the Marble Betrothed, 1831), now remembered only by its rousing overture.

HINDEMITH, PAUL (1895–1963). German. After several one-act operas, he made his name with *Cardillac* (1926), a tragic piece from a Hoffmann story about a 17th-century goldsmith who murders his clients to repossess his creations. It was revived and improved by the composer in 1952, musically and dramatically. *Neues vom Tage* (News of the Day, 1929) is a satire on the Press, which landed the opera in trouble with the Gas Company: the heroine sings that electric heating is better than gas—while in the bath. By far Hindemith's best-known opera is *Mathis der Maler* (Mathis the Painter, 1934, produced 1938). It got the composer exiled from Germany as it dared to show 16th-century peasants rebelling on stage. It is a serious, impressive work, reflecting Hindemith's own views on the relation of the artist to his society, and is a significant statement, full of musical riches, rather than a popular repertoire piece. It is based on a real painter, while *Die Harmonie der Welt* (The Harmony of the World, 1957), as clearly constructed and richly musical as the former, is about the astronomer Kepler. His last opera was *Der lange Wei-*

nachtsmahl (The Long Christmas Dinner, 1961), from Thornton Wilder's play.

HOFFMANN, E. T. A. (1776–1822). German composer, conductor, critic, novelist, poet, painter who believed that 'Romantic opera is the only genuine opera'. Best known outside Germany as the hero of Offenbach's *Contes d'Hoffmann*, he wrote ten operas, including *Undine* (1816), which he hoped would lay the foundations of German Romantic opera, but this was to be Weber's later achievement.

HOLST, GUSTAV (1874–1934). English. *Savitri* (1916), on an Indian subject, has many admirers, while *The Perfect Fool* (1923), best known for its ballet music, was once very popular, not least for its parodies of Verdi and Wagner. Other operas include *At The Boar's Head* (1925) about the Falstaff of *Henry IV*, and the comic *The Tale of the Wandering Scholar* (1934). It is hard to imagine a British composer in more urgent need of reappraisal, or, indeed, of a hearing.

HONEGGER, ARTHUR (1892–1955). French composer of Swiss parentage, who made his name with the oratorio *King David* (1921), a stage work of striking power and simplicity, and with spoken dialogue. *Antigone* (1927), with a text by Cocteau after Sophocles, is not considered dramatically convincing, partly because it began as oratorio. He also wrote *Judith* (1926), *Amphion* (1931), *Cris du Monde* (1931), and then his most famous work, the stage oratorio, *Jeanne d'Arc au Bucher* (Joan of Arc at the Stake, 1936), a large-scale work in several styles, with a heroine whose part is spoken, and who is at the stake the entire performance, looking back on her life. The score is medieval sounding and modern, and the effect is most impressive. Later stage works include the opera, *Charles le Téméraire* (Charles the Reckless, 1944).

HUMPERDINCK, ENGELBERT (1854–1921). German, ironically up-staged by a modern British pop star who has 'stolen' his name. Fortunately, this friend of Wagner, who helped the Master in preparing the first *Parsifal* (1880–1), is immortal in his own right as the composer of the perfect opera for children, *Hänsel und Gretel* (1893), whose richly Wagnerian orchestration cannot daunt even young listeners, so full of charm and sheer delight is the music. Humperdinck went on trying to repeat the formula, but only *Königskinder* (The Royal Children, 1910) has had real success in Germany, if scarcely any outside.

IBERT, JACQUES (1890–1962). French. His most successful opera was his first (of nine), a one-acter, *Angélique* (1927).

JANÁČEK, LEOŠ (1854–1928). Czech. His operas are gradually becoming recognized, though not fast enough for his growing band of devotees, who are continually dismayed to find how difficult it is to convince doubting conservatives how *enjoyable* they are, and that they are no more difficult to absorb than Richard Strauss or late Puccini. His plots alienate some, while his words are so tied to the Czech language that inevitably, translations rarely catch their full flavour. Indeed, he was passionately obsessed with speech-rhythms. A humanist who embraced all nature in his love of life, he did not find himself operatically until *Jenufa* (finished 1903, produced 1904) taken from a drama by Gabriella Preissová. This superb lyrical, tragic and dramatic masterpiece is surely the ideal way to discover Janáček. It is discussed earlier on page 33. There followed *Osud* (Fate), crippled by its libretto; *The Excursions of Mr Brouček* (1920), a fantasy about a Czech bourgeois on the Moon and set in the 15th century, which contains much fine music; then another masterpiece, *Kátya Kabanová* (1921), from Ostrovsky's *The Storm*, the guilt-wracked heroine being only one of a number of memorable characters.

The Cunning Little Vixen (1924), a paen of praise to Nature, has a cast of animals (and humans) and an ending which matches Beethoven's *Pastoral Symphony* in its pantheism. *The Makropoulos Case* (1926), from Capek's play, is about a woman possessing the secret of 'eternal life'. Its first act packs too much (legal) plot for its own operatic good, but the opera is splendidly theatrical, given a major star performer in the lead, and its ending—with her longed-for death—is magnificent. Janáček's last opera, *From the House of the Dead* (produced 1930), from Dostoyevsky's book, is hard going for those geared to at least one love duet, being set in a Siberian labour camp. However, it is intensely theatrical, often very moving, and has at the head of the score Dostoyevsky's words, 'In every human being there is a divine spark.' Episodic—occasionally to a degree—there are moments when the tension slackens, and some small parts have to be brilliantly acted and sung to counterbalance this. Yet from the harrowingly melodic introduction onwards, this masterpiece has an atmosphere which is not only unique in opera, but is also totally unforgettable and thrilling. Janáček is not a cult figure: he is a major master.

KABALEVSKY, DMITRI (1904–   ). Russian. His straightforward, tuneful operas, include *The Craftsman of Clamecy* (1938); *Before Moscow* (1942); *The Family of Taras* (1944/9), about the German occupation; and *Armoured Train 14–69* (1956).

KODÁLY, ZOLTÁN (1882–1967). Hungarian. A monumental figure in his country's musical history. Best-known abroad for his *Háry János* suite, the fortunate few have seen the work staged as an opera (1926) with separate numbers and much dialogue. About a splendid Hungarian liar who, amongst other things, claims to have defeated Napoleon's army single-handed, it is popular entertainment as well as brilliant music. He also wrote *The Spinning Room of the Székelys* (1932), a one-acter, and *Czinka Panna* (1948), an historical work to commemmorate the Revolution of 1848.

KORNGOLD, ERICH WOLFGANG (1897–1957). Austrian, now a cult figure with movie buffs for his incredibly fluent scores: *The Adventures of Robin Hood* (1938/Errol Flynn), *The Sea Hawk* (1940/ditto), etc. He began as a child-prodigy at 11, his pantomime *Der Schneemann* being given at the Vienna Court Opera. There followed a number of operas including his greatest success, *Die tote Stadt* (The Dead City, 1920). His music—according to Gerhart von Westerman—seems like a synthesis between Richard Strauss and Puccini.

KŘENEK, ERNST (1900–). Austrian-born American of partly Czech descent, his best-known works being composed before he moved to America in 1938. By far his most famous piece is the jazz opera, *Jonny spielt auf* (Johnny strikes up, 1927), the first of its kind, in which Jonny, a Black, steals a violin from Daniello, then conquers the world with his dance music from it. Excellently constructed, and a sensation at first, it now seems banal to some. After *Jonny*, he composed in neo-Schubertian vein, as in *Leben des Orest* (The Life of Orestes, 1930), an attempt to condense the *Orestia* into a single evening. *Karl V* (1938) is an epic and atonal music drama, mixing drama, film and mime, while *Pallas Athene Weint* (Pallas Athene Weeps, 1956) is a brutally dramatic work in 12-note form.

LALO, ÉDOUARD (1823–92). French. One of his three operas is still given in France, *Le Roi d'Ys* (1888).

LECOCQ, CHARLES (1832–1918). French. The best known of some fifty operettas (and one attempted serious work) is *La Fille de Mme Angot* (1872).

LEHÁR, FRANZ (1870–1948). Hungarian composer of operettas, including one masterpiece, *Die lustige Witwe* (The Merry Widow, 1905). In Britain, this most melodious of skilful confections was turned (1907) into musical comedy and remained as such until the Sadler's Wells production (1958). Other works, some of which come within hailing distance of *The Merry Widow*, are *Der Graf von Luxembourg* (1909); *Gipsy Love* (1910); *Frasquita* (1922); *Paganini* (1925); *Frederica* (1928) and *Das Land des Lächelns* (The Land of Smiles, 1929). Lehár was the last great operetta composer.

LEONCAVALLO, RUGGIERO (1858–1919). Italian composer of *Pagliacci* (1892), the unsinkable, dramatic and melodic two-act twin of Mascagni's *Cavalleria Rusticana* (*Cav* and *Pag* colloquially), and, frustratingly for him, the 'other' *La Bohème* (1897). It is an enjoyable work, fascinating for obvious reasons, and with Marcello and Musetta more prominent than Mimi and Rodolfo. His other works include *Chatterton* (1896); *I Medici* (1893) whose failure made him abandon a projected trilogy about Renaissance Italy; *Zazà* (1900), which is sometimes revived; *Roland von Berlin* (1904); several operettas, and a valiant attempt to re-establish himself with *Edipo Re* (1920). He is guaranteed immortality solely on *Pagliacci* (Clowns) based on an incident when an actor killed his wife in mid-performance, the judge at the trial being Leoncavallo's father. This admirable work is a splendid introduction to opera for

newcomers and the magnificent aria, 'Vesti la giubba' (On with the Motley) has one unique claim to fame. Caruso's incomparable version of it was the first record to achieve the magic figure of a million sales.

LIEBERMANN, ROLF (1910–). Swiss. His experimental music ranges from 12-note technique to jazz and includes clever use of pastiche. His *Leonore/40/45* (1952)—the link with *Fidelio* is intentional—charmingly portrays the love of a German soldier and a Parisienne during the Second World War. There followed *Penelope* (1954) about Odysseus's wife, successfully premièred at Salzburg, and *The School For Wives* (1955), after Molière's play. He became Intendant of the Hamburg Opera (1959) and the Paris Opera in 1973 (*see* p. 279).

LORTZING, ALBERT (1801–51). German composer, actor, singer, and librettist who is little known outside Germany, except by the titles of two of his works, *Zar und Zimmermann* (Tsar and Carpenter, 1837) about Peter the Great, and *Der Wildschütz* (The Poacher, 1842). Crippled by the lack of a copyright law, which prevented his earning the money his great popularity deserved, he yet managed to retain his musical spirits in a series of charming comic operas. *Undine* (1845) is a romantic piece and less successful, while the grand opera *Regina* was far too revolutionary in theme and liberal in sentiment to be given in the aftermath of the revolutions of 1848. *Der Wildschütz* is considered his masterpiece and is musically more elegant than *Zar und Zimmermann*, while *Der Waffenenschmied* (The Armourer, 1846) is now very popular in Germany.

LULLY, JEAN-BAPTISE (1632–87). French composer of Italian birth, famous for his opera-ballets for the court of Louis XIV. A born intriguer who rose from scullion to total domination of opera production, he aimed at creating a French national opera, and, despite the formality of his methods, his music lives on. A dancer, speculator and versatile man-of-the-theatre, he died from an abscess brought about from a foot injury sustained when he hit himself instead of the floor with the staff he used for beating time. Lully became the head of music and court in 1662, then collaborated with Molière (1664–71) in opera-ballets and music for plays, including *Le Bourgeois Gentil-homme* (1670). Collaborating with the poet Quinault (see page 271), he wrote twenty operas, perhaps the finest being *Alceste* (1674), *Thésée* (1675) and *Armide* (1686), all of which were popular for a century. He directed and choreographed his works to a peak of perfection and supervised their décor. He

inaugurated the French style of overture, used short accompanied recitatives and many simple, tuneful arias, some tunes being repeated in later scenes and anticipating the *leitmotiv*. His orchestral palette was notably richer than had been usual in Italy because of the size of his orchestra, which allowed him to experiment in sounds.

MALPIERO, GIAN FRANCESCO (1882–1973). Italian, much influenced by early Italian music, and editor of works by Monteverdi, Vivaldi, etc. Many of his large output of operas have been first given abroad, including his trilogy, *Il Mistero di Venezia* (The Secret of Venice, Coburg, 1933). His *La Favola del Figlio Cambiato* (1934), to a fine politico-satiric libretto by Pirandello, had the distinction of being banned by Mussolini after its first performance in Rome as it allegedly (and in modern dress) mocked the Cabinet. Two of the most successful operas of this experimental composer have been *Giulio Cesare* (1936) and *Antonio e Cleopatra* (1938).

MARSCHNER, HEINRICH (1795–1861). German. A leading figure in the history of German Romantic opera. Nature, the macabre, humour and the life of ordinary people are all present in his work, which was influenced by Weber but is dramatic in its own right. His two best-known operas are *Der Vampyr* (1828) and *Hans Heiling* (1833), the latter his masterpiece about the gnome king who courts a human girl. This tragedy is a link between Weber and early Wagner.

MARTIN, FRANK (1890–). Swiss. His oratorio *Le Vin Herbé* (The Love Potion, 1941) has been staged. His *Der Sturm* (1956) is an almost word-for-word setting of *The Tempest* in Schlegel's translation with much *parlando* and with jazz elements.

MARTINŮ, BOHUSLAV (1890–1959). Czech. From 1932, he worked in France, then in the U.S.A. Of his dozen operas, the most successful has been *Comedy on the Bridge* (1951), which satirizes frontier restrictions.

MASCAGNI, PIETRO (1863–1945). Italian composer of the first famous *verismo* (realism) opera, the one-act *Cavalleria Rusticana* (Rustic Chivalry), doyen of second-rate operas, and based on Verga's celebrated play. Set in Sicily, it is a lurid and splendidly melodic melodrama, its music grateful for singers and audiences alike; for all that it is direct to the point of primitiveness. *Cav* (its colloquial name) won its composer first prize in a competition organized by the publishers Sanzogno, and the rest of his life was spent in trying to write another winner. *L'Amico Fritz*

(1891), a work full of charm, is still given. Its stirring intermezzo is almost as easy on the ear as *Cav*'s. *Iris* (1898), too, is sometimes given, but *Le Maschere* (The Masks, 1901), a *commedia dell'arte* inspired work, was premièred simultaneously in six Italian cities, hissed in four of them, halted in a fifth, and only completed unscathed in Rome where Mascagni was conducting it. *Il Picolo Marat* (1921), set in the French Revolution, is considered by many who know it to contain his finest music. Pre-*Cav* operas were *Guglielmo Ratcliff* and *Pinotta*. Mascagni's later life was blighted by having elected to become Mussolini's musical spokesman, composing *Nerone* in his honour and other politically inspired works, and he died under a cloud not long after his patron.

MASSENET, JULES (1842–1912). French. Arguably the most neglected minor master of our day. It is amazing that at a time when many operagoers can sing gems from the lesser works of Donizetti in the bath, the small, exquisite talent of Massenet gets so pitiful a hearing. His strengths are melodic charm, craftsmanship and Gallic sensibility, and good performances disguise any alleged over-sentimentality, as do good performances of *Butterfly*. Unfotunately, Massenet's talent is less robust than

Puccini's and, unlike the resilient Italian's, cannot always survive bad performances of his works.

His first success was *Le Roi de Lahore* (1877), and his twenty-six other operas include *Hérodiade* (1881); *Manon* (1884); *Werther* (1892); *Thaïs* (1894); *Le Jongleur de Notre-Dame* (1902) and *Don Quichotte* (1910). All are quite well known outside France, especially *Manon*, which even breaks down a certain British prejudice against what d'Indy called Massenet's 'discreet and semi-religious eroticism'. *Manon* is, of course, an accepted masterpiece, though a minority, given courage by the late Constant Lambert, ultimately prefer the less refined, but more dramatic and melodically vivid, *Manon Lescaut* by Puccini. Massenet's later works have been less successful, perhaps because he did not develop but continued to produce less-inspired versions of his earlier operas. He did not live to enjoy the triumphs of his most famous 20th-century interpreter, the Scottish soprano Mary Garden, especially in America. On occasions, Massenet could rise to the grand manner. Proof that the heights were not beyond him can be most easily found by listening to the aria, 'Pleurez, mes yeux', from *Le Cid*.

MAW, NICHOLAS (1935–). English composer of the entertaining and successful *The Ris-*ing of the Moon* (Glyndebourne, 1970), with an amusing libretto by Beverley Cross.

MÉHUL, ÉTIENNE (1763–1817). French. Admired by Napoleon, having earlier been befriended by Gluck and later admired by Beethoven and Weber, this has not ensured his immortality, for, apart from a few of his overtures, and some of his patriotic pieces, it is hard to hear any of his output today. He brought a new seriousness and power to *opéra comique*, and one of his dramas, *Joseph* (1807), about the Biblical character, was given in France and Germany long after his death.

MENOTTI, GIAN CARLO (1911–). American, born in Italy, where he created the superb Festival of Two Worlds at Spoleto in 1958 (see page 323). His operas find no favour with those who will not allow them to exist as valid music theatre, but damn them as sub-Puccinian. His musical talent is indeed limited, though he uses it skilfully, without Puccini's musical imagination or creative flair, but with an easy sense of lyricism. His real gift is in allying a small talent to extreme theatrical flair. There is a place for such works as his, and it is sheer humbug to damn him— he has been damned almost to the point of giving up composition—but praise deadly dull unoperatic pieces by 'better' modern composers.

His first success was *Amelia Goes to the Ball* (1937), while *The Telephone* (1947), a delightful one-act piece with two characters, is admired even by his fervent detractors. This work and *The Medium* (1946), a brilliantly atmospheric short work about a phoney medium faced with the unknown, made his reputation, and *The Consul* (1950), tragically topical, being set in a nameless European country after the Second World War and showing the plight of the ordinary person faced with totalitarian authority, confirmed it. The best known of his other operas has been *Amahl and the Night Visitors*. His later works include *The Saint of Bleecker Street* (1954), *Maria Golovin* (1958) and *The Last Savage* (1963).

MERCADANTE, SAVERIO (1795–1870). Italian. He produced several operas each year in Naples until, with *Il Giuramento* (The Oath, 1837), he began to change his style and, influenced by Meyerbeer, aspire to greater dramatic power and more ambitious orchestration. He failed and finally returned to his older methods.

MESSAGER, ANDRÉ (1853–1929). French conductor of the first *Pelléas et Mélisande* (1902). He wrote a number of operettas and light operas, including *Véronique* (1898) and *Monsieur Beaucaire* (1919).

MEYERBEER, GIACOMO (1791–1864). German, of Jewish parentage, who dominated the French operatic scene for a number of years and helped create French grand opera. A rich man, he was envied and resented, and has been much criticized as a musician down the years, especially by those who have never seen one of his operas sung by the sort of stellar cast that he demanded and expected in his own day. If his talent was a trifle shallow and external, it was also effective, grand and impressive. Wagner was one of the musicians Meyerbeer helped, actually getting both *Rienzi* and *The Flying Dutchman* staged in Berlin. The former shows his influence strongly. For his pains he was later grossly abused in print by Wagner at his most anti-Jewish.

The rise in the fortunes of many early 19th-century operas has not greatly assisted Meyerbeer, for the combination of superb casts and colossal spectacle is a daunting one for managements in an inflationary age. Yet his most famous works are still remembered by name and from favourite arias. After early successes in Venice writing Italian operas, he went to Paris and began a notable collaboration with Scribe, having busily absorbed all he could about every aspect of French culture and history. Together they produced *Robert le Diable* (1831), a huge success at the Opéra, with Meyerbeer, who had studied in Berlin, providing German methods and adding Italianate tunes and his new sense of French identity. There followed *Les Huguenots* (1836), the Everest of French grand operas, full of musical riches if the singers are present to seize them. He became the King of Prussia's musical director in 1842, writing *Ein Feldlager* for Jenny Lind (1844), who also sang other roles of his in Berlin. *Le Prophète* (1849) and *L'Étoile du Nord* (1854) were given in Paris and also *Le Pardon de Ploermel* or *Dinorah* (1859), best known for its Shadow Song. These two more lightweight pieces were followed by *L'Africaine*, produced the year after his death and usually considered his masterpiece.

MILHAUD, DARIUS (1892–1974). French. Wide-ranging and possessor of a superb technique, opera was his favourite medium. His works include several children's operas, also *Le Pauvre Matelot* (1927), which has a libretto by Jean Cocteau and was his first success. It is a gloomy story, most economically and skilfully handled by the composer. His large-scale *Christophe Colomb* (1930) was first given in Berlin and presents the hero's life in twenty-seven scenes. It demands a lecturer and chorus, film sequences as well as acted scenes, ballet and mime, choral sequences on one vowel, etc., along with a mix-

ture of symbolism, allegory and reality. The libretto is by Paul Claudel. It greatly impresses some, others find it short on dramatic development and suffering from an excess of happenings. *Bolivar* (1943) did not create such an effect when given in Paris in 1950. *David* (1954), a colossal work to celebrate the 3,000th anniversary of Israel, has been more successful despite its demands, which include forty-three singers, two large choruses, dancers and a vast orchestra. In these huge works, Milhaud has revived the tradition of French grand opera. In striking contrast are his three one-act pieces, roughly eight minutes in length each. These entertaining *opéras-minutes* are *L'Enlèvement d'Europe*, *L'Abandon d'Ariane* and *La Délivrance de Thésée*, first given together in 1928.

MILLÖCKER, KARL (1842–99). Austrian composer and conductor, the most famous of whose operettas are *Der Bettelstudent* (The Beggar Student, 1882) and *Der arme Jonathan* (Poor Jonathan, 1890).

MONIUSZKO, STANISLAW (1819–72). Polish composer of his country's national opera, *Halka* (1848), a romantic tragedy still very popular today and recognizably Polish in idiom.

MONTEMEZZI, ITALO (1875–1952). Italian. Little known

outside Italy except for his masterpiece, *L'Amore dei Tre Re* (1913), which was often given in America. Not one of the *verismo* school, he was more in the tradition of Boito.

MONTEVERDI, CLAUDIO (?1567–1643). Italian. The first great master, more honoured in the texts than in performance until recently, but now, though most of his output is lost, he is much loved by many operagoers. A turning point was the Glyndebourne production of *L'Incoronazione di Poppea* (1642) in 1962, realized by Raymond Leppard, who has done so much to make him and his pupil, Cavalli, popular. Other realizations during this century have included versions by d' Indy and Malpiero.

Monteverdi's first opera, and the first to have some hold in the repertoire, is *La Favola d' Orfeo*, 1607 (see page 13). After this superb outburst of passionate dramatic recitative, his fellow countrymen presumably enjoyed a stream of his endless melody in many operas that are lost to us. Of all the operas he wrote before moving from Mantua to Venice in 1613, only part of one, the sublime Lamento from *Arianna* (1608) survives. We have the short dramatic cantata, *Il Combattimento di Tancredi e Clorinda* (1624), complete with a brilliant evocation of a battle, then another large group of operas was lost when Mantua

was sacked. When the world's first public opera house opened in Venice in 1637, Monteverdi, now in holy orders, began to work for the stage again. Only two pieces survive, the first of which is *Il Ritorno d'Ulisse in Patria* (1641), a magnificent work, surpassed by Monteverdi's final opera, *L'Incoronazione di Poppea* (1642). This is one of the supreme glories of Italian opera. Totally amoral, as befits the love story of Nero and Poppea, the pair bring down the curtain with the first great love duet, as sweetly sensuous as any later ones. The Nurse has a scene of self-congratulation that her mistress's success will turn her into a 'ladyship', too, and her music has a colloquial speed and humour rarely matched again in Italy until Verdi's *Falstaff*; while, in a totally different vein, Seneca's scene in which he prepares for death is as stirring as it is noble. Monteverdi is able to follow this marvel with a scene of rejoicing at Seneca's death, with Nero and Lucan singing joyfully at the removal of such a blot on their happiness: 'Now that Seneca is dead, let us sing love songs'. The felicities are endless. Not until Mozart's day did a composer produce such a blazing operatic masterpiece, and one that can so stir the feelings of modern audiences.

Monteverdi was the father of *bel canto* and *buffo*; his use of recitative was a sublime example for posterity to follow; he invented the tremolo effect, whose throbbing so much increases the suggestion of excitement and feeling, and he may have been the first to use pizzicato to add to orchestral colour. None of this would matter, except to musicologists, if it had not been for the fact that he was a genius. We have little more than the vocal and bass lines of *Poppea* on which realizers must provide their versions, and these versions and the problems of orchestration must be worked out with scholarship, imagination and love. Yet even with these problems, this astonishing work comes down to us as perhaps the only Italian opera to match Verdi at his greatest.

MOZART, WOLFGANG AMADEUS (1756–91). Austrian. The incomparable musician who, with Verdi and Wagner, is one of opera's supreme trinity. It is the inestimable good fortune of operagoers that he reserved so much of his most deeply felt and personal music for his operas. Only parts of his concertos have something of this personal feeling also. It is not that his theatre music is his 'best' work; simply that, except for those poor lost souls whose tragedy it is not to like the human singing voice, it is some of his most emotional and moving. Goethe compared him with Shakespeare. Both

were artistically all things to all men, divinely ambivalent, middle of the road men rather than reformers, with matchless sympathy for humanity. In their greatest works they are concerned not with heroes and villains but with people, who may be heroic or villainous but are all drawn in the round.

Mozart's early operas, full of delights, are naturally remembered mainly because they are by him: *La Finta Semplice* (1767) after Goldoni; *Bastien und Bastienne* (1768), based on Favart's parody of Jean Jacques Rousseau's *Le Devin du Village*, and with a German text; *Mitridate, Rè di Ponto* (1770), an *opera seria*; *Ascanio in Alba* (1771); and *Lucio Silla* (1772), in which the true Mozart starts to show itself at times. *La Finta Giardiniera* (The Pretended Garden-Girl, 1775) has delightful moments, improved characterization and the beginnings of a symphonic operatic style, while *Il Rè Pastore* (1775) is a succession of arias. *Zaide* (1779) anticipates *Die Entführung* in its plot and, though unfinished, is a fine singspiel. Then came the first masterpiece, *Idomeneo* (1781), discussed on page 15, and a sublime example of *opera seria*.

There followed the utterly delightful *Die Entführung aus dem Serail* (The Abduction from the Seraglio, 1782), an irresistible musical comedy with spoken dialogue and several superb characters, most notably Osmin, in charge of the Pasha's harem, and one of the finest comic creations in all opera. His mock villainous music is marvellous, his drinking duet with Pedrillo is (one may legitimately claim) utterly intoxicating, while in more serious vein, Constanze's 'Martern aller Arten' (Torture me and flay me) is a coloratura showstopper. There is a lighthearted rapture about this opera which Mozart never again attempted except at suitable moments, for now he entered his matchless maturity. After three minor works, one of which, a parody of the world of opera, *Der Schauspieldirektor* (The Impresario, 1786), is sometimes rightly given, he wrote the first of four late masterpieces, three of them with the great librettist, Lorenzo da Ponte.

The first was *Le Nozze di Figaro* (1786), discussed on page 16. It was followed by *Don Giovanni* (1787) which, like Hamlet, is the subject of constant argument. The 19th century overplayed the tragic side of the opera, usually ending it with the Don's descent to Hell, but this flatly contradicts da Ponte's description of the work as a *dramma giocoso* (a gay—in the old sense of the word—drama). Not as tidy a work as *Figaro*, it is even more ambitious, not so much because of its superb characterization, but because, like Shakespeare, Mozart is able to overlap comedy and tragedy with astonishing facility: his idea of *dramma giocoso* transfigures da Ponte into something sublime, while in the last act he displays a quite astonishing power. He may not have been a revolutionary, but this opera presages the musical revolution to come.

There followed the most sensuous of his operas, and one that is at last widely understood, as well as adored, *Così fan tutte* (Thus do they all/All women do it, 1790). The plot is pure farcical comedy, though this tale of two lovers who go away only to return disguised as Albanians to test the constancy of their mistresses, is allegedly based on a true incident. In all music there are few more extraordinary feats than the way Mozart, working within the classical idiom, gradually warms his scores until, when the two women succumb in their beautifully contrasted ways, a most passionate atmosphere is created. *Così fan tutte* disturbs as well as enchants. Its felicities are too many to list here. Suffice it to state that cynical and wryly comic as the opera may be, Mozart's music, for all its outward gaiety, is as profound and stirring as anything he or anyone else has written. Over-pretty productions with arch acting do the opera great harm (for the opposite, see page 254).

The last of this quartet was *Die Zauberflöte* (The Magic

Flute, 1791). Its fantastical fairy tale plot was concocted by a most versatile man-of-the-theatre, Emmanuel Schikaneder, whose efforts have been abused and hailed with equal vigour. As the opera was an instant hit and its characters at once became and have remained favourites, those who mock the libretto are on dangerous ground. Arthur Jacobs has summed it up as an opera 'of Masonic and humanistic symbolism', whereas some regard it as a silly pantomime redeemed by divine music. The latter choose to ignore that Mozart was making a statement on his own and humanity's religious and spiritual aspirations and on the search for truth. Though the opera lives because of Mozart, his actor-singer-manager librettist must have his share of credit. Goethe thought so, being so impressed by Schikaneder's efforts that he felt inspired to write a sequel.

Also in 1791 came *La Clemenza di Tito*, an *opera seria* full of musical riches, but lacking the dramatic vitality and characterization which Mozart breathed into the dying form so memorably in *Idomeneo*. Yet the opera, when done as finely as Covent Garden's 1974 production, can achieve a tremendous effect.

Nine weeks after the première of *Die Zauberflöte*, before which, according to Wagner, German opera scarcely existed,

Mozart died in circumstances known even to the tone-deaf. It is useless, if fascinating, to imagine the masterpieces he should have lived to write. The miracle is that, amongst all his vast output, he had the time to produce so much opera. As for the mystery of his genius, that is the supreme miracle.

MUSGRAVE, THEA (1928–). English composer of *The Decision* and the admired *The Voice of Ariadne* (1974).

MUSSORGSKY, MODEST (1839–81). Russian. His one completed opera, *Boris Godunov* (1870), is discussed on page 26. This genius, untidy in his life as well as his work, completed nothing else. His early works were experimental and gave little evidence of the glory to come, though *Salammbo* (1863–6) has moments of steely realism and *The Marriage* (unfinished but performed 1909), from Gogol's comedy, already shows his mastery of setting speech inflections to music and creating character. After *Boris Godunov* —his sudden and only ascent to the Olympian heights of Shakespeare and Michelangelo —he achieved one more masterpiece, *Khovanshchina* (1872–80), which was completed and orchestrated by Rimsky-Korsakov. Though it is theatrically less effective than *Boris*, lacking characters to equal the Tsar or, indeed, the Russian people (they appear, but less memorably), there are scenes of tremendous power and emotion, and of beauty. For those who revel in the sound and depths of feeling that Mussorgsky provides, as well as his deeply felt melodies, a performance of this opera is always a major event if (it would sadly seem) only for a minority. From 1874 to 1880 he worked on *Sorochinsky Fair*, after Gogol's comedy and using Ukrainian folk-melodies. He left it unfinished and there are several versions of it. His life makes sad reading and his death from drink deprived Russia of her greatest composer. Grandeur, originality and greatness of soul, qualities found in *Boris* and the finest of the songs, justify this claim. Only he among native composers was able not only to penetrate the very soul of Russia and her people, but express it majestically, starkly, lyrically, humorously and with devastating emotion.

NESSLER, VICTOR (1841–90). German composer and conductor, very popular in his own day, his best-known work being *Der Trompeter von Säckingen* (1884).

NICOLAI, OTTO (1810–49). German composer and conductor and a Kappellmeister in Vienna and Berlin. Only one of his operas is remembered, his masterpiece, *Die lustigen Weiber*

von Windsor (The Merry Wives of Windsor, 1849), from Shakespeare's play.

NIELSEN, CARL (1865–1931). Danish. His two operas are *Saul and David* (1902) and the comedy *Maskarade* (1906), Denmark's national opera.

NOVÁK, VITĚZLAV (1870–1949). Czech. He has been compared to Janáček in his view of humanity and nature. His operas include *The Imp of Zvíkov* (1915), the patriotic *Karlstejn* (1916) and *The Grandfather's Heritage* (1926), full of Slovak colour.

OFFENBACH, JACQUES (1819–80). German-born French composer of incomparable operettas and one famous opera, *Les Contes d'Hoffmann*. It is a mattter of taste whether one prefers him to Johann Strauss, who allegedly wrote better tunes: both rank—and one may add Sullivan—as the supreme masters of operetta. Offenbach's inspired nickname, 'The Mozart of the Champs Élysées', given him by Rossini, sums him up as does nothing else. His high spirits, via his most famous Can-Can, are known to millions who have never seen his works in the theatre, and no operetta composer, except perhaps Lehár, and few opera composers, can match his sweetly sensual music at its best: the Letter Song from *La Perichole* and the Hymn to

Bacchus from *Orpheus in the Underworld*. His music is in turn exhilarating, cynical, tender, funny, sexy and happy, and his orchestration is superb.

Born Jakob Eberst in Cologne, he went to Paris as a youth, made a reputation as a cellist and a conductor, became manager of the Théâtre des Champs-Élysées in 1855, which saw his first triumphs, then changed the tiny Théâtre Comte into Les Bouffes-Parisiens and became an immortal. He turned Johann Strauss's thoughts to operetta, and Sullivan was influenced by him except in the taboo matter (in Victorian Britain) of sex. His finest works (assuming there are no forgotten masterpieces among his ninety-odd operettas) are *Orphée aux Enfers* (1858), *La Belle Hélène* (1864), *La Vie Parisienne* at the Palais Royal (1866), and, at the Varietés, *La Grande Duchesse de Gérolstein* (1867) and *La Périchole* (1868), also his one romantic opera, *Les Contes d'Hoffmann*, posthumously given in 1881. A lesser work of art than his finest operettas, it nevertheless is enormously popular because of its tunes and chances for spectacle. Owing to his death, it was revised, orchestrated and given recitatives by Guiraud. As the composer-entertainer *in excelsis* of the Second Empire, Offenbach suffered an eclipse after its fall, and today some of his most topical pieces present problems—all of which are banished by the scintillating sound of him.

ORFF, CARL (1895–). German. His solution to the estrangement of modern music and the public has been to go back to essentials: vibrant rhythms, folk-song, strikingly exciting and primitive effects and, whatever progressives may say, a distinct and 'meaningful' style. This was first heard in *Carmina Burana* (1937), a cantata rather than an opera but which is most effective when staged, using chorus and dancers and three soloists. These minstrels' songs of the 13th century are racy, sensual, amusing and simple paens to life, love and nature, and Orff's music to them is notable for its powerful percussive effects. *Carmina Burana* is his best-known work though opinions of it vary widely. There followed *Der Mond* (The Moon, 1939) a fairy-tale opera along the same lines as *Carmina Burana*, but even more melodic; *Catulli Carmina* (1943), a scenic cantata dealing with Catullus's love for Lesbia; the tragic opera *Antigonae* (1949), and *Trionfi dell'Afrodite* (1953). His other works include *Oedipus der Tyrann* (1959), from Sophocles's tragedy, and what is generally considered his masterpiece, *Die Kluge* (The Clever Woman, 1943) after a story by Grimm. This opera is theatrically his greatest achievement and the score, as simple as ever, is spirited, delightful and often funny.

PACINI, GIOVANNI (1769–1867). Italian. His more than seventy operas, popular in their day, were Rossinian in manner, including the speed in which they were written.

PAËR, FERDINANDO (1771–1839). Italian. His most successful work was *Le Maître de Chapelle* (The Precentor, 1831). In 1812 he succeeded Spontini at the Italian Opera in Paris. His forty operas include a sequel to *Le Nozze di Figaro*.

PAISIELLO, GIOVANNI (1740–1816). Italian. He composed a *Barbiere di Siviglia* (1782) so popular that Rossini was considered to be committing *lèse-majesté* by using the same play.

PEDRELL, FELIPE (1841–1922). Spanish. Though the 'founder of Spanish music-drama' wrote a number of operas, first wrongly dubbed Wagnerian, none has become widely popular, but his influence and inspiration fired later composers.

PENDERECKI, KRZYSTOF (1933–). Polish composer whose *The Devils of Loudun* is an astonishing, searing piece of music theatre, though musically it has disappointed many of his admirers.

PERGOLESI, GIOVANNI BATTISTA (1710–36). Italian. He wrote the famous intermezzo (an interlude set between the acts of a serious opera), *La Serva Padrona* (The Maid as Mistress, 1733). This sparkling work was particularly influential in French opera and is given today, when the serious piece surrounding it originally, *Il Prigionier Superbo*, is forgotten. His comic talent was far superior to his more serious work, but note his early death.

PERI, JACOPO (1561–1633). Italian composer of the first opera, *Dafne* (1597), whose music is lost. *Euridice* (1600), in which he sang Orpheus, survives, complete with the expressive dramatic recitative which later composers were to use so strikingly. It was his finest work, and he and his rival Caccini rank as the founding fathers of opera, *Euridice* in particular proving the viability of the new art form. Also see *Camerata*, page 328.

PFITZNER, HANS (1869–1949). German. Only one of his four operas is known outside Germany, *Palestrina* (1917). This is about the famous Italian composer, but based on the legend that by composing *Missa Papae Marcelli* after being inspired by angels, he managed to persuade the Council of Trent not to ban polyphony. A Wagnerian and Romantic nationalist, the angelic scene in *Palestrina* is considered a supreme example of 20th-century music by his admirers. Other works include *Der arme Heinrich* (Poor Henry, 1895), *Die Rose vom Liebesgarten* (The Rose from the Garden of Love, 1901), *Christelflein* (The Little Elf of Christ, 1906) and *Das Herz* (The Heart, 1931).

PICCINNI, NICCOLÒ (1728–1800). Italian. Against his wishes, the rival of Gluck, whom he admired. His *La Cecchina, ossia La Buona Figliuola* (The Good Daughter, 1760), witty, touching and well characterized, was a huge success and has been revived in Italy. Later, the rival followers of himself and Gluck divided Paris, where he had settled, into two camps. A director had both men compose an *Iphigénie en Tauride*, Piccinni's fine effort (1781) not matching Gluck's. A later success was *Didon* (Dido, 1783).

PIZZETTI, ILDEBRANDO (1880–1968). Italian. One of the most distinguished of the generation after Puccini who reacted against *verismo* and extreme Italianate lyricism. Pizzetti adhered 'to a pervasive declamation of the voice part' and reduced 'the static lyric element to a minimum' (Mosco Carner). *Debora e Jaele* (1922) is considered the finest of his music dramas. His other works include *Fedra* (1905) to a text by d'Annunzio, *Fra Gherardo*

(1928), *Vanna Lupa* (The Vain She-Wolf, 1950), *La Figlia di Jorio* (1954) and *L'Assassinio nella Cattedrale* (1958). The last two works were taken respectively from a d'Annunzio play and T. S. Eliot's *Murder in the Cathedral*. Both have been successfully given outside Italy, where he ended his distinguished career with *Clitennestra* (1965).

PONCHIELLI, AMILCARE (1834–86). Italian. His nine operas include *La Gioconda* (The Joyful Girl, 1876), the sort of second-rate masterpiece which brings out the Puritan worst in most British opera critics, yet, given a fine cast, is utterly irresistible to the majority of opera-lovers.

POULENC, FRANCIS (1899–1963). French. His operas include the comic *Le Gendarme Incompris* (The Misunderstood Gendarme, 1920, the amusingly satiric *Les Mamelles de Tirésias* (The Breasts of Tiresias, 1944), and *Les Dialogues des Carmélites* (1957), with a text by Bernanos, about the fate of the Carmelite nuns in Revolutionary Paris. A serious opera, much of it in *arioso*, it has an unforgettable last scene when the nuns mount the guillotine, singing the 'Salve Regina'.

PROKOFIEV, SERGEY SERGEYEVICH (1891–1953). Russian. He started composing operas at nine and achieved at least four major works. Official Soviet policy towards music was at its most unfortunate in the 1940s when he returned from a long exile abroad, and this no doubt robbed the world of several masterpieces. His four finest operas are *The Love of the Three Oranges* (1921), *The Fiery Angel*, written in the 1920s and produced in 1955, *The Duenna*, written 1940–1 and produced in 1946, and *War and Peace*, written in 1941–2 and produced in 1946.

The first of these, a fantastical anti-romantic entertainment, was premièred in Chicago, while *The Fiery Angel* was first staged in Venice. It is a thrillingly theatrical story of possession and passion culminating in an electrifying scene in a convent. *The Duenna* is a charming version of Sheridan's text for Linley's opera, while *War and Peace* is a colossal epic. Admittedly it is necessary to know something of Tolstoy's masterpiece, an advantage enjoyed by all Russians, but there are no complications in the music, the opera being a rare example of successful use of conventional sound in a modern work. Part I, *Peace*, is the most admired section, harking back to late 19th-century Russian romanticism, while Part 2, *War*, has been accused of banality, but is strikingly effective. With the opera conquering London and Sydney in the early 1970s, however, such criticisms are academic for many thousands who recognize the 'genuine article' when they hear it.

PUCCINI, GIACOMO (1858–1924). Italian. The saviour of innumerable opera companies, thanks to three adored house-fillers, *La Bohème*, *Tosca* and *Madama Butterfly*. Half a century after his death, he remains, as Desmond Shawe-Taylor has written, 'the only operatic composer since Verdi and Wagner to make a large and effective contribution to the regular international repertoire', and the abuse once heaped on him by the austere and the jealous, abuse that can sometimes be heard even today, seems more fatuous than ever. Spike Hughes wrote in *Famous Puccini Operas* that his music 'was considered "sickly" and one has heard his long and infectious soaring tunes described as "cheap" and "empty"'. Hughes noted that Puccini was granted at best a sense of theatre, 'a not inconsiderable asset, let us admit, to a composer who hoped to earn a living in the opera house'. In *Opera* by Edward Dent, possibly the best short book on the subject ever written in English, the author descends to sheer bitchery about Puccini's capacity for making money, also repeating the old chestnut that all the operas (including those written when the phonograph had only just ceased being an idea in Edison's multi-purpose brain) were written so that they could be divided up into sections for the gramophone. He even alleges that Puccini's American operas were written to exploit the new American market, not, as was the actual case, that this self-confessed hunter of wildfowl, libretti and women liked the stories.

Puccini was Verdi's natural successor though he wisely never tried to match his great predecessor, who, like Shakespeare, could handle themes of heroism, honour, friendship, revenge, patriotism and epic love. But Puccini's more limited world suited his more limited talent, which was none the less a colossal one. To a gift for melody which is superbly lyrical, sensuously and deeply appealing and strongly projected, and to a quite exceptional theatrical flair, he was able to add masterly and often enchanting orchestration. A keen student of contemporary music, including Debussy (*La Fanciulla del West* had Debussian harmonies) and Stravinsky, he was also influenced by the immediate past, not only by Verdi but by Wagner, including the latter's *leitmotiv* technique. Yet he remained and remains unique, for all his influence on would-be imitators and on the lighter stage, most notably late Lehár, and composers, good and bad, of film music. He is not thought of primarily as a choral composer, yet the first act of

Turandot is the direct, but totally Puccinian, descendant of Mussorgsky's choral writing.

Born in Lucca, Puccini was one of a line of musicians. His teacher in Milan was Ponchielli and his first opera was *Le Villi* (1883). Set in *Giselle* country (complete with the Wilis who dance faithless swains to death), it was a success, even with the highly critical Verdi, who yet was worried abut Puccini's apparent symphonic tendencies. The short opera has a middle section entirely given over, a few bars of choral writing apart, to mime and dance and speech—and music. The R.C.A. recording (1974) has revealed the score to be full of exciting anticipations, for all the non-Puccinian nature of the story. *Edgar* (1889) has a ghastly libretto and the opera failed badly, though, again, it is full of interest for the devout.

At last, with *Manon Lescaut* (1893) came mastery which justified the House of Ricordi's faith in Puccini's talent and provided the operatic repertoire with a work of intoxicating lyricism though only one scene, the third act, has genius. That the characterization does not always reach later standards is forgotten in the flood of melody, and the allegedly anti-climatic last act never fails with the right singers.

La Bohème (1896), the most universally admired and loved of the operas, is discussed on page 31. *Tosca* (1900) rapidly conquered the world, and ivory-tower Puritans like Joseph Kerman, author of the essential *Opera as Drama*, who condemned it as a 'shabby little shocker', cannot stop its gigantic popularity. Because of its Grand Guignol moments in Act II and ultra-dramatic plot, its admirers sometimes allow that Puccini lowered his standards by, as he admitted, colouring the drama, not illuminating it from within. Yet its atmospheric power and melodic and dramatic strength have gripped thousands of audiences and overwhelmed them when the singers do the opera justice. It is a far more *verismo* opera than the poetic, episodic *Bohème*, less of a tear-jerker, more of a theatrical body-blow. The play by Sardou on which it is based is forgotten, but *Tosca* lives.

Madama Butterfly (1904) was a famous flop at its first appearance, after which a few revisions were made and, in front of a friendly as opposed to a deliberately hostile audience, it triumphed. It is a true tragedy, as every excellent performance reveals. The actress-singer of Butterfly fails if she cannot reveal the part as tragic, but only provides sentiment and sentimentality. Based on Belasco's play, which in turn was drawn from a short story by John Luther Long, it has a heroine who is the ultimate Puccinian 'little woman/girl' whose love is expiated in death.

Subtly and sometimes exotically orchestrated, the opera is and has been quite simply adored by millions. Even critics who know its music far too well, are occasionally seen dabbing their eyes at key moments, and let no one mistake Puccini's extraordinarily powerful achievement at the end of the opera. The whole of Butterfly's final scene reveals a capacity for grandeur that he rarely attempted in his career.

La Fanciulla del West (The Girl of the Golden West, 1910) is given less often than it deserves. Based on Belasco's melodrama set in the Californian Gold Rush period, and with a heroine, Minnie, angelically pure, but quite prepared to cheat at cards to save her man, it is thinly characterized by Puccinian standards and short of the procession of arias conservative Puccinians expect. Yet this *verismo* work has an expert and evocatively atmospheric score, and its comparative lack of success cannot be put down to its Wild West setting and resulting, alleged, lack of credibility. Given a good Minnie and a fine cast it always makes an effect.

La Rondine (1917) is rarely given. Puccini's creative genius is not at its best, yet, in performance (except in London in 1974) and on disc, its melodic quality is happily evident and the crowd scenes are masterly. Insults such as 'the poor man's Traviata' tend to misfire when so much typical Puccinian charm is on display.

There followed the far better-known *Il Trittico* (1918), the triple-bill consisting of *Il Tabarro* (The Cloak), *Suor Angelica* and *Gianni Schicchi*. *Il Tabarro*, set on a Seine barge, is a *verismo* masterpiece. The atmosphere created from the opening bars of the music is as vivid as the characters are perceptively drawn, especially, perhaps, Michele. He is the skipper of the barge who, having first appeared sinister, then deeply sympathetic and finally murderous, kills his wife's lover. The score is as passionate (and not just sexually so) as anything Puccini ever wrote. *Suor Angelica* is the least popular of the three. It is at first steeped in the placid atmosphere of a convent, then superbly dramatic and melodic in the great scene when the heroine is confronted by her iron-hearted aunt bearing news of the death of Angelica's illegitimate child, and, finally, bathed in religious bathos of the Cecil B. de Mille kind when the opera ends with a miracle which is too much for the averge Catholic, let alone everyone else. *Gianni Schicchi*, featuring Dante's lovable rogue, is a scintillating end to *Il Trittico*. Puccinians resent its being over-praised at the expense of the Master's other operas, yet it is hard not to over-praise such supreme skill.

Turandot (1926), finished after Puccini's death by Franco Alfano, is his grandest work, a black fairy story complete with a 'little woman' in Liu whose story provides the tragedy, while the ice-cold Princess Turandot gives sopranos one of the toughest roles in the whole of opera. Calaf is a conventional enough hero and none the worse for that; Ping, Pong and Pang are marvellous creations. The score, passionately Italian with totally successful oriental interpolations, is beyond praise in Act I, thrilling in Act II, and so fine in Act III up to the point where Puccini died, when his Liu was dead, that the loss of the final love scene as the icy princess turns to fire will always seem tragic. Alfano's efforts are excellent, but remain a valiant try. Adami's libretto from Gozzi's play is a fine springboard for greatness (he had written the excellent one for *Il Tabarro*), but, like Illica and Giacosa who provided libretti for Puccini's most famous works, he was dominated by the composer, more a master of the theatre, physical as well as lyric, than any of them.

PURCELL, HENRY (*c.* 1659–95). English. His one true opera, *Dido and Aeneas* (1689 or 1690) is an outright masterpiece. His other works were essentially magnificent incidental pieces for theatrical spectacles, including *The Fairy Queen*, an 'improved' version of Shakespeare's *Dream*. *Dido* is a short work and a complete operatic experience, in three acts, which culminates in Dido's incomparable lament, 'When I am dead and laid in earth'.

RACHMANINOV, SERGEY (1873–1943). Russian composer and pianist. He wrote three operas including *Aleko* (1893), an effective piece which is occasionally heard.

RAMEAU, JEAN-PHILIPPE (1683–1764). French. He became famous when he was 50 despite critical doubts, after his first opera, *Hippolyte et Aricie* (1733). He is regarded as the founder of the modern theory of harmony and at his finest— in his tragic operas—he rivalled his mighty contemporaries, Bach and Handel. He reached his creative peak with *Les Indes Galantes* (The Courtly Indies, 1735), *Castor et Pollux* (1737), *Dardanus* (1737) and *Zoroastre* (1739), the first of these being revived with tremendous success at the Paris Opéra in 1952. In the *guerre des bouffons* (1752–4), he represented the French, as opposed to the Italian, tradition at a time when Paris was divided into two camps. He breathed new life into baroque music and made recitative more flexible than it had been in his great predecessor Lully's music, increasing the depth of characterization. French classical opera in his hands became more

exciting and dramatic and, indeed, entertaining. He was much criticized, but later in the century, Gluck was to begin his reforms along the same thrillingly austere lines.

RAVEL, MAURICE (1875–1937). French. He wrote two operas, both brilliant and still popular miniatures. They are *L'Heure Espagnole* (1907), a racy one-acter set in a clockmaker's shop, and *L'Enfant et les Sortilèges* (The Child and the Spells, 1925), an enchanting piece, to a Collette libretto, in which furniture, books and toys come to life to rebel against a naughty child.

RESPIGHI, OTTORINO (1879–1936). Italian. One of the group born a generation after Puccini who rebelled against *verismo*. More drawn to German trends as well as earlier Italian forms, Respighi's nine operas, mostly richly scored, have not stayed in the repertoire. However, *Belfagor* (1923), *Maria Egizica* (1932) and *La Fiamma* (The Flame, 1934), were considerable successes in their day.

REUTTER, HERMANN (1900–). German. His eight operas are notably bold in theme—Faust, Don Juan, etc.—and carefully constructed to his own fine librettos, though lacking spontaneity. A famous accompanist, he writes gratefully for the voice. His biggest success has been *Dr Johannes Faust* (1936), a folk-opera drawn from an old puppet play.

REYER, ERNEST (1823–1909). French. After having his *opéra-comique Maître Wolfram*, praised by his friend Berlioz he later became a Wagnerian to the extent of basing his great success, *Sigurd* (produced 1883), on the *Neiblunglied*.

REZNIČEK, EMIL NICOLAUS VON (1860–1945). Austrian composer and conductor, best known abroad for the overture to his sparkling *Donna Diana* (1894).

RIMSKY-KORSAKOV, NIKOLAY (1844–1908). Russian. The master orchestrator who provided versions of his friends' operas, notably *Boris Godunov* (the most famous orchestration, though too bright for purists) and *Khovanschchina* (orchestration and completion) by Mussorgsky, and *Prince Igor* (completion with Glazunov) by Borodin. Most of his own operas are on Russian themes, and his penchant for the fantastic and mythical, while making for colourful entertainment, also causes a lack of heart and humanity in many of his works. These include *The Maid of Pskov* (1873) which does display human emotions; *May Night* (1880), a colourful folk-story full of dance and spectacle, but short on storyline and character; and *The Snow*

Maiden (1882), the best known of his early operas, which embraces fairies and humans. There followed *Mlada* (1892), *Christmas Eve* (1895) and the spectacular *Sadko* (1898), a favourite work in Russia, with a feeling for history giving it a new dimension. *Mozart and Salieri* (1898), the first neo-classical opera, is based on the legend that Mozart was poisoned by his rival. *Kashchey the Immortal* (1902) returns to the fairy world, after *The Tsar's Bride* (1899) had displayed the first ordinary human emotions since *The Maid of Pskov*. *The Invisible City of Kitezh* (1907) is rich in lyrical music, while *The Golden Cockerel* (1909) is the composer's best-known opera outside Russia. It is an entertaining mixture of fantasy, lyricism, spectacle and almost totally obscure satire. The orchestration is brilliant even by Rimsky-Korsakov's standards, but the work is shallow because of the lack of humanity on display.

ROSSINI, GIOACCHINO (1792–1868). Italian composer and wit, and first master of the age of glory. Few things have been more delightful for opera-goers over the past quarter-century than the rediscovery of work after work by him of surpassing delight, for it seemed that he was to be remembered as an Interesting Historical Personality, Monument even, who was destined to live by a single opera. Stendhal in his galloping, inaccurate, captivating biography may have exaggerated when he wrote that (after *Tancredi*, 1813) 'the glory of the man is only limited by the limits of civilization itself; and he is not yet 22', but the hero-worshipping biographer's heart was in the right place.

After sensibly obtaining a town trumpeter as a father and a singer as a mother, Rossini rapidly progressed via the Bologna Conservatory, where he wrote his first opera, *Demetrio e Polibio* (produced 1812). Mostly buffo pieces followed, including the delightful one-act *La Scala di Seta* (The Silken Ladder) which, oddly, was a failure. His first success was *La Pietra del Paragone* (The Touchstone, 1812), complete with the first chance to hear his crescendo, but, after two more works, it was *Tancredi* which made him internationally famous. Its most famous aria, 'Di tanti palpiti', swept Italy and, indeed, Europe like a pop hit today. To be noted in *Tancredi* is the most feeling love music he ever wrote (it was not his speciality) and an increasing mastery of orchestration.

There followed *L'Italiana in Algeri* (1813), composed in three weeks and a particular favourite of many Rossinians for its intoxicating tunes. It was his first great *opera buffa*. Less successful were *Aureliana in Palmira* (1813), some of its music, including the overture, being later used in *Il Barbiere*, and *Il Turco in Italia* (1814), which was (rightly) unfavourably compared with *L'Italiana*. *Sigismondo* also failed. Rossini, now in charge of both Naples' opera houses, wrote the lead in *Elisabetta, Regina d'Inghilterra* (1815) for Isabella Colbran, his mistress, later his wife. This enjoyable, if minor, work was the first occasion on which recitatives were accompanied by strings and ornaments were fully written out. The next year —at Rome—came the disastrous first night of *Il Barbiere di Siviglia*. (The opera is discussed on page 18.) Another highlight of this period was *Otello* (1816), a very fine work not entirely submerged by Verdi's masterpiece. Its happy ending was 'By Public Demand': the original ending was too much for them.

Rossini was now at the peak of his creative ardour, his operas including *Armida* (1817); *La Cenerentola* (Cinderella, 1817), like *The Barber* written originally for a coloratura contralto (or mezzo); *Mosè in Egitto* (later *Moise* in France) in 1818, a most impressive work; *La Donna del Lago* (The Lady of the Lake, 1819); and *Maometto* (1820), better known by its later Parisian title, *Le Siège de Corinthe*. Other operas of this period include the enjoyable comedy drama, *La Gazza Ladra* (The Thieving Magpie, 1817) and the monumental *Semiramide* (1823), best known for its overture until Sutherland reclaimed it. So ended Rossini's Italian period in which he had composed twenty-five operas in ten years (since *Tancredi*).

Rossini visited Vienna and England (duets with the musical Prince Regent), then settled in Paris until his death. His operatic works produced in that city, the two revisions apart, were two masterpieces, the first of which is *Le Comte Ory*, a ravishing *opera buffa*, well-known today since its revivals at Florence and Edinburgh/Glyndebourne in the 1950s. This intoxicating, sophisticated score reaches a pinnacle of Rossinian art in the last act with the trio, 'A la faveur de cette nuit obscure', worthy of Mozart at his finest. The second is *Guillaume Tell*, far more impressive than its popular overture suggests. It is a long work. 'Ah, Maestro,' gushed one admirer to Rossini, 'I heard your William Tell at the Opéra last night!' 'What?' queried the composer. 'The whole of it?' Yet for all its length, it is a profoundly stirring opera, with dramatic passages which foreshadow Verdi. Donizetti, who never equalled it, except in certain scenes, said: 'The first and last acts were written by Rossini; the second by God!'

The Revolution of 1830 led to the cancellation of a contract for four other operas and Rossini became instead one of the sights of Paris and a noted gourmet, composing delicious trifles and occasional religious works. He was buried in Paris, but his body was taken to Florence in 1887 and thousands of mourner-celebrators marched through the streets escorting it, along with military bands and a 300-strong chorus who sang the glorious Prayer from *Mosè*. So taken were the crowd in front of the burial church with this performance that they demanded and got an encore.

ROUSSEAU, JEAN-JACQUES (1712–78). French philosopher and composer, who also wrote about music. His most famous work was *Le Devin du Village* (The Village Soothsayer, 1752), a simple, delightful and influential piece, written after hearing Pergolesi's *La Serva Padrona* and proving that French was a suitable vehicle for singing.

RUBINSTEIN, ANTON (1830–94). Russian composer and pianist who wrote twenty operas, most notably *The Demon* (1875), which demonstrated his belief that Russian music must imitate Western composers.

SAINT-SAËNS, CAMILLE (1835–1921). French. One of his twelve operas, *Samson et Dalila* (1877), works very effectively in the theatre, though it has been criticized for lacking genuine drama. The two principals at least are finely drawn, there is a wealth of melody, much skilful musicianship and a committed attitude to the story. With fine singers, this highly enjoyable opera banishes sneers of 'dramatized oratorio' and 'Biblical colour plates', and seems a minor masterpiece.

SALIERI, ANTONIO (1750–1825). Italian. Best remembered now for the rumour that he poisoned his rival Mozart, yet he was thought much of by no mean judges: Gluck, Beethoven, Schubert, etc. teaching the last two as well as Liszt. His best-known operas are *Les Danaides* (1784) and *Tarare* (1787), to Beaumarchais's libretto.

SCARLATTI, ALESSANDRO (1660–1725). Italian. Father of Domenico (1685–1757), who was best known as a keyboard composer. Alessandro composed more than 100 operas and, more importantly, created the style of opera which dominated 18th-century Europe. Forced to please the Church and Aristocracy, he yet achieved his ends: the use of the Italian overture and the *da capo* aria, having accompanied recitatives to heighten the drama and also secco recitatives. For all his reputation, he is more honoured by scholars than in performance. Two are occasionally given: his masterpiece, *Mitridate Eupatore* (1707) and his comic opera, *Il Trionfo dell' Onore*

(1718). Most of his career was in Naples, with a brief stay in Rome. He often used popular songs and rhythms when the occasion demanded it, and his style gradually became less rigidly austere. Ironically, this serious master has been accused of indulging singers by allowing them a free hand with their embellishments, musical ornaments that they were to cling on to, often for better, more often for worse, for more than a century.

SCHOENBERG, ARNOLD (1874–1951). Austrian. His atonality, followed by use of the 12-note technique and speech song (which he invented), are widely enough mentioned in print to scare the average operagoer out of his wits, even ones who will admit that *Wozzeck* by Schoenberg's pupil, Berg, is a remarkable piece of musical theatre. In fact, opera was a small part of the composer's output, but an important one. The first of his four was *Erwartung* (1909, produced 1924), a short, powerful monodrama about a woman looking for her lover in a forest and finally finding his body. Musically it is an extraordinary glimpse of a frantic woman's mind. Marie Pappenheim's libretto is highly effective and the nervous operagoer, if prepared for some homework in advance and granted a major performer, can be guaranteed a remarkable experience. *Die glückliche Hand*

(The Lucky Hand, 1913, produced 1924) has a baritone, two silent parts and a chorus, who inhabit a nightmare world which could be said to be a compound of Strindberg and a Beckett out to shock. Its theme is a man's quest for happiness. *Von Heute auf Morgen* (From one day to the next, 1930) was the first 12-note comic opera, in the event an undaunting prospect, for it wittily shows a woman out to save her marriage. Finally came *Moses und Aron*, whose third act was not finished, and which was first heard in 1954 and first staged in Zürich in 1957. This masterpiece about communication between God and Man, is discussed on page 39. Thanks to *Moses*, Schoenberg's later works are at last ceasing to terrify a growing number of ordinary music- and opera-lovers.

SCHREKER, FRANZ (1878–1934). Austrian. Like so many others, he was greatly overpraised and is now unfairly forgotten. *Der Ferne Klang* (The Distant Sound, 1912) was a limited success, notably with Schoenberg and Berg, and later operas, especially *Die Gezeichneten* (The Stigmata, 1918) and *Der Schatzgräber* (The Treasure-Seeker, 1920) increased his fame if not with a really wide public.

SCHUBERT, FRANZ (1797–1828). Austrian. If he had lived, he would surely have achieved what he so longed for—a successful career in the theatre. Of his ten operas and five operettas, none are considered stageworthy (their books being mediocre or bad) except, perhaps, *Die Verschworenen* (The Conspirators, 1823), which is sometimes heard. *Alfonso und Estrella*, his only all-sung opera, is occasionally broadcast.

SCHUMANN, ROBERT (1810–56). German composer whose only opera, *Genoveva*, has nothing to commend it except (naturally) some fine music. He could well have learnt from some of the Italian operas he despised.

SEROV, ALEXANDER NIKOLAYEVICH (1820–71). Russian. A Wagnerian who was an opponent of the growing nationalism amongst his fellow composers. *Judith* (1863) was both Wagnerian and successful.

SHAPORIN, YURY (1889–1966). Russian. His *The Decembrists* (1953), about an 1825 revolutionary movement, was socialist realist, up-beat and heroic enough to satisfy his demanding official guardians of music.

SHOSTAKOVICH, DMITRI (1906–). Russian. He has had more trouble than Shaporin (above). His first opera was *The Nose* (1930) from the story by Gogol. This delightful satire was too experimental for the authorities and helped bring about the fossilizing theory of Socialist Realism as a guideline for Soviet composers. The ruling was concocted in 1932 and the composer's *Lady Macbeth of Mtsensk* (now known as *Katerina Ismailova*) was produced in 1934. This highly dramatic, erotic and powerfully melodic work has a heroine who takes one of her husband's workers as a lover, kills her father-in-law with rat poison and strangles her husband. She is deserted by her lover on the journey to Siberia and kills his new woman and herself. Yet this lurid plot is redeemed by Shostakovich's deeply felt portrait of his heroine, in striking contrast to the satirical treatment of the rest of the characters. It was hailed with delight by Press and Public alike in Russia and played in America, Sweden and Czechoslovakia over the next two years. Then, in January 1936, there was a sudden *volteface* by authority and a *Pravda* article condemned it as 'Confusion instead of Music'. It has to be admitted that the music has too many styles, but that, of course, was not the reason for the change. Suddenly it became liable to corrupt the morals of the public, its libretto in particular being attacked for daring to show 'Love, in its most vulgar form'. The fact that the pre-Revolutionary past was attacked was not enough to save it against the charge of sex. After Stalin's death, the opera was revived in Russia in slightly altered form, including the new title.

SMETANA, BEDŘICH (1824–84). Czech. The musical leader of his country's new-found nationalism after the slackening of Austrian rule. At the then recently established Provisional Theatre, his patriotic *The Brandenbergers in Bohemia* was given in the same year (1866) as his—and his country's—most famous and popular opera, *The Bartered Bride*. This happy lyric comedy did not at once capture the public, and only became popular outside Czechoslovakia in the 1890s. *Dalibor* (1868) is a return to heroic, as opposed to folksy, nationalism, and was alleged to be too Wagnerian. The best known of his later operas are the delightful comedy, *The Two Widows* (1874), the not very dramatic but musically charming, *The Kiss* (1876), and *The Secret* (1878). Only *The Bartered Bride* is widely known outside Czechoslovakia, but his other operas are all given there, being the foundation stones of his very operatically minded country's repertoire.

SMYTH, (DAME) ETHEL (1858–1944). English composer and ardent suffragette, whose best-known operas are *The Wreckers* (1906), set on the Cornish coast, and *The Boatswain's Mate* (1916).

SPOHR, LOUIS (1784–1859). German composer, violinist and conductor, one of the first to use a baton. Though this master of Romantic opera is now a mere name to music-lovers, he was once famous and very popular. His *Faust* (1816), not from Goethe's play, has been claimed as the first true Romantic opera, and it was followed by the even more successful *Zemire und Azor*. His biggest success was *Jessonda* (1823), which is still sometimes revived. Its tunes are apparently too straightforward and sugary for sophisticated Germans.

SPONTINI, GASPARO (1774–1851). Italian. After early successes in Naples, he went to Paris in 1803 where, having overcome prejudice, he won the patronage of Josephine and wrote his masterpiece, *La Vestale* (1807), which made his name throughout Europe. *Fernand Cortez* (1809) followed, which Napoleon hoped might be of propaganda value for his war in Spain and, indeed, it had a major success. The work he considered his masterpiece, *Olympie* (1819), was an even grander grand opera than the earlier works, costing a fortune to stage.

Spontini next went to Berlin to become head of the Court Opera at the invitation of the Emperor of Prussia. Two years later came the historic first night of *Der Freischütz* and,

though the Court sided with Spontini, the people welcomed Weber as a musical saviour. He survived in Berlin for twenty years, however, not an easy man to deal with, and finally he lost his supporters, even though he tried to write a German opera, *Agnes von Hohenstaufen* (1829). Too prone to the grandiose, he remains a fascinating bridge between the classical and romantic eras.

STANFORD, (SIR) CHARLES (1852–1924). Irish. The most successful of his ten operas, now forgotten, were *Shamus O'Brien* (1896) and *The Travelling Companion* (1925), given posthumously).

STRADELLA, ALESSANDRO (1642–82). Italian. His operas influenced Scarlatti and other Neapolitans, and may have influenced Purcell. He was murdered, having earlier, according to legend and Flotow's opera, *Alessandro Stradella* (1844), escaped being killed after an elopement. How different, how very different, from the lives of our own dear composers.

STRAUSS, JOHANN (The Younger) (1825–99). Austrian composer, the son of the famous Waltz King. Offenbach directed his steps towards operetta and he wrote three which are still greatly loved: *Die Fledermaus* (The Bat, 1874), *Eine Nacht in Venedig* (One Night in Venice,

1883) and *Der Zigeunerbaron* (The Gypsy Baron, 1885). The first of these is quite simply the finest of all operettas, though all three are beautifully orchestrated and melodious in the extreme. Some may prefer the champagne high spirits of Offenbach at his best, and his sensuous charm, but *Die Fledermaus*, complete with its own hymn to champagne, remains unequalled.

STRAUSS, RICHARD (1864–1949). German composer, the last of a short line to have written operas that are still part of the international repertoire. Perhaps only *Der Rosenkavalier* is greatly loved internationally, though a number of others fill the house when the principals are right. The son of a famous horn player, Strauss made his reputation with his orchestral music and conducting before turning to opera with *Guntram* (1894) and *Feuersnot* (Beltane Fire, 1900), whose closing love music is a foretaste of sumptuous things to come. There followed *Salome* (1905), from Oscar Wilde's play, a great scandal in its day and still with the power to stun if properly done, claustrophobic sensuality, violent music and passions, and sickly sweet melody sometimes being among the ingredients. With the orchestra given an exceptional importance beyond even Wagner's demands, the opera yet stands or falls by its heroine, the 16-year-old

with the voice of an Isolde and the looks of a 'sex kitten'. Miraculously, these requirements are sometimes met, as when Gwyneth Jones took the role at Covent Garden in 1974. 'Louder! louder! I can still hear the singers', is the legendary quote from Strauss at a rehearsal of *Salome*. It must surely have been a teasing remark, for he loved the soprano voice this side of idolatory.

Elektra (1909), discussed on page 34, was the first of his fertile collaboration with the poet and dramatist, Hugo von Hofmannsthal. Having outstripped even *Salome*, he turned to comedy with *Der Rosenkavalier* (1911), a masterpiece which is discussed on page 36. There followed *Ariadne auf Naxos* (1912), whose first version followed a performance of Molière's *Le Bourgeois Gentilhomme*, complete with Strauss's incidental music. Splendid as this is, the expense of hiring an opera and an acting troupe was prohibitive even in less inflationary times, so in 1916 came the second, more usual, version, in which the would-be gentleman, having hired an opera company and *commedia dell'arte* players, orders them to give the opera simultaneously to get it over in time for fireworks. The advantage of this version is the introduction of the Composer, one of Strauss's most magical soprano (in trousers) roles. Moreover, the comments of the players on the opera in which they join are happily and expertly blended with the Ariadne story. The final love duet enraptures Strauss-ians and many others, though not all feel it is vintage. Zerbin-etta, the *commedia* heroine, has one of the most taxing and stunning of all coloratura arias.

Die Frau ohne Schatten (The Woman without a Shadow, 1919) has many champions, though some consider it a failure. Hofmannsthal set great store by it, but Strauss did not attempt to put across its complicated allegories. The prodigious score is full of riches, not least parts of Barak's music which admirably pre-sents a good man. *Intermezzo* (1924) is based on a misunder-standing between Strauss and his wife and, indeed, the original hero and heroine at Dresden were made up like them. By now Strauss's powers were waning, some would say that they had been since *Ariadne auf Naxos*. Certainly, *Die Aegypt-ische Helena* (The Egyptian Helen, 1928), for all its beautiful music, is dramatically ineffective, yet *Arabella* (1931), a second Viennese comedy, is for many an enchantment, and not only when a glorious artist like Lisa della Casa is on hand to play the heroine. It was Strauss's last opera with his incomparable librettist. *Die schweigsame Frau* (The Silent Woman, 1935), from a Ben Jonson play, is full of comic

invention if short on lyrical splendour. Stefan Zweig col-laborated with the composer, but the Nazis banned further use of the Jewish writer. Strauss, incidentally, was not, as Ken Russell depicted him in his travesty of a film, anti-Jewish. With Josef Gregor, Strauss wrote *Friedenstag* (The Day of Peace, 1938), a one-act histori-cal opera; *Daphne* (1938), a 'bucolic' opera; and *Die Liebe der Danae* (1938–40, produced 1952), which contains some of his most beautiful music. His final work was *Capriccio* (1942) which dramatizes the argument as to the relative importance of words and music in opera. Not surprisingly, this lovely work has the most effect when the audience can follow every word of it. At the end, the Countess (Opera) cannot decide between her two suitors, who represent Poetry and Music. On this suitably indecisive note, Strauss ended a wonderful operatic career. The majority only accept a handful of his works as being masterpieces and he has many detractors, including those who not only resented his ability to make money (see the entry on Puccini, a fellow moneymaker), but the ease with which he made it. And, sadly, he is banned in Israel for not having been brave enough to stand up and be counted against Hitler.

STRAVINSKY, IGOR (1882–1971). Russian. He became French,

then American without losing his essential Russianness. This supreme ballet composer only wrote two full-length operas, *Le Rossignol* (The Nightingale, 1914) and *The Rake's Progress* (1951), but a number of his other works are at least partly operatic. *The Nightingale*, Stravinsky's first opera, was started in 1914. It is as opulent and spectacular as his famous Diaghilev ballets of the period, though his rapid development and consequent change of style is evident between Acts I and II. *Les Noces* (produced 1923) is the ballet's property, but is full of solo and choral music, while *Renard* (1922), starring a fox, has singers and chorus in the orchestra pit and dancers on the stage. *Mavra* (1922) is a one-act *opera buffa* in the Italo-Russian style. It is based on a Pushkin poem and was a deliberate counterblast to the 'inflated arrogance' of Wagner.

There followed the neo-classical, fiercely passionate opera-oratorio, *Oedipus Rex* (1927), with a text in Latin by Cocteau after Sophocles, and a speaker introducing each episode. Movement is minimal and the chorus and cast are masked. A number of other works bears some relation to opera, but only one is the real thing, *The Rake's Progress* (1951), scintillating and loosely following Hogarth's famous paintings, with a libretto by W. H. Auden and Chester Kallman. The typically unexpected music recalls Mozart, the *bel canto* Italian and other influences, while, at the end, characters come forward as in *Don Giovanni* and point the moral. The Rake is convincingly drawn and, before it, the scene in Bedlam finds Stravinsky in his most human vein. The orchestra is of classical dimensions, less trombones and with a harpsichord for recitatives. The opera divides opinion sharply, but that is not unusual for post-1914 Stravinsky.

SULLIVAN, (SIR) ARTHUR (1842–1900). English composer, with Offenbach and Strauss, one of the supreme masters of operetta. Obsessed with serious longings, his colossally successful partnership with W. S. Gilbert often frustrated him, and until the copyright on his music expired in 1950, too many people who should have known better underrated his music because of often inadequate performances. His musical style developed, while remaining delightfully fresh and individual, though the opera- and music-lover can have much enjoyment from his loving glances back at Handel, Mendelssohn, Verdi and others. An essential difference between Sullivan and Offenbach is that the former, outwardly a conforming Victorian, allowed next to no sex to creep into his delicious but chaste music. He collaborated with Gilbert from

1871, their first success being *Trial by Jury* (1875), their only piece without spoken dialogue. Being full of parodies of Italian opera of forty years earlier, it is a particular favourite with operagoers. There followed *The Sorcerer* (1877), the delectable *H.M.S. Pinafore* (1878) and, even more popular, *The Pirates of Penzance* (1880). From 1881, their manager and peace-keeper, Rupert D'Oyly Carte, moved them to the new Savoy Theatre. Gilbert was a brilliant lyricist, if some of his wit is dated now, while Sullivan's settings are by turns witty, pretty and sentimental, and never less than ingeniously inventive. As for his gift for parody, it is masterly.

Later operas included *Patience* (1881), a satire on the cult of the aesthetic, with Bunthorne a caricature of Wilde; the ravishing *Iolanthe* (1882), complete with a satire on the House of Lords; *Princess Ida* (1884), which lives by Sullivan's music; *The Mikado* (1885), the most popular of all the Savoy Operas; *Ruddigore* (1887), with Sullivan surpassing himself in 'The Ghosts' High Noon'; *The Yeomen of the Guard* (1888), the nearest the pair came to grand opera; and *The Gondoliers* (1889), a jolly throw-back to earlier works, and during which, the pair fell out. Sullivan achieved his dream of a grand opera, *Ivanhoe* (1891), which had a long initial run but is now very rarely heard. G. and S.

were reunited but neither *Utopia Unlimited* (1893) nor *The Grand Duke* (1896) were vintage pieces, and works he wrote with others are now forgotten. The Savoy Operas are probably immortal.

SUPPÉ, FRANZ VON (1819–95). Austrian. In his day a very popular writer of operettas, etc. His most famous one is *Boccaccio* (1879), the hero being a mezzo-soprano role, while another operetta, now remembered for its overture but probably his finest work, is *Die Schöne Galathee* (The Beautiful Galatea, 1865).

SUTERMEISTER, HEINRICH (1910–). Swiss. His best-known opera is his first, *Romeo und Julia* (1940), which concentrates on the love-story of Shakespeare's *Romeo*. A traditionalist, he is not afraid of tunes. *Die Zauberinsel* (The Magic Island, 1942) stems from *The Tempest* and was less popular, but *Raskolnikoff* (1948), from *Crime and Punishment*, was a great success and, like *Romeo*, has had many performances. Its atmospheric power has been much admired. Other works have included *Die schwarze Spinne* (1936, revised 1949) and *Titus Feuerfuchs* (1958), a delightful comic opera. His operas are often given in Germany.

TCHAIKOVSKY, PETER ILYICH (1840–93). Russian. He loved

opera, but only achieved two major successes, *Eugene Onegin* (1879) and *The Queen of Spades* (1890). He had little sympathy with the nationalist school in Russia, though both these works are set in Russia, which brought out the best in him. His other operas include *Voyevode* (1869), the unproduced *Undine* (1869), some of whose music he later used, notably for Odette's adagio in *Swan Lake*, and *Vakula the Smith* (1876), which later became *The Little Shoes* (1887), and which uses a number of delightful Russian and Ukrainian folktunes. It is occasionally heard abroad. *Eugene Onegin*, discussed on page 29, followed, after which masterpiece Tchaikovsky inadequately set Schiller's *The Maid of Orleans* (1881), the characterization, Joan apart, being poor. Her 'Farewell' is sometimes heard. Like *Undine*, it is a Meyerbeerian work, whereas *Mazeppa* (1884) finds him on his home ground and in more typical form. *The Sorceress* (1887) is melodramatic and poorly characterized, but *The Queen of Spades* (1890), taken like *Onegin* from Pushkin, finds the composer, if not at his best— it is not melodically in the first rank—in superb dramatic form and able to provide a magnificent 18th-century pastiche. The Countess is a creation worthy of Puskin's, given a singer who can act, and the opera is a splendid example of operatic entertainment for newcomers and old hands alike. *Iolanta* (1892), a one-acter, is weak structurally, but brimming with musical invention.

TELEMANN, GEORG PHILIPP (1681–1767). German. Some of his forty operas were popular in his day. *Don Quichote* and *Pimpione* have been revived in modern times.

THOMAS, AMBROISE (1811–96). French. Of his two famous operas, one, the romantic and tuneful *Mignon* (1866), is still popular in France and occasionally given elsewhere. Collectors can sometimes hear his *Hamlet* (1868), an entertaining opera as long as one forgets Shakespeare, with a most enjoyable mad scene aria for Ophelia.

THOMSON, VIRGIL (1896–). American composer and critic, he has written two operas, *Four Saints in Three Acts* (1928) and *The Mother of Us All* (1947), both with librettos by Gertrude Stein. The first is a surrealist work, easy on the ear and with more than four saints in it, and was written for an all-black cast.

TIPPETT, (SIR) MICHAEL (1905–). English. The reputation of his three operas is due to their often magnificent scores. His librettos are more controversial and his first opera, *The Midsummer Marriage* (1955), was held back by this when it appeared. It applies an ancient myth to modern characters, but the warmth of the music and its richness has now been realized. *King Priam* (1962), set in the Trojan War and a much sparser score, had a magnificent first production (Wanamaker, with Sean Kenny as designer), but has yet to establish itself. It is about 'the mysterious nature of human choice'. However, *The Knot Garden* (1970), again brilliantly staged (Peter Hall/Timothy O'Brien), already has many admirers. It is about the need to reconcile the dark and light aspects of human nature to obtain growth and peace, and the music abandons the economy of *Priam*. Many find it a dazzling score.

VAUGHAN WILLIAMS, RALPH (1872–1958). English. None of his six operas has escaped criticism, yet the first act of his ballad opera, *Hugh the Drover* (1924), is stirring and lyrical, even though the rest is less inspired. *Sir John in Love* (1929), Sir John being the Falstaff of the Merry Wives, is tuneful, affectionate and leisurely, even if no match for Verdi's *Falstaff*. *Riders to the Sea* (1937), an exact setting of Synge's tragedy, is generally regarded as the composer's masterpiece, while *The Poisoned Kiss* (1936), despite a libretto resembling Gilbert on a very 'off' night, is full of vital and delightfully satirical music. *The Pilgrim's Progress* (1951) includes a one-act opera Vaughan Williams had written in 1922, *The Shepherds of the Delectable Mountains*, but though lovers of the composer's music are drawn to it, it is the 'Morality' it claims to be, not an opera.

VERDI, GIUSEPPE (1813–1901). Italian. If it is the duty of a genius to be born at the right moment, Verdi's timing must be considered immaculate. Just as Shakespeare had the scene set for him by Marlowe, Kyd and others, so Verdi had Rossini, Bellini and Donizetti. Like Shakespeare, his early works were comparatively crude, yet he was already blazing with the vitality which Bellini and Donizetti rarely achieved, and instinct for superb melodic invention. Today, Verdi stands with Wagner and Mozart at the pinnacle of operatic supremacy. In Italy, his fortunes never really waned, though many works dropped out of the regular repertoire, but elsewhere for many decades he was adored for four works: *Rigoletto, La Traviata, Il Trovatore* and *Aida*; and respected by many musicians only for the *Requiem, Otello* and, especially *Falstaff*. Reappraisal began in Germany in the 1920s and gathered momentum, although many of his works remained almost totally unknown. Operas like *La Forza del Destino* and *Don*

Carlos were damned for daring to be Italian rather than Wagnerian. The reviews of the great critic, Ernest Newman, of pre-Requiem Verdi often make incredible reading today and, ironically, many distinguished critics imagined that Verdi was influenced by his great contemporary, hence the 'improvement' in his last works. Now it is understood that Verdi was Italian to the core, more, indeed, than Puccini who was susceptible to outside influences. The 1950s saw the climate change totally in Verdi's favour, and now regular operagoers happily swallow Verdi whole, and even the most primitive early works are hailed as worthy of attention.

Verdi's origins were humble but he had the luck to be helped by the rich, music-loving Antonio Barezzi of Bussetto, the town nearest his birthplace, Le Roncole, in Parma. Notoriously, he failed to gain admission to the Conservatory in Milan, so settled in Bussetto as *maestro di musica*, marrying his patron's daughter. His first (lost) opera, *Rochester* (1836), was followed in 1839 by his first staged work, *Oberto, Conte di San Bonifacio*, which was given at La Scala. Its soprano lead was sung by Giuseppina Strepponi, who was to become successively his mistress and second wife, and at all times his most sympathetic friend.

A contract for three more operas was now offered Verdi by Merelli, the manager of La Scala. Tragedy, however, struck him when his first wife and two children died in quick succession, and then his first comic opera, *Un Giorno di Regno* (King for a Day, 1840), was a total failure, though, as a few thousand operagoers know, it is an enjoyable piece, full of anticipations of later glories. His career seemed to him to be at an end, but Merelli tempted him with a libretto, *Nabucodonosor*, known better as *Nabucco* (1842). It fell open at the words where the Jews long for their homeland as they sadly lament by the waters of Babylon. It was a turning point in operatic history, for at that moment he returned to opera, while the words inspired his most loved chorus, 'Va, pensiero, sull' ali dorate' ('Go my thoughts, on golden wings'), which was to become almost a national anthem in the Italian struggle for freedom. *Nabucco* was a musical and patriotic triumph, and even in the darkest days of his early operas' fortunes, it was never forgotten. It and the works which followed are stirring and simple, though even in their own day too stark for the taste of some of those brought up on his less vigorous forerunners. The immediate successor was *I Lombardi alli Prima Crociata* (Crusade), which followed in 1843, then the even finer *Ernani* (1844), a supreme example of very early Verdi, and the composer was now in great demand. Later he was to describe this time of his life as his 'years in the galleys' and, rightly, for he was a musical slave, *I due Foscari* (1844) had Donizetti hailing Verdi as a genius and was followed by *Giovanna d'Arco* (1845), *Alzira* (1845) and *Attila* (1846). All the works of this period are full of what can only be described as great swinging melodies, often in slow waltz or march tempo: beautiful arias followed by fiery cabalettas.

Perhaps the first masterpiece was *Macbeth* (1847, revised 1865), which is only worthy of Shakespeare at certain times (notably in the Sleepwalking Scene) but which is full of feeling, nobility and grandeur, a sign of things to come. *I Masnaderi* (1847) was written for Jenny Lind and premièred in London, and, though rarely given, contains superb and forceful music. *Il Corsaro* (1848) is interesting only because it is Verdi, but *La Battaglia di Legnano* (1849) is finer and is also part of operatic history for the tumultuous scenes at its première in Rome: the fourth act was encored, a soldier threw first his accoutrements and then himself from a box, and the entire proceedings helped fan the flames of revolution, a very rare event in artistic history.

There followed one of the finest of all Verdi's early works, *Luisa Miller* (1849). Francis Toye has written of its inti-

mate pathos, and it is certainly a most human and warm score, much loved by true Verdians. *Stiffelio* (later *Aroldo*, 1850/ 1857) was the last work of Verdi's early period. It has few champions but many fine moments.

These 'galley years' may have been rugged ones, but they were made more so by Verdi's exacting standards, best demonstrated when *Macbeth* was in production at Naples. His famous letter to the librettist, Cammarano, is full of production notes, but best known for its demands for Lady Macbeth. The singer, Tadlini, was beautiful and sang to perfection, whereas Verdi dreamt of an ugly, wicked woman with a hard, stifled, dark voice, the voice of a devil—which, of course, meant character before beauty of tone. The original Lady Macbeth, Barbieri-Nini, practised her sleepwalking scene for three months to meet Verdi's exacting standards. But perhaps these early years are equally well summed up by Verdi the patriot who roused audiences regularly to frenzy with moments like 'Avrai tu l'universo Resti l'Italia a me' in *Attila*—'You may have the universe, but let Italy remain mine'. Soon Italy was to be his and to remain so.

The first masterwork was *Rigoletto* (1851), discussed on page 22. In 1853 came *Il Trovatore* (The Troubador) and *La Traviata*. The first is the final trumpet blast of the old Verdi, its tunes forged in steel or swooningly beautiful. The mocked-at libretto is, in fact, admirable because the main characters are simply but superbly effective, and dramatic situations abound which are transfigured by the composer working at white-hot, passionate speed. Given the four or five best singers in the world, the result would be a thunderbolt, and even with mere great singers, the effect is dynamite. Whereas *La Traviata* is a beautiful, strong, theatrically effective masterpiece, with a heroine, Violetta, who must range from coloratura to dramatic soprano and, pray God, be able to act and look the part. Far better than the novel and play which inspired it, and improved by Verdi's own emotional problems with his Giuseppina and his father-in-law, Barezzi, it has survived transfers to Louis XIII's day, shoddy performances, and visually absurd performances early this century (McCormack/Tetrazzini, etc.), but is now treated as often as not as a major work of art, an intimate music drama of infinite compassion.

Les Vêpres Siciliennes (Paris, 1853), though shot through with grandeur and glory, is the only one of Verdi's later operas which looks like remaining comparatively neglected. He was not happy with conditions at the Opéra, which he was to call 'La Grande Boutique', nor was he happy with the libretto by Scribe and Duveyrier, and the liberation he had achieved in *Traviata*, extending his style away from the old conventions, though not abandoning the best in them, suffered a setback. *Simon Boccanegra* (1857, revised 1881) is much finer, despite a tortuous plot and a sombre atmosphere. Verdi called the early version monotonous and cold, and today's combined versions tend inevitably to show its two different dates. Its finest scene, in the council chamber, with text by Boito, belongs entirely to the revision, and anticipates the wonders to come in *Otello*. It is admired rather than greatly popular, but Verdians prize it very highly.

Verdi sat in the Italian parliament from 1861 to 1865 at the request of Cavour, the great statesman and architect of national unity. Not only had Verdi's operas been symbols of the spirit of the Risorgimento, his very name had been used as a slogan. 'Viva VERDI' on a wall was safe, but it meant 'Viva Vittorio Emanuele, Re d'Italia'. Before he settled down somewhat reluctantly to politics, he had written one of his most melodious works, *Un Ballo in Maschera* (1859), which the censors did their best to strangle, and which even today causes confusion. It was staged with a 17th-century Boston setting to prevent a king, the historical Gustavus III of Sweden, being killed on stage. Now it is most often set as Verdi intended: in and around Stockholm. Tuneful, dramatic and often light-hearted and amusing, it is now a most popular opera with singers and audiences.

While in parliament Verdi wrote *La Forza del Destino* for production in St Petersburg (1862). The force of coincidence is very strong, but the situations are springboards for magnificent, often ravishing, music and meaty dramatic situations. Time and again doubts about the stageworthiness of the opera are banished by good or great performances, and Friar Melitone gave advance notice that the composer had a comic masterpiece in him. After this grand opera, and the revision of *Macbeth*, he wrote an even grander one, for Paris again, *Don Carlos* (1867). For many years this was neglected and even misunderstood, but now it ranks with the greatest of Verdi's works and is many Verdians' favourite opera. It is perhaps a greater work of art than *Aida* for one reason: the characters are more deeply drawn, musically and dramatically. Never had Verdi created such a teeming world on stage, and one scene, which begins with King Philip's matchless aria, 'Ella giammai m'amo' ('She has no love for me'), then has an extraordinary duel of wills between the king and the Grand Inquisitor, and culminates in Eboli's 'O Don fatale' (O fatal gift), is arguably as fine as any scene in opera. The work is rarely given complete and sometimes has its superb and important first act lopped off. It is a subtle, psychologically true, majestic, epic, but deeply human work.

Aida (1871) is Verdi's grandest opera, written not on commission to celebrate the opening of the Suez Canal, but to open the Italian Theatre in Cairo. It is one of the most popular of all operas, an impresario's friend, and a fine first opera for newcomers, not least because of its spectacle and choral writing. But it lives through the more private relationships of its leading characters. Old *Aida* hands tend to look forward to the incomparable Act III: the Nile Scene, and also Amneris's passionate outburst of jealous emotion in the penultimate scene. The spectacle can pall unless superbly done or given in the open air, preferably in the Verona Arena.

Otello (1887), the most perfect of tragic operas, is discussed on page 30. Perhaps only those who know *Othello* well appreciate just how great Boito's masterly condensation of play into opera is. Boito again provided a matchless libretto for Verdi's last opera, *Falstaff* (1894), from *The Merry Wives of Windsor*, but with additions from the Falstaff of *Henry IV*, most notably the splendidly cynical Honour speech. This opera is the delight of most musicians, who consider it Verdi's masterpiece. The public has never warmed to it so much, though it is now a house-filler with the right cast. Perhaps it is too quicksilver for the average Italian opera lover, and lacking in the expected arias, duets, etc. Yet what depths of emotion it contains, as befits a man who in his old age became the only operatic composer ever to match Shakespeare's greatness, actually surpassing it in *Falstaff*, *The Merry Wives* not being a great play by Shakespearean standards. Ford's jealous outburst in Act II Scene 1, the finest scene in the opera perhaps, is one of the supreme moments in opera, and is given—Shakespearean touch—to a supporting part. Even more than the marvel of a choral fugue to end the work is Falstaff's 'Va, vecchio John', a triumphant affirmation of Man, the eternal optimist.

Verdi's greatness of spirit, his home for aged musicians, fierce peasant love of the land and glorious career, added to the marvellous 'look' of him in old age, have combined to make the very thought of him moving, though a study of *The Man Verdi* by Frank Walker reveals that the hero was only too mortal. Of all operatic composers he is at once the most virile and melodious. He died 'magnificently, like a fighter, formidable but mute', wrote Boito. 'We had all basked in the sunshine of that Olympian old age': Boito again. Millions have basked since in the warmth of his whole incomparable career.

VIVALDI, ANTONIO (*c* 1675–1741). Italian. He wrote over forty operas, usually hastily, but producing them very efficiently. Some have moments of the musical scene-painting for which he is well-known.

WAGNER, RICHARD (1813–83). German. His career is the most astounding in the history of opera. It is hard to believe that he will ever cease to be controversial, and he is a rare case of a musician whose life ought to be studied fully to comprehend his art. The ideal solution is a period of unfeverish illness, with Ernest Newman's monumental, four-volume *Life* of the composer to hand. This, incidentally, introduces us to a delightful young man-about-the-theatre before the iron entered his soul, iron which enabled him to survive shattering setbacks and conquer, with the help, when his fortunes were at their blackest, of Ludwig the Great of Bavaria. Could Wagner have achieved what he did without at times behaving like a near monster? Probably not. He aimed at the *Gesamtkunstwerk*, the complete work of art uniting all the arts, which for him was his form of music drama. Visually, he never met his own near-impossible demands, but happily his grandson Wieland achieved the impossible at post-war Bayreuth by lighting, by symbolic scenery rather than realism, and by inheriting the theatrical and operatic flair of his grandfather. Wagner's success artistically can be seen as a slow climb to the summit, and his revolution sprang from old as well as new values. He was no iconoclast, though he seemed it in his day.

Beethoven was an early influence, most notably the choral finale of the Ninth Symphony. Wagner, as Arthur Jacobs and Stanley Sadie have written in *Opera, A Modern Guide*, 'wished his operas similarly to be "music fertilized by poetry", not merely poetry set to music'. He was his own librettist. Other influences were Weber, the Romanticism of whose *Der Freischütz* so inspired composers in his day and later, while Schröder-Devrient's Leonore in *Fidelio* also had a decisive effect in turning Wagner to music drama (see page 192). Wagner did not invent the *leitmotiv* (leading motive) with which he is so emphatically associated. These motives, which are musical figures identifying and characterizing a person, thing or idea, had been used most notably by Weber

before him, but it was Wagner who transformed them by the time he reached *Götterdämmerung* into most potently expressive, variable and intricate musical ideas. They were an essential part of his equipment, not an end in themselves: it was his ardent disciples who became obsessed with them and brought them into disrepute in some circles. His greatest operas can be enjoyed without knowing any but the most famous of them, but as every Wagnerite, Perfect or Imperfect, knows, they are infinitely worth studying. Wagner did not label them: later disciples did that, the ninety themes of *The Ring* being labelled up to the hilt. All Wagner's operas have stories which their author meant to be followed closely. *The Ring*, like the character of Hamlet, can be taken to mean all manner of things, but to think that all that matters is the music is gravely wrong. As William Mann wrote in the introduction to his excellent translation of *The Ring* for the Friends of Covent Garden, 'Wagner would turn in his grave at the idea'.

Wagner, wrote Ernest Newman, was a better actor than any of his actors, though his players have to discipline themselves to long stationary spells, often on steep slopes these days, which are unkind to calf muscles. This statuesque form of acting, broken by slow motion and occasional burst of activity, is at once easier and more difficult than working in 'faster' pieces. What matters is that it should be done well.

His early training was erratic, but he studied at Leipzig in 1831, becoming chorus master at Würzburg in 1833 and conductor at Magdeburg in 1834. At the former he began working on *Die Feen* (The Fairies), first given in 1888. For all its echoes of Beethoven and Weber, it shows no signs of latent genius. *Das Liebesverbot* (Love's denial), based on *Measure for Measure*, failed at Magdeburg in 1836 and shows the influence of the Italians whose works he was then conducting. He now married his unfortunate Minna, who got him a job at Könisberg, after which they went to Riga. They fled from there to avoid his creditors, and the tempestuous sea voyage they made to London later inspired the seas which surge through *Der fliegende Holländer* (1843). The year before, *Rienzi* had been given in Dresden, where he had arrived after spells in London and Paris. This long opera, very much of its time, and 'grand' in the tradition of Spontini, Meyerbeer and others, had a triumph and got him the job as Dresden's music director. Only its stirring overture is well-known.

Wagner's *Holländer*, however, is a popular favourite and the first true Wagner opera, for all its echoes of Weber.

Redemption through Love, a theme which obsessed the composer, makes its first appearance. It is a poor spirit which does not respond to this virile, tuneful work.

There followed *Tannhäuser* (1845), a step towards Valhalla, though the characters are a step back if anything. It was revised for Paris in 1861 and had a notorious fiasco which disgraced the Opéra. The opening scene on the Venusberg was extended by the composer who had by now written *Tristan und Isolde*, so when the Paris version is given the work lacks unity for all the gain in splendour. Its Dresden première had Wagner's niece, Johanna, as Elizabeth and Schröder-Devrient as Venus (she had also been Adriano in *Rienzi*). The hero was Tichatschek, also the first Rienzi.

In 1848 Wagner was forced to flee to Zürich after being involved in Dresden's revolution. Naturally, his growing fame increased, and Liszt was the most influential of his new allies, giving the first performance of *Lohengrin* at Weimar in 1850. For the first time Wagner had completed a wholly unified work, not all on the same level of achievement, but, like all his operas to come, a work which exists in a unique world of its own. It is the last singers' opera that he wrote (only parts of *Meistersinger* fall into that category: basically, it is music drama). Like

Tannhäuser, Lohengrin was once very popular, even with second-rate touring companies and their audiences, but now both need help to capture the public, for all their many glories. The processions alone present problems, yet with fine casts, first-rate conducting and inspired direction, they can be unforgettable.

The 1850s saw Wagner working on the text of *The Ring* (mainly completed as we have it by 1852), sponging off whoever he could to try and get out of financial difficulties, conducting his music in front of an approving Victoria and Albert, becoming steadily more famous, and, amongst other entanglements, having an affair with Frau Wesendonck which was to help in inspiring *Tristan*. Poor Minna died in 1860 after he had begun his most notable and artistically fruitful liaison, with Liszt's daughter, Cosima, then married to Hans von Bülow, a heroic man who never ceased to champion the Master even after this colossal hurt.

Meanwhile, Wagner's financial affairs and artistic hopes were in desperate straits when one of the supreme miracles in the history of Art occurred; he found a patron in poor, lonely Ludwig of Bavaria, no great music-lover, but a fanatical Wagnerian because of the composer's vision and choice of subjects. All Wagner's financial problems were solved for the time, and *Tristan und Isolde* (discussed on page 24) was first presented in Munich in 1865. But Wagner's luck was running out. His extravagance, political interfering and hold over Ludwig so outraged ministers that he was forced to retire to Switzerland again, where in 1870 he married Cosima, which alienated him from Ludwig. This second exile of six years was a most creative period, for he finished *Die Meistersinger von Nürnberg*, *Siegfried* and most of *Götterdämmerung*. The first of these masterpieces is featured on page 25. This monumental comedy about ordinary people had its première in Munich in 1868. *Das Rheingold* was given there the next year, then the build-up began—thanks to Ludwig's loyalty to the composer if not now to the man— towards the foundation of the Bayreuth Festival Theatre. The complete *Ring* was given in 1876.

It would be insulting to suggest that this most colossal of all musical works can be even remotely discussed in a reference book entry. There is nothing like it in all theatre. The nearest equivalent is Shakespeare's History cycle, but this was not conceived as an entity. That the *Ring* most certainly was, from the low E flat which begins the cosmic drama on the bed of the Rhine, to the cataclysmic fall of Valhalla at the end of *Götterdämmerung*, which in its final moments returns to *the* theme of Wagnerian themes, Redemption through Love. Never believe that the drama is about gods and goddesses, dwarfs and dragons, legendary Norse heroes and villains, except on the physical surface. It is a dateless story of Mankind, as relevant today in every part of the world as it was in 1876. Wagner, the lucky magician, had at last achieved 'unending melody': he had permutated his *leitmotivs* into musical riches of quite extraordinary intellectual and emotional power and beauty. Along with a prologue in one act, *Rheingold*, Wagner had conceived three of the longest operas ever written: *Die Walküre*, *Siegfried* and *Götterdämmerung*. Yet once they are mastered, they seem not a moment too long. Most opera-goers, apart from born Wagnerites (who sometimes take very little other music), reach the summit slowly, enduring hours of travail enlivened by 'easy' highspots. Once the summit is scaled it is hard to remember the climb, and this applies to all Wagner's output from *Tristan* to *Parsifal* (1882). *Parsifal*, this 'stage dedication festival play', harmonically beyond even *Tristan*, is the least accessible of Wagner's masterpieces. An astonishing mixture of sexuality and spirituality, its hero is a 'simpleton without guile' who is the Percival of Malory's *Morte d'Arthur*. Compared with *The Ring*, it has few *leitmotivs*, and its heroine is a part-Virgin, part Venus, Kundry. For many years it was only given at Bayreuth, a suitable theatre/temple, and its atmosphere of ecstatic mysticism is for some Wagnerites the composer's supreme achievement. Except when it burst out of Bayreuth when the copyright expired in 1914, it has never been as widely popular as the other supreme masterpieces.

Wagner's influence was colossal. The sheer number of musicians who reacted against him is as significant as the legion of his disciples. In opera's supreme trinity, Mozart, Verdi and Wagner, each one of them a genius, Mozart was surely the most perfect musician, Verdi the most remarkable human being, and Wagner was a phenomenon.

WAGNER-RÉGENY, RUDOLF (1903–69). Hungarian/German. His first opera, *Der Günstling* (The Favourite, 1935), had considerable success in Germany. Set in Mary Tudor's London, with the Queen as a main character, it has a powerful story but its music is formal and subdued, though essentially modern. Other operas are *Die Bürger von Calais* (1939), *Johanna Balk* (1941), *Prometheus* (1959) and *Das Bergwerk zu Falun* (The Mine at Falun, 1961).

WALLACE, VINCENT (1812–65). Irish composer whose *Maritana*

(1845) was very popular for more than half a century.

WALTON, (SIR) WILLIAM (1902–). English. His *Troilus and Cressida* (1954), a richly romantic work, had some success not only in Britain, then was neglected. It awaits reappraisal at the forthcoming (1976) revival. *The Bear* (1967) is an amusing romp from Chekov's one-act play.

WEBER, CARL MARIA VON (1786–1826). German. His *Der Freischütz* (1821) is discussed on page 19. Before this landmark in German operatic history, he had written several pieces, including *Peter Schmoll* (1803) and the delightful operetta *Abu Hassan* (1811). His *Euryanthe* (1825), saddled with an impossible libretto, is full of beautiful music, but his failure to repeat his great triumph, plus health and money troubles, snapped his will to continue his reforming crusade. In 1824, Charles Kemble invited him to write an opera for Covent Garden, which he ran. The result was *Oberon* (1826), a romantic work set by J. R. Planché in the time of Charlemagne, and full of lovely music. Weber died soon after conducting the première. This fairy tale with much spoken dialogue needs plenty of production.

WEILL, KURT (1900–50). German composer of every type of stage work. Thanks to his collaboration with Bertholt Brecht, as well as his deliberately popular, straightforward, sourly romantic style, he reached far beyond the opera house, his most famous works being *Die Dreigroschenoper* (The Threepenny Opera, 1928), a transposition of *The Beggar's Opera* of 1728 to Edwardian London, and *Mahagonny* (1930), more properly *The Rise and Fall of the City of Mahagonny*, a brilliant work about a city of material pleasure, totally topical and set in an imaginary American city. Settling in America in 1935 because of the Nazis, he wrote the opera, *Down in the Valley* (1948).

WEINBERGER, JAROMIR (1896–1967). Czech. His *Schwanda the Bagpiper* (1927) is a minor, but delightful successor to *The Bartered Bride*.

WELLESZ, EGON (1885–1975). Austrian. A pupil of Schoenberg, who influenced his *Alkestis* (1924), an attempt to revive baroque opera. *Incognita* (1951) looks back to Mozart.

WILLIAMSON, MALCOLM (1931–). Australian. His *Our Man in Havana* (1963) and *The Violins of St. Jacques* (1966) are enjoyable and contain actual melodies.

WOLF, HUGO (1860–1903). Austrian. His one completed opera is *Der Corregidor* (The Magistrate, 1895), a delightful but undramatic small-scale work.

WOLF-FERRARI, ERMANNO (1876–1948). Italian composer of German as well as Italian descent. He is best known for his comic operas, very Italian plus German motifs and thoroughness. The most famous are the captivating *I Quatro Rusteghi* (The Four Boors, 1906), known in Britain as *The School for Fathers*, and the one-act *Il Segreto di Susanna* (Susanna's Secret, 1909). His best-known serious opera is a *verismo* piece, *I Gioielli dell Madonna* (The Jewels of the Madonna, 1911).

ZANDONAI, RICCARDO (1883–1944). Italian. One of the *verismo* school. His operas include *Conchita* (1911), his first big success, and *Francesca da Rimini* (1914), which was even more popular. Later successes included *Giulietta e Romeo* (1922) and *I Cavalieri di Ekubu* (1925).

SINGERS

Legendary Performances

Originally this section was to have begun with a trio as sublime as *Rosenkavalier's*, those supreme superstars of the early 19th century, Pasta, Malibran and Schröder-Devrient. This proved impossible, for, with a limited allowance, it was not even feasible to get beyond 1914. Finally, the list of glory has been confined to the last quarter of a century, just missing Flagstad, with acting ability tipping the balance in some cases.

Some omissions appal the author and will outrage many readers. No Björling, Tucker, Di Stefano, Tebaldi, Ludwig, Placido Domingo ... and it is no consolation to note that the chosen few are considered legendary, not always the best, though this makes selection slightly easier, for, as one opera-maniac called in to help asked: 'How can anyone be better than Marion Studholme as Gretel at the Wells in the 1950s?' How indeed! How can anyone be better than Ann Pashley as Boris's son Feodor?

This helpful friend recalled Victoria de Los Angeles's Mélisande at the Met in 1959 as perfection, while the author babbled ecstatically of Kiri Te Kanawa's Desdemona. But it is time to begin—in alphabetical order—then head for Outer Mongolia.

GRACE BUMBRY   EBOLI
Nowadays Grace Bumbry is a glamorous superstar complete with a soprano voice greatly cherished in two continents, acting ability of a high order and a stage personality like a sleek pantheress. In 1963, when she made her début at Covent Garden as Eboli in a revival of Visconti's famous production of *Don Carlos*, she was a mezzo, best-known before that sensational April night for her Venus in *Tannhäuser* at Bayreuth in 1961, which stirred up controversy (because of her colour) until she actually performed.

Word of her prowess as Eboli raced around operatic London

after the dress rehearsal, during which the Friends of Covent Garden were successively astounded and thrilled by her Veil Song and so overwhelmed by her 'O don fatale' that they burst into a forbidden storm of applause to the annoyance of authority. The first night, with a cast which included Christoff and Gobbi, was Bumbry's (with a thought for her glorious teacher, Lotte Lehmann). This was the night that made her a major star, highlights being the fast coloratura of the Veil Song and the passionate account of 'O don fatale', deeply moving in the grief-stricken middle section. It resulted in an eruption of applause and cheers. Most of the legendary performances selected for inclusion here do not concern a single night, but, as this one does, the date must be stated: April 6, 1963.

MARIA CALLAS   NORMA

Choosing a legendary Callas role is like selecting a representative novel by Dickens: at least six immediately spring to mind. Reluctantly turning from her Violetta, her Anna Bolena, Tosca, etc. one may legitimately select her grandest tragic role, Norma, in which she made her Covent Garden and Met débuts. The great tenor, Lauri-Volpi, writing in his *A viso aperto*, said of the 26-year-old Callas's 1950 performance of Norma: 'Voice, style, bearing, power of concentration and that vital surge of the spirit—all these rise to a rare height in this artist ... In the last act, Norma's imploring voice seemed to me art's purest joy.'

Callas was never at her vocal best in 'Casta diva' it seems, even in her prime, but has anyone since the days of Pasta and Malibran, even Rosa Ponselle, delivered the dramatic recitative leading up to it more vividly? From the second act, she nearly always had her audiences enslaved (give or take hired assassins and over-zealous supporters of rivals—see *Claque*, page 329), until the last Normas in Paris in the mid-1960s when the part was becoming beyond her. Even that toughest of her débuts, the Met in 1957, became 'a royal progress' from Act II onwards. She only failed in one area of Norma, trying to have us believe that any man would leave her for any of the Adalgisas, for Callas's Druid priestess was glamorous, noble, flashing-eyed, womanly, passionate, tigerish, loving, valiant and dangerous.

Almost as remarkable as her powers of vocal characterization and dramatic genius was her phrasing and, indeed, gift for making a single word memorable; so one remembers 'Tremi tu? e per chi?' (You are trembling? For whom?) fired like a thunderbolt at her faithless lover, who later received 'In mia man alfin tu sei' (At last you are in my hands) like a whiplash. But there were also so many long sublime stretches: the great duets, the scene where she nearly kills her children, and the finale where Norma ascends into a new dimension in 'Qual cor tradisti' (The heart that you betrayed), upbraiding her lover, yet inspiring him to die gladly with her. Records mercifully preserve these Olympian memories. Just once in his life, Bellini joined the great creative gods—with *Norma*—but he provided a role only to be conquered fully by a goddess chaste in devotion to her art. Such a one was Callas.

BORIS CHRISTOFF   BORIS GODUNOV
He has everything going for him as Boris: a dark, Slavonic voice, superb musicality, eyes to threaten and command, height, an overwhelming personality with acting ability to match, and, like Olivier, the rare gift of bringing a sense of danger into the theatre. Down the years his vocal prowess has varied, but at the time of writing, just a quarter of a century since his first Covent Garden Boris, his magnificent voice, the very essence of drama and capable of the most winning lyricism, seems as good as ever it was. It is surely no longer in order to say that his Boris is of the school of Chaliapin, for he is now the Tsar in his own right from his first towering, majestic entrance, through the Macbeth-like torments of 'I have attained the highest power' and the terrifying, hyterical passion he brings to the Clock scene, to his final shattering death fall. His farewell to his son Feodor, of which Harold Rosenthal wrote in 1971 that his 'ravishingly beautiful *mezza voce* was fined down to a whisper', is a sequence when composer and actor-singer hypnotize an entire audience totally. The recollection of that great, great-eyed kneeling figure haunts the imagination for days after a performance. One cannot state that a whole audience at a Christoff Boris is spellbound, only pity anyone who is not.

KATHLEEN FERRIER   ORFEO
This most radiant of contraltos and adored artist first sang Gluck's Orfeo at Glyndebourne in 1947. In 1953, under

Barbirolli at Covent Garden, she returned to the role—in English—when she was already desperately ill. Yet her performance was nobility itself, not just of utterance and appearance—that was expected—but of movement, to such an extent that the ballet critic, Richard Buckle, stated that it was an object lesson to the Sadler's Wells Ballet. Off-stage, it was later revealed, she was hardly able to move, indeed the author remembers seeing her having to be supported to her car afterwards by the Barbirollis, her warm voice joking away as she went. The second performance could not be finished, the rest were cancelled and soon she was dead. So it is fair to claim that some 2,200 people on that opening night experienced a miracle, though at the time most of them merely thought it was a miracle of art. They gave Kathleen Ferrier the first volcanic ovation accorded to a British singer in the post-war years and one that has been rarely equalled or surpassed since by anyone of any nationality.

TITO GOBBI   SCARPIA

Gobbi is too good an actor and too naturally inventive not to have altered his interpretation of Puccini's corrupt, lustful, evil and splendidly theatrical chief of police in *Tosca* down the years in matters of detail, but in essence it has remained the same: aristocratic, dangerous and totally compelling. The voice has lost its bloom but seemingly none of its power—the iron-hard, thrilling, commanding tone which is so much more attractive than the average, conventionally beautiful baritone voice. Indeed, his Scarpia has positively gained by the passing of the years, and not only in artistry. Few singers act vocally as well as he, and his Scarpia sets a standard of vocal and physical impact which makes nearly all his rivals seem pale shadows. Sometimes, when marching into strange or non-existent productions, his Scarpia has seemed 'external', 'melodramatic' at moments in the wrong way, but never so in the Zeffirelli production with Callas at Covent Garden in 1964, mercifully preserved in part on film, and, one suspects, never since then. His restraint made the passion boiling beneath all the more powerful until, in the classic confrontation with Tosca in Act II, passion finally got the upper hand. He died, like Olivier's Richard III, fighting for his life, his arm stretched up as if he was trying to keep death at bay. Scarpia is Gobbi's part by right now until he finally retires, and at his finest, it is hard to imagine anyone succeeding to his title.

HANS HOTTER   WOTAN

Playing a great Wagner role is like performing in slow motion with sudden bursts of activity. Dignity, repose and magnificence of presence are ideally essentials before a note has been sung, especially with Wotan, the ruler of the gods, and no one in modern times has matched up more to the great role than Hotter. Merely to see him holding a spear was an education. True, his voice, especially towards the end of his career, had 'wobble' at times, and, sadly, some of those who never saw and heard him will hear his later recordings and wonder, despite his dramatically resonant voice and superb phrasing, just how good he was. Others will recognize in him what Kent saw in Lear—authority.

He finally retired in Paris in 1972, suitably as Wotan in *Die Walküre*. For the last time, an audience heard him sing his Farewell to Brünnhilde. Perhaps some made allowances for the march of time and its effect on a once great voice, but no allowances were needed in the final moments, when all the old beauty seemed to return and became moving beyond words. Then the curtain came down on a matchless career.

SENA JURINAC   BUTTERFLY

After establishing herself as one of the great Mozartian singers of the age in the late 1940s and the 1950s, also as an incomparable Octavian and Composer in *Ariadne auf Naxos*, Sena Jurinac added a number of Italian roles to her repertoire, including Butterfly. Hers was a dramatic soprano's Cio-Cio-San (Butterfly's Japanese name) in the tradition of Emmy Destinn, as opposed to a lighter lyric soprano's interpretation, and it ranks with her other masterpieces. Like Callas, Jurinac has a number of legendary performances for a compiler to choose from.

Madame Butterfly is a genuine tragedy, and however much that fact is obscured by conductors, producers and designers, a great soprano sees to it that Puccini's tragic masterpiece comes across as just that and not merely—for the opera is unsinkable—a splendid and tuneful tearjerker. Jurinac brought extreme beauty of voice to the role, superb artistry and rare dramatic ability. She was a deeply moving Butterfly, over-whelming in her Act II 'triumph' after Pinkerton's ship has been heard and before the Flower Duet, and again tremendous and monumental in her death scene. When she first sang the role at Covent Garden in 1958, some claimed that her acting was too contrived at times, lacking spontaneity. If this was so, it must have been first night anxiety—though she had a triumph —for, at later performances, a great actress-singer brought additional glory to a glorious role.

VICTORIA DE LOS ANGELES   MANON

In 1950, when the young Covent Garden company was at a stage of development which rarely extended beyond the well-meaning, one of the few triumphant happenings was the appearance of the Spanish soprano, Victoria de los Angeles, in three roles: Mimi, Massenet's Manon and Elsa. The last was the finest, indeed it is hard to believe that anyone has equalled her in the post-war period, but it is her Manon which remains the legend, a legend reinforced by her recording of the role. Her characterization was vocally brilliant and physic-ally never less than adequate because of her extreme charm and natural dignity. She gave us the young, inexperienced girl in Act I, an almost brazen hedonist in her singing and phrasing in the Cours la Reine scene and elsewhere, and finally she gave passion. The Earl of Harewood wrote in *Opera*: 'This great singer rose to the heights of the celebrated vocal moments of the score'; while J. B. Steane has since written (about her Manon) of the 'warm heart of de los Angeles's voice'. That warmth, allied to Massenet's delicate yet committed and know-ing talent, made her Manon sheer magic, unequalled since by anyone except the singer in other countries. In this year of years, she was only 26.

BIRGIT NILSSON   ISOLDE

The hard core of Nilsson worshippers will very reasonably ask, why no Brünnhilde as well? The answer must be that most of the singers featured here achieved more than one legendary performance, so only one of hers—for many, her supreme role —is allowed. The word 'worshipper' is chosen with care. The combination of Nilsson and Wagner reduced one *Opera* critic to such an enviable state of total abandon that, after her

1970 Isolde at Bayreuth, he hailed her as the greatest singing-actress now before the public. But a great actress-singer (the phrase used throughout this book) convinces a deaf man that he is in the presence of a great actress in the strict theatrical sense, a quality which belongs to only a handful of singers in any age. The miracle is that Nilsson is such a good actress, for only those who find her a cold personality (there are those, dear God, who find that Olivier lacks 'heart'!) are not conquered by her ardent, seriously conceived, physical portrayal of Isolde.

Which brings us to the crux of the matter, an Isolde who sings magnificently, subtly, gloriously, with measureless reserves of power, superb dramatic feeling, depths of emotion and searing passion. She has never had Tristan to match her which, whatever the unknowing may think, hardly helps an artist. (When was Chaliapin at his best? Before 1914, with a great Russian company.) Yet her relationship with her Tristans has been utterly convincing whenever possible, from the anger and sorrow at the beginning to the heightened rapture at the end. She is the most dynamic Wagnerian of modern times, an embodiment of the operatic life force. Wagnerites spend much of their lives making allowances for singers because the Master asked so much of them. No one has needed to make allowances for Nilsson as Isolde, the phenomenal performance of a phenomenal artist.

LEONTYNE PRICE   AIDA
It is hard to imagine a finer Aida than Leontyne Price in the late 1950s, the morning glory of her career. Today she ranks as one of the supreme Verdians of the century, with her Aida the role that her legions of admirers most treasure, for it has been her masterpiece. In the 1950s she was a much more dedicated actress than she is today, and her physical allure was almost as strong as her voice was beautiful. Those who caught her few performances at Covent Garden in the role are still spellbound at the memory of them. Voice, phrasing, deep sincerity and emotional power made them pinnacles of lyric art. Her high, soft, floated notes held the house breathless, that stage beyond mere pin-drop silence, while her sultry looks matched the sometimes smoky tone of her voice. This was the apotheosis of Miss Price, the girl from Mississippi who had come up by way of Bess in *Porgy and Bess*. She has become an

even greater singer and artist since then, but her Aidas in America and Europe in those days remain legends.

JOAN SUTHERLAND   LUCIA DI LAMMERMOOR
After the event there were many to say that they foresaw Joan Sutherland's leap to superstardom, missing mere stardom on the way, and, indeed, some operagoers had been prophesying great things for her, especially after her Gilda and her stunning Israelite Woman in *Samson*. But how could even Serafin, Zeffirelli, Sir David Webster, how even could her husband, Richard Bonynge, who had first realized that her truest home was as a dramatic coloratura in the roles of the golden age of *bel canto* opera, have foreseen the phenomenal triumph she enjoyed at Covent Garden that legendary night, February 17, 1959. She emerged from it an actress-singer and a beautiful woman. Philip Hope-Wallace put it bluntly: 'Miss Sutherland used to look gauche. Last night she looked beautiful.' He then proclaimed her singing intensely musical and accurate. Andrew Porter found her spellbinding: 'Tears and fire co-mingled', and Desmond Shawe-Taylor introduced his readers to a newly minted creation, 'Joan Sutherland, the tragic actress' And along the way Messrs Bonynge, Serafin and Webster were vindicated and Donizetti's grand old work given a British boost strong enough to silence those who considered him beyond the musical pale.

Since then, Lucia has always been La Stupenda's supreme role; indeed, it was amusing to note the astonishment of her detractors when exposed to it at Covent Garden in 1973. Their doubts were confounded: class will out.

Every great interpretation has peaks of achievement and most some unique touch. Such a moment occurred in the astounding Mad Scene (O, that first hearing of her 'Alfin son tua'—'at last I am yours'—so long ago!), when Zeffirelli gave her a difficult piece of 'business', carried out to perfection. It was he who inspired her into becoming an actress, and Lucia has always been her best acted part since. He had her swooping about the stage in her echoing duet with the flute, perfection of swift movement without any loss of spectacular vocal virtu-osity. She was chasing the sound of the flute: her head had jerked round to follow it and, as Russell Braddon has written: 'Instantly the audience recognized it for what it was—a sound that existed only in Lucia's flawed mind.' And there came a moment in the unique coloratura display that followed, on the move all the time, when she was directed to turn full upstage for an entire electric phrase. As thousands know, it is now part of her Lucia, but those who were there that night of nights hear it as they heard it and saw it as they saw it then, however many times they have returned to Sutherland's Lucia since.

SHIRLEY VERRETT   EBOLI

To include another black singer's Eboli is sheer accident or perhaps, British bias, for many London operagoers cite *Don Carlos* as their favourite Verdi opera. Like Bumbry, Verrett is also a famous Amneris and Carmen, while her Azucena is totally believable—no mean feat—and gloriously sung, and her Orfeo, some would say, ranks as a legend. But Eboli is her most legendary role. Typically, she became 'a star of the first order' (Joseph Wechsberg) after her house début at the Vienna State Opera in 1970, her 'subtle phrasing and *bel canto* delivery of the Veil Song' delighting *Opera*'s Austrian-based critic. She apparently overacted on that great night, but as there was a planned and disgusting demonstration against the unfortunate conductor, Horst Stein, and the producer was no better than he should have been, who can blame her if she deserted her own high dramatic standards? Yet she still created a local legend. Her earlier Eboli at Covent Garden (1968), a first on any stage, was also a sensational success, all tonal beauty and dramatic fire, plus memorable phrasing and the equally memorable use of words. There are few more vivid singers than Verrett, and when this quality is added to an already most vivid role, the result is thunder and lightning.

JON VICKERS   FLORESTAN

Jon Vickers' commitment to his roles is so total, and his virile, craggy personality, plus his sensitive artistry, so memorable, that he always makes a strong impression. This has been the case since his very first Riccardo in *Un Ballo in Maschera* at Covent Garden in 1957. It is hard to choose between his Peter Grimes and his Florestan (*Fidelio*) when deciding which is his most legendary performance, but perhaps because some find his Grimes controversial, one may escape from a quandary and hail his Florestan as even more indisputably a master-piece. Not, though, for a handful of booers one April night at Covent Garden in 1976; but perhaps the fact that his voice is now liable to splay out accounted for their absurd demonstration, or perhaps they were canary-fanciers who could not endure Art on display. For Vickers' Florestan is a work of art from the first sight of him lying squalidly in chains to the joyous moment when his Leonore unlocks them in the last scene and they crash to the ground. (When Hildegard Behrens sang the role opposite him, matching his high quality, the result was a double legend.) Vickers alone almost of modern Florestans *is* a prisoner and has suffered deeply, which is not easy to transmit in Covent Garden's negatively effective production, originated by Klemperer. The fervour of his opening aria may have been equalled, but as a piece of total music theatre can never have been excelled, and such is his intensity that he can risk big effects, big facial expressions without ever coming near operatic ham. The conviction is total, the result, matching Beethoven's vision, is shattering.

Selected Singers

The majority of artists chosen for this section have become famous in the last thirty years or are legendary figures from opera's past.

See the Index of Operatic Roles, pages 341–6 for the roles, the operas they belong to, and voices.

ABBOTT, EMMA (1850–91). American soprano who made her Covent Garden (1876) and New York (1877) débuts as Marie in *La Fille du Régiment*. With her husband, Eugene Wetherell, she ran the Emma Abbott English Grand Opera Company, which toured the U.S.A. from 1878.

ACKTÉ, AINO (1876–1944). Finnish soprano, born into an operatic family, her début was as Marguerite in Paris (1897). She was Salome in the first British production, and Beecham described her as 'a slim and beautiful creature with an adequate voice and a remarkable understanding of her part' (*A Mingled Chime*). This excellent actress-singer became Director of the Finnish National Opera in 1938.

ADAM, THEO. German bass who first appeared at Bayreuth in 1952, having made his début in Dresden. He has sung at the leading German opera houses, also at Vienna, London, Russia, Rome and at the Met. A musical if not a majestic Wotan, his Sachs at Bayreuth (1974), warmly human and vocally superb, was a peak of achievement in a distinguished career.

ALEXANDER, JOHN. American tenor, best known for stylish and vigorous performances opposite Sutherland, Sills, etc. in Italian roles as well as Faust, Hoffmann. A famous Pollione in *Norma*.

ALBANESE, LICIA (1913–). Italian-American soprano, a major star of the Metropolitan from 1940–66, and well known to millions in America and Europe for her Mimi opposite Gigli in the first complete recording of *La Bohème*.

ALBANI, (DAME) EMMA (1847–1930). Canadian soprano whose real name was Marie Louise Lajeunesse. Though she studied in Paris and Milan, and sang at the Met, her career is essentially a notable part of Covent Garden history, being its first Mignon (Thomas), Elsa, Elisabeth (*Tannhaüser*), Senta and Desdemona (1872–96). She had a perfect legato.

ALBONI, MARIETTA (1823–94). Italian contralto who was taught roles in Rossini's operas by the composer himself, and was the greatest contralto of her age. When she sang Arsace in *Semiramide* at Covent Garden in 1847, *The Times* said that perhaps 'a more perfect singer was never heard'. Her legs were very good, which presumably increased her affection for *travesti* parts, including Tancredi and Cherubino, and Urbano in *Les Huguenots*, which Meyerbeer wrote for her. She even sang Carlos in the first Covent Garden *Ernani* after two famous baritones had turned the role down. Alas, the sylph became an elephant and she was forced to sing, so Richard Bonynge tells us (*Opera Annual* 7), 'from a semi-recumbent posture'. A critic—they did not mince matters in the last century—wrote how her voice 'issued forth from the throat of a hippopotamus like the trill of a nightingale'.

ALDA, FRANCES (1883–1952). New Zealand-born soprano, a pupil of Mathilde Marchesi, her début being as Manon in Paris (1904). After European successes, including impressing Toscanini, she became a star of the Metropolitan, marrying Gatti-Casazza, the manager. Her career there spanned 1908 to 1930 and was a stormy one off-stage.

ALLEN, THOMAS (1944–). English baritone, one of the fastest-rising young actor-singers of the 1970s, notably with the Welsh National Opera (including Billy Budd, 1972), and at Glyndebourne where he was a fine Papageno (1973) and an even finer Figaro (1974). The first Count in Musgrave's *The Voice of Ariadne* (Aldeburgh, 1974) and a sterling Sid in *Albert Herring*. His Covent Garden roles include a stirring Valentine in *Faust* (1974). An excellent Marcello (1976).

ALLIN, NORMAN (1884–1973). English bass who worked with the Beecham Company singing King Mark, Méphistophélès, etc. and at Covent Garden (1919), including Gurnemanz. A pillar and director of the British National Opera Company (1922–9), he later sang at Glyndebourne and for the Carl Rosa.

ALTHOUSE, PAUL (1889–1954). American tenor, the first American to be engaged at the Met without European experience (1913). The Company's Heldentenor (1934–40), he was the first American Tristan at the Met.

ALVA, LUIGI (1927–). Peruvian tenor with an international reputation, especially in Mozart and Rossini (his Count in *Il Barbieri* is only one of many fine roles). To an ingratiating voice, used with style, he brings a good appearance and acting ability. It is hard to imagine a better Fenton in *Falstaff* than his at Covent Garden in 1961.

ALVARY, MAX (1856–98). German tenor, notorious in England for demanding that the first English *Ring* (1892) should begin with *Siegfried* so that he could make an advantageous début at Covent Garden. Previously he had been at the Met (1885–9), and was the Bayreuth Tristan and Tannhäuser in 1891.

ANDERS, PETER (1908–54). German tenor who, as his voice grew heavier, passed from Offenbach, through Mozart to Walther and Otello, both in Hamburg in 1950. A much admired artist.

ANDERSON, MARIAN (1902–). American contralto, whose magnificent voice was not heard at the Met (because of prejudice against Black singers) until 1955, when she sang Ulrica.

ANDRÉSEN, IVAR (1896–1940). Norwegian bass, whose very fine voice was heard in Wagnerian and other roles in Dresden, Bayreuth (1927–36), Covent Garden and the Met. A superb Osmin at Glyndebourne in 1935.

ARIÉ, RAPHAEL (1920–). Bulgarian bass, who after singing at the Sofia Opera, made his La Scala début as the King in *The Love of the Three Oranges* (1947). The original Trulove in *The Rake's Progress* (1951). A leading bass at the major Italian houses, a more recent success was his Ivan Khovansky in *Khovanshchina* at the Florence Maggio Musicale of 1973.

ARMSTRONG, SHEILA. English soprano, a very attractive actress-singer who made her name at Glyndebourne in the late 1960s, her début being Belinda in *Dido and Aeneas* (1967). Her Covent Garden Nanetta (1974) was perfection.

ARNOLDSON, SIGRID (1861–1943) Swedish soprano, who made her début in Moscow as Rosina. Sang in London in the 1880s and 1890s, including Charlotte in *Werther* at Covent Garden (1894).

ARROYO, MARTINO. American soprano, a magnificent lyric-dramatic singer, especially in Verdi (Lady Macbeth at the Met in 1973 excepted). Her phrasing, breath control and musicianship, allied to a beautiful voice and a pleasant personality, have given this black artist a huge following on both sides of the Atlantic.

ARTÔT, DÉSIRÉE (1835–1907). Belgian mezzo-soprano who became a soprano, her roles included Marie in *La Fille du*

Régiment and Violetta, in London and elsewhere. Proposed to by Tchaikovsky, she married instead a Spanish baritone, Mariano Padilla y Ramos, and their daughter, Lola Artôt de Padilla (1880–1933), was the first Berlin Octavian.

AUSTIN, FREDERICK (1872–1952). English baritone. Gunther in the Covent Garden English *Ring* (1908) under Richter. He was the Peacham of the famous *The Beggar's Opera* (1920) at the Lyric, Hammersmith, then became Artistic Director of the British National Opera Company in 1924.

AUSTRAL, FLORENCE (1894–1968). Australian soprano whose actual name was Wilson. A famous Brünnhilde from the time she first sang the role in *Die Walküre* for the British National Opera Company (1922), later singing in the rest of *The Ring*. She also excelled as Isolde and Aida. She sang Brünnhilde in International Seasons as well, including Berlin and Australia. Her voice was warm and strong, her technique superb.

BACCALONI, SALVATORE (1900–69). Italian bass, one of the greatest buffos in operatic history, at La Scala for Toscanini, Covent Garden, the Met (from 1940) and Glyndebourne (1936–9). Don Pasquale was his masterpiece, though his Leporello, garlic-scented and richly sung, was another marvel, along with Bartolo and Osmin. A natural comic, short, fat and with a comedian's face, his other roles included Falstaff, Melitone and Gianni Schicchi. He was with the Met until 1962.

BACQUIER, GABRIEL (1924–). French baritone who made his début as Rossini's Figaro at the Monnaie, Brussels in 1953. From 1956, at the Opéra-Comique and Opéra as Rigoletto, Méphistophélès, Scarpia, etc. He has sung at La Scala and the Met, also at Covent Garden as Sir Richard in *I Puritani* (1964) and a very fine Scarpia on a number of occasions since.

BAHR-MILDENBURG, ANNA (1872–1947). Austrian soprano, a noted Wagnerian at Bayreuth, Vienna, etc. and London's first Klytemnestra (1910).

BAILEY, NORMAN (1933–). English bass-baritone who played a wide range of roles from 1960 in Germany before joining Sadler's Wells, where his second role, Hans Sachs, made his name (1968). In 1969, he stood in as Sachs at Covent Garden with resounding success, singing the role that year in Hamburg, Brussels, Munich and Bayreuth. From 1970, he has been the Wotan of the Goodall *Ring* at the Coliseum. Since then, his roles at the Coliseum and Covent Garden have included Pizarro, Kurnewal, the Dutchman and other Wagner roles; also Ford in *Falstaff*, and Kutuzov in *War and Peace*. A totally committed artist whose best is yet to come.

BAINBRIDGE, ELIZABETH. English mezzo-soprano whose fine voice has been heard in a wide range of roles at Covent Garden, including Suzuki, Ann in *The Trojans*, Amneris, also Emilia (1974) and Ulrica (1975).

BAKER, JANET (1933–). English mezzo-soprano whose voice is a great one. Its beauty and emotional power, allied to a winning personality and dedication to her art, make her increasingly frequent operatic performances exceptional occasions. Her Dido for Scottish Opera and at Covent Garden is already a legend, and other roles include Marguerite in Berlioz's *Faust*, Monteverdi's Poppea and Donizetti's Mary Stuart, all three for the English National Opera. Her Dorabella for Scottish Opera (1967) proved her to be a comedienne as well as an irresistible Mozartian. An exciting, impassioned Vitellia in *La Clemenza di Tito* at Covent Garden (1974) and La Scala (1976).

BAKLANOV, GEORGE (1882–1938). Russian baritone, whose most famous roles included Rigoletto and Scarpia. An exile after the Revolution, he was at Chicago from 1917–26.

BAMPTON, ROSE (1908–). American soprano, earlier contralto, whose Met début was as Laura in Ponchielli's *La Gioconda* (1932). Her soprano début there was as Leonora in *Il Trovatore* (1937), though the same year she was Covent Garden's Amneris. Other roles included a much admired Donna Anna, and Sieglinde and Kundry.

BARBIERI, FEDORA (1920–). Italian mezzo, one of the most admired Italian singers since the war. Azucena, Amneris, Eboli and Mistress Quickly have been among her triumphs in Italy and elsewhere, and she was Eboli on the opening night of the Bing regime at the Met in 1950, singing a number of seasons there. She was first heard at Covent Garden in La Scala's visit in 1950, and in Italy she was a famous Carmen. She sang with Callas in many now legendary performances.

BARBIERI-NINI, MARIANNA (*c* 1820–87). Italian soprano who created Lady Macbeth as well as the soprano leads in *I Due Foscari* and *Il Corsaro*, proving Verdi's high regard for her. A magnificent dramatic soprano and a most conscientious artist, she studied the sleep-walking scene in *Macbeth* for three months to get it right.

BARRIENTOS, MARIA (1883–1946). Spanish soprano remembered

best for her period at the Met (1916–20), where *Lakmé*, *Puritani* and *Sonnambula* were staged for her.

BARSOVA, VALERIJA (1892–1967). Russian soprano, a leading singer at the Bolshoi (1920–48). Her roles included Violetta, Gilda, Ludmilla and Rosina.

BARSTOW, JOSEPHINE (1940–). English soprano whose performances for Sadler's Wells/ English National Opera in the 1870s as Natasha in *War and Peace*, Violetta, and the obsessed prioress Jeanne in *The Devils of Loudun* have proclaimed a major actress-singer of great achievement and greater promise. Since then she has given a superb Octavian (1975). Her Denise in *The Knot Garden* (1970) at Covent Garden was another triumph, as were her Salome (1975) and Elisabeth de Valois and Tosca (1976) for the English National Opera.

BASSI, AMEDEO (1874–1949). Italian tenor whose notable career included Radamès at the opening of the Colón, Buenos Aires (1908); Covent Garden's first Walther in *Loreley*; Frederico in *Germania* and Dick Johnson in *La Fanciulla del West* (1907–11); and Parsifal, Siegfried and Loge for Toscanini at La Scala (1921–6).

BASSI, LUIGI (1766–1825). Italian baritone for whom Mozart wrote Don Giovanni after he had sung the Count in *Figaro*.

BASTIANINI, ETTORE (1922–67). Italian baritone, much admired in Verdi, who died of cancer at the height of his career. He made his début as a bass, but changed to a lyric baritone after singing some of the tenor part in *La Forza del Destino*. At the Met, 1953–9.

BATTISTINI, MATTIA (1856–1928). Italian baritone, one of the greatest in operatic history, especially renowned as a high baritone of remarkable range. So well-schooled that he was singing in his seventies, and he had a repertoire of eighty operas. His European and South American reputation was immense, but he never sang in the U.S.A. Massenet rewrote *Werther* for him.

BEGG, HEATHER (1932–). New Zealand mezzo-soprano whose repertoire ranges from an hilarious Queen of the Fairies in *Iolanthe* to Azucena.

BELCOURT, ÉMILE (1926–). Canadian tenor, best known for his excellent performances in operetta, including Pluto in *Orpheus in the Underworld* for Sadler's Wells, but, since 1972, renowned for his Loge in *Rheingold* in the Goodall *Ring* at the Coliseum, London. Other roles include Pelléas and Shuisky.

BELLINICIONI, GEMMA (1864–1950). Italian soprano, the first Santuzza (1890) and Fedora (1898). This fine-looking actress-singer married Robert Stagno, the first Turiddu.

BELLOC, TERESA GIORGI (1784–1855). Italian mezzo for whom Rossini wrote roles in *Tancredi* and *La Gazza Ladra*. The index of Coe's English translation of Stendhal's *Life of Rossini* tells us that the writer thought her voice ugly and coarse-grained, in flat contradiction to the references to her in the book, where she seems a superior singer whose voice got better and better.

BENDER, PAUL (1875–1947). German bass, a notable Wagnerian in Europe and at the Met, also well known for his Osmin, Sarastro and Ochs. He was Covent Garden's first Amfortas (1914).

BENELLI, UGO. Italian tenor, renowned for his stylish use of a delightful light voice, and for his looks and acting ability, especially in Rossini and Donizetti. Indeed, his Glyndebourne Nemorino (1967) and Covent Garden Ernesto (1974) could hardly have been bettered. Lindoro in *L'Italiana in Algeri* at La Scala (1973).

BENUCCI, FRANCESCO (c 1745–1824). Italian bass, the first Figaro (1786) and Guglielmo in *Così fan tutte* (1790).

BERGANZA, TERESA (1934–). Spanish mezzo-soprano whose début was as Dorabella at Aix-en-Provence (1957). Blessed with looks, personality and a rich voice, particularly at home in Rossini's most florid moments, she is a famous Rosina and Cenerentola. Recordings do not quite capture her sense of fun, notably her Isabella in *L'Italiana in Algeri*. Spike Hughes said of her 1958 début at Glyndebourne in his book of that name: 'With a face like something out of a Murillo, her Cherubino was a complete joy!'

BERGER, ERNA (1900–). German soprano, one of the most famous singers of the 1930s and 1940s: Bayreuth, Salzburg, Berlin, Covent Garden and the Met. She retired to become a teacher in 1955. Her astonishingly youthful voice never deserted her. A famous Queen of the Night.

BERGLUND, JOEL (1903–). Swedish bass-baritone and a major Wagnerian in the 1930s and 1940s. On leaving the Met in 1949, he became Director of the Stockholm Royal Opera (1949–52). His roles included Hans Sachs, Wotan and the Dutchman, the last of which he sang at Bayreuth in 1942.

BERGONZI, CARLO (1924–). Italian tenor, one of the most stylish of the century, who began as a baritone, making his début as Rossini's Figaro in 1948. His second début was as Andrea Chénier (1951). His technique is as masterly as his voice is ingratiating, and fortunately his recordings of Verdi, Puccini, etc. do him justice. His long Met career began in 1956. Without physical and dramatic advantages, he reached the top by voice and sheer artistry.

BESANZONI, GABRIELLA (1890–1962). Italian mezzo-soprano, who, after her début as Adalgisa at Viterbo (1911), appeared all over Italy and sang Carmen and Orfeo for Toscanini at La Scala. Also sang in Chicago, South America and at the Met. Her Isabella in *L'Italiana in Algieri* and Cenerentola were much admired.

BETZ, FRANZ (1835–1900). German baritone whose firsts are awe-inspiring: the original Hans Sachs (Munich, 1868), and the Wotan of the first complete *Ring* (Bayreuth, 1876); also the first Berlin Falstaff.

BILLINGTON, ELIZABETH (*c* 1765–1818). English soprano, as famous in Italy as in Britain where her admirers included the Prince Regent, who may even have been her lover. Bianchi's *Ines de Castro* (1794) was written for her after the King of Naples had her engaged at the San Carlo, Naples, while in 1806 she became the first English Vitellia in *La Clemenza di Tito*. Mrs Billington—her husband was a bass player and teacher—had a pure, not overpowerful voice and was also a composer and pianist. Her Naples engagement was not without incident, for Vesuvius promptly erupted, which caused some Neapolitans to think that the Almighty was criticizing the choice of a Protestant as prima donna. Fortunately, the majority of local opera buffs were untroubled by the thought of a heretic on their sacred stage.

BJÖRLING, JUSSI (1911–60). Swedish tenor, one of the most admired and popular of his day, technically admirable and whose rich voice was—one cannot avoid the not altogether happy word—most tastefully used. His lack of involvement dramatically would have upset Verdi and Puccini, but his singing disarmed criticism. His repertoire was vast and included French and Russian roles, though no German ones except for Mozart's. The Met enjoyed his services from 1938 to 1960, but he only appeared at Covent Garden in 1939 and 1960.

BJÖRLING, SIGURD (1907–). Swedish baritone, unrelated to the above, who gave many fine Wagnerian performances in the early 1950s in London, Bayreuth and New York.

BLACHUT, BENO (1913–). Czech tenor who joined the Prague National Theatre in 1941 and rapidly became well known for his work in 'local' operas by Smetana, Dvořák and Janáček.

BLACKHAM, JOYCE (1934–). English mezzo-soprano, one of the finest post-war Carmens and very successful in operetta. Married to Peter Glossop (see page 149).

BLANC, ERNEST (1923–). French baritone, with the Opéra from 1954, he has sung in Britain and America and at Bayreuth. At his peak in the 1950s and early 1960s, his roles included Rigoletto, Germont and Wolfram.

BOCKELMANN, RUDOLF (1892–1958). German bass-baritone who appeared at Bayreuth from 1929–42, also at Covent Garden and Chicago, and at the Berlin Staatsoper (1932–45). His finest roles were Sachs and Wotan, sung with authority and power.

BÖHME, KURT (1908–). German bass who was at Dresden, 1930–50, since when he has been a permanent member of the Munich State Opera, while appearing all over Europe, North and South America as well as Japan. A Bayreuth regular since 1963. His masterpiece is Baron Ochs.

BOHNEN, MICHAEL (1887–1965). German bass-baritone, and an actor-singer of remarkable range vocally, whose repertoire included Jonny in Křenek's jazz opera, *Jonny spielt auf*. Much of his career was spent at the Met (1922–32) and in Berlin's Deutsches Opernhaus (1933–45).

BONCI, ALESSANDRO (1870–1940). Italian tenor, renowned for his elegant singing of Rossini, Bellini and Donizetti.

BONINSEGNA, CELESTINA (1877–1947). Italian soprano who made her début virtually untrained as Norina aged 15, then became a notably powerful and artistic dramatic soprano.

BORGIOLI, ARMANDO (1898–1945). Italian baritone, famous in Italy, at Covent Garden and the Met in the late 1920s and 1930s, especially for his Verdi roles.

BORGIOLI, DINO (1891–1960). Italian tenor, famous for his singing in Mozart and Rossini in Italy, and at Salzburg, Glyndebourne, Covent Garden and San Francisco. This admirable stylist put opera-starved Londoners in his eternal debt by his work as vocal director and producer (on occasion) of the New London Opera Company (1946–9).

BORI, LUCREZIA (1887–1960). Spanish soprano, much of whose career was spent at the

Met, where she made her début as Manon Lescaut in 1912, having the previous year been the first Italian Octavian. A charming, strong and most artistic singer.

BORKH, INGE (1917–). German soprano who began as an actress. Her Magda Sorel in Menotti's *The Consul* in Switzerland was the turning point of her career (1952), since when she has sung in Germany, England and at the Met. Her most remarkable performances have been as Elektra, Lady Macbeth and, many feel, as the Dyer's Wife in *Die Frau ohne Schatten*.

BORONAT, OLIMPIA (1867– 1934). Italian soprano whose beautiful voice was abetted by a superb technique, her roles including Violetta, Rosina and Elvira in *I Puritani*.

BOURDIN, ROGER (1900–). French baritone, with the Opéra-Comique and the Opéra from 1922; also Pelléas at Covent Garden (1930) and other engagements outside France. His wife, Géori Boué (1918–), beautiful enough to be Offenbach's Helen, made her début as Thaïs in 1942.

BOWMAN, JAMES. English counter-tenor whose unusually strong voice, allied to fine technique, has made him an admirable Oberon in Britten's *A Midsummer Night's Dream* (Covent Garden, 1974).

BRAHAM, JOHN (1774–1856). English tenor of Jewish extraction who had a European reputation, especially in Italy. A famous Handel singer, he was the first English Max in Weber's *Der Freishütz* (1824) and the creator of Huon in Weber's *Oberon* (1826). Later, his voice lowered and he sang Don Giovanni and William Tell. A very fine, if not over refined, singer, he was described by Sir Walter Scott as 'a beast of an actor, but an angel of a singer'.

BRAMBILLA. Family of Italian singers, including Marietta (1807–75), a contralto who created Orsini in *Lucrezia Borgia* and other roles; Teresa (1813–95) was the first Gilda (1850), and her niece, Teresina (1845–1921) created the role of Lucia in *I Promessi Sposi* (1872) and married its composer, Ponchielli.

BRANNIGAN, OWEN (1908–73). English bass renowned for his buffo performances. For Britten, he was the first Swallow in *Peter Grimes* (1945), Collatinus in *The Rape of Lucretia* (1946), Noye in *Noye's Fludde* (1958) and Bottom in *A Midsummer Night's Dream*, all also firsts.

BRANZELL, KARIN (1891–). Swedish mezzo-soprano, one of the finest of her day. She was at the Met, 1924–44 and at Covent Garden, 1935–8.

BRAUN, VICTOR. Canadian baritone, creator of Serle's Hamlet at Covent Garden (1969). He has sung at La Scala, San Francisco and in Canada, in Verdi, Mozart and Wagner. Eugene Onegin at Covent Garden (1972) and elsewhere.

BREMA, MARIE (1856–1925). English mezzo-soprano, Lola in the first English *Cavalleria Rusticana* (1891). Later, she became a Wagnerian, singing Kundry, Ortrud and Fricka at Bayreuth, and having the range to sing Brünnhilde in Paris for Richter. She gave an opera season at the Savoy (1910), singing Orfeo herself in English.

BROUWENSTIJN, GRÉ (1915–). Dutch soprano, blessed with a beautiful voice, artistry and a most attractive womanly warmth which made her widely popular in many countries as well as her own. Her Elisabeth de Valois at Covent Garden (1958) remains unequalled, while at Bayreuth (1954–6) her roles included Elisabeth, Eva, Gutrune and Sieglinde. She sang Leonore in *Fidelio* at Stuttgart for Wieland Wagner.

BROWNLEE, JOHN (1900–69). Australian baritone, brought to London by Melba. At the Paris Opéra, 1927–36, and a fine Almaviva, Don Giovanni and Don Alfonso in early Glyndebourne seasons. From 1937 to 1957, a member of the Met.

BRUSCANTINI, SESTO (1919–). Italian baritone and superb buffo who could happily make a living on the straight stage. A Glyndebourne regular from 1951, where his Mozart and Rossini performances were among the finest ever seen and heard there, and his Covent Garden Malatesta in 1974 must have come as a revelation to those who had never experienced his comic art. In the 1960s he added serious Verdian roles to his repertoire. A delightful Gianni Schicchi at Covent Garden in 1976.

BRYN-JONES, DELME. Welsh baritone. Macbeth for the Welsh National Opera (1963), joining Covent Garden (1964), since when he has also sung in San Francisco and Santa Fé. A fine voice.

BUCKMAN, ROSANA (?–1948). New Zealand soprano, a famous star of the Beecham company (1915–20), her roles including Aida, Isolde and Butterfly.

BUMBRY, GRACE (1937–). American soprano, originally a mezzo, now an international superstar and a major actress-singer. For her Covent Garden début as Eboli in *Don Carlos* (1963), see page 107. Other major successes have included Amneris and Salome, also

Lady Macbeth for which (at the Met) she was coached by Judith Anderson.

BURIAN, KAREL (1870–1924). Czech tenor who sang Wagnerian leads at Covent Garden and the Met before the First World War, and created—sensationally—a lust-ridden Salome at Dresden (1905).

BURROWS, STUART (1933–). Welsh tenor, now an international star, whose début was with the Welsh National Opera as Ismael in *Nabucco* (1963). His repertoire is very wide, including Verdi and Puccini, but he is perhaps best known as a Mozartian (Tamino, Don Ottavio) and in *bel canto* roles, including Ernesto and Nemorino.

CABALLÉ, MONTSERRAT (1933–). Spanish soprano, possessor of a very beautiful, true legato voice, and the ability to project considerable emotion. A major Verdian and Donizettian and a superb Norma vocally, she is no great actress, but has personality. Her pianissimi are national assets.

CAFFARELLI (1710–83). Italian male soprano who made a big enough fortune to buy a dukedom and two palaces, and was considered one of the greatest of all castrati.

CAHILL, TERESA. English soprano, a rising and attractive singer whose roles include Zerlina and an enchanting Servilia in *La Clemenza di Tito* at Covent Garden (1974).

CALLAS, MARIA (1923–). Greek soprano, born Kalogeropoulou, the only operatic singer since the war to become and remain an international household word for several decades, and one of the most important and influential in operatic history. The fact that she has been a controversial figure does not alter her achievement, which her many detractors normally allow. Even allowing for the changing musical climate about 1950, she more than anyone revived interest in early 19th-century Italian opera, and her magnificent championship of Spontini's *La Vestale* and Cherubini's *Medea* saved them from near oblivion. Her vocal dramatic genius, including memorable phrasing and vivid use of words, has hopefully killed the bird-like, pretty, shallow style of singing roles such as Lucia for ever; while her phyical acting (especially after Visconti worked with her at La Scala in the 1950s) has notably raised acting standards generally. Her sensational slimming in the mid-1950s, at some cost to her voice, perhaps, has helped force singers to realize that, today, the ordinary opera public, as opposed to the totally hooked, will not accept acres of flesh unless the voice is a great one. That some found her voice the most haunting sound of the 1950s, even though its top became gradually more suspect, and that others, who allowed her intense musicianship, never liked it, was and remains a fact of operatic life. Another fact was her extraordinary ability to characterize vocally, as records remind us. It was beyond mere colouring, being a mixture of dramatic instinct and intense thought. Even her Puccini heroines all sound different.

Born in New York, she made her début as Santuzza in Athens (1938), becoming famous in 1947 after singing Gioconda in the Verona Arena. In 1948 she sang Brünnhilde and Elvira in *I Puritani* (learnt rapidly in an emergency) with a day in between, having previously triumphed as Isolde. International fame far beyond the opera house came in the 1950s, though she was basically a child of La Scala (1951–8: 1960–2). Serafin was her most valuable conductor. Her Norma is discussed on page 108, while other masterpieces included Medea, Anna Bolena, Lucia and Violetta. Débuts include Covent Garden in 1952, Chicago in 1954, the Met in 1957 and Dallas, where she reigned as queen, in 1958. Controversies raged (see Jellinek's *Callas*, etc.), many because of her determination to 'do Art', and the few performances she missed, fewer than most singers, were blown up into international incidents. Her last masterpiece was Tosca in Zeffirelli's production at Covent Garden in 1964, the second act (with Gobbi), for all her vocal troubles, being arguably the most remarkable piece of music theatre in the Garden's history. A year later she virtually retired from the battlefield, though rumours of a return to the stage, as opposed to the concert platform, are regularly rife. La Divina remains the only world-famous opera singer a decade after ceasing to sing in the opera house.

CALVÉ, EMMA (1858–1942). French soprano, born Rose Calvet, for many years a major star of Covent Garden, the Met, etc. The creator of Suzel in Mascagni's *L'Amico Fritz* (Rome, 1891), the title role in Massenet's *Sapho* and Anita in his *La Navarraise*, she is best remembered for her Carmen, the most famous in the opera's history.

CANIGLIA, MARIA (1906–). Italian soprano, at the height of her fame—La Scala, Covent Garden, the Met—in the 1930s, especially as Adriana Lecouvreur and Tosca. She was Italy's finest lyric-dramatic soprano, her lower register being particularly rich.

CAPECCHI, RENATO (1923–). Italian bass, one of the finest buffos of the last half-century:

Bartolo, Gianni Schicchi, Melitone, Pasquale, etc. A great comic singer. Of his Dandini at La Scala (1973), Peter Hoffer noted in *Opera* that 'it proved once again that real professionals are worth going a long way to see and hear'.

CAPPUCILLI, PIERO (1927–). Italian baritone who was at first content to use his remarkable voice and no more, especially in Verdi, but has now become a major actor-singer because of Visconti, Zeffirelli and, especially, Strehler. Hence his magnificent La Scala Boccanegra and the authority of his Covent Garden Iago (1974).

CARLYLE, JOAN (1931–). English soprano, an attractive actress-singer, whose many admirable performances at Covent Garden and elsewhere from the 1960s have included Mimi, Donna Anna, Britten's Titania (*A Midsummer Night's Dream*) and a superb and moving Suor Angelica (1965).

CAROSIO, MARGHERITA (1908–). Italian soprano at La Scala, Covent Garden, etc. from the late 1920s. A famous and beautiful Violetta, including when the San Carlo visited Covent Garden in 1946.

CARRÉ, MARGUERITE (1880– 1947). French soprano, a noted singer at the Opéra-Comique, whose director, Albert Carré, she married. Best known for her Louise (Charpentier), Manon and Mélisande.

CARRERAS, JOSE. Spanish tenor whose voice, technique, looks and acting have shot him to deserved stardom in 1976. Already a Covent Garden idol for his Nemorino, Rodolfo, etc.

CARRON, ARTHUR (1900–67). English tenor, first known as Cox, who made his name as a dramatic tenor in London, then in America, including the Met (1935–46), and Covent Garden (1947–51), when past his best.

CARTERI, ROSANNA (1930–). Italian soprano whose career flourished in the 1950s but who was later absent from the stage for some years. Natasha in *War and Peace* at Florence (1953).

CARUSO, ENRICO (1873–1921). Italian tenor, the most famous in operatic history, a household word even to the tone deaf, and the possessor of one of the most beautiful tenor voices, mercifully preserved on many discs made between 1902–20. He was not simply the first 'gramophone tenor', for it could be claimed that he *made* the gramophone. His 'Vesti la giubba' was the first record to sell a million copies (though with more than one recording). Born in Naples, where he made his début in 1894, he rapidly became world famous. He was *the* tenor of Edwardian Covent Garden and sang at the Met from 1903–20, including Dick

Johnson at the first *La Fanciulla del West*. He also created Maurizio in *Adriana Lecouvreur* (La Scala, 1902) and other roles, and had a vast repertoire. No oil painting (though an excellent caricaturist) except in his youth, he yet was a sincere actor, especially in roles such as Canio, Eleazar (the part he sang when taken fatally ill), and Vasco da Gama in Meyerbeer's *L'Africaine*, in which role his 'O Paradiso' was paradise indeed, as his 1910 recording reveals.

His lower register had a baritone timbre in his early career, while later his voice darkened, by which time his style and phrasing had made him a matchless artist to all except that Puritanical handful who will always find traces of vulgarity in even the best Italian tenors. Those who remember him in the flesh regard him as unique, and the glamour which still surrounds his name is never likely to disappear.

CASSILLY, RICHARD. American tenor, at Hamburg State Opera and elsewhere (Parsifal, Siegmund, etc.). One of his finest roles is Laca in *Jenufa* at Covent Garden, first given there by him in 1968.

CASTELLAN, JEANNE ANAIS (1819–?). French soprano who created Bertha in Meyerbeer's *Le Prophète* at the Opéra (1849); also several firsts in London including Glicera in

Gounod's *Sapho*. She was a famous Leonore in *Fidelio*.

CATALANI, ANGELICA (1780–1849). Italian soprano and a prima donna *in excelsis*, vain, jealous and with a manager husband who, when asked who else was to be in a certain cast, said: 'My wife and five dolls will suffice.' London's first Susanna (1812), she had earlier made her début there as Semiramide. She was a fine actress-singer, much admired by connoisseurs as well as by ordinary operagoers.

CAVALIERI, KATHARINA (1760–1801). Austrian soprano and, according to Mozart, a singer of whom Germany might well be proud. He wrote Constanze for her as well as Silberklang in *Der Schauspieldirektor*, and, for the Vienna première of *Don Giovanni*, especially added 'Mi tradi' for her.

CEBOTARI, MARIA (1910–49). Russian soprano, at Dresden from 1931 to 1941, later at Vienna and Berlin. Appearances at Covent Garden 1936 and 1947, first with the Dresden company, later with the Vienna State Opera (including Donna Anna and Salome). This fine and good-looking artist created Aminta in Strauss's *Schweigsame Frau* (1935), and other roles.

CERQUETTI, ANITA (1931–). Italian soprano whose short,

spectacular career began at Spoleto as Aïda (1951) and was ended by illness in 1958. Norma and Abigaille (*Nabucco*) were two of her most famous roles.

CHIARA, MARIA (1942–). Italian soprano who made her début as Desdemona at Venice (1965) and became internationally famous in the early 1970s, her beautiful lyric soprano, dramatic sense and looks making her an ideal Puccini heroine. Giuletta in Zandonai's *Giuletta e Romeo* (Naples, 1972), coached by Olivero.

CHALIAPIN, FEODOR (1873–1938). Russian bass, a unique phenomenon in operatic history. Using the adjective in the narrowest sense of the word, he was a 'great' singer and a 'great' actor with a 'great' voice, allied to which was a magnificent physique, a superb head and total magnetism. His education, musical and otherwise, was limited; he came from peasant stock and stories of his temperamental nature are legion. Stanislavsky based his theories of acting on Chaliapin's work, Nijinsky watched him in the wings whenever possible, and generations who never experienced him can revel in recordings of exceptional vividness and grandeur. He made his name in Mamontov's private company in Moscow, especially as Boris Godunov, making the opera, and his

interpretation of it, world famous. He sang at La Scala (1901) and the Met (1907), where his art was misunderstood. The peak of his career followed his joining the Diaghilev company, an artistic ensemble where he was surrounded by dedication and talent. He conquered Paris in 1908 as surely as the Diaghilev Ballet the following year, and in 1913, was the chief attraction in Sir Joseph Beecham's Russian season at Drury Lane, singing in London's first *Boris Godunov*, *Khovanshchina*, *Ivan the Terrible* and *Prince Igor* (in the two roles of Galitsky and Khan Kontchak).

After the Revolution, he was a wandering comet, often surrounded by enforced mediocrity. He was at the Met, 1922–9, he also sang in four London seasons and made a curious film in several languages of *Don Quixote* with music by Ibert and with George Robey as Sancho Panza. He wrote *Pages From My Life* and *Man and Mask* and 'told' his autobiography to his friend Maxim Gorky. Stories about him, many of them true, are told in countless books including Beecham's *A Mingled Chime*. Most moving impressions of him can be found in Karsavina's *Theatre Street*, and Rachmaninov spoke of his 'limitless phenomenal talent'. When he died in Paris, Russian exiles thought that their world had ended indeed, while in

Russia itself he is remembered with love and awe, for he was a supreme national glory.

CHRISTOFF, BORIS (1918–). Bulgarian bass, upstaged by being considered immediately after Chaliapin, whose successor he has been since the 1950s. His superbly dark voice and striking presence has made him a renowned Boris, an equally famous King Philip in *Don Carlos* in Italy, London and elsewhere, and Attila is one of his many other roles. His main American base has been Chicago (1958–63). His splendidly Slavonic temperament has occasionally erupted, as when he literally crossed swords with Franco Corelli during rehearsals of *Don Carlos* and had moments of tension with Callas. His voice is not a vast one, but used with exceptional skill, and when at its best is one of the noblest sounds of our time. See also page 109.

CIGNA, GINA (1900–). French–Italian soprano, internationally famous in the 1930s in Europe and America, especially as Turandot and Gioconda.

CIONI, RENATO (1931–). Italian tenor, who has often sung with Sutherland and Callas, including a stirring Cavaradossi opposite Callas at Covent Garden in 1964.

COATES, EDITH (1908–). English mezzo-soprano, a striking actress-singer with Sadler's Wells (1931–46). At Covent Garden before and after the war. A popular Carmen for many years, her most famous later role was the Countess in Tchaikovsky's *The Queen of Spades*. Married to the tenor, producer and designer, Powell Lloyd (1900–).

COATES, JOHN (1865–1941). English tenor much admired by Beecham, not least for his ability to sing clearly in English. A considerable artist with a fine appearance, he was excellent as Tristan and Siegfried for Beecham.

COLBRAN, ISABELLA (1785–1845). Spanish soprano, the mistress and, later, wife of Rossini, who wrote many roles for her. Her début was in Paris (1801) and Rossini met her in Naples where she was the mistress of the San Carlo's manager and a Royal 'favourite'. He wrote the title role of *Elizabetta, Regina d'Inghilterra* for her, and she created leading roles in his *Otello, Armida, La Donna del Lago, Mosè in Egitto, Semiramide* and *Maometto II*.

COLLIER, MARIE (1927–71). Australian soprano, a magnificent and glamorous actress-singer who died accidentally at the height of her career. She made her Covent Garden début in 1956 and some of her finest roles were Santuzza, Butterfly,

Katerina Ismailova (Shosta-kovich), Giorgetta and Chryso-themis, also Tosca. Her most famous Wells role was Emilia Marty in *The Makropoulos Case*, while her Renata for the New London Opera's *The Fiery Angel* was electrifying. She sang Minnie in San Francisco and appeared at the Met and in many European houses.

COLZANI, ANSELMO (1918–) Italian baritone, with La Scala from 1953 and the Met from 1960. Noted for his perform-ances in modern works as well as the standard repertoire, he created the title role in Mil-haud's *David* at La Scala (1955).

CORELLI, FRANCO (1923–). Italian tenor, tall, dark and handsome, with a big voice to match, thrilling to listen to, if not always used with great art. At La Scala since 1954 and the Met since 1961, he occa-sionally appears outside Italy and America. His heroic tenor is particularly suited to Man-rico, Calaf, Dick Johnson, etc. and on the right night he is quite irresistible.

CORENA, FERNANDO (1916–). Swiss–Italian bass and a born comedian, Baccaloni's logical successor at the Met, and with a big following in Europe as one of the supreme basso-buffos of the age. A superb Falstaff, including a famous performance for Glyndebourne

at the Edinburgh Festival in 1955, his Bartolo in *Il Barbiere* is instinct with the very spirit of vocal and physical comedy.

CORNELIUS, PETER (1865–1934). Danish tenor, formerly a bari-tone, who, apart from his distinguished career in Copen-hagen, sung at Bayreuth (1906) and at Covent Garden (1907–14), notably as Siegfried in Richter's famous English *Ring* (1908–9).

CORTIS, ANTONIO (1891–1952). Spanish tenor who became internationally famous in the 1920s, notably at Chicago (1924–32). Very successful as Dick Johnson in *La Fanciulla del West*.

COSSOTO, FIORENZA (1935–). Italian mezzo-soprano whose splendidly powerful voice and strong if simple acting has brought down the house at La Scala, Covent Garden and the Met. Amneris, Eboli, Azucena and Adalgisa are among her famous roles.

COSSUTA, CARLO (1932–). Italian tenor who, after stirring performances in Verdi and Puccini in Italy, Covent Gar-den, etc. astonished even his warmest admirers with a sup-erbly sung, moving and com-mitted Otello at Covent Garden (1974), his first on any stage.

CORTRUBAS, ILEANA. Ruman-ian soprano, one of the fastest

rising actress-singers of the 1970s, having been at Frankfurt, and a Glyndebourne Mélisande in the late 1960s. Her Susanna is non-soubrettish and ideal, her Tatyana most appealing, and her Violetta, twice interrupted by bomb scares at Covent Garden in 1974, deeply moving. An enchanting artist.

CRAIG, CHARLES (1922–). English tenor, very fine in many Italian roles from his Carl Rosa days in the 1950s. At the Wells, Covent Garden and, later internationally, his successes have included Turiddu, Canio and, in Italy and for Scottish Opera, Otello.

CRESPIN, RÉGINE (1927–). French soprano, internationally famous since the 1950s, and one who has notably increased the prestige of French singing. Her most famous roles include the Marschallin, Tosca and Elsa, and she sang Kundry at Bayreuth (1958). She has sung both Cassandra and Dido in *Les Troyens*.

CROOKS, RICHARD (1900–). American tenor, at the Met, 1933–43, and also sang elsewhere in America. His début had been in Hamburg. His most famous roles included Faust, Roméo and Massenet's Des Grieux.

CROSS, JOAN (1900–). English singer, producer and teacher who was director of Sadler's Wells Opera, 1943–5. One of the very finest operatic artists and a genuine actress-singer, she began in the Old Vic chorus and was a principal of Sadler's Wells, 1931–46, also singing at Covent Garden before and after the war. She was a founder member of the English Opera Group (1945) and founded (with Anne Wood) the Opera School, later National School of Opera, in 1948. She has produced opera at Sadler's Wells and Covent Garden, and in Holland and for Phoenix Opera. Though famous in Verdi, Wagner, etc. in the 1930s, she has been best known since the war for her Britten performances. The first Ellen Orford in *Peter Grimes* (1945), Female Chorus in *The Rape of Lucretia* (1946), Lady Billows in *Albert Herring* (1947) and Queen Elizabeth in *Gloriana* (1953).

CUÉNOD, HUGUES (1902–). Swiss tenor, particularly associated with Glyndebourne since 1954). A marvellous player of eccentrics, including Sellem in *The Rake's Progress*, Basilio in *Figaro* and the Astrologer in *The Golden Cockerel*, an extraordinary creation.

CURPHEY, MARGARET. English soprano, a most useful, musical member of the English National Opera: Eva, Leonore, Elisabeth de Valois, etc.

CURTIN, PHYLLIS (1930–). American soprano, a gifted and

striking looking actress-singer, particularly associated with the New York City Center (since 1953). Creator of Cathy in Floyd's *Wuthering Heights* (1958). New York's first Cressida in Walton's *Troilus and Cressida*, a fine Mozartian and Salome.

CZERWENKA, OSCAR (1924–). Austrian bass who first sang at Salzburg in 1953 and was a brilliant Ochs at Glyndebourne in 1959. An excellent comedian.

DALIS, IRENE (1929–). American mezzo-soprano much of whose career has been at the Met (since 1956) and in Germany. An actress-singer of quality, she sang Kundry at Bayreuth (1962).

DALLA RIZZA, GILDA (1892–1975). Italian soprano, a great favourite of Puccini whose best Minnie she was. He wrote the part of Magda in *La Rondine* for her (1917). She was the first Italian and London Suor Angelica and the first Italian Lauretta in *Gianni Schicchi*. She also created roles by Vittadini, Zandonai and Mascagni. Greatly admired by Toscanini, she sang a superb Violetta for him at La Scala.

DAL MONTE, TOTI (1893–1975). Italian soprano who sang Gilda for Toscanini at La Scala in 1922 and from then on used her small and amazingly agile voice in Donizetti, Bellini, etc.

robbing roles of some of their true drama, but singing with great purity. She was heard at Covent Garden and the Met in the 1920s.

DAMOREAU, LAURE CINTHIE (1801–63). French soprano who, at the Paris Opéra (1826–35), created major Rossini roles in *Mosè in Egitto, Comte Ory, Guillaume Tell*, etc. and was the first Isabelle in *Robert le Diable* and the first Elvira in *Masaniello*.

DANCO, SUZANNE (1911–). Belgian soprano whose wide range of parts include Ellen Orford at La Scala (1947) and a splendid Donna Elvira in Edinburgh for Glyndebourne in 1951.

DARCLÉE, HARICLEA (?1868–1929). Bulgarian soprano who replaced Patti as Juliette at the Opéra, Paris (1889), then enjoyed a major career at La Scala, Rome, etc. The first Wally in Catalini's *La Wally* (1892).

DAVIDE, GIOVANNI (1790–1864). Italian tenor, son of the tenor Giacomo Davide, who taught him. Giovanni was the first Narciso in Rossini's *Il Turco in Italia* (1814) and Rossini gave him roles in *Otello* and *La Donna del Lago*. Stendhal thought the world of him.

DAVIES, RYLAND (1943–). Welsh tenor who made his

name with the Glyndebourne Touring Company as Nemorino (1968), making his début at Covent Garden in 1969. A good-looking, light-voiced lyric tenor, one of his finest roles is Almaviva, and he is an admirable Fenton. Cassio for Karajan at Salzburg (1970/1). He is married to the English mezzo, Anne Howells, *see* page 155.

DAVIES, TUDOR (1892–1958). Welsh tenor of British National Opera Company and Old Vic/Sadler's Wells and Carl Rosa fame. The creator of Vaughan Williams's Hugh the Drover (1924), and other roles, he taxed his fine voice singing to many heroic parts.

DEAN, STAFFORD (1937–). English bass who made his name with the Wells in the 1960s (Leporello, the first Samuel Breeze in *Penny for a Song*). A fine Leporello in Munich (1973–4).

DE ANGELIS, NAZZARENO (1881–1962). Italian bass, one of the finest of his day all over Italy and in Chicago (1910–11 and 1915–20). A famous Mosè, Mefistofele, etc. and a notable Wagnerian, he retired in 1959.

DELLA CASA, LISA (1919–). Swiss soprano, especially famous for her Strauss and Mozart performances, and for her charm. A favourite artist at Salzburg, Vienna, the Met, Glyndebourne and Covent Garden, she has gone from Sophie to the Marschallin via Octavian, and is the most notable exponent of Arabella. One of the greatest and most magical of all Strauss sopranos.

DEL MONACO, MARIO (1915–). Italian tenor, at his peak in the 1950s in Italy and at the Met. Not the most artistic singer, he yet had such an exciting voice, so full of power and passion that his popularity in Verdi and Puccini was rightly enormous. Something of the old quality has lasted until the 1970s.

DE LOS ANGELES. See LOS ANGELES.

DE LUCA, GIUSEPPE (1876–1950). Italian baritone, particularly associated with the Met (1915–35/1939–40), where he appeared in over a hundred different operas, one of his creations being Gianni Schicchi (1918). So well-schooled was he that he could sing Rigoletto at 70.

DE LUCIA, FERNANDO (?1860–1925). Italian tenor, Covent Garden's first Cavaradossi, Canio, Turiddu, etc. and creator of the title role in Mascagni's *L'Amico Fritz* (Rome, 1891). However, he was also renowned as a *bel canto* singer.

DE LUSSAN, ZÉLIE (1861–1949). American soprano who played Carmen more than a thousand times in Britain and New York, and was also a fine Mozartian.

DEMEUR, ANNE (1824–92). French soprano who, after a fine career in London, including the first London Countess in *Comte Ory*, became a close friend of Berlioz, creating Béatrice in *Béatrice et Bénédict* (1862) and Dido in *Les Troyens à Cathage* (1863).

DEMPSEY, GREGORY. Australian tenor, an exceptionally gifted actor-singer since coming to Britain in 1963. The excellent Mime of the Wells *Ring*, his other parts include Jimmy in *Mahagonny*, Albert Gregor in *The Makropoulos Case*, Don José, David and, for Scottish Opera, Albert Herring and Aeneas. He has also sung in Europe and America.

DE RESZKE, ÉDOUARD (1853–1917). Polish bass, brother of Jean (below). Blessed with height and a most striking appearance, he had a magnificent voice, rich and huge, which he could use with remarkable dexterity, taking even the fastest passages in his stride, and in addition he had brains. He was one of the greatest of all basses. He made his début as the King in *Aïda* (1876) at its Parisian première under Verdi. He became a leading figure in the legendary operatic circuit of the later 19th century, the Opéra, the Met and Covent Garden, his roles including

Méphistophélès, Leporello, Frère Laurent in *Roméo et Juliette*, Marcel and St Bris in *Les Huguenots*, and, later, Hans Sachs, Hagen and King Mark. His Wagnerian roles were first sung in Italian.

DE RESZKE, JEAN (1850–1925). Polish tenor, brother of Édouard (above) and—what in an ideal world every tenor should be—tall, handsome, with a voice of great beauty which he used with superb musicianship, and an excellent actor. He looked and was every inch a gentleman, his charm was immense, and he was one of the greatest of all tenors.

However, he began as a baritone in Italy, London and Paris (roles included Don Giovanni), then, thanks to his brother's advice, re-studied as a tenor, with no great success at first. The turning point came in 1884 when he sang John the Baptist at the Paris première of Massenet's *Hérodiade* after several years as a concert singer. His success was so great that Massenet promptly completed *Le Cid* for him. Like his brother, he was a superstar of the Opéra, Met and Covent Garden circuit, his roles including Roméo, Raoul in *Les Huguenots*, Faust, Vasco da Gama and, later, the logical Wagnerian roles, Lohengrin, Tristan, Walther and Siegfried. He became a great teacher. The brothers had a sister, Josephine (1855–91), who became a star of the Opéra, but retired to marry a baron.

DERMOTA, ANTON (1910–). Yugoslav tenor, a star of Vienna's fabulous post-war Mozart ensemble, having made his début there as Alfredo in 1936. Also a Salzburg regular for many years.

DERNESH, HELGA (1939–). Austrian soprano, a beautiful actress-singer whose sometimes suspect top of the voice has not prevented Wagnerian successes at Bayreuth (since 1967) and Salzburg (since 1969), also at Covent Garden and with Scottish Opera. Roles include Brünnhilde, Isolde, Marschallin, Leonore and Cassandra. Her Dyer's Wife in *Die Frau ohne Schatten* at Covent Garden (1975) was a triumph.

DESTINN, EMMY (1878–1930). Czech soprano, originally Ema Kittl, whose début was in Berlin (1898) as Santuzza. She rapidly became a major actress-singer in Berlin, Covent Garden, the Met, etc. and is remembered for some legendary 'firsts': Bayreuth's first Senta (1901); Berlin's first Salome (1906); and four at Covent Garden— Butterfly (1905), Tatyana in *Eugene Onegin* (1906), Tess in d'Erlanger's *Tess of the d'Urbevilles* (1908) and Minnie in *La Fanciulla del West* (1911). She was one of the greatest of all Aidas and a famous Marenka in *The Bartered Bride*. The

First World War badly interrupted her career and, being a great patriot, she changed her name to Destinova when her country became independent, singing under that name after the war until she retired in 1921. She was adored.

DEUTEKON, CRISTINA. Dutch soprano who made her name as the Queen of the Night in Holland (1963). Her voice divides opinion, except at the top; however, her Lucia (1973) in Dallas and Sinadie in *Mosè in Egitto* (1973) in Florence were acclaimed.

DICKIE, MURRAY (1924–). Scottish tenor who was a leading member of the New London Opera Company and Covent Garden Opera (1947–52), then began a long career in Vienna, singing Pedrillo, Jacquino, David, etc. His brother, the baritone William Dickie, was also a leading member of the New London Opera Company.

DI STEFANO, GIUSEPPE (1921–). Italian tenor who made his début in Reggio Emilia as Massenet's Des Grieux (1946) and rapidly became one of the most popular singers in the world, his singing until the early 1950s being ravishing. The Toscanini recording of Verdi's *Requiem* is a perfect example of his art at that period, when he excelled as Nadir in *Les Pêcheurs des Perles* and Elvino in *La Sonnambula*. His tone was smooth and rich, and his pianissimo was a marvel. From 1953, he sang heavier roles at La Scala and the Met, many with Callas, with whom he made several historic recordings, including the de Sabata *Tosca* (1953). Turiddu, Canio, Don José and Radamès were among his new roles, and by the end of the 1950s, his voice was no longer so glorious. Yet even today his technique is such that he can give much pleasure, while his place in operatic history is assured, for his long partnership—not without its stormy moments—with Callas, and for his sheer vocal glamour.

DOBBS, MATTIWILDA (1925–). American soprano, one of the first black artists to triumph in opera, notably in coloratura roles. Not until 1957 did she reach the Met, after a brilliant Glyndebourne Zerbinetta (1953) and a stunning Queen of the Night (1956), and a seductive Queen of Shemakhan in Rimsky-Korsakov's *The Golden Cockerel* at Covent Garden (1954).

DOMGRAF-FASSBÄNDER, WILLI (1897–). German baritone at the Berlin Staatsoper from the 1920s to the mid-1940s, and the Figaro of the first performance of Glyndebourne Opera (1934), also singing Guglielmo and Papageno there as well. Later, this splendid actor-singer became chief resident producer at Nuremberg. His daughter Brigitte Fassbänder is one of the finest young German actress-singers, an excellent Mozartian and a totally believable Octavian at the Bavarian State Opera, Covent Garden, etc.

DOMINGO, PLACIDO (1941–). Mexican tenor, born in Spain, and one of the most stylish and exciting tenors, a good actor, fine-looking and (since 1974) slim. Not surprisingly, he is a superstar. At the Met (since 1968) and in Europe, he is a renowned Verdian, his 1974 Radamès at Covent Garden (followed by a perfect Rodolfo) was a triumph, even in 'Celeste Aïda'. Not so much a heroic tenor as a lyric one of great power, yet he is now a magnificent Otello.

DONZELLI, DOMENICO (1790–1873). Italian tenor, admired by Rossini, and the creator of Pollione in *Norma* at La Scala.

DORUS-GRAS, JULIE (1805–96). Belgian soprano. She created Alice in *Robert le Diable* (1831) and Marguerite in *Les Huguenots* (1836).

DOWD, RONALD. Australian tenor, whose notable roles for Sadlers Wells in the 1950s and 60s included Idomeneo and Dick Johnson. A most expressive voice.

DOWLING, DENIS. New Zealand baritone with the Wells since 1947. A fine actor-singer, especially in comedy: Rossini's Figaro, Guglielmo, etc.

DUPREZ, GILBERT (1806–96). French tenor and composer (of eight operas), the first Edgardo in *Lucia* (1835) at Naples, then at the Opéra (1837–45) where his creations included the title-role in *Benvenuto Cellini* (1838) and Fernando in *La Favorite* (1840). Another of his famous roles was Arnold in *Guillaume Tell*.

DUVAL, DENISE (1921–). French soprano, mainly in Paris, but a most notable Glyndebourne Mélisande (1962). Other roles included Blanche in *Les Dialogues des Carmélites* (La Scala, 1957), which she created, along with other Poulenc roles; Thérèse in *Les Mamelles de Tirésias* and Elle in *La Voix Humaine*, one of her most famous performances, not least because the opera is a forty-five-minute solo.

DUX, CLAIRE (1885–1967). Polish soprano with 'a perfect legato and a phenomenal breath control' (Beecham). At Berlin from 1911–18, she was Covent Garden's first Sophie in *Der Rosenkavalier* (1913), also Eva, but it was her Pamina for Beecham (1914) which made her name to the extent that, at the second performance, Melba with Caruso, Chaliapin and Destinn in the audience, hailed her as 'My Successor!'. Alas for art, this paragon married a rich American when starring in Chicago (1921–3) and retired.

DVORAKOVA, LUDMILA. Czech soprano, internationally famous since the mid-1960s in Wagner (Bayreuth, Covent Garden, the Met) and as Leonore. A beautiful woman, her Brünnhilde is intensely human and likeable, her Isolde, except at the top of her voice at climaxes, deeply moving. She is based at the State Opera, East Berlin.

DYCK, ERNEST VAN (1861–1923). Belgian tenor and a famous Wagnerian who was Bayreuth's ideal Parsifal from 1888 to 1912, Covent Garden (1891–1907) and the Met (1898–1902). He was also famous as Massenet's Des Grieux and Werther.

EAMES, EMMA (1865–1952). American soprano whose remarkable repertoire ranged from Mozart to Verdi, Puccini and Wagner. Coached by Gounod as Juliette for her Paris début (1889), this beautiful woman, blessed with a superb voice and artistry, left Paris because of intrigues, and was at Covent Garden (1891–1901) fairly regularly, where Melba became jealous of her. A star of the Met from 1891 to 1909. Her most famous roles included Aida, Donna Anna, Tosca and Desdemona.

EASTON, FLORENCE (1884–1955). English soprano whose repertoire embraced 150 roles ranging from Brünnhilde to

Carmen. Her long career included the Berlin Royal Opera (1907–13), the Met (1917–29, 1935–6), where she created Lauretta in *Gianni Schicchi*, Turandot at Covent Garden (1927), and, later, Brünnhilde and Isolde there, and Tosca at Sadler's Wells (1934).

EDELMANN, OTTO (1916–). Austrian bass, a major star of the Vienna Opera from 1947, and a regular singer at the Met and San Francisco in the 1950s and 1960s. His most famous part has been Baron Ochs.

EDVINA, LOUISE (*c* 1880–1938). French Canadian soprano, a Covent Garden regular, 1908–24, London's first Louise, Mariella in Wolf-Ferrari's *I Gioielli della Madonna*, and the creator of other roles. She also sang in America. Slim and charming, she was a stylish singer.

ELIAS, ROSALIND (1931–). American mezzo-soprano, at the Met since 1954. This attractive actress-singer created Erika in *Vanessa* (1958). Her roles include Carmen, Dorabella and Rosina.

ELLIOTT, VICTORIA (1922–). English soprano, especially with Sadler's Wells (1951–63), where her roles included Violetta, Tosca and Lady Hamilton in Berkeley's *Nelson*.

ELMO, CLOË (1910–62). Italian mezzo-soprano who sang at La Scala, 1936–43, and at the Met, 1947–9.

ERB, KARL (1877–1958). German tenor, a fine Mozartian and the creator of the title role in *Palestrina* at Munich (1917). Married to Maria Ivogün (see page 142).

ESSER, HERMIN. German tenor whose Wagnerian roles include Tannhäuser (at Bayreuth, where he has also sung Loge, etc.), Tristan for Scottish Opera (1973).

ETCHEVERRY, BERTRAND (1900–60). French bass-baritone, famous in Paris for his Boris, Méphistophélès, St Bris in *Les Huguenots* and, above all, for his Golaud in *Pelléas et Mélisande*.

EVANS, (SIR) GERAINT (1922–). Welsh baritone and the first British opera singer to be knighted (1969) since Santley. With Covent Garden since 1948, he was one of the first British singers to break on to the post-war international scene: Glyndebourne from 1949, La Scala in 1960, San Francisco and other American centres from 1961, Vienna, 1961, and Salzburg from 1962. A most talented and delightful actor-singer, his Falstaff is one of the finest in the opera's history, and he is a famous Leporello, Figaro, Papageno, Don Pasquale, etc. and a marvellous Bottom in Britten's

A Midsummer Night's Dream. His straight roles include Edgardo, Wozzeck and the first Mr Flint in *Billy Budd,* but it is as a born comedian with a warmly lyrical voice that this superb artist will always be remembered.

FABBRI, GUERRINA (1868–1946). Italian contralto, famous for her Rossini heroines, especially Cenerentola.

FALCON, MARIE CORNÉLIE (1814–97). French soprano whose career only lasted from 1832–8, during which she created Rachel in Halévy's *La Juive* and Valentine in *Les Huguenots.* She also excelled as Donna Anna and as Guilia in *La Vestale,* and left her name to a type of voice, a *falcon* being, in Andrew Porter's words, a 'kind of dramatic-soprano-cum-mezzo voice'. A beauty, she had to retire because she lost her voice.

FARINELLI (1705–82). Italian male soprano with a huge following in London, Vienna and Spain, where he stayed twenty-five years, singing the same four songs every night to Philip V to help keep the king's depression at bay.

FARRAR, GERALDINE (1882–1967). American soprano, beauty and film star (including a silent Carmen), whose popularity was such that she had a following of girls known as 'Gerry-flappers'. After making her name in Berlin, she was a supreme attraction at the Met (1906–22), especially as Butterfly, Manon, Carmen and Zaza. Her creations included Suor Angelica (1918). At the Met, she appeared 493 times in thirty different roles, and she retired at the height of her powers.

FARRELL, EILEEN (1920–). American soprano whose sumptuous voice (in Wagner, Verdi, Poncielli, etc.) has more often been heard in the concert hall than at the Met and other American houses.

FASSBÄNDER, ZDENKA (1880–1954). Bohemian soprano, a famous Wagner and Strauss singer at Munich (1906–19).

FAURÉ, JEAN-BAPTISTE (1830–1914). French baritone, famous in London, but particularly associated with the Opéra from 1861. In his seventeen seasons there he created, amongst others, Nelusko in *L'Africane,* Posa in *Don Carlos* and Hamlet in Thomas's opera of that name. He was also a renowned Don Giovanni and William Tell.

FEINHALS, FRITZ (1869–1940). German baritone, at Munich from 1898–1927, plus pre-1914 seasons at the Met and Covent Garden. Best remembered for his fine Wagnerian roles.

FERRIER, KATHLEEN (1912–53). English contralto whose supremely beautiful voice, radiant personality and warm and moving sincerity made her one of the most beloved of all singers. Most of her career was on the concert platform, but she made her operatic début as Lucretia in *The Rape of Lucretia* at Glyndebourne, creating the role, and sang Gluck's Orfeo there (1947), also in Holland and at Covent Garden, being forced to retire after her second performance (see page 109).

FIGNER, NIKOLAY (1857–1919). Russian tenor, the creator of Herman in *The Queen of Spades* at St Petersburg (1890), and also a renowned Otello, Don José, Lensky, etc. He was married to Medea Mei-Figner (1858–1952), a famous Lisa in *The Queen of Spades*, Tatyana and Carmen.

FINE, WENDY. South African soprano, a rising star whose successes have included a brilliant Marie in *Wozzeck* at Munich (1971) and a triumph as Giuletta in *Hoffmann* there (1973). Her finest Covent Garden role to date has been Fiordiligi.

FISCHER, EMIL (1838–1914). German bass-baritone at the Met, 1885–91, where he was America's first Sachs, Wotan, Mark, Hagen; also a Covent Garden Sachs (1884).

FISCHER, LUDWIG (1745–1825). German bass, the original Osmin for his friend Mozart in *Entführung* (1782).

FISCHER-DIESKAU, DIETRICH (1925–). German baritone, one of the greatest of the century. Much of his splendid career has been with the Berlin Stadische Oper (from 1948), and he has sung at Salzburg since 1957 and at Covent Garden, where he was a superb Mandryka in *Arabella* (1965). Occasionally criticized outside Germany for his unidiomatic singing of Italian roles, his repertoire includes Busoni's Dr Faust, Falstaff, Jochanaan, Mathis der Maler, Onegin, Don Giovanni, Wozzeck and Amfortas. A fine-looking actor-singer.

FISHER, SYLVIA (1910–). Australian soprano, the young Covent Garden company's leading dramatic soprano from 1949–58. Her finest performances have included the Marschallin, the Kostelnička in *Jenufa*, and Queen Elizabeth in *Gloriana*.

FLAGSTAD, KIRSTEN (1895–1962). Norwegian soprano, a supreme Wagnerian who brought to the great roles a warmly radiant and very powerful voice, physical beauty in her younger days, and womanly grace in her later years. Until 1933, she only sang in Scandinavia in a huge repertoire, which included operetta, and was about to retire when hired to sing small parts at Bayreuth. In 1934 she sang Sieglinde and in 1935 sang it again at the Met. At short notice she found herself singing Brünnhilde and Kundry in New York and at once, though not so superb an artist as she later became, was established as *the* Wagnerian soprano of the day. Until she retired in 1954, she held this position, not least because she had what Variety and Vaudeville players call 'heart'. She sang at pre-war Covent Garden and, more than any other singer, made the house a leading Wagnerian one after the Second World War, singing Brünnhilde, Sieglinde, Kundry and Isolde. She also sang Leonore in *Fidelio* there, and Purcell's Dido at Bernard Miles's Mermaid Theatre in London—for a pint of beer per performance. Director of the Norwegian Opera (1959–60).

FLETA, MIGUEL (1893–1938). Spanish tenor, at La Scala from 1923–6, where he created Calaf in *Turandot* (1924), also Romeo in Zandonai's *Giulietta e Romeo* (1922).

FODOR-MAINVIELLE, JOSÉPHINE (1789–1870). French soprano, a very famous Mozart and Rossini singer in London, Paris Naples, Vienna, etc.

FRANTZ, FERDINAND (1906–59). German bass-baritone, especially well known in Munich and at the Met, who began as a Wagnerian bass, but became a famous Sachs, Wotan, Pizarro, etc.

FREMSTAD, OLIVE (1871–1951). Swedish, then American, soprano, especially famous as Isolde and Brünnhilde. She sang at the Met from 1903–14, including Kundry, Carmen opposite Caruso, and a single Salome (1907), the opera being considered too strong meat for sensitive New Yorkers. At her Farewell, she received 21 minutes of applause. A great artist.

FRENI, MIRELLA (1936–). Italian soprano of extreme charm and considerable musicality. The early 1960s saw her at Glyndebourne, Covent Garden, La Scala, and Chicago after a season with the Netherlands Opera (1959–60). Her roles included Zerlina, Susanna, Adina, Mimi, Elvira and Marguerite, and a Nanetta opposite Alva at Covent Garden (1961) which can soberly be described as ravishing. Her Desdemona at Salzburg (1970) revealed a major dramatic actress-singer. One of her recent triumphs was an even more passionate Susanna than usual in the Solti–Strehler *Figaro* at Versailles (1973). A most moving Amelia in *Boccanegra* with La Scala at Covent Garden (1976).

FRETWELL, ELIZABETH (1922–). Australian soprano who

made her name at Sadler's Wells as an excellent Violetta (1955), her other roles including Minnie. Now a leading soprano with Australian Opera.

FREZZOLINI, ERMINIA (1818–84). Italian soprano, daughter of Giuseppe Frezzolini, the first Dulcamara in *L'Elisir d' Amore* (1832). She created Viclinda in Verdi's *I Lombardi* (1843), and the composer thought well enough of her to give her the lead in *Giovanna d'Arco* (1845). She was New York's first Gilda.

FRICK, GOTTLOB (1906–). German bass, one of the finest of modern times, his voice retaining its richness, cavernous quality and drama until his sixties. A famous Wagnerian in Dresden, Vienna, Munich and London—his Hagen is only one of several memorable roles —he has also distinguished himself in Mozart and Verdi.

FRYATT, JOHN. English tenor, an excellent actor-singer in operetta and opera, an early success being Menelaus in *Belle Hélène* at the Wells. Comic roles at Glyndebourne in the 1970s have included Don Basilio and Mercury in *La Calisto* (Cavalli).

FUCHS, MARTA (1898–). German soprano who began as a mezzo. A famous Bayreuth Isolde, Brünnhilde and Kundry, she sang at Dresden (1930–6), after which she was with the Berlin State Opera and, later, Stuttgart. A very fine dramatic soprano.

GABRIELLI, ADRIANA (1755–?). Italian soprano, much admired by Mozart. She was the first Fiordiligi in *Così fan tutte* (1790).

GABRIELLI, CATERINA (1730–96). Italian soprano, the beautiful daughter of Prince Gabrielli's cook. Between liaisons with royalty and the aristocracy all over Europe, she managed to create roles in Gluck's Italian operas (1755–60), and was renowned for her thrilling voice and temperamental nature.

GALE, ELIZABETH. English soprano, a rising actress-singer as those who in 1973 saw her Glyndebourne (touring) Susanna and Flora in *The Turn of the Screw* for the English Opera group will know. More recent successes have included Anna in *Intermezzo* at Glyndebourne.

GALLI, FILIPPO (1783–1853). Italian tenor, later bass, one of the finest of his day. Rossini wrote Fernando in *La Gazza Ladra* for him (1817) and other roles, and he created Henry VIII in Donizetti's *Anna Bolena* (1830).

GALLI-CURCI, AMELITA (1882–1963). Italian soprano, a famous Gilda, Violetta and Elvira in *I Puritani*, whose pure, astoundingly acrobatic voice made her a major recording star. Enormously popular in Chicago (from 1916) and at the Met (1921–30). Illness forced her to retire and a come-back in 1936 was not a success.

GALLI-MARIÉ, CÉLESTINE (1840–1905). French mezzo-soprano, the creator of Thomas's Mignon at the Opéra-Comique (1866) and the first Carmen there at its historic and melancholy première in 1875, where she was much too good for the staid audience.

GARCIA family. One of the most famous of all operatic families, the founding father being Manuel Garcia (1775–1832), a Spanish tenor, composer and teacher (a ferocious one of his daughter Maria), with gypsy blood in his veins. He made his début in Paris (1808), created Norfolk in Rossini's *Elizabetta, Regina d'Inghilterra* (1815), and Almaviva (1816) at the notorious première of *Il Barbiere* (1816). He and his family (who also appeared with him in London) founded Italian opera in New York (1825) and gave *Don Giovanni* its première there in 1826, a performance made more legendary because da Ponte was in the audience. The family were later robbed by Mexican bandits. A great teacher. Maria can be found under her immortal name Malibran, her young sister Pauline under Viardot. Manuel II (1805–1906) was also a bass and a great teacher, and was the first to make a scientific study of voice production and invented the laryngoscope. He was New York's first Figaro (1825) and his pupils included Jenny Lind, Mathilde Marchesi and Santley. His son Gustave Garcia (1837–1925) was a baritone and teacher who sang at La Scala after making his début in London as Don Giovanni, and his son was Albert Garcia, yet another baritone and teacher.

GARDEN, MARY (1874–1967). Scottish soprano and a famous actress-singer and shrewd woman. Trained in Paris, she made a sensational début at the Opéra-Comique, taking over Louise in mid-performance from Rioton. The first Mélisande (1902), she overrode a hostile audience moved to laughter by her British accent. She created other roles, including Massenet's Sapho, then became a major American star, most notably at Chicago from 1910, becoming its director (1919–20), running up debts as huge as her figure was slim. She sang there until 1931.

GARRARD, DON. Canadian bass at Sadler's Wells, in Canada, etc. His many roles include the Wanderer in *Siegfried* at the Coliseum (1973) and a brilliant Pastor in *The Visit of the Old Lady* at Glyndebourne (1973).

GEDDA, NICOLAI (1925–). Swedish tenor, of Russian parentage, a very fine and most musical singer, at home in a number of languages, including Russian. Much in demand since the mid-1950s, not least because of his acting ability and looks, he created Anatol in *Vanessa* at the Met (1957), later singing it in Salzburg, and is an ideal Benvenuto Cellini. A recent triumph was a superb Nemorino at Salzburg (1973) and his Cellini with the Royal Opera at La Scala (1976) was perfection.

GENCER, LEYLA (1928–). Turkish soprano with an international reputation as an actress-singer, especially in the later 1950s and the 1960s. Madame Lidoine in the first *Carmélites* (Poulenc) at La Scala (1957) and First Woman of Canterbury in Pizzetti's *Murder in the Cathedral* (1959). She has sung in San Francisco, Salzburg, Covent Garden and Glyndebourne, and her roles include Elisabeth de Valois, Donna Anna, Anna Bolena, Norma, and Renata in Prokofiev's *The Fiery Angel*.

GERL, THADDEUS (1766–1844). German bass, the original Sarastro (1791), his wife Franziska creating Papagena.

GERSTER, ETELKA (1855–1920). Hungarian soprano who sang Gilda at the Fenice on Verdi's recommendation (1876). Sang in France, Germany and London, and in America (1878–87) was almost as popular as Patti, the two ladies cordially disliking each other.

GIANNINI, DUSOLINA (1902–). American soprano, her singer father Ferruccio having gone to the U.S.A. from Italy in 1891. In his Philadelphia theatre, the 11-year-old Dusolina sang La Cieca in *La Gioconda*. Appeared in many European cities between the wars, notably as Donna Anna and Alice Ford at Salzburg (1934–6), and at the Met from 1935–42. The first Hester in her brother Vittorio's *The Scarlet Letter* (Hamburg, 1938).

GIAUROV, NICOLAI (1929–). Bulgarian bass, at the Scala since 1959. A superb lyric-dramatic voice, less 'dark' than his only rival, Boris Christoff. He is almost as striking-looking, and an excellent actor, without Christoff's power to bring an element of danger to the stage. If Boris Godunov is his most famous role, he is also a renowned Verdian, notably as King Philip and Attila. A splendid Méphistophélès.

GIGLI, BENIAMINO (1890–1957). Italian tenor, possessor of a most beautiful voice which was used so well and easily that he was singing superbly in his sixties. He was well-known, thanks to discs and radio and concert appearances, far beyond the world's opera houses.

At La Scala from 1918, the Met (1920–32 and 1938–9), and in several seasons at Covent Garden. His voice did not darken as much as Caruso's during his career. No actor, and sometimes lacrymose, his voice was his—and his audience's—fortune, especially as Des Grieux, the Duke in *Rigoletto*, Andrea Chénier (Giordano), Lionel in von Flotow's *Martha* and Canio. With the San Carlo at Covent Garden in 1946, he sang Turiddu and Canio in the same evening, and Rodolfo opposite his daughter, Rina, as Mimi.

GILIBERT, CHARLES (1866–1910). French baritone, well-known pre-1914 in Paris, London and New York. London's first Le Père in *Louise* (1909).

GLOSSOP, PETER (1928–). English baritone who made his name at the Wells in the 1950s, especially in Verdi, since when he has become internationally famous in Europe and America. Recent major successes of this fine singer and sometimes first-rate, always committed actor at Covent Garden have been Don Giovanni (1973–4), Rigoletto and Marcello (1974).

GLUCK, ALMA (1884–1938). American soprano, born in Rumania, and a brilliant singer whose small voice was beautifully projected. At the Met (1909–11). Sophie in *Werther*

and Mimi were among her roles.

GLYNNE, HOWELL (1907–69). Welsh bass, particularly fine in buffo roles, especially Mr Crusty in *The School for Fathers* (*I Quatro Rusteghi*) at Sadler's Wells. His Popoff in *The Merry Widow* and Jailer in *Die Fledermaus* were hilarious.

GOBBI, TITO (1915–). Italian baritone, the greatest since the war, and one of the finest actor-singers in operatic history. Even in his sixties, his voice is still abounding in drama, and combined with his dramatic skill, musical intelligence and personality, has made him enormously popular, especially, perhaps, at Covent Garden, where he is adored. His repertoire is immense, three of his greatest roles being Iago, Falstaff and Scarpia (though at least six more could be added). Outside the Italian repertoire, he has been a memorable Wozzeck. He has played both Figaro and the Count, has made twenty-six films and has often been on television. He is also a fine artist. Chicago (from 1954) has been his chief American base, while he is known all over Italy and in Vienna. His Scarpia opposite Callas in the Zeffirelli production of *Tosca* at Covent Garden in 1964 was a classic justification of opera as an art form (see page 110).

Fortunately, many of his recordings do him justice. It should be noted that the 1953 recording of *Tosca* under de Sabata is the one to get. Also see page 110.

GOLTZ, CHRISTEL (1912–). German soprano, at Dresden 1936–50, and a famous postwar Salome and Elektra in Germany and Austria, including Munich, Vienna, Salzburg and Berlin. Covent Garden has heard her Salome and Marie in *Wozzeck*, and she has sung at the Met (1954). A true actress-singer with a brilliant voice, at her peak in the 1950s.

GOMEZ, JILL. Anglo-Spanish soprano. This striking-looking actress-singer made her name in the late 1960s at Glyndebourne and elsewhere, and gave a beautiful Calisto (Cavalli) there in 1970, the year she created Flora in Tippett's *The Knot Garden*. Recent successes include Ilia in *Idomeneo* for the English Opera Group and a ravishing Titania in Britten's *A Midsummer Night's Dream* at Covent Garden (1974/76).

GORR, RITA (1926–). Belgian mezzo-soprano who in her prime, in the late 1950s and early 1960s, could rouse audiences to a frenzy with the fire and total commitment of her performances in Europe and America. Her Amneris and Azucena were two such roles, though she has been notable in most schools: Fricka and Kundry, Dalila, Charlotte and Herodias, also Orphée. Has sung at Bayreuth, Naples, Rome and Lisbon, having been engaged at the Paris Opéra in 1952, and has been a popular visitor to Covent Garden.

GRANDI, MARGHERITA (1899–). Italo-Irish soprano, born in Tasmania and educated in France, and one of the few famous Lady Macbeths in operatic history, notably at Glyndebourne (1939). Her Tosca was in the grand manner, vocally and dramatically.

GRANT, CLIFFORD. English bass, at the Wells, English National Opera, San Francisco (Hagen and Hunding). The Hunding and Hagen of the Goodall *Ring*, an impressive Philip in *Don Carlos* (1974). His many other roles include Don Basilio and Seneca in *Poppea*.

GREINDL, JOSEF (1912–). German bass, particularly well-known at Bayreuth where he first appeared in 1943, singing leads, including Hagen and Hunding, since 1951. First appeared in Berlin in 1942, and has sung in London, Italy and North and South America.

GRISI, GIUDITTA (1805–40). Italian mezzo-soprano. The niece of Josephina Grassini (1773–1850), the singer and teacher, and Carlotta the dancer's cousin, she made her début in Vienna (1826). Bellini composed Romeo in *I Capuletti ed i Montecchi* (1830) for her, but she was inevitably overshadowed by Giulia (below).

GRISI, GIULIA (1811–69). Italian soprano, sister of the above, who created Juliet opposite Giuditta in *I Capuletti ed i Montecchi* (1830), also Adalgisa in *Norma* (1831) at La Scala. This superb and beautiful actress-singer became frustrated at La Scala and escaped to Paris, breaking her contract, to join her sister and aunt Grassini, who were at the Théâtre-Italien. There she created Elvira in *I Puritani* (1835) and Norina in *Don Pasquale* (1843), singing in the latter opposite Mario (see below, page 169), whom she married the following year. She sang in London from 1834 until 1861 (except in 1842), other famous and passionately played roles including Lucrezia Borgia, Semiramide, Anna Bolena and Donna Anna. 'What a soprano voice was hers!' raved Chorley, 'rich, sweet, equal throughout its compass of two octaves (from C to C) without a break or a note which had to be managed.' Richard Bonynge has noted that she lacked the creative originality of Pasta and Malibran, though possessing much of the former's nobility and the latter's fire.

GRIST, RERI. American soprano at the Met, Glyndebourne, etc.

A fine artist with a delightful stage presence and most agile voice, her most famous role (Vienna 1973 and in many houses previously) is Zerbinetta in *Ariadne auf Naxos*.

GROB-PRANDL, GERTRUD (1917–). Austrian soprano, at the Vienna State Opera (from 1948) and elsewhere in Europe, also in South America. A dramatic soprano whose best-known roles were Isolde, Brünnhilde, Ortrud and Turandot.

GRUMMER, ELISABETH (1911–). German soprano, originally an actress. Best known for her Mozart and Strauss, she joined the Berlin Städtische Oper in 1946, and first sang at Bayreuth in 1957, also singing regularly in Hamburg and Vienna.

GUADAGNI, GAETANO (*c* 1725–92). Italian male soprano who sang for Handel in London and created the title role in Gluck's *Orfeo* (1762).

GÜDEN, HILDE (1917–). Austrian soprano, with the Vienna State Opera from 1946, a very attractive singer, delightful in Mozart, Strauss (R. and J.) and Lehár. At the Met for many years from 1950. Her modern roles included Anne in *The Rake's Progress* (1953).

GUTHEIL-SCHODER, MARIE (1874–1935). German soprano, allegedly a 'singer without a voice' at first after Mahler had chosen her for Vienna (1900), but overcoming this to such an extent that she remained until 1926. Her most famous roles included Carmen, Octavian, Pamina and Elektra, also Elvira, an interesting role for a voiceless wonder.

HÄFLIGER, ERNST (1919–). Swiss tenor, in Berlin (since 1953) and elsewhere, and best known for his Mozartian and modern roles.

HAMMOND, JOAN (1912–). Australian soprano, and champion golfer, with a huge following via records and radio outside the opera house. She sang with British companies in the 1940s and 1950s as a guest after work with Carl Rosa (1942–5), and was the first British Rusalka (Dvořák) at the Wells (1959). Sang Aida at the Bolshoi, Moscow.

HAMMOND-STROUD, DEREK. English baritone and a fine actor-singer, especially in comic roles for the Wells, etc. Parts include a brilliant Beckmesser, Melitone and Alberich, and another triumph, Bartolo.

HANN, GEORGE (1897–1950). Austrian bass-baritone and a brilliant buffo, especially at Munich (1927–50). Famous for Falstaff, Ochs and Leporello.

HARGREAVES, JOHN (1914–). English baritone, for many years singing leads at Sadler's Wells. Creator of Strickland in Gardner's *The Moon and Sixpence* (1957).

HARPER, HEATHER. Irish soprano who since 1962 has given a number of memorable performances at Covent Garden and elsewhere, especially Ellen Orford in *Peter Grimes*. Her overseas roles have included Elsa at Bayreuth. An excellent Empress in *Die Frau ohne Schatten* at Covent Garden (1976). Equally successful in the concert hall.

HARSHAW, MARGARET (1912–). American soprano, earlier a mezzo, who made her Met début in 1942 and from 1951 was a major Wagnerian, her roles including Brünnhilde, which she also sang at Covent Garden.

HARWOOD, ELIZABETH. English soprano who made her name at the Wells from 1961 in Mozart, Verdi and Strauss, becoming internationally known in the late 1960s. In 1972 she was a superb Countess (*Marriage of Figaro*) for Karajan at Salzburg, a role in which she excelled on television in 1974. A welcome regular for Scottish opera, where she was the Fiordiligi of the legendary *Così fan tutte* of 1967, and Lucia.

HAUK, MINNIE (1851–1929). American soprano, her country's first Juliette, aged 16 less a day, and London's first —and passionate—Carman (1878). She appeared in France, Belgium, Russia and Germany, sang a season at the Met (1890–1), ran her own company for a season, then retired in her vocal prime.

HEDMONT, CHARLES (1857–1940). American tenor, Bayreuth's David (1886), then with Carl Rosa from 1891 to 1909. Presented London's first English *Walküre* in 1895, singing Siegmund, and sang Loge in the English *Ring* at Covent Garden in 1908.

HELDY, FANNY (1888–1973). Belgian soprano, chosen by Toscanini for La Scala's Louise and Mélisande at La Scala, and a renowned Massenet singer in Paris and elsewhere between the wars.

HEMING, PERCY (1883–1956). English baritone who made his début for Beecham as Mercutio at Covent Garden (1915) and became a distinguished member of the British National Opera Company, later acting as Artistic Adviser (1946–8) to the young Covent Garden Company. A famous Scarpia.

HEMPEL, FRIEDA (1885–1955). German soprano of versatility who in the decade before the First World War ranged (in Berlin, New York, London, etc.) from Eva to the Queen of the Night and Rosina, and was

Berlin's and New York's first Marschallin.

HEMSLEY, THOMAS (1927–). English baritone, mainly in Germany (1953–63) and at Zürich, making his début at Bayreuth in 1968 as Beckmesser. In Britain he has sung at Sadler's Wells, Glyndebourne and with the English Opera Group, creating the Ferryman in *Curlew River* and the Astrologer in *The Burning Fiery Furnace*. A notable Covent Garden début as Mangus in *The Knot Garden* (1970). His multi-role as the Traveller in *Death in Venice* (1975) was a superb tour-de-force.

HENDERSON, ROY (1899–). Scottish baritone, in the first Glyndebourne Company (1934–9), his roles including the Count in *Figaro*, Guglielmo and Papageno. Later a famous teacher.

HERINCX, RAYMOND. English bass-baritone whose many fine performances for the Wells/English National Opera have included Rance in *La Fanciulla del West* (1962) and Berlioz's Méphistophélès (1972). His magnificent Wotan for the English National Opera (1976) came as a revelation.

HIDALGO, ELVIRA DE (1882–). Spanish soprano, famous at La Scala, the Met, etc. and, later, the only teacher (in Athens) of Callas.

HINES, JEROME (1921–). American bass who joined the Met in 1947. His most famous roles include Boris, the Grand Inquisitor in *Don Carlos*, and Gurnemanz (Bayreuth, 1958), also Attila (Newark, 1973).

HOENGEN, ELISABETH (1906–). German mezzo-soprano and notable actress-singer, especially as Klytemnestra, Herodias, Lady Macbeth and Ortrud. At Düsseldorf and Dresden in the 1930s and early 1940s, she became especially famous in Vienna after the war.

HOFFMAN, GRACE (1925–). American mezzo-soprano who has sung in many European and American cities, most notably at Stuttgart from 1955, at Bayreuth from 1957. Her most famous roles include Brangäne, Kundry and Eboli.

HOFMANN, LUDWIG (1895–1963). German bass-baritone at Bayreuth, Vienna, Covent Garden and the Met, most notably in the 1930s, in Wagnerian, Italian and French roles.

HOLM, RICHARD (1912–). German tenor at Munich, the Met, etc. where his finest roles have included David, Tom Rakewell in *The Rake's Progress*, and Loge.

HOMER, LOUISE (1871–1947). American contralto, especially famous at the Met (1900–19)

where she sang Orfeo and Hate (in *Armide*) for Toscanini. A fine Wagnerian.

HOPF, HANS (1916–). German tenor who joined Munich Opera in 1949 and has since sung at Salzburg and Bayreuth, and at Covent Garden and the Met in the 1950s. As well as Wagnerian leads, he has been a distinguished Otello and Max in *Der Freischütz*.

HORNE, MARILYN (1934–). American mezzo-soprano whose rich voice and remarkable technique have made her a famous *bel canto* singer, including Adalgisa opposite Sutherland. Marie in *Wozzeck* at San Francisco (1960) and Covent Garden (1964). An unexpectedly successful Carmen at the Met (1972).

HOTTER, HANS (1909–). German bass-baritone, a great actor-singer and one of the most famous Wotans in history (see page 111). In the 1930s, his various engagements included Hamburg (1934–8). He then became a pillar of the Vienna and Munich Operas for the rest of his glorious career. Few singers have enjoyed such a long and triumphant reign at Covent Garden in modern times as Hotter (1947–67). He was at the Met, 1950–4, and *the* Wotan of post-war Bayreuth. Famous non-Wagnerian roles have included Borromeo in *Palestrina* and the

Grand Inquisitor in *Don Carlos*, and he created the Kommandant in *Friedenstag* (1938) and Olivier in *Capriccio* (1942). The great age of Wagner recordings found his voice past its splendid best, but his keen intelligence and musicianship remained as undimmed as his acting powers until the end of his career. That he has only proved a competent producer who can get good acting out of casts (as in his *Ring* at Covent Garden) can only surprise those who naïvely suppose that a greater actor is necessarily a great producer.

HOWARD, ANN. British mezzo, one of the finest Carmens since the war (for Sadler's Wells) and a notable Cassandra in *Les Troyens* for Scottish Opera (1967).

HOWELL, GLYNNE. Welsh bass, with Sadler's Wells from 1968 and the Royal Opera from 1970. His fine voice and authoritative manner make him a notable asset to a company. Roles include Monterone, Timur and Colline, and, in 1974, King Philip in *Don Carlos* for the English National Opera.

HOWELLS, ANNE (1941–). English mezzo, a most attractive actress-singer who has sung Dorabella at Covent Garden, Chicago, etc. and also soprano parts, including Poppea for Scottish Opera, and Mélisande. At Glyndebourne,

where her roles include a delightful Minerva in *Il Ritorno d'Ulisse* (1973), she has brilliantly created Cathleen in Maw's *The Rising of the Moon* (1970). An ideal Offenbach's Helen (1975). Married to the tenor Ryland Davies (p. 136).

HÜNI-MIHACSEK, FELICE (1891–). Hungarian soprano and a famous Mozartian between the wars, especially at Munich (1926–45). As well as Donna Anna, Fiordiligi and the Queen of the Night, she was a renowned Eva and Marschallin.

HUNTER, RITA (1933–). English soprano, the (now internationally) famous Brünnhilde of Goodall's *Ring* at the Coliseum. Already a great Wagnerian (her diction apart), her finest Italian roles to date are Leonora in *Il Trovatore* and Elisabeth de Valois in *Don Carlos*. Despite physical disadvantages, a winning personality and a sincere actress.

HYDE, WALTER (1875–1951). English tenor. Siegmund in the English *Ring* at Covent Garden (1908), where he appeared until 1923—with Beecham and the British National Opera Company. The first English Parsifal (1919).

INGHILLERI, GIOVANNI (1894–1959). Italian baritone, well known between the wars in Rome and elsewhere in Italy.

Gérard in *Andrea Chénier* at the 50th anniversary celebration (1946) of the première at La Scala, under Giordano's direction.

IVOGÜN, MARIA (1891–). Hungarian soprano, the first Ighino in *Palestrina* (1917) and a famous coloratura soprano between the wars in Germany, at Covent Garden, etc. her roles including Zerbinetta, Gilda and Constanze.

JANSSEN, HERBERT (1895–1965). German, later American, baritone at Covent Garden, 1926–39 and the Met, 1939–51. His most famous roles included Gunther, Kurwenal, Wolfram and Amfortas, which he sang in Bayreuth and elsewhere, and his Kothner in *Die Meistersinger* is regarded as definitive.

JANOWITZ, GUNDALA (1937–). Czech soprano, born in Berlin, who rapidly made her name after joining the Vienna State Opera in 1960. Her roles include Sieglinde, Desdemona, Ariadne, the Countess, and Agathe in *Freischütz* in Germany, Austria, France, etc. Her acting has improved down the years. Though she divides opinion, at her best she is superb.

JERGER, ALFRED (1889–). Austrian baritone, famous between the wars at Vienna and elsewhere, and the original Mandryka in *Arabella* (1933).

JERITZA, MARIA (1887–). Czech soprano and a stunningly beautiful actress-singer, equally famous in Europe and America. Her legendary Tosca included 'Vissi d'arte' flat on the floor and face down, while other famous roles were Thaïs, Carmen, Minnie and Fedora. She was the Met's first Jenufa (1924) and Turandot (1926), and Vienna's first Die Kaiserin in *Die Frau ohne Schatten* (1919), its world première. 'One of the most original artists I have ever known,' said Puccini of her, whose favourite Tosca she was. He thoroughly approved of her horizontal aria, which occurred originally in her tussle with Scarpia.

JOBIN, RAOUL (1906–). Canadian tenor, best known in Paris and at the Met from the 1930s to the 1950s. His roles included Don José, Samson, Werther and Hoffmann.

JOHNSON, EDWARD (1878–1959). Canadian tenor, manager of the Met from 1935 to 1950. The first Parsifal in Italy (La Scala, 1913), he also created a number of Italian roles. The first Italian Luigi and Rinunccio in *Il Trittico* (1918). He was also a noted Wagnerian, including Siegfried. Between the wars, he was mainly at the Met, creating various roles in American operas, and being notably successful as Pelléas and Romeo.

JOHNSTON, JAMES (*c* 1900–). Irish tenor, at Sadler's Wells (1945–50) and Covent Garden (1950–8). In a period when British dramatic tenors were rare, he provided sterling performances, lyrical as well as dramatic, as Radamès, Calaf, Manrico and Don José.

JONES, GWYNETH (1936–). Welsh soprano, a beautiful and, at her best, superb actress-singer, who made her name as Leonore in *Fidelio* with the Welsh National Opera in the early 1960s, having been a mezzo at Zürich. After a ravishing Leonora in *Il Trovatore* at Covent Garden (1964), she rapidly became internationally famous, but her voice was liable to be variable. Her roles include Sieglinde, Desdemona, Donna Anna and Senta. Vocally, as well as physically, she was in electrifying form as Salome at Covent Garden (1974), a performance which, together with her Bayreuth triumphs, ranks her as a superstar.

JOURNET, MARCEL (1867–1933). French bass, at Covent Garden (1897–1907) and the Met (1900–8), whose voice was so superb and technique so fine that he sang major leads for Toscanini at La Scala in the 1920s, including Hans Sachs, Mefistofele and Escamillo.

JUNE, AVA. English soprano, especially known for her Butter-fly at Sadler's Wells/English National Opera.

JURINAC, SENA (1921–). Yugoslav soprano, with the Vienna State Opera from 1944, at Glyndebourne (1949–56), and elsewhere. One of the greatest Mozartian singers of the century, and a great Octavian and later memorable Marschallin, she is for many the finest Composer in the history of *Ariadne auf Naxos*. Best known originally for Cherubino, Fiordiligi and Pamina, she became, as her voice grew heavier, a famous Donna Anna and Countess, while, outside Mozart, other roles apart from those mentioned have included Butterfly, Desdemona and Elisabeth de Valois. See also page 111.

KABAIVANSKA, RAINA (1934–). Bulgarian soprano, a notable and beautiful actress-singer who, in the 1970s, has become one of the great Verdi and Puccini interpreters of the age. Giorgio Gualerzi (*Opera*, August 1973) has written of the 'overwhelming authority' of her Turin Manon Lescaut, her 'immense dramatic talent and rare intensity of expression', but, like others, warned against an excess of vocal and physical energy. Desdemona is one of her finest roles.

KAPPEL, GERTRUDE (1884–1971). German soprano, famous, especially in Munich and at the

Met between the wars, for her Wagnerian and Strauss performances, most notably Isolde and Brünnhilde.

KELLY, MICHAEL (1762–1826). Irish tenor who created Don Basilio and Curzio in *Le Nozze di Figaro* (1786) in Vienna. Earlier he had sung in Italy and later in London, but his most valuable service was to write his engaging *Reminiscences* (1826). He was also a composer.

KEMBLE, ADELAIDE (1814–79). English soprano, the operatic representative of a most famous acting family. Her aunt was the immortal Sarah Siddons. After a début in Venice as Norma (1839), she was the main attraction at Covent Garden (1841–2), her roles including Norma, Amina, Semiramide, Susanna, and Caroline in *Il Matrimonio Segreto*.

KEMP, BARBARA (1881–1959). German soprano, best known in Berlin (1913–30) and at Bayreuth (1914–27) where she sang Kundry and Senta. Married to the manager, Max von Shillings. She created the title role in his *Mona Lisa* at Berlin (1915).

KERN, ADELE (1901–). German soprano, a famous Mozartian, Sophie and Zerbinetta, in Vienna, Munich and at Salzburg, where she sang from 1927 to 1935.

KERN, PATRICIA. Welsh mezzo-soprano who made her name at the Wells as Rossini's Cinderella (*La Cenerentola*) and a definitive Isolier in his *Count Ory* (1963). She is an excellent Cherubino, while her Octavia in *Poppea* for Scottish Opera (1973) was typical of what a major artist can do with a small part.

KERNS, ROBERT. American bari-baritone, a fine Billy Budd at Covent Garden (1964) and now a distinguished Mozartian in the U.S.A., Covent Garden, etc.; an amusing Belcore at Vienna (1973).

KIEPURA, JAN (1902–66). Polish tenor and film star, blessed with voice and remarkably good looks. A famous Danilo in *The Merry Widow* in Europe and America, a role for which he was ideally suited. His 'Widow' was his wife, the Hungarian soprano Martha Eggerth. His operatic career between the wars took in Vienna, Berlin, the Met and Chicago, Milan, Paris, and he was a renowned Rodolfo, Cavaradossi, Calaf, Des Grieux, and Don José.

KINDERMANN, AUGUST (1817–91). German bass-baritone whose career as a soloist (after being in the Berlin Opera chorus) began in Leipzig in 1839 and ended in Munich in the year of his death. Bayreuth's first Titurel in *Parsifal* (1882).

KING, JAMES (1925–). American tenor, originally a baritone. Joined the Deutshe Oper in 1961, making his Bayreuth début as Siegmund (1965), one of his most famous parts. The Emperor in *Die Frau ohne Schatten* (1967) at Covent Garden, in which Harold Rosenthal wrote that he sounded like a young Melchior, and he was equally fine in the role in Paris (1973). A Covent Garden and Met Florestan. Despite strain and hardness of voice occasionally, he is a major artist. A magnificent Florestan at Munich (1974).

KIPNIS, ALEXANDER (1891–). Russian bass whose beautiful, flexible voice and musicianship made him one of the most admired singers of the interwar years at Berlin, Chicago, the Met, Covent Garden, Bayreuth, Glyndebourne and Salzburg. He became an American citizen in 1934. His career from his Hamburg début (1915) was essentially German, and he was a famous Hagen, Gurnemanz, Mark and Sarastro. Steane calls him a 'miracle among singers', the voice 'grandly sonorous'.

KIRSTEN, DOROTHY (1917–). American soprano and a very attractive and committed actress-singer whose notable career began at the Chicago Opera. At the Met from 1945, her roles have included Louise, Butterfly, Marguerite and Manon Lescaut, while her Tosca, as reported in *Opera*, February, 1973, was still superb in San Francisco the previous November.

KLEIN, PETER (1907–). German tenor, with Hamburg Opera (1937–41), after which he joined the Vienna Opera (1942) and sang for many years at Salzburg. His large repertoire has included Shuisky, Don Basilio, the Captain in *Wozzeck*, David and Jacquino; also, a famous Mime, which he sang regularly at Covent Garden (1947–60) and elsewhere.

KLOSE, MARGARETE (1902–65). German mezzo-soprano, one of the finest of the 1930s to 1950s in Berlin and elsewhere. She sang at Bayreuth (1936–42), appeared in London, and was admired for her Verdi as well as her Wagner, also excelling as Carmen, Klytemnestra, Orfeo and the Kostelnička in *Jenufa*.

KNOTE, HEINRICH (1870–1953). German tenor, a major Wagnerian in Germany, at Covent Garden and the Met before 1914, having made his début in Munich in 1892. His Tristan, Siegfried and Tannhäuser were not only famous but a feast for the eyes.

KOLLO, RENÉ. German tenor whose roles range from Parsifal at Bayreuth to Danilo, having started as a pop singer.

KONETZNI, ANNY (1902–68). Austrian soprano, at the Berlin State Opera from 1931 to 1935, and the Vienna State Opera from 1935 to 1954. She also sang at Covent Garden and the Met and is remembered as a major Wagnerian (Brünnhilde, Isolde, etc.), but she was also heard as Santuzza, Eboli, Elena in *I Vespri Siciliani* and the Marschallin.

KONETZNI, HILDE (1905–). Austrian soprano, sister of the above, who joined the Vienna State Opera in 1936 and is still with the company at the time of writing. A brilliant Wagnerian with a beautiful voice, her other roles include Donna Anna and Leonore in *Fidelio*.

KÓNYA, SÁNDOR (1923–). Hungarian tenor who made his name in Germany in the 1950s at the Berlin Stadtische Oper (1955) and Bayreuth as Lohengrin (1958). In the 1960s he appeared frequently at La Scala, San Francisco and the Met. Calaf in *Turandot* is one of his best known non-Wagnerian roles.

KÖTH, ERIKA (1927–). German soprano, especially associated with Munich and Vienna from 1953 onwards. A famous high coloratura, her Zerbinetta has been particularly notable.

KRAUS, ALFREDO. Spanish tenor who has become a most stylish singer of *bel canto* roles in Europe and America, including Edgardo at the Met (1972). Elegant-looking and a good actor, his Duke in *Rigoletto* at Covent Garden (1974) was perfection.

KRAUS, ERNST (1863–1941). German tenor, a Bayreuth Siegfried, Walther, etc. and London's first Herod in *Salome* (1910).

KRAUS, OTAKAR (1909–). Czech, then British, baritone who created Tarquinius in *The Rape of Lucretia* (1946), and was the first Nick Shadow in *The Rake's Progress* (Venice, 1951). This splendid actor-singer was a Covent Garden stalwart through the 1950s and 1960s, a famous Alberich, also singing the role at Bayreuth (1960–2), and the first Iago thousands of post-war London operagoers heard (1955).

KRAUSS, FELIX VON (1870–1937). German bass, at Bayreuth (1899–1909) and elsewhere, his roles including Hagen. He became Artistic Director of Munich Opera. His wife, Adrienne von Krauss-Osborne (1873–1951) was a noted Wagnerian.

KRAUSS, GABRIELLE (1842–1906). Austrian soprano, especially famous at the Opéra, Paris (1875–88), where she sang Rachel in Halévy's *La Juive* on the opening night of the new building. A remarkable actress-singer, nick-named 'La Rachel Chantante' (Rachel was the greatest of all French actresses), her roles included Norma, Lucia, Aida and Donna Anna.

KRUSCENISKI, SALOMEA (c 1872–1953). Polish soprano, Butterfly at the opera's first successful performance (Brescia, 1904). She was Italy's first Elektra at La Scala (1907). Also a noted Brünnhilde, Isolde and Salome.

KUBIAK, TERESA. Polish soprano who made her début in Łódz (1965). Now an international artist, a Covent Garden Butterfly, Tosca and Aida, Lisa in *Queen of Spades* at the Met (1973), and, at her best, a fine actress. A superb Jenufa at the Met (1974).

KULLMAN, CHARLES (1903–). American tenor who made his name in Berlin, London and at the Met in the 1930s. Sang at the Met, 1935–62, in a wide range of leading roles.

KUNZ, ERICH (1909–). Austrian bass-baritone, one of the now legendary Vienna State Opera ensemble of the postwar period, having made his début there in 1940. His Leporello, Figaro and Guglielmo have been vastly enjoyed there, in London and at Salzburg, and he has sung Papageno and Beckmesser (at Bayreuth and elewhere). At the Met, 1952–4. This born comedian has been accused of occasionally going too far, even clowning roles. Having had so few chances to see him, I cannot comment adequately on the alleged pecadillos of a first-rate actor.

KUPPER, ANNELIES (1906–). German soprano at Hamburg (1940–6) and then Munich, famous as a Strauss singer creating Danae in *Die Liebe der Danae* (1952) at the composer's request.

KURT, MELANIE (1880–1941). Austrian soprano, originally a pianist. A famous Wagnerian, especially in Berlin (1908–12) and at the Met (1915–17) where she lost her job when America joined in the war. Her roles included Isolde, Brünnhilde, Pamina and Leonore.

KURZ, SELMA (1874–1933). Austrian soprano whose now legendary trill upset Melba, as did her success, leading to her absence from Covent Garden from 1907 to 1924, having first sung there in 1904. However, she was a famous star of the Vienna Opera (from 1899) in Mahler's day, as a lyric-dramatic soprano (Eva, Sieglinde, etc.), then as a coloratura, her roles including Lucia and Violetta.

KUSCHE, BENNO (1916–). German bass-baritone, a noted actor-singer in Germany and elsewhere, his roles including

Falstaff, Beckmesser and Leporello, especially at Munich since 1946.

KUZNETSOVA, MARIA (1880–1966). Russian soprano, originally a dancer, making her singing début at St Petersburg (1905). Mimi, Marguerite and Manon at Covent Garden (1909–10). By now famous in Russia and in Chicago (1915–17) she escaped from Russia in 1920 (dressed as a boy, then hidden in a trunk) to reappear at Covent Garden, later directing the Opéra Russe de Paris. Note for sceptics: in *Opera*'s 1966 obituary the word 'allegedly' is used about her trunk.

LABLACHE, LUIGI (1794–1858). Italian bass of French and Irish parentage, one of the most famous singers of the century, who taught Queen Victoria and was so gigantic that he used to exit with his Masettos under his arm. First making his name in Italy and Vienna (where he sang in Mozart's *Requiem* at Beethoven's funeral), he made his London and Paris débuts in 1830 and regularly sang in both until 1856. The first Riccardo in *I Puritani* (1835) and *Don Pasquale* (1843), amongst his other creations were Karl von Moor in *I Masnadieri* (1847) in London under Verdi's baton.

LAMMERS, GERDA (1915–). German soprano, a concert artist for many years, who made her stage début at Bayreuth (1955), the year she joined Kassel Opera. A notable Wagnerian, she also sang Gluck's Alceste and Medea, but it was her Elektra that made her famous, especially in London (1957).

LANGDON, MICHAEL (1921–). English bass, with Covent Garden Opera Company/Royal Opera from 1950. His most notable parts include Ochs, which he has sung in Vienna, and Britten's Peter Quince.

LANIGAN, JOHN (1921–). Australian tenor, with Covent Garden Opera from 1951, singing romantic leads at first, including Des Grieux (*Manon*), then making a name in character parts, including a brilliant Mime and an equally fine Shuisky.

LARSEN-TODSEN, NANNY (1884–). Swedish soprano, Stockholm's leading lyric, then dramatic, soprano (1907–22). Isolde in Milan (1923–4), and a major Wagnerian at the Met (1924–7), also singing Leonore and La Gioconda.

LASSALLE, JEAN (1847–1909). French baritone, one of the most celebrated of his day from his début as Guillaume Tell at the Opéra (1872) until the 1890s, when he was a star of the Met, having also triumphed at Covent Garden (from 1879).

LASZLÒ, MAGDA (1919–). Hungarian soprano, creator of Cressida in Walton's *Troilus and Cressida* (1954) in which her looks and musicianship almost compensated for her too small voice (for the part), and the incomparable Poppea in Monteverdi's *Poppea* at Glyndebourne (1962).

LAURI-VOLPI, GIACOMO (1892–). Italian tenor, one of the most famous of the century, especially in lyric-dramatic roles. Though between the two world wars was his great period, he was singing as late as 1959. At the Met he sang 232 performances of twenty-six operas from 1923 to 1934, and was the first American Calaf, a role which particularly suited his ringing tone and top notes, while in 1936 he was Covent Garden's Duke of Mantua, Cavaradossi and Radamès. Gigli's artistic and personal rival at the Met, he allegedly got ten cents more per performance so as to be officially higher paid.

LAWRENCE, MARJORIE (1909–). Australian soprano whose career was hit by polio during *Walküre* in Mexico City (1941), after which she recovered enough to appear as Isolde, Venus and Amneris in specially produced performances for her in America and Paris. A major star of the Opéra and the Met in the 1930s, her roles included Brünnhilde, Salome, Tosca and Thaïs.

LAZZARI, VIRGILIO (1887–1953). Italian, later American, bass and an actor-singer who made his name in Chicago (1918–33), the Met (1933–50) and as a Salzburg Leporello, Pistol, etc. (1934–9).

LEAR, EVELYN. American soprano, well-known in Germany and elsewhere in a wide range of roles including Fiordiligi and the Marschallin (Berlin, 1972). Married to Thomas Stewart.

LEGROS, JOSEPH (1730–93). French tenor (and composer) who sang at the Opéra, 1764–83. Created Gluck's Achilles in *Iphigénie en Aulide*, Admète in *Alceste*, Pylades in *Iphigénie en Tauride*, also the tenor role Orphée.

LEHMANN, LILLI (1848–1921). German soprano who sang 170 roles in 119 operas and ranged majestically, powerfully and triumphantly from Wagner to Mozart, also excelling in Bellini. After working in Danzig, Leipzig, etc. she was a lyric and coloratura in Berlin (1870–85), having meanwhile been a Rhinemaiden, etc. at the first Bayreuth Festival (1876), and sung Isolde for Richter at Covent Garden (1884). Made her Met début as Carmen (1885) and was America's first Isolde and Brünnhilde in *Götterdämmerung*. Bayreuth's Brünnhilde in 1896, she was singing Mozart at the Salzburg Mozart Festival in 1905, and became Artistic Director there and a famous teacher. Her sister Marie (1851–1931) was overshadowed, but sang excellently with the Vienna Opera (1881–1902), having been an original Rhinemaiden with Lilli in 1876.

LEHMANN, LOTTE (1888–1976). German, later American, soprano, about whom no one over the age of 50 is less than ecstatic, her Marschallin being regarded as definitive. At Vienna, 1914–38, her creations included the Composer in *Ariadne auf Naxos* (1916) and the Dyer's Wife in *Die Frau ohne Schatten* (1919), and, for all her fame as Eva, Sieglinde, Else and Leonore, she was also renowned as Turandot, Manon and Mimi, and Vienna's first Suor Angelica. The first Christine in *Intermezzo* at Dresden (1924), she was adored at Covent Garden in the 1920s and 1930s, and at the Met (1934–45), being forced to leave Vienna in 1938. This warmly tender, highly intelligent great singer—though, in view of her Marschallin, 'actress-singer' would be more accurate—became an inspirational teacher.

LEIDER, FRIDA (1888–1975). German soprano, the greatest Brünnhilde and Isolde of the inter-war years, and a magnificent actress-singer into the bargain. Even under pressure,

her glorious voice 'nearly always remained keen and expressive', as Philip Hope-Wallace has written. Berlin, London, Chicago, New York and Bayreuth were the chief stages for her warm, thrilling art, while her non-Wagnerian roles included the Marschallin and Donna Anna. According to Eva Turner, 'the greatest Isolde and Brünnhilde of our time', and 'as an artist she was supreme' (*Opera*, August 1975).

LEIGH, ADÈLE (1928–). English soprano, at Covent Garden (1948–56), where she graduated to Massenet's Manon, and Pamina. From 1963, a member of the Vienna Volksoper.

LEMNITZ, TIANA (1897–). German soprano, at Hanover (1929–33), Berlin (1934–57), and elsewhere, including Covent Garden in 1936 and 1938. One of the finest of all Octavians, her Eva was also a delight, and both parts were well acted. Her range was remarkable, her roles including Jenufa, Aïda, Sieglinde and Pamina, in which her famous pianissimo was heard to advantage.

LEMSHEV, SERGEY (1902–). Russian tenor, famous at the Bolshoi (from 1932) for his Lensky, and Italian and French roles, including Roméo.

LEVASSEUR, ROSALIE (1749–1826). French soprano and a

fine actress-singer who created many roles, including the title roles in Gluck's *Armide* (1777) and *Iphigénie en Tauride* (1779), both in Paris.

LEWIS, RICHARD (1914–). English tenor, an admirable artist whose début was as the Male Chorus in *The Rape of Lucretia* at Glyndebourne (1947). Regularly at Glyndebourne (from 1948 with the Company, beginning with Don Ottavio), he has often sung at Covent Garden and in San Francisco (from 1955). His roles have included Tom Rakewell, Idomeneo, Don José, Hoffmann, Florestan and Des Grieux, and his creations have been Troilus in Walton's *Troilus and Cressida* (1954) and Achilles in *King Priam* (1962).

LIGABUE, ILVA. Italian soprano at La Scala and elsewhere since 1950. Her roles at Glyndebourne included a superb Fiordiligi (1959), and she is a notable Verdian and Puccinian in Europe and America, Alice Ford and Elisabeth de Valois being among her finest roles. Her personality is delightful.

LIGENDZA, CATERINA (1937–). Swedish soprano who made her name in Germany and elsewhere in the mid-1960s and later (1974) reached the heights with an Isolde at Bayreuth which for many was perfection: 'for the most part the Isolde of one's dreams', wrote Alan Blyth

in *Opera*. 'With no hint of wobble in her glinting tone, she offered a *bel canto* reading.' A beauty into the bargain.

LIND, JENNY (1820–87). Swedish soprano of colossal popularity, her voice being remarkably agile and pure in quality, with a sympathetic quality about it which, allied to her personality and true and evident good nature, led to the Lind Mania of the 1840s. She touched so many hearts and gave so many thousands to charity, that it becomes hard to discover enough about her as an artist. She was a lyric-coloratura soprano, a little weak in the middle, powerful at the top, and always in tune, while her pianissimo notes had an extraordinary echo effect.

'The Swedish Nightingale' made her début in Stockholm in 1838 and retired from the stage in 1852. After her Berlin début as Norma (1844), she rapidly captured Germany, Scandinavia and Austria, then came to Her Majesty's, London, in 1847 as a rival attraction to Covent Garden's stellar roster. Her roles included Amelia in *I Masnadieri* under Verdi's baton (1847), while her most famous portrayals were Alice in *Robert le Diable* and Amina in *La Sonnambula*, two simple girls—roles that suited her personality. She triumphed in America as well as Europe, hypnotizing audiences despite unremarkable looks, and it was a black day for opera when she was persuaded by an English clergyman that God and the stage were incompatible.

LIPP, WILMA (1925–). Austrian soprano, with the Vienna State Opera from 1945, singing coloratura and soubrette roles, later *lyrico-spinto* parts (see *Soprano*, page 336).

LISITSYAN, PAVEL (1911–). Russian baritone, at the Bolshoi since 1940, and Amonasro at the Met (1960). His roles include Eugene Onegin and Escamillo.

LITVINNE, FÉLIA (1860–1936). Franco-Russian soprano, a famous Wagnerian, the first Paris Isolde (1899) and the La Monnaie Brünnhilde in the first Belgian *Ring* (1903). Earlier, with Mapleson in America, several seasons at Covent Garden from 1899.

LONDON, GEORGE (1920–). Canadian bass-baritone who made his début in Vienna as Amonasro in 1949 and joined the Met in 1951, singing Boris, Don Giovanni, etc. the same year singing the Dutchman and Amfortas at Bayreuth. An impressive actor-singer, he has now become a producer.

LORENGAR, PILAR. Spanish soprano who made her name in the mid-1950s, including a delightful Pamina at Glyndebourne, and has since become an international singer, best known for her Mozartian roles and Violetta. A superb Fiordiligi.

LORENZ, MAX (1901–75). German tenor, a famous Wagnerian between the wars in Berlin, London, Bayreuth, and also at the Met, where he sang from 1947–50. A musicianly *Heldentenor*, his roles included a magnificent Otello.

LOS ANGELES, VICTORIA DE (1923–). Spanish soprano with a most beautiful voice and great charm, one of the most loved singers of the post-war era, often heard at Covent Garden and a Met regular from 1951. Her London début in 1950 as Mimi created a sensation. Her other roles have been Butterfly, Salud in Falla's *La Vida Breve*, a superb Elsa in *Lohengrin*, Mélisande, etc. and her Manon (Massenet) which is featured on page 112.

LUBIN, GERMAINE (1890–). French soprano, at the Opéra from 1914 to 1944, and the first French Kundry and Isolde at Bayreuth. A fine actress-singer with a lovely voice.

LUCCA, PAULINE (1841–1908). Austrian soprano who used her pure, powerful voice, which spanned two-and-a-half octaves, expressively and passionately, and almost rivalled Patti in popularity in the 1860s. Internationally famous, her best-known roles were Marguerite, Carmen and Cherubino.

LUDIKAR, PAVEL (1882–1970). Czech bass-baritone who sang widely in Europe, then joined the Met (1926–32) where he sang Figaro well over one hundred times.

LUDWIG, CHRISTA (1928–). German mezzo-soprano, a striking actress-singer with a rich, powerful voice, renowned for her Eboli, Amneris, Octavian and Composer, and, from 1962, Leonore. Joined Vienna State Opera in 1955. She has graduated to Ariadne and the Marschallin, and one of her supreme roles is the Dyer's Wife in *Die Frau ohne Schatten*, notably under Karajan in Vienna (1964) and in Paris in 1972.

LUNN, LOUISE KIRKBY (1873–1930). English mezzo-soprano whose voice was large and face was handsome. At Covent Garden (1901–14 and 1919–22), she excelled as Ortrud, Fricka, Brangäne, Delilah and Amneris.

LUXON, BENJAMIN. English baritone who, since creating the title-role in Britten's *Owen Wingrave* on television (1970) and in the theatre, has rapidly become a notable actor-singer. Recent parts have included a striking Count in *Figaro* at Glyndebourne (1973), Posa in the English National Opera's

Don Carlos (1974), the outstanding performance in the production, and an admirably strong, sympathetic Marcello in *La Bohème* at Covent Garden.

MACINTYRE, DONALD (1934–). New Zealand-born bass-baritone who made his London début as Nabucco in 1959 with the Welsh National Opera, then joined Sadler's Wells, where his roles included the Dutchman, Guglielmo, Attila and Figaro. Made his Covent Garden début in 1967, one of his most memorable roles there being Barak in *Die Frau ohne Schatten*. In 1973, he became the first British baritone to sing Wotan in a complete *Ring* cycle at Bayreuth. A striking Pizarro in *Fidelio* at Covent Garden in 1976.

MCCORMACK, JOHN (1884–1943). Irish tenor, only in opera from 1906 to 1913, after which he became one of the most beloved singers in history, not least when he essayed native and sometimes pseudo-native ballads. He was a feeble actor, which was one reason why he left the stage, but his voice and technique were exceptional, as recordings show: his 'Il mio tesoro', if lacking in passion, is a classic piece of singing, not least for its phenomenal breath control. He sang in opera mainly at Covent Garden and in America, the best known of his roles being Rodolfo, Elvino,

Edgardo, the Duke of Mantua and Don Ottavio.

MCCRACKEN, JAMES. American tenor, one of the few true Otellos of modern times. His interpetation is notable for superb use of words, acting well above operatic standards, brilliant use of his beautiful voice (whose only weakness is at the top), and total commitment to the role. His Covent Garden début at the proverbial moment's notice in 1964 was a legendary triumph.

MADIERA, JEAN (1924–72). American contralto, at the Met from 1948, her roles including Amneris, Erda, Suzuki and Preziosilla in *La Forza del Destino*. She later sang Carmen in Munich, Erda at Covent Garden and Bayreuth, and Klytemnestra at Salzburg (1956), her last role at the Met in 1971. She had striking looks and a richly dramatic voice.

MALIBRAN, MARIA (1808–36). Spanish mezzo-contralto with the range of a soprano, a few carefully concealed notes in the middle of her voice apart. The daughter of Manuel Garcia (featured page 147), she was the most exciting member of a fabulous family, and, one suspects, the most thrilling singer in operatic history, an incomparable actress into the bargain, who, like David Garrick and few more, excelled in tragedy and comedy. Her early death,

resulting from complications after a fall from a horse, helped increase her legend, but the testimony of musicians and non-musicians alike, including Rossini, Lamartine, de Musset and Bellini, justifies such a claim. The only doubter was Delacroix, an arch-romantic in art, who preferred the more classical genius of Pasta. Living life at fever pitch, she summed up for many the whole Romantic movement.

Ferociously taught by her father, she made her début as Rosina in London in 1825, becoming New York's first prima donna the same year when the Garcia family went there. Perhaps to escape from her father, she married a banker named Malibran, but soon left him and returned to Europe where she conquered Paris, London, Milan, Rome, etc. At Venice, she was greeted with trumpets, while her Norma in Milan in 1835 caused such a sensation that the police were called in by the Mayor. Her Leonore was famous, while her Amina in *La Sonnambula*, in English at Drury Lane in 1833, sent Bellini into ecstasies. An instinctive actress rather than a studied one, she was compared with the great French actor, Talma, and Rachel, the actress who conquered Paris after Malibran's death. Théophile Gautier said that she had the genius to die young, while Rossini claimed her as one of three geniuses of his time, the others being Lablache and Rubini. Malibran, he said, was a spoiled child of nature, while Lablache said of her: 'Son grand esprit était trop fort pour son petit corps.'

MALLINGER, MATHILDE (1847–1920). Croatian soprano, the first Eva in *Die Meistersinger* (Munich, 1868).

MALTEN, THERESE (1855–1930). German soprano, at Dresden for thirty years from 1873, and at Bayreuth from 1882 to 1894, her most famous role being Kundry.

MANNERS, CHARLES (1857–1955). Irish bass, with D'Oyly Carte, Carl Rosa and Covent Garden, where he was London's first Gremin in *Eugene Onegin* (1892). With his wife, the soprano Fanny Moody (see below), started the Moody-Manners Company (see page 290).

MANOWARDA, JOSEF VON (1890–1942). Austrian bass, at the Vienna State Opera (1919–42) and Berlin State Opera (1934–42), also singing at Bayreuth in the 1930s.

MARCHESI FAMILY. Salvatore Marchesi, Cavaliere de Castrone (1822–1908), was an Italian baritone and teacher who married Mathilde (Graumann) in 1852. She was a German mezzo-soprano, and one of the greatest of all teachers in Germany, then, finally, in Paris from 1861–5 and from 1881. Her pupils included Calvé, Melba and Mary Garden. Her daughter Blanche (1863–1940) was a French soprano, for some years with the Moody-Manners Co., after which she, too, became a (London) teacher.

MARCOUX, VANNI (1877–1962). French bass-baritone, at Covent Garden, 1905–14, where his roles included a superb Marcel in *Les Huguenots* (1908). At Chicago, 1913–14 and 1925–32. He had a repertoire of 240 roles, including Massenet's Don Quichotte which he created (1910).

MARIO, GIOVANNI (1810–83). Italian tenor, possessor of a beautiful voice, used with immense style, and a handsome actor-singer, whose popularity was naturally and rightly immense. London saw more of him than any other city: he was at Her Majesty's, 1839–46, and at Covent Garden, 1847–67, making a farewell appearance there in 1871. He made an excellent operatic match in Giulia Grisi (see page 151), having been with her, Tamburini and Lablache in the legendary première of *Don Pasquale* in Paris (1843), and he was London's first Gennaro in *Lucrezia Borgia*, Ernesto in *Don Pasquale*, the Duke of Mantua, Roméo, etc.

MARTINELLI, GIOVANNI (1885–1969). Italian tenor eminently worthy to be the entry after Mario. Making his début as Ernani in Milan (1910), he so impressed Puccini that he was cast as Johnson for the first European *La Fanciulla del West* (Rome, 1911), and was hailed as a second Caruso at Covent Garden (1912), singing Cavaradossi opposite Edvina. Stylish, technically perfect, with a resonant silvery voice, not very large but large enough, he sang several seasons at Covent Garden, including a now legendary Otello (1937), though his voice could never be ideal for the most heroic moments, and in the same season a superb Calaf. At the Met, 1913–46, he sang in over fifty operas. He sang Tristan opposite Flagstad in Chicago (1939) and, having retired in 1950, took over the part of the Emperor in *Turandot* in Seattle in an emergency in 1967 when over 80.

MASINI, ANGELO (1844–1926). Italian tenor, admired by Verdi in whose *Requiem* he sang under the composer's baton in London, Paris and Vienna, also singing Radamès for him in Paris. However, he refused to create Fenton in Falstaff, even with the carrot of a suggested extended aria.

MASON, EDITH (1893–). American soprano, well known between the wars especially in Italy and Chicago.

MASTERSON, VALERIE. English soprano, who, after working with the D'Oyly Carte Company, then brilliantly singing Tancredi at Camden Festival, London (1971), joined Sadler's Wells Opera, where she quickly made her name as a most attractive actress-singer, her roles including Manon (Massenet's), Violetta, Adele and Sophie.

MASTILOVIC, DANICA. Yugoslav soprano, at Bayreuth, Munich, etc., where her Elektra at the latter (1972) was a triumph.

MATERNA, AMALIE (1844–1918). Austrian soprano, who graduated from operetta to Bayreuth's first (and very great) Brünnhilde (1876), also Kundry (1882). She was also the Met's first *Walküre* Brünnhilde.

MATHIS, EDITH. American soprano, at Salzburg, Glyndebourne, Covent Garden, Vienna, etc. her roles including Cherubino, Despina, Ilia in *Idomeneo* and a wonderful Mélisande at Munich (1973). An attractive and very gifted actress-singer.

MATTERS, ARNOLD (1903–). Australian baritone, notably at the Wells and Covent Garden from the 1930s to the mid-1950s, except the war years. The first British Boccanegra (Sadler's Wells, 1948), he created Pilgrim in Vaughan Williams's *Pilgrim's Progress* at Covent Garden (1951).

MATZENAUER, MARGARETE (1881–1963). Hungarian contralto, later soprano, especially noted for her Wagnerian roles in Germany (including Bayreuth) and at the Met (1911–30). These included Kundry, Isolde, Brünnhilde and Ortrud. The Met's first Eboli, and first Kostelnička in *Jenufa* (1924), opposite Jeritza.

MAUREL, VICTOR (1848–1923). French baritone, one of the greatest actor-singers in operatic history, a conceited man with plenty to be conceited about. His voice was not exceptional, but his technique and artistry were superb. He had the fire of his native Marseilles, so Philip Hope-Wallace has written, and his firsts included the American Amonasro (1880) and, immortally, Iago (1887) and Falstaff (1893). He was also a painter, designer, lecturer and teacher, and acted in the straight theatre for a time. He was not only London's first Iago and Falstaff, but also Covent Garden's first Dutchman (1877), and he was the Met's first Falstaff.

MAYR, RICHARD (1877–1935). Austrian bass-baritone who made his début as Hagen (Bayreuth, 1902) and was a notable Gurnemantz. However, his most famous role was Baron Ochs in which we are told he has never been equalled. In Vienna (1902–35), at Covent Garden (1924–31) and at the Met (1927–30), this glorious creation was seen and heard, while he was also a renowned Salzburg Figaro, Leporello and Sarastro, and in Vienna the first Barak in *Die Frau ohne Schatten* (1919).

MEI-FIGNER, MEDEA (1858–1952). See Nikolay Figner, page 144.

MELBA, (DAME) NELLIE (1861–1931). Australian soprano and one of the most famous singers in history. Born Helen Mitchell, her name came from her native Melbourne. Technically brilliant, her voice remained fresh and pure until her epic Farewell at Covent Garden (1926). Verdi was one of many composers who admired her singing, but her acting was more than somewhat basic. As to her alleged cold interpretations, many were so carried away with her vocal art that they will not admit this failing. Her last note of Act I in *La Bohème* is a Covent Garden legend, but then everything about her is now legendary including her say in casting at the same theatre. A Marchesi student, her début was in Brussels as Gilda (1887), while her Covent Garden début was as Lucia (1888), a success, but not in the same class as her Juliette the following season. She was rarely absent from the Garden until her retirement, beginning as a coloratura, including Violetta and Rosina, then turning to Desdemona, Marguerite, etc. and the role she made her own in London —some would say cornered— Mimi. She also sang Aida and was the first London Nedda (1893). She sang most seasons at the Met from 1893–1911 and at La Scala, Chicago, St Petersburg, Paris, etc. She was a Sacred Monster if ever there was one, but also a Dinkum Aussie who did much to encourage young singers, even female ones *after* she had retired.

MELCHIOR, LAURITZ (1890–1973). Danish, later American, tenor, one of the greatest of all *Heldentenors*, who sang Tristan over 200 times. He began as a baritone in Copenhagen, making a second début as Tannhäuser (1918). His career facts speak for themselves: Covent Garden, 1924 and 1926–39, Bayreuth, 1924–31, and the Met, 1926–50, singing at the last over 500 times. His thrilling, untiring voice was beyond criticism, though his artistry and sensitivity as a musician was occasionally questioned. But Frida Leider, who sang opposite him so often, recalled for *Opera* (May 1973): 'To me he was always the perfect Tristan ... and the greatest *Heldentenor* of his time.' Apart from Tristan and Siegfried, he was also a notable Otello, despite difficulty with his words, and he sang all the great heroic Wagner roles.

MELNIKOV, IVAN (1832–1906). Russian baritone, the first Boris Godunov (1874), Don Juan in Dargomizhsky's *The Stone Guest* (1872), etc.

MERLI, FRANCESCO (1887–). Italian tenor, regularly at La Scala and Rome between the two world wars, and at Covent Garden and the Met. He was Covent Garden's first Calaf (1926) and other famous roles included Otello.

MERRILL, ROBERT (1917–). American baritone, at the Met (1945–) except when Bing suspended him for a season for going to Hollywood instead of touring. His rich voice is best known outside the U.S.A. by his many records. He was admired by Toscanini, for whom he sang Germont and Renato in broadcasts and recordings.

MERRIMAN, NAN (1920–). American mezzo-soprano, chosen by Toscanini for broadcasts and recordings, including Gluck's Orfeo. She was Britain's first Baba the Turk in *The Rake's Progress* (Glyndebourne at Edinburgh, 1953).

MEYER, KERSTIN (1928–). Swedish mezzo-soprano, a most notable and attractive actress-singer, whose début at Stockholm was as Azucena (1952) to her 58-year-old 'son', Set Svanholm. Regularly at Bayreuth since 1964, her roles include Dido in Berlioz's *The Trojans* (London, 1960) and Carmen, Octavian and Brangäne. Her 1973 performances included a superb (if incomprehensible in English) Claire in Einem's *The Visit of the Old Lady* and a delightfully funny Clairon in *Capriccio*, both at Glyndebourne. A striking Kostelnička in *Jenufa* at the Edinburgh Festival (1974).

MICHEAU, JANINE (1914–76). French soprano, the Opéra-Comique's first Zerbinetta and Anne Trulove (*The Rake's Progress*) and, at the Opéra (from 1936), the creator of the title role in Milhaud's *Médée*.

MIKHAILOV, MAXIM (1893–). Russian bass, a leading singer at the Bolshoi from 1932.

MILANOV, ZINKA (1906–). Yugoslav soprano at the Met from 1937–66. A magnificent dramatic soprano with a most beautiful voice.

MILDMAY, AUDREY (1900–53). English soprano, with the Carl Rosa, etc.; then she married John Christie (see page 319 and was the inspiration behind Glyndebourne where she delightfully sang Susanna, Zerlina and Norina. *See also* p. 318.

MILNES, SHERRILL (1935–). American baritone whose formidable voice and fine physique

have made him greatly in demand since the mid-1960s. Especially renowned for his Verdi roles at the Met and elsewhere, including Miller in *Luisa Miller*, this stirring singer and no-nonsense actor is an asset to any performance. He created the role of Adam Brant in David Levy's *Mourning Becomes Electra* at the Met (1967).

MIOLAN-CARVALHO, MARIE (1827–95). French soprano, a great favourite in Paris at the Opéra-Comique (1949–55) and the Théâtre-Lyrique (1856–67), and also at Covent Garden (1859–64, 1871–2). Much admired by Gounod, she created Marguerite in *Faust*, Juliette in *Roméo et Juliette* and the title role in *Mireille*. An attractive woman, her husband was the impresario Léon Carvalho.

MIURA, TAMAKI (1884–1946). Japanese soprano and a famous Butterfly in Boston, Chicago, etc. having previously sung the role in London. She created Messager's *Madame Chrysanthème* in Chicago (1920) and also sang in Japan, Mimi being one of her roles.

MINTON, YVONNE (1938–). Australian mezzo-soprano who joined the Covent Garden Company in 1965 and rapidly established herself as an attractive and gifted actress-singer. Outstanding roles include Octavian, Dorabella,

Marina in *Boris Godunov*, Orfeo, etc. The first Thea in *The Knot Garden* (Tippett). In 1974 she made a successful Bayreuth début as Brangäne, and her Sestro in *La Clemenza di Tito* at Covent Garden, 1974–6, is a masterpiece.

MODL, MARTHA (1912–). German mezzo, then soprano, now mezzo again, and one of the most exciting singers to appear since the war. She became a Bayreuth regular in 1951, singing Kundry and, later, Brünnhilde, Isolde, Gutrune and Sieglinde, and she was Leonore in *Fidelio* at the re-opening of the Vienna State Opera (1955). She has also been one of the finest Carmens of modern times, dedicated enough to learn the part in English for Covent Garden (1949). First sang at the Met in 1956. One of her greatest roles has been Klytemnestra in Strauss's *Elektra*. Her Covent Garden performance (1966) was accurately summed up by Harold Rosenthal as shattering, and he wrote in *Opera* of her powerful personality, wonderful diction, use of tone colour and complete abandonment to the role. This superb actress-singer has also appeared in modern works and as Ruth in *The Pirates of Penzance* (Cassel, 1973).

MOFFO, ANNO (1935–). American soprano who made her début as Butterfly on Italian television (1956), her looks being very photogenic (and her cleavage once making President Nixon blush). At the Met since 1961, she has also sung elsewhere in America, at Covent Garden, etc. her most famous roles including Violetta.

MONGINI, PIETRO (1830–74). Italian tenor, the creator of Radamès at Cairo (1871). He sang regularly in London in the 1860s and 1870s.

MOODY, FANNY (1866–1945). English soprano who married Charles Manners (see above, page 169) and formed the Moody-Manners Co. with him. The first English Tatiana (1892). She was a noted Mignon, Marguerite and Arline in *The Bohemian Girl*, and sang Wagner's earlier heroines in English. A fine artist.

MOORE, GRACE (1901–47). American soprano, ex-musical comedy and night club star, a Met regular from her début there as Mimi in 1928, and also well known in Paris. Mimi at Covent Garden in 1935. Her glamour more than compensated most people for her ordinary, though not negligible, vocal talent, and she rendered opera a great service through her films, most notably *One Night of Love*. Killed in a plane crash.

MORENA, BERTA (1878–1952). German soprano and beauty,

at Munich from 1898 to 1924, and also at the Met. Isolde and Brünnhilde were her most famous roles.

MORISON, ELSIE (1924–). Australian soprano, at Sadler's Wells (1948–54) and Covent Garden from 1953 until the 1960s. An enchanting Susanna and an outstanding Mimi, she was the first British Blanche in *The Carmelites* (1958) and the first British Anne Trulove in *The Rake's Progress* (Glyndebourne at Edinburgh, 1953).

MÜLLER, MARIA (1898–1958). Austrian soprano, best known in Wagner (Bayreuth, 1930–9) but a famous Iphigénie (Gluck) and Jenufa also. Eva was one of her finest roles. This actress-singer was at Berlin (1926–43, 1950–2), the Met (1925–35), Salzburg (1931–4) and Covent Garden in 1934 and 1937.

MULLINGS, FRANK (1881–1953). English tenor, the greatest of native Otellos. He was also a famous Wagnerian. With Beecham (1916–21) and the British National Opera Company (1922–6).

MUNSEL, PATRICE (1925–). American soprano, at the Met from 1943 for many years, and especially successful in coloratura roles, including Filine in Thomas's *Mignon*, also popular as Despina, Adele, etc.

MUZIO, CLAUDIA (1889–1936). Italian soprano, famous in Europe and America for her lovely voice, intelligence, depth of feeling and warm personality. The daughter of the stage manager of Covent Garden and the Met, she triumphed in both houses. New York (1916–22, 1933–4) and Chicago (1922–31) knew her best and she was also immensely popular in Buenos Aires and Rome. Her creations included Giorgetta in Puccini's *Il Tabarro* at the Met (1918), while her most famous roles included Violetta and Desdemona. Her single season at Covent Garden is legendary: Manon Lescaut; Tosca, brilliantly replacing Edvina; Desdemona, succeeding Melba; Mimi; and Alice in *Falstaff*.

NASH, HEDDLE (1896–1961). English tenor. Between the two world wars, he sang at the Old Vic, Sadler's Wells, Covent Garden and Glyndebourne, and was later with the Carl Rosa and New Opera Company. The possessor of a beautiful lyric voice, his most famous parts were Don Ottavio and David in *Die Meistersinger*. His son is the baritone, John Heddle Nash.

NEIDLINGER, GUSTAV (1912–). German bass-baritone, for many years at Bayreuth (from 1952), Hamburg (1936–50) and Stuttgart (from 1950). Particularly fine as Alberich and Pizarro.

NEMETH, MARIA (1899–1967).
Hungarian soprano, a famous
Turandot, Tosca and Donna
Anna between the wars, especi-
ally in Vienna.

NESSI, GIUSEPPE (1887–1961).
Italian tenor, La Scala's famous
comprimàrio (see page 330),
1921–59, at Covent Garden
from 1927–37. His creations
included Pang in *Turandot*
(1926).

NEVADA, EMMA (1859–1940).
American soprano, one of the
greatest of all Bellini singers,
whose medallion was put beside Pasta's and Malibran's on
his statue in Catania. Her
London début was as Amina in
1880 and, five years later (with
Mapleson), she was singing it
in St Joseph, Missouri.

NEWAY, PATRICIA (1919–).
American soprano, the first
and greatest Magda Sorel in
The Consul (1948). This striking
looking actress-singer has also
been a notable Marie in *Wozzeck*, Tosca, and Katiusha in
Alfano's *Risurrezione* at the
Opéra-Comique, where it was
revived for her (1954).

NICHOLLS, AGNES (1877–
1959). English soprano. She
sang with Beecham and for the
British National Opera Company, and was the Sieglinde
and *Siegfried* Brünnhilde of
Richter's English *Ring* (1908).

NIEMANN, ALBERT (1831–1917).
German tenor, and a legendary
Wagnerian who was the first
Paris Tannhäuser (1861), the
first Siegmund (1876) at Bayreuth and in London (1882),
and the Met's first Tristan and
Siegfried in *Götterdämmerung*
(1886–8).

NILSSON, BIRGIT (1918–).
Swedish soprano, the natural
successor as a supreme Wagnerian to Flagstad, though a
trumpet to the latter's warm
French horn. Her Isolde is
discussed on page 112, but her
Brünnhilde is as famous, not
least for the matchless reserves
of power she can muster. At
the Royal Opera Stockholm
(1946–), she has sung in a
variety of roles, including much
Verdi, was Glyndebourne's
Electra in *Idomeneo* (1951),
then became famous at Munich
as Brünnhilde and Salome,
since when she has been Europe
and America's leading Wagnerian soprano. Too cold in
voice and personality for some
tastes in Italian roles, her Turandot, however, is all ice and
fire. Not an actress-singer in
the true sense, she does not
neglect the dramatic side of her
work. Records have guaranteed
her immortality, though she
would be legendary because of
her voice whenever she had
lived.

NILSSON, CHRISTINE (1843–
1921). Swedish soprano who
made her début as Violetta in
Paris (1864) and created Ophélie in Thomas's *Hamlet* there

in 1868. She was the finest Mignon (Thomas) of her day, and sang Marguerite on the Met's opening night in 1883. This legendary lady also had beauty and charm in abundance.

NISSEN, HANS HERMANN (1893–). German bass-baritone, one of the finest performers of Sachs and Wotan, between the wars, in Munich and many European cities, and in America.

NOBLE, DENNIS (1899–1966). English baritone who sang regularly at Covent Garden and with the Carl Rosa and British National Opera Company. He excelled in the highest company, notably as Amonasro in 1937.

NONI, ALDA (1916–). Italian soprano with the Vienna State Opera during the war, then captivating London as Norina in the long run of *Don Pasquale* at the Cambridge Theatre (1946). Strauss chose her for Zerbinetta for his 80th birthday treat, *Ariadne auf Naxos* (Vienna, 1943), but she later became best known as a delicious soubrette, notably at Glyndebourne.

NORDICA, LILLIAN (1857–1914). American soprano who broke out of a New England puritan upbringing to make her début as Donna Elvira in Milan (1879). Her cosmopolitan career included Marguerite and Ophélie (Thomas's *Hamlet*) in Russia, and Verdi and, later, Wagner at Covent Garden, including Brünnhilde, Isolde, Venus and Aida, all in 1902. Elsa at Bayreuth (1894), the first American to sing there, and many triumphs at the Met between 1891 and 1910.

NORDMO-LØVBERG, AASE (1923–). Norwegian soprano. A notable Wagnerian in the 1950s and 1960s in Stockholm, Vienna (from 1958) and elsewhere, also singing Italian roles. A distinguished Eva, Sieglinde and Elsa.

NORENA, EIDÉ (1884–1968). Norwegian soprano, well known between the wars at La Scala, where she made her début as Gilda for Toscanini (1924), also Covent Garden and the Met.

NOURRIT, ADOLPHE (1802–39). French tenor who succeeded his father, Louis, at the Paris Opéra after making his début there, but left in 1837 when Duprez was engaged. The first Robert the Devil (1831—Meyerbeer), Masaniello in Auber's *La Muette de Portici*, Count Ory, Arnold in *William Tell*, etc.

NOVELLO, CLARA (1818–1908). English soprano, fine enough to excel in a very golden age. Rossini thought highly of her and she was one of the elect who were dragged home in a carriage (after *I Puritani* in Rome, 1842). Her roles included Bellini's Norma, Amina and Beatrice di Tenda, but she had doubts about Gilda because of the male clothes in the last scene. However, she relented, for 'all exposure was obviated in the costume arranged with my husband's help'.

NOVOTNÁ, JARMILA (1907–). Czech soprano, famous between the two world wars in Europe, and at the Met from 1939 to 1953, especially as Octavian and Donna Elvira.

OBER, MARGARET ARNDT (1885–1971). German mezzo-soprano, at Berlin (1906–44) and elsewhere, including the Met (1913–17) where she was the first to sing Octavian, also Eglantine in *Euryanthe* under Toscanini.

OESTVIG, KARL (1889–1968). Norwegian tenor, at the Vienna State Opera (1919–27) and elsewhere between the wars. A notable Wagnerian.

OHMS, ELISABETH (1888–). Dutch soprano, especially successful in Wagner at Munich (1926–36) and elsewhere, including Covent Garden. Toscanini's Leonore (*Fidelio*) and Kundry at La Scala (1927–9).

OLCZEWSKA, MARIA (1892–1969). German mezzo-soprano, famous between the wars, especially at Vienna (1923–36) and Covent Garden (1924–32), her roles including Fricka, Herodias and a splendidly repulsive Klytemnestra; also Amneris, Brangäne, Carmen, etc. She also sang in Chicago and at the Met.

OLIVERO, MAGDA (1914–). Italian soprano, a very famous actress-singer, the supreme Adriana Lecouvreur (Cilèa), also excelling in Puccini and Verdi. At the time of writing, her long career continues.

O'MARA, JOSEPH (1866–1927). Irish tenor, Sullivan's Ivanhoe in 1891 and the leading tenor of the Moody-Manners Company, finally running the O'Mara Company.

ONCINA, JUAN (1925–). Spanish tenor, a notable singer of Rossini and Donizetti, especially at Glyndebourne (1952–61), where his acting ability was much in evidence.

ONEGIN, SIGRID (1891–1943). Swedish contralto, well known between the two world wars in Europe especially for her Lady Macbeth, Fricka, Eboli, Orfeo, etc. She sang at Berlin from 1926–33.

OSTEN, EVA VON DER (1881–1936). German soprano, the creator of Octavian at Dresden, where she sang, 1902–30. She

was Covent Garden's first Oct-
avian, also its first Kundry
(1913–14), and was also a
famous Tosca and Tatiana.
Her husband was the singer
Friedrich Plaschke (1875–1951).
Her Octavian was hailed as
'sheer delight' in London,
where she also sang Ariadne,
Sieglinde and a wonderful
Isolde, while her husband sang
Amfortas, Kurwenal, etc.

O'SULLIVAN, JOHN (1878–1955).
Irish tenor, at the Paris Opéra
(1914–22 and 1929–30), also
singing at La Scala, Covent
Garden, Chicago, etc. his finest
parts being Arnold in *William
Tell*, Raoul in *Les Huguenots*
and Manrico.

OTTO, LISA (1919–). German
soprano, best known for her
excellent soubrette performances in Germany, at Salzburg
and at Glyndebourne (1957),
where her Blonde was out-
standing. At the Stadtische
Opera Berlin from 1952.

PACCHIEROTTI, GASPARO (1740–
1821). Italian male soprano
who conquered Italy in the
1770s and was hailed by Lord
Mount-Edgcumbe in 1778 as
'the most perfect singer it ever
fell to my lot to hear'.

PAGLIUGHI, LINA (1910–).
Italian soprano, especially famous for her Rossini, Bellini and
Donizetti roles in Italy and
elsewhere, though she was a

singer with a beautiful voice
and notable technique rather
than a dramatic vocalist.

PAMPANINI, ROSETTA (1900–).
Italian soprano, well known in
Italy and elsewhere between
the wars after Toscanini chose
her as Butterfly for La Scala.
When she sang the part at
Covent Garden (1928), Ernest
Newman noted her 'lovely
voice, of the genuine dramatic
timbre and bigness, capable of
the finest nuance'. Her other
famous roles included Mimi,
Liu and Desdemona, and the
title role in Mascagni's *Iris*.

PANERAI, ROLANDO (1924–).
Italian baritone with a most
engaging personality allied to
a fine voice, at his best in the
1950s and 1960s. A Salzburg
Figaro and Guglielmo.

PARETO, GRAZIELLA (1888–).
Spanish soprano, highly
regarded by Beecham and well-
known in the 1920s in Italy and
elsewhere. Her Leila (1920) in
The Pearl Fishers at Covent
Garden was much admired,
while her Violetta was magnifi-
ent.

PASERO, TANCREDI (1893–).
Italian bass, at La Scala (1926–
52) and elsewhere, whose fine
voice was used to great effect
in Italian, French, Russian and
German roles, including Boris
Godunov, Mefistofele, and
Wagnerian and Verdian parts.

PASTA, GIUDITTA (1798–1865). Italian soprano, one of the greatest and most famous singers in history, and the creator of Bellini's Norma and Adina in *La Sonnambula*, and Donizetti's Anna Bolena. This great actress-singer, 'classical' in the sense that her greatest successor, Malibran, was 'romantic' in her acting, was not a perfect singer, having, like Malibran, weak spots in her range, but less able to conceal them. Though she made her début in 1815, her fame dates from 1821 in Paris (see Stendhal's *Life of Rossini* for opera-maniac eulogies of her), and she was a great favourite in London, also triumphing in Russia. Tragically, she risked a come-back in London (1850) when she was 'the shadow of a shade' (Lumley) in scenes from *Anna Bolena*. Rachel laughed and Pauline Viardot-Garcia wept.

PATTI, ADELINA (1843–1919). Italian soprano whose stage début (as Little Florinda) was in New York (1859), singing Lucia. It was in the 1860s that she became famous and was soon a living legend, for without being a true actress-singer —she avoided rehearsals whenever possible, thanks to a clause in her contracts—and without, indeed, being a notable musician, she had an extraordinary voice, plus charm and looks. She excelled in coloratura and lyric roles, singing twenty-five consecutive seasons at Covent Garden in Rossini, Bellini, Donizetti, Verdi, Meyerbeer and Gounod, including the first London Juliette (1867) and the first London Aida (1876). She was such a superstar in Paris that, in Offenbach's *La Vie Parisienne*, the tourists long above all to hear Patti in *Don Pasquale*, while she gave her Violetta complete with her own diamonds and two detectives in the chorus keeping an eye on them. She got £200 per performance at Covent Garden, and 5,000 dollars in America where she occasionally appeared, as she sometimes did in Italy. Her return to Covent Garden for a Farewell Season saw her wearing £200,000 worth of diamonds (hence those detectives) and scoring a tremendous success as Violetta once again, then as Rosina, Zerlina (she had sung it with Grisi in 1861), and finally as Rosina just over thirty-four years after making her début in 1861. In 1894, she sang a song by Wagner to Bernard Shaw's delight, but then she even sang *God Save the Queen* as if it was a masterpiece.

PATZAK, JULIUS (1898–1973). Austrian tenor, at Munich (1928–45) and Vienna (1945–60), and elsewhere, and particularly famous in two roles: Pfitzner's Palestrina and Florestan (*Fidelio*), the latter much admired at Covent Garden. His voice was not an exceptional one, and was rather reedy in tone, but he was a great artist, first making his name as a Mozartian in the 1930s. He was able to range from operetta to the Evangelist in Bach's Passions, but perhaps the climax of his career was his Florestan under Furtwängler at Salzburg (1948–50).

PAULY, ROSA (1894–1975). Hungarian soprano, especially famous between the wars in Europe (including Vienna, 1931–8) and America. A fine actress, her Elektra was one of the greatest, and she was a noted Salome and Marie in *Wozzeck*.

PAVAROTTI, LUCIANO (1935–). Italian tenor, possessor of a big bold voice with stunning top notes. He is equally well known for his *bel canto* roles (Edgardo, Arturo in *I Puritani*, Tonio in *La Fille du Régiment*, often opposite Sutherland), and for his Rodolfo, Alfredo and Duke of Mantua. An international singer since the mid-60s, his great and deserved fame is due entirely to his voice and technique, though his personality is engaging and he acts pleasantly.

PEARS, PETER (1910–). English tenor who after singing with the Glyndebourne chorus (1938) and with Sadler's Wells in Mozartian and other roles, created Peter Grimes at the Wells in 1945. From 1946 Pears was with the English Opera Group, and it was he who originally conceived the idea of the Aldeburgh Festival. His other creations of Britten roles have been Male Chorus in *The Rape of Lucretia* (1947), Albert Herring (1947), Captain Vere in *Billy Budd* (1951), Essex in *Gloriana* (1953), Quint in *The Turn of the Screw* (1954), Flute in *A Midsummer Night's Dream* (1960), roles in the Church Parables, Sir Philip in *Owen Wingrave* (television, 1971), and Aschenbach in *Death in Venice*, a superb performance. One of the most musical and intelligent artists of our time. Not a born actor, his commitment to his art, including its theatrical side, is total. One of his most brilliant non-Britten performances was as Pandarus in Walton's *Troilus and Cressida* (1954).

PEASE, JAMES (1916–67). American bass-baritone who gave many notable performances at New York's City Center, Hamburg, Covent Garden and elsewhere, especially as a not-too-mature Wotan and Hans Sachs.

PEDERZINI, GIANNA (1906–). Italian mezzo-soprano, especially famous between the wars at La Scala, Rome and elsewhere, in Rossini, and as Carmen and Mignon. After the Second World War, she was particularly associated with roles which stressed her talents as an actress-singer, including Menotti's Medium and the

Countess in Tchaikovsky's *The Queen of Spades.*

PEERCE, JAN (1904–). American tenor who graduated from playing the violin and singing in dance bands to the Met (from 1941 until the 1960s). He has sung elsewhere in America and also in Europe and, significantly, for Toscanini in broadcasts which were recorded: *La Traviata, Un Ballo in Maschera, Fidelio, La Bohème.*

PERSIANI, FANNY (1812–67). Italian soprano, daughter of the hunchback tenor, Tacchinardi, and notable, sometimes notorious, for her dazzling ornamentation, brilliantly invented and executed. The first Lucia, written for her by Donizetti (San Carlo, Naples, 1835), and a favourite in London (1838–49) and Paris (1837–48). Her voice was thin in quality but clear and capable of the most astonishing effects. Her roles included Bellini's Amina, Norma and Elvira, and Camile in Hérold's *Zampa.* Her husband, the composer, Persiani, put up much of the money for the Royal Italian Opera which Covent Garden became in 1847, and she helped make it famous as such.

PERTILE, AURELIANO (1885–1952). Italian tenor, famous between the wars, especially at La Scala (1921–37), where he became Toscanini's favourite tenor. His voice was big but not beautiful, yet his artistry was such that he made a tremendous impression on audiences, not least at Covent Garden (1927–31) from his début as Radamès onward. An outstanding singer whose acting was not negligible, he created the title roles in Boito's *Nerone* (1924) and Wolf-Ferrari's *Sly* (1927).

PETERS, ROBERTA (1930–). American soprano, at the Met since 1950 and a famous coloratura, also blessed with charm and looks. At her peak in the 1950s and 1960s, her roles include Gilda and Rosina, and, at Salzburg (1963), the Queen of the Night.

PETRELLA, CLARA (1919–). Italian soprano and an actress-singer so brilliant that she was dubbed 'the Duse of Singers'. At her finest in the 1950s and 1960s after joining La Scala in 1947. One of her most famous roles was Giorgetta in Puccini's *Il Tabarro,* while her performance in the title-role of Pizzetti's *Clitennestra* (La Scala, 1965) was a triumph.

PETROV, IVAN (1920–). Russian bass, at the Bolshoi (since 1943) and elsewhere, including European opera houses outside Russia. His most famous role is Boris Godunov.

PETROV, OSSIP (1807–78). Russian bass, engaged for St Petersburg after being heard singing at a market fair. He created Ivan Susanin, Russlan and Varlaam.

PICCAVER, ALFRED (1884–1958). English tenor, for many years a major star in Vienna (1910–37), where he used his big voice to perfection, his phrasing and legato being famous. London, alas, only heard of him in 1924 (as Cavaradossi and the Duke in *Rigoletto*). He was Austria's first Johnson in *La Fanciulla del West* and Luigi in *Il Tabarro*.

PICCOLOMINI, MARIETTA (1834–99). Italian soprano, London's first Violetta (1856) and Luisa Miller (1858). She was from an ancient family and left the stage to marry an aristocrat in 1860, and was famous for her looks and acting rather than her voice.

PILARCZYK, HELGA (1925–). German soprano, at Hamburg (from 1954), and famous for her modern roles, notably Marie in *Wozzeck*, Lulu (Berg), the Woman in Schoenberg's *Erwartung*, also in Verdi and Strauss. An excellent actress-singer.

PINI-CORSI, ANTONIO (1858–1918). Italian baritone, the first Ford in *Falstaff* (1893) and Happy in *La Fanciulla del West* at the Met (1910). He was also a famous Bartolo, Pasquale and Leporello. His brother, Gaetano, was a successful Mime in *Siegfried*.

PINZA, EZIO (1892–1957). Italian bass, a magnificent actor-singer, striking looking and the possessor of a rich *basso-cantante* voice. He was the most famous Don Giovanni between the wars (and no slouch in the role off-stage), first making his name at Salzburg (1934) when Bruno Walter conducted the opera. At La Scala in the early 1920s, he sang at the Met from 1926 to 1948 and at Covent Garden, 1930–9. He was the Met's first Fiesco in *Simon Boccanegra* (1932), and operagoers could enjoy his art in such roles as Colline and Ramfis: he had a repertoire of ninety-five roles and sang in all the great houses. One of the greatest of all Italian basses, certainly the finest between the wars, he later became a Broadway superstar in *South Pacific*, being the man that Ensign Nellie Forbush hoped to wash out of her hair. He also played Chaliapin in *Tonight We Sing*, a film about Sol Hurok. This performance must be seen at all costs, not simply because it includes Pinza singing Boris, but because it is brilliantly acted and often hilarious. Track it down.

PIROGOV, ALEXANDER (1899–1964). Russian bass, at the Bolshoi from 1924, noted for his Boris, Méphistophélès, etc.

PLANÇON, POL (1854–1914). French bass, one of the few 'perfect' singers in operatic history, not simply because his voice was smooth, flexible and of enormous range; his runs and trills [*sic*] made sopranos green with envy. At the Opéra (1883–93), Covent Garden (1891–1904) and the Met (1893–1908), his most famous role was Méphistophélès.

POLLAK, ANNA (1915–). English mezzo-soprano, with Sadler's Wells from 1945 to the 1960s, also singing at Glyndebourne (Dorabella, 1953) and with the English Opera Group, creating Berkeley's Ruth (1956). Several of her performances were perfection, notably Hansel, Orlofsky and the Secretary in *The Consul*. Her Carmen, Cherubino, Dorabella, Suzuki, Calliope in *Orpheus in the Underworld*, etc., were much admired. A superb actress-singer.

PONS, LILY (1904–76). French soprano, at the Met from 1931 to 1959, where her coloratura, petite figure and charm brought her an enormous following as an enjoyable Lakmé (Delibes), Rosina, etc., and an undramatic Lucia. She also appeared in films.

PONSELLE, ROSA (1897–). American soprano (of Neapolitan parents), one of the greatest singers in operatic history, her voice being a thrilling dramatic soprano true throughout its range. At the Met (1918–37), Covent Garden

(1929–31) and elsewhere, she electrified audiences, her striking looks and acting ability adding to the tremendous impression she made as Violetta, Norma, La Gioconda, La Vestale, Leonora in *La Forza del Destino*, etc. She did the operatic state some extra service at Covent Garden for, in a period when Italian opera was considered by many to be inferior to German, and when *Norma* especially was regarded as a museum piece, she rekindled a flame which still has opera-lovers now in their 50s and more babbling happily to their juniors. She retired at the height of her powers, the nervous strain at the top having diminished (for her) the pleasure to be had.

PRANDELLI, GIACINTO (1916–). Italian tenor, one of those chosen by Toscanini to reopen La Scala (1946) and chosen by de Sabata for the 50th anniversary performance of Giordano's *Fedora* (1948), singing Loris.

PREY, HERMANN (1929–). German baritone, internationally famous especially in Mozart (Papageno and Guglielmo at Salzburg, 1974). A Bayreuth Wolfram (1965), the role he had sung in his Met début in 1960 after seasons with the Hamburg State Opera. This good-looking actor-singer is also noted in lieder.

PRICE, LEONTYNE (1927–). American soprano, at the Met since 1960 after earlier triumphing as Bess in *Porgy and Bess* (1952–4) on a world tour; also at Covent Garden, San Francisco and Chicago in Italian and French roles, including Aida (see page 113), Liu, Pamina and Thaïs (Massenet). Salzburg's Donna Anna (1960) and at La Scala since 1962, her rich creamy voice is one of the finest to be heard in recent times. Dramatic involvement has diminished with the years if a Covent Garden *Il Trovatore* (1970) is anything to go by, but she remains a thrilling artist. Created Cleopatra in Barber's *Antony and Cleopatra* at the opening of the new Met in Lincoln Center (1966).

PRICE, MARGARET. Welsh soprano, one of the supreme Mozart singers of the day, possessing a beautiful, thrilling, creamy voice, and dramatic ability. Now internationally famous as Fiordiligi, Constanze and, especially, Donna Anna. Her performance as the last at Cologne in 1971 shot her to superstardom. Vienna and Munich have heard her great interpretation since.

PRING, KATHERINE. English mezzo-soprano, at Sadler's Wells since 1968. Already a notable actress-singer: Thea in Tippett's *The Knot Garden* (1972) at Covent Garden, Car-

men, Eboli (1974), etc. at the Coliseum.

PROHASKA, JARO (1891–1965). Austrian bass-baritone, well known between the wars and later, especially in Berlin and at Bayreuth, his most notable parts being Wotan, the Dutchman, Hans Sachs and Amfortas.

QUILICO, LOUIS. Canadian baritone whose large and beautiful voice was heard to advantage in Italian roles at Covent Garden and Paris in the 1960s, and who is now a principal singer at the Met.

RADFORD, ROBERT (1874–1933). English bass, one of the finest native singers of the century, who made his Covent Garden début as the Commendatore in *Don Giovanni* in 1904. Hagen and Hunding in Richter's English *Ring* and, later, a leading singer for Beecham and the British National Opera Company, of which he was a founder and director.

RAIMONDI, GIANNI (1925–). Italian tenor, notable since the 1950s, especially in early Verdi and Donizetti at La Scala (since 1955) and elsewhere in Europe and America. Typical of his artistry at its best was his Carlo in *I Masnadieri* (Rome, 1972). Occasionally, a lack of subtlety has been noted against him, but his career has been a very fine one.

RAIMONDI, RUGGERO (1941–). Italian bass, a notable Don Giovanni who sings all the notes in the Champagne aria and who looks the part; also a fine Boris Godunov (Venice, 1973), Banquo, Fiesco in *Simon Boccanegra*. A magnificent Silva in *Ernani* at Verona (1972) and a stirring Attila at Edinburgh (1972). Italy's leading bass (1976).

RAISA, ROSA (1893–1963). Polish soprano who, after being forced to flee from persecution (being Jewish), reached Naples, making her début as Leonora in Verdi's *Oberto* (Parma, 1913). At Chicago 1913–37, she also sang seasons at La Scala and Covent Garden. Her creations included Turandot (La Scala, 1926), and this exciting actress-singer was also much admired as Norma and Tosca.

RALF, TORSTEN (1901–54). Swedish tenor, a famous Wagnerian at Dresden (1935–44), Covent Garden (1935–9, 1948) and at the Met (1945–8). His finest parts included Lohengrin, Walther, Parsifal, Otello and Radamès.

RANALOW, FREDERICK (1873–1953). Irish baritone, with Beecham as Figaro, Sachs, Papageno, etc. then the most famous of the Macheaths in the enormous run of *The Beggar's Opera* (1922–3) at the Lyric, Hammersmith.

RANKIN, NELL (1926–). American mezzo-soprano, with the Met (from 1951) and other American companies, and at Covent Garden (1953) where her singing as Carmen was admired more than her acting, and whose Ortrud was notable.

RASA, LINA (1907–). Italian soprano and Mascagni's favourite Santuzza; also a notable Tosca.

REEVES, SIMS (1818–1900). English tenor, a famous and handsome Edgardo in *Lucia* at La Scala (1846) and Drury Lane (1847), also a notable Faust (1864).

REICHER-KINDERMANN, HEDWIG (1853–83). German soprano, daughter of August Kindermann (see page 158), the baritone, and Erda and Grimgerde in the first Bayreuth *Ring* (1876). She was Fricka in the first London *Ring* (1882) and Brünnhilde in the second, both at Her Majesty's.

REICHMANN, THEODOR (1849–1903). German baritone, the first Amfortas (Bayreuth, 1882), also singing Wolfram and Hans Sachs there.

REINHARDT, DELIA (1892–1974). German soprano, well known in Germany, London and New York in the 1920s, especially as Octavian in the incomparable Lehmann, Schumann and Mayr performances of *Der Rosenkavalier* under Walter. She was a fine Cherubino and a famous Elsa, Eva and Pamina, also shining as Mimi and Butterfly, even if not Italianate enough for some tastes. Desdemona was another notable role, and she made much of Micaela (Covent Garden, 1927), always a sign of a good singer with personality.

REINING, MARIA (1905–). Austrian soprano, notably at the Vienna State Opera (1931–3 and 1937–55), also at Salzburg from 1937 (when she sang Eva for Toscanini) until 1949, her other most famous parts being Strauss's Arabella and the Marschallin.

REIZEN, MARK (1895–). Russian bass, at the Bolshoi from 1930. His famous parts included Boris, Gremin in *Eugene Onegin* and Dosifey in *Khovanshchina.*

REMEDIOS, ALBERTO (1935–). English tenor who joined the Wells in 1957, singing Erik in *The Flying Dutchman*, Bacchus in *Ariadne auf Naxos*, Samson, etc. without giving much indication (whatever is said now) that a great Wagnerian tenor was waiting in the wings. His Walther (1968) was the beginning of his sensational climb. Then, after a spell in Frankfurt, came his Siegfried in the Goodall *Ring*, lyrical, yet powerful, well-acted, good-looking, altogether admirable.

RENAUD, MAURICE (1861–1933). French baritone, a notable actor-singer from the 1880s until the First World War, in Brussels, Paris, London and with several American companies. A most distinguished singer, though his voice was neither very big nor remarkable for its range. He created a number of roles, and was the Opéra's first Beckmesser and Alberich.

RESNIK, REGINA (1924–). 1976). German, later American first-rate actress-singer, at the Met since 1944, and a popular visitor to Covent Garden since 1957. Her Mistress Quickly in *Falstaff* is a masterpiece, not least her 'Reverenza'. Other successes have been Carmen, Hérodias and Amneris, while her creations include the Baroness in Barber's *Vanessa* (1958). She was New York's first Ellen Orford.

RETHBERG, ELISABETH (1894–1976). German, later American soprano, a lyric-dramatic singer with a lovely voice, and one of the finest artists of the 1920s and 1930s. At the Met, 1922–42, and Covent Garden, 1926 and 1934–9, she also appeared in Milan and Salzburg, having made her début in Dresden in 1915. It was in Dresden that she created the title role in *Die Aegyptische Helena* (1928). Her Covent Garden roles included Mimi, Butterfly, Dorota in Weinberger's *Schwanda the*

Bagpiper, Jaroslavna in *Prince Igor*, the Marschallin, Elsa—one of her greatest roles—and Aida, the finest of her time, but not, alas, Desdemona, another of her major triumphs. Toscanini is said to have agreed with the result of a ballot voting her the world's perfect singer.

REYNOLDS, ANNA. English mezzo-soprano, a Bayreuth Fricka, Waltraute and Magdalene of the 1970s, best known in Britain for her fine work with Scottish Opera.

RICCIARELLI, KATIA (1946–). Italian soprano of promise but, at the time of writing, still controversial, her Mimi in Turin and at Covent Garden, like her La Scala début as Suor Angelica, suggesting that she is not a Puccinian, but her Elsa in Turin (1973), despite 'almost totally incomprehensible diction' (Giorgio Gualerzi), was something of a triumph, and her Amelia in *Simon Boccanegra* at Verona (1973) was superb.

RIDDERBUSCH, KARL. German bass who first appeared at Bayreuth in 1967 where he has sung Hunding, Hagen, etc. King Mark at Salzburg (1972), a most moving performance. He has appeared at Vienna, Covent Garden, the Met and Buenos Aires, other notable roles including Ochs, Fasolt and Sachs. A commanding presence.

ROBIN, MADO (1918–60). French soprano, a famous Lucia and Lakmé (Delibes), singing in Paris, Brussels, San Francisco and elsewhere, and able, apparently, to reach the highest note ever, one for the bats, the C above top C.

ROBINSON, FORBES (1926–). English bass, at Covent Garden since 1954, his most famous parts being Moses in *Moses and Aaron*, Claggart in *Billy Budd*, and the title-role in Tippett's *King Priam*. Has appeared widely in Britain and Europe, and America. An asset to any company.

RODE, WILHELM (1887–1959). German bass-baritone, regarded by some as the finest heroic baritone of the 1920s and 1930s. At Munich, Vienna, Salzburg, Berlin, etc. his roles including Wotan, the Dutchman and Hans Sachs.

ROSING, VLADIMIR (1890–1963). Russian tenor who made his début as Lensky in *Eugene Onegin* in St Petersburg and sang Herman in the British première of *The Queen of Spades* (1915). Ran the British Music-Drama Opera Company with Albert Coates (1936), which lasted one season and produced, amongst other works, the latter's *Pickwick*. Later Rosing produced opera in New York and Chicago.

Boris Christoff as Boris Godunov and Anne Pashley as Feodor at Covent Garden in 1974. The great Bulgarian's first Boris on any stage had been there in 1949.

Above left. Luigi Lablache as Caliban in Halévy's *The Tempest.*
Above right. Maria Malibran. *Below left.* Malibran's sister, Pauline
Viardot-Garcia. *Below right.* Christine Nilsson.

Adelina Patti (1843–1919), the superstar who made her début as Lucia in 1859 under the name of 'Little Florinda'. She sang in 25 consecutive seasons at Covent Garden and saw to it that her contract included a 'no-rehearsals' clause.

Left. Jean de Reszke as Siegfried. *Right.* Alberto Remedios as Siegfried and Clifford Grant as Hagen in the English National Opera's *The Twilight of the Gods. Below.* Ludmila Dvorakova as Isolde and Jess Thomas as Tristan in the Solti–Hall *Tristan and Isolde* at Covent Garden in 1971.

Callas, La Divina, as Tosca at Covent Garden in 1964.

Sutherland, La Stupenda, as Lucia at La Scala in 1961.

Above left. Wolfgang Amadeus Mozart. *Above right*. Richard Strauss. *Below*. Giuseppe Verdi and his incomparable librettist Arrigo Boito at the time of *Falstaff* (1893).

Above. Richard Wagner. *Above right*. Enrico Caruso as seen by himself. *Right*. Puccini with his Girl of the Golden West in his clutches, as seen by Caruso, the original Dick Johnson.

Above left. Beverly Sills. *Above.*
Shirley Verrett as Carmen. *Left.*
Leontyne Price. *Right.* Sherrill
Milnes. An all-American galaxy.

Above. The legendary *Così fan tutte* of Scottish Opera, 1967. (Left to right) Janet Baker, Elizabeth Harwood, Jennifer Eddy, Ryland Davies, Peter van der Bilt. *Below.* The ultimate *Tosca*: Callas and Gobbi in Act II of the Zeffirelli production at Covent Garden in 1964.

Placido Domingo as Turiddu and Pauline Tinsley as Santuzza in
Cavalleria Rusticana at Covent Garden in 1976, when Domingo also
sang Canio in *Pagliacci*.

Above. Benjamin Britten and Peter Pears. *Below.* Jon Vickers as Peter Grimes, Heather Harper as Ellen Orford and John Maguire as John at Covent Garden in 1975 in the Davis–Elijah Moshinsky production.

Above. Marie Collier as Emilia Marty and Gregory Dempsey as Albert Gregor in the Sadler's Wells production of Janacek's *The Makropoulos Case*. *Below*. The Welsh National Opera's production in Cardiff of *Jenufa*, a joint production (1975) with Scottish Opera.

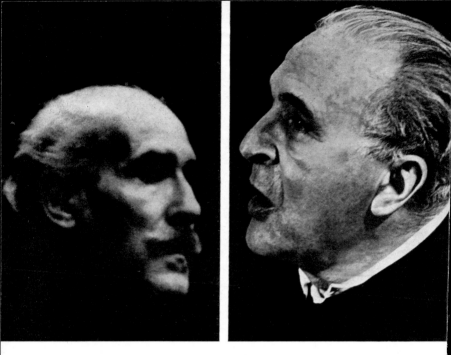

Above left. Arturo Toscanini. *Above right*. Bruno Walter.
Below left. Georg Solti. *Below right*. Carlo Maria Giulini.

ROSSI-LEMINI, NICOLA (1920–).
Italian bass, now also a producer. Not one of the greatest bass
voices of our day, he has more
than made up for it by a notable
career as an actor-singer, allied
to striking looks. At La Scala
(from 1947) and other leading
houses, he has been a famous
Boris and Méphistophélès
(Gounod's and Boito's),
while also giving fine performances as Gruenberg's *The Emperor Jones* and Bloch's *Macbeth*,
being less happily cast vocally
and stylistically as Don Giovanni. Memorably created the
title-role in Zafred's *Wallen-
stein* at Trieste (1970). For his
wife, Virginia Zeani, see p. 213.

ROSWAENGE, HELGE (1897–).
Danish tenor, at his peak from
the 1920s to the late 1940s, in
Berlin, Salzburg, etc. his most
famous roles including Florestan and Tamino, though he has
also been an exciting singer of
Italian roles, including Radamès, Manrico and Calaf. He
was Bayreuth's Parsifal, 1934–
6, and was regarded as a
magnificent lyric-dramatic
tenor.

ROTHENBERGER, ANNELIESE
(1924–). German soprano, an
excellent artist, pretty enough
to have played Adele in a film,
and who has been delighting
European audiences since joining Hamburg Opera in 1949
and Vienna 1956. Glynde-
bourne's enchanting Sophie in
Der Rosenkavalier (1959), and

a favourite at Salzburg and the
Met. She has had great success
as Lulu (Berg) and as Zdenka
in *Arabella*.

ROTHMÜLLER, MARKO (1908–
). Yugoslav baritone who
made his début in Hamburg
(1932), but became famous as
a fine actor-singer in the 1940s,
notably at Covent Garden
(1948–55) and with Glyndebourne (1949–52). He also
appeared at the New York City
Center (1948–52), at the Met,
and in Vienna and Berlin, his
most famous roles being Rigoletto, Scarpia and Wozzeck.

ROULEAU, JOSEPH (1929–).
Canadian bass, with Covent
Garden since 1957: King Philip,
Timur (*Turandot*), Fiesco in
Simon Boccanegra; also, the
finest Sparafucile for decades.
He has sung widely abroad,
including Russia, and Boris for
Scottish Opera.

RUBINI, GIOVANNI (1794–1854).
Italian tenor, one of the most
famous in operatic history, for
whom the tenor leads in
Bellini's *Il Pirata*, *La Sonnambula* and *I Puritani*, and Donizetti's *Anna Bolena* were
written. His truly fabulous career began in Italy, was boosted
when he went to Paris (1825)
and caused sensations with his
Rossini singing, then grew
even more spectacular with
his successes in London and
St Petersburg. His sweet
yet powerful voice ascended

happily to high **D**, much to the discomfort of later tenors in his roles, and he was a magnificent singer of even the most florid music. He was, however, accused of mannerisms, too much vibrato and of being the first great singer to sob (musically). But Rossini called him incomparable.

RUFFO, TITTA (1877–1953). Italian baritone whose voice was one of the most beautiful and biggest of his day, a day that extended from his début in Rome in 1898 as the Herald in *Lohengrin*, until the 1930s, though his voice was still in grand shape when he died. His most famous parts were the great Verdi roles, also Scarpia (*Tosca*), Thomas's Hamlet and Tonio (*Pagliacci*). He fell foul of Melba at her worst, for he was so fine as Edgardo at the dress rehearsal of *Lucia di Lammermoor* in 1903 that Melba, down for the heroine, had him removed from the cast because he was too young to play her father. Years later, he was able to object to her in the same role at another house, as being too old to be his daughter.

RYSANEK, LEONIE (1926–). Austrian soprano, at the Vienna State Opera (since 1954) and elsewhere, including London and New York. Sieglinde in the first post-war Bayreuth (1951), also singing Senta and Elsa there in later festivals. This major lyric-dramatic sop-

rano rapidly made her name also as a Verdian and a famous singer of Strauss roles, notably Danae (*Die Liebe der Danae*), Aegyptische Helena and the Kaiserin in *Die Frau ohne Schatten*. Superb in this last role at Salzburg (1974), while her 1972 Medea (Cherubini) in Vienna was acclaimed as a masterpiece.

SALIGNAC, THOMAS (1867–1945). French tenor who, in the 1890s and early 1900s, sang in Paris (creating many roles by Massenet, Milhaud, etc.), at Covent Garden and the Met as Don José, Canio, Roméo, Don Ottavio, etc. A fine actor-singer.

SALTZMANN-STEVENS, MINNIE (1874–1950). American soprano, a magnificent Brünnhilde in the first English *Ring* (1909) and, later, a Bayreuth Kundry and Sieglinde.

SAMMARCO, MARIO (1868–1930). Italian baritone whose beautiful voice was heard in the 1890s and early years of this century at La Scala, other Italian houses, and in London and New York. He quickly made his name at Covent Garden, after his début as Scarpia (1904), in other Puccini roles, as well as roles in operas of Giordano and Verdi.

SANDERSON, SYBIL (1865–1903). American soprano, a favourite

of Massenet's who wrote *Esclarmonde* and *Thaïs* for her. An actress-singer, renowned for her high notes and looks.

SANTLEY, (SIR) CHARLES (1834–1922). English baritone, knighted in 1907, and one of the most renowned singers ever produced by Britain. His Valentin in *Faust* (1863), the first in England, so pleased Gounod that he wrote 'Even bravest heart' for him. He was the first Dutchman in the first production of any Wagner opera in England (1870). He also sang in Europe, including La Scala, and in America.

SAYÃO, BIDU (1902–   ). Brazilian soprano, at the Met, 1937–51, where she was a noted Mimi, Manon, Juliette, Mélisande, etc. also singing in Europe and South America.

SCARIA, EMILIA (1838–86). Austrian bass at Dresden, Vienna, etc. and the first Gurnemanz at Bayreuth (1882), and London's first Wotan (1882).

SCHACK, BENEDIKT (1758–1826). Bohemian-German tenor, also composer, the first Tamino in *The Magic Flute* (1792), with his wife as one of the Three Ladies. He played his own flute.

SCHEFF, FRITZI (1879–1954). Austrian soprano who, after a notable career in Germany, at Covent Garden and the Met, became a major Broadway star. She was a famous Nedda, Zerlina and Musetta, and, singing the last at Covent Garden in 1903, was the victim of Melba at her bitchiest. At the climax of her Act II waltz song, the Diva's voice was heard 'helping her out', after which Miss Scheff very properly tried to scratch Melba's eyes out, then had hysterics. She was 'unable to continue' and Melba, ever game, marched on stage to sing the Mad Scene from *Lucia*.

SCHEIDEMANTEL, KARL (1859–1923). German baritone, notably at Bayreuth (1886–92), where his Amfortas, Wolfram and Sachs were much admired. He also sang at Covent Garden, and for many years in Dresden.

SCHIPA, TITO (1888–1965). Italian tenor. 'When Schipa sang, we all had to bow down to his greatness,' said Gigli. His technique, style, taste, enunciation, vocal colouring and phrasing bespoke the great artist, even though his actual voice was not large, and, from his La Scala début in 1915, until the 1950s, his career was as satisfying as a Rolls-Royce. At Chicago (1920–32), the Met for several seasons, Italy continually, while, at Monte Carlo in 1917, he created Ruggero in Puccini's *La Rondine*.

SCHIPPER, EMIL (1882–1957). Austrian bass-baritone, at Vienna, 1922–40, and in London and Chicago in the 1920s. A notable Wagner and Strauss singer.

SCHLUSNUS, HEINRICH (1888–1952). German baritone, at the Berlin State Opera, 1917–51. Between the wars, he was Germany's leading Verdi baritone.

SCHMEDES, ERIK (1866–1931). Danish tenor, at first a baritone, and at the Vienna Opera from 1898 to 1924. A Bayreuth Siegfried and Parsifal, he was one of the stars of the Mahler regime in Vienna.

SCHNORR VON CAROLSFELD, LUDWIG (1836–65). German tenor who became famous at Dresden (1860–5), then immortal as the first Tristan (Munich, 1865), dying soon after of rheumatic fever and heart failure. His wife, the Danish soprano Malvina Schnorr von Carolsfeld (1832–1904) was the first Isolde, and was not treated very kindly by Wagner after her husband's death. She sang in Hamburg and Karlsruhe and later taught.

SCHOEFFLER, PAUL (1897–). German baritone, of remarkable authority, whose début was as the Herald in *Lohengrin* in Dresden in 1925, and who was only prevented by injury from playing Antonio in *The Marriage of Figaro* in Paris in 1973. At Dresden until 193? when he joined the Vienna State Opera, he was famous before and after the war at Covent Garden and at the Met in the 1950s, also appearing at Bayreuth, Salzburg, etc. His creations include Danton in Einem's *Dantons Tod* (1947) and Jupiter in Strauss's *Die Liebe der Danae* (1952), while many consider that his greatest role was Hans Sachs.

SCHÖNE, LOTTE (1891– Austrian soprano, London first and excellent Liu (1927) and a notable Blonde, Zerlina and Despina at Salzburg (1922–34).

SCHORR, FRIEDRICH (1888–1953). Hungarian, then American, bass-baritone, outstanding as Wotan, Hans Sachs and the Dutchman in the 1920s and 1930s, at Bayreuth, Covent Garden and the Met; also Daniello in the first American *Jonny spielt auf* (1929). Not the least of his assets was the projection of a warm humanity, though his Wotan was splendidly god-like. His voice was richly dramatic and renowned for its beauty when singing *mezza voce*. A magnificent artist.

SCHRÖDER-DEVRIENT, WILHELMINE (1804–60). German soprano, the third of a matchless trio of incomparable actress-singers—the others being Pasta and Malibran—in an age when glory would scarcely be believable if it were not so well documented. Her most important single achievement was to stir the young Wagner so profoundly, totally ravaging his emotions by her performance of Leonore in *Fidelio*, that he was inspired to create his form of music drama. Ill-trained, her splendid, wide-ranging voice lost its top notes, and, like other supreme artists, her singing was less than perfect, but her acting ability, riveting personality and total commitment made 'the Queen of Tears' the most thrilling singer in Germany's operatic history. Her roles included Donna Anna in *Don Giovanni* and Weber's Euryanthe, and she was a legendary interpreter of Gluck and Bellini. She came from a family of actors and singers—indeed her mother, Antoinette Burger, was called 'the German Siddons'—but she was not a member of the famous Devrient family: that name came from her husband Karl, whom she later divorced. Past her best, she memorably created Adriano in *Rienzi*, Senta and Venus for Wagner, having earlier conquered London in the 1830s when Malibran was doing the same.

SCHUMANN, ELISABETH (1885–1952). German soprano who, thanks to the Nazis, settled in the U.S.A. Inter-war operagoers often claim her as the perfect Sophie, to which some would add her perfection as Adele, Susanna, Zerlina, Blonde. She sang in Vienna (1919–37), at Covent Garden (1924–31), Salzburg, Munich, etc. later becoming a teacher in America, where she had sung a season at the Met (1914–15). A bewitching personality.

SCHUMANN-HEINK, ERNESTINE (1861–1936). Czech, then American, contralto. At Hamburg (1883–98), then an international star at the Met, Covent Garden, Bayreuth etc. from the 1890s until 1932 (at the Met). A formidable-looking actress-singer, her voice was powerful and flexible, and her temperament dramatic, as befitted the first Klytemnestra in Strauss's *Elektra* (1909). Her 150 roles included Erda, Fricka, Brangäne and Amneris.

SCHWARZKOPF, ELISABETH (1915–). German soprano and beauty who made her name in Berlin and Vienna during the Second World War, including Susanna and Zerbinetta, then from 1947 became a lyric soprano, singing with the Vienna State Opera in London as Donna Elvira (1947). She joined the young Covent Garden Company (until 1951), singing Violetta, Pamina, Mimi, Eva and Butterfly, also a delightful Sophie, later (1959) singing the Marschallin to critical disapproval and public cheers. At Salzburg from 1947 and La Scala since 1948, she has been one of the most famous Mozart singers of the day, and was the first Anne Trulove in *The Rake's Progress* (Venice, 1951).

SCIUTTI, GRAZIELLA (1932–). Italian soprano, the perfect soubrette, her looks and acting being as delightful as her voice. Her parts include Susanna, Zerlina, Norina, Nanetta and Despina, and she has been with La Scala and the Piccola Scala since 1956. A Glyndebourne favourite (1954–9) and equally adored at Covent Garden (1956–62), also at Aix-en-Provence, where she made her début (1951) as Lucy in Menotti's *The Telephone*.

SCOTTI, ANTONIO (1866–1936). Italian baritone, one of the most famous actor-singers of his day at Covent Garden, especially the Met (1899–1933), and in Italy and elsewhere. London and New York's first Scarpia, London's first Sharpless and a famous Falstaff and Iago, he often sang with Caruso. His flexible voice was beautiful, if not big, and used with the utmost artistry. Like so many others, he was not a great Don Giovanni.

SCOTTO, RENATA (1934–). Italian soprano whose fine career began in the early 1950s, when she rapidly developed into a major singer. If her acting was not so obviously 'worked out', she would also rank as a major actress-singer: as it is, she is a considerable artist, her finest roles including Butterfly, Manon, Mimi, Adina and Violetta. At the Scala since 1953, she has appeared very successfully in London and elsewhere, including Edinburgh (1957), replacing an ailing Callas as Amina in *La Sonnambula*.

SEEFRIED, IRMGARD (1919–). German soprano, one of the legendary Vienna ensemble just after the war, having sung the Composer in *Ariadne auf Naxos* for Strauss's 80th birthday in 1944—it was one of her greatest roles. She was a famous Susanna, Pamina and Zerlina at Salzburg, complete with imaginative intensity, a lovely voice and delightful personality, but gradually turned more to concert work.

SEINEMEYER, META (1895–1929). German soprano, a noted lyric-dramatic soprano of the 1920s in Dresden, at Covent Garden, etc. in Verdi and Wagner, including Sieglinde.

SEMBRICH, MARCELLA (1858–1935). Polish soprano, famous in Europe and America from the 1880s and at the Met until 1909, her favourite part being Violetta. She was also a superb Lucia, Amina and Marguerite de Valois.

SENESINO (*c* 1680–*c* 1750). Italian male mezzo-soprano who created leading roles in many Handel operas. He seems to have been the perfect castrato, with a clear, penetrating voice and faultless technique, a flawless shake included.

SHACKLOCK, CONSTANCE (1913–). English mezzo-soprano, a pillar of the young Covent Garden Opera (1947–56), being a good-looking actress-singer with a wide range, including an excellent Brangäne and a fine Carmen, Ortrud, Octavian and Amneris. She has also sung in Russia, Australia and Holland.

SHARP, FREDERICK. English baritone, an actor-singer whose excellent performances at the Wells in the 1950s and 1960s included the Count in *Figaro*, Onegin, Germont and Sharpless.

SHAW, JOHN (1921–). Australian baritone, at Covent Garden (since 1958) and elsewhere. His many roles include Scarpia and Rigoletto, but he will live in operatic memory for his superb Ford in *Falstaff*.

SHERIDAN, MARGARET (1889–1958). Irish soprano, a good-looking actress-singer whom Toscanini chose for Catalani's La Wally at La Scala (1922), and who sang Mimi, Butterfly, etc. in the 1920s and 1930s at Covent Garden.

SHILLING, ERIC (1920–). English baritone, renowned for his brilliant operetta performances for the Wells, including Jupiter in *Orpheus in the Underworld* and the Lord Chancellor in *Iolanthe*.

SHIRLEY, GEORGE (1934–). American tenor, the first internationally famous black male opera singer. A superb and attractive artist who has appeared at Glyndebourne, Covent Garden, and with the Scottish Opera, in Europe, at the Met. His most notable roles include Tamino, Pelléas, Rodolfo, and Tom in *The Rake's Progress*.

SHIRLEY-QUIRK, JOHN (1931–). English baritone whose roles include Don Alfonso in *Così fan tutte*, the Count in *Figaro* and Coyle in *Owen Wingrave*, one of many Britten works in which he has sung with the English Opera Group. A fine actor-singer, he brilliantly played a number of parts in *Death in Venice* (1973). He has often performed with the Scottish Opera.

SHUARD, AMY (1924–1975). English soprano, at Sadler's Wells (1949–55) and Covent Garden from 1954, who also sang at La Scala, Bayreuth and Vienna, and in America. Though a renowned Turandot, as would befit a pupil of Eva Turner, and a notable Brünnhilde, Elektra and Kundry,

English opera-lovers now in their forties-plus have the happiest memories of her Santuzza, Butterfly, and, especially, her Magda Sorel in *The Consul* at the Wells in the 1950s. She added an impressive Kostelnička in Janáček's *Jenufa*, having earlier played the title role.

SIEMS, MARGARETHE (1879–1952). German soprano, at Dresden (1908–22), Covent Garden (1913) and Drury Lane (1914). Though her extraordinary voice and expressive art could range from Bellini roles to Amelia, Aida and Isolde, she is best remembered as a famous Strauss singer, creating Chrysothemis, the Marschallin (she was Strauss's favourite in the part) and Zerbinetta.

SIEPI, CESARE (1923–). Italian bass, at La Scala since 1946, the Met since 1950, Salzburg in the 1950s and elsewhere, including Covent Garden. Blessed with a superb appearance and considerable power, his most famous roles are Boris Godunov, Don Giovanni and Verdi's great bass parts.

SILJA, ANJA (1940–). German soprano, an exceptional actress-singer, who sang Senta at Bayreuth, aged 20, then, under the guidance of Wieland Wagner, triumphed not only in Wagner (Eva, Elisabeth), but as Leonore, Marie in *Wozzeck*, Lulu,

and a Salome (first at Stuttgart, 1962) which was 'Lilith and Lulu, virgin and death-goddess in one person' (Wieland Wagner). In her total commitment to music and drama, including grippingly vivid phrasing, she resembles Callas.

SILLS, BEVERLY (1929–). American soprano, internationally famous, but especially associated with the New York City Opera, a particular highlight of her career there being the 'Tudor Ring' (1973), with herself as Donizetti's Anna Bolena, Maria Stuarda and Queen Elizabeth (*Roberto Devereux*). A legendary figure in America, her fame, especially in *bel canto* roles, is based on her powers as an actress-singer. Her voice is exceptionally agile and most satisfying at the top (though she is a renowned lingerer on decorative moments), not as warm and opulent as some, but, allied to her personality and ability to project different characters dramatically, it makes her a superstar. Lucia and Violetta are among her roles, though it was her Cleopatra in Handel's *Giulio Cesare* (1966) which first made her a legend. She reached the Met in 1975.

SILVERI, PAOLO (1913–). Italian baritone whose short career in the 1940s and 1950s was a major one, notably in Verdi and Puccini. A fine Boris Godunov at Covent Garden (1948).

He served the young Covent Garden Opera Company well, especially as Rigoletto, Marcello, Amonasro and Di Luna.

SIMIONATO, GIULETTA (1910–). Italian mezzo-soprano who first sang at La Scala in 1939 and became internationally known in the late 1940s. At the Met from 1949, and Chicago from 1953, the year in which she sang three of her most famous roles at Covent Garden: Amneris, Azucena and Adalgisa. Her skill in coloratura also made her a famous singer of Rossini and Donizetti, including a splendid portrayal of Jane Seymour in *Anna Bolena* opposite Callas (La Scala, 1957), with whom she sang on many now legendary occasions. An impassioned Valentine in *Les Huguenots* (La Scala, 1963).

SIMONEAU, LÉOPOLD (1920–). Canadian tenor, well known for his distinguished Mozartian and French roles (including Meister in Thomas's *Mignon* and Nadir in *Les Pêcheurs des Perles*). From the late 1940s until the 1960s at Glyndebourne, Aix-en-Provence, Paris and elsewhere, including Covent Garden (1947–9).

SLADEN, VICTORIA (1910–). English soprano, with Sadler's Wells (1943–50) and also at Covent Garden (1947–52). Butterfly and, especially, Tosca, were her most notable roles.

SLEZAK, LEO (1873–1946). Austrian tenor, a big man with a big voice and a penchant for practical jokes on stage. At Vienna (1901–26), he also sang seasons at the Met (1909–13) and Covent Garden, his most famous roles being Lohengrin, Otello, Radamès, and Raoul in *Les Huguenots*. Renowned for his mezzo voce and for making the Met chorus laugh so much in *Aida* that they were fined. He paid. At the Met, he was the Hermann of the first American *Queen of Spades*.

SLOBODSKAYA, ODA (1895– 1970). Russian soprano, at St Petersburg from 1918 to 1922, when she left Russia, singing in Paris, London and Milan. Her Russian repertoire included Tatyana, and she sang Natasha opposite Chaliapin in Dargomizhsky's *Rusalka* at the Lyceum, London, in 1931. She also created Palmyra in Delius's *Koanga* at Covent Garden (1935).

SOBINOV, LEONID (1873–1934). Russian tenor, an admirable artist, whose warm ringing tone was heard to advantage as Lohengrin, Roméo and Werther, and, especially, as a magnificent Lensky, at St Petersburg and elsewhere in Russia.

SÖDERSTRÖM, ELISABETH (1927–). Swedish soprano, at the time of writing (1974), Christine in *Intermezzo* at Glyndebourne, and drawing from Desmond Shawe-Taylor, in *The Sunday Times*, such phrases as 'the pile and sheen of (her) beautifully managed voice', and 'this delightful actress and enormously charming singer looked ravishing'. She first sang at Glyndebourne in 1957, making her début as the Composer in *Ariadne auf Naxos*, and her repertoire in Sweden and abroad includes all three soprano roles in *Der Rosenkavalier*, Marie in *Wozzeck*, Elisabeth in *Elegy for Young Lovers*, and Puccini roles.

SONTAG, HENRIETTE (1806–54). German soprano who created Weber's Euryanthe in 1823, aged only 18, having been heard by him in *La Donna del Lago*. A superb singer with a winning voice, 'a real, pure and unalloyed soprano of the highest possible register; likewise ... she accomplishes her marvels of execution with perfect ease'. So wrote a critic. Catalani, whom some claimed she excelled, admired her greatly. In the 1820s she often sang with Malibran, being particularly noted for her singing and acting of roles such as Norina, Zerlina, Susanna, Amina and Donna Elvira, though she was also a famous Donna Anna and Semiramide. She gave up the stage to marry a Count Rossi in Berlin, but returned when the revolutions of 1848 ate into their combined fortunes, conquering London again as Linda di Chamounix (Donizetti), which was considered a very suitable role for a simple girl who had married well. A glorious artist, one of the greatest of all German singers.

SOYER, ROGER (1939–). French bass whose magnificent voice can take in baritone roles. One of the few successful Don Giovanni's of recent times at Edinburgh (1973) and elsewhere, he is also a notable Méphistophélès (Berlioz), Arkel in *Pelléas*, and Escamillo, in Europe and America.

SPANI, HINA (1896–1969). Argentinian soprano, noted for the technique and emotional power of her singing between the wars in Milan, Buenos Aires, etc. Her repertoire was enormous, including the Countess in *Figaro*, Turandot, Lady Macbeth and a famous Tosca.

STABILE, MARIANO (1888–1968). Italian baritone, one of the most famous Falstaffs, singing the role for Toscanini at La Scala in 1922 and as late as 1961. Other famous parts included Don Giovanni, both Figaros, Iago, Scarpia and Malatesta. His mastery of singing and powers of acting completely compensated for a voice which was by no means exceptional, and he was enormously popular at Covent Garden (1926–31), Salzburg (1935–9) and at Glyndebourne (1936–9). He returned to London after the war, singing at the Cambridge and the Stoll (1946–8), and his last British performance was as Don Alfonso for Glyndebourne at the Edinburgh Festival in 1948.

STEBER, ELEANOR (1916–). American soprano, at the Met from 1940 to the 1960s, where she sang notably well in Verdi, Puccini, Mozart, Strauss, etc. including Sophie and the Marschallin, and created the title-role in Barber's *Vanessa* (1958).

STEHLE, SOPHIE (1838–1921). German soprano, the first Fricka in *Rheingold* (1869) and Brünnhilde in *Walküre* (1870), both at Munich.

STELLA, ANTONIETTA (1929–). Italian soprano who made her début as Leonora in Il *Trovatore* (Spoleto, 1950), joined La Scala in 1953, and the Met (1956–60). Her large, warm voice and intensity (in Verdi, Puccini, Giordano) compensates for imperfect technique and a sometimes suspect upper register. Tosca and Butterfly are among her most noted roles.

STEVENS, RISË (1913–). American mezzo-soprano, a most attractive and notable actress-singer, one of the few operatic artists that Tyrone Guthrie praised wholeheartedly (see his *A Life in the Theatre*). At the Met from 1938, and Glyndebourne's Cherubino and Dora-

bella in 1939, her most famous roles have included Dalila, Octavian, Orlofsky and, most acclaimed of all, Carmen.

STEWART, THOMAS. American baritone, especially well known in Germany, first singing at Bayreuth in 1960. A notable Wagnerian and Orest in *Elektra*. Married to Evelyn Lear (see page 63).

STICH-RANDALL, TERESA (1927–). American soprano, an Aida at 15 and, later, one of the finest Mozartians of her day, at Aix-en-Provence (from 1953) and elsewhere. An early success was as Nanetta in the N.B.C. *Falstaff* conducted by Toscanini. Fiordiligi and Donna Anna are two of her most famous roles.

STIGNANI, EBE (1904–74). Italian mezzo-soprano, famous for 'streams of beautiful tone', to quote from one of many versions of the same praise. At La Scala (1925–56), Covent Garden before and after the war, and elsewhere, she thrilled audiences by sheer singing, if minimal acting, though she presented a dignified appearance. Eboli, Azucena, Laura in *La Gioconda* and Leonora in *La Favorita* (Donizetti), were some of her greatest roles, her Adalgisa with Callas at Covent Garden (1952 and 1957) being unforgettable.

STOLZ, TERESA (1834–1902). Czech soprano whose Italian

début was as Mathilde in *William Tell* (1864), conducted by Verdi's friend, Mariani, whose mistress she became. Her flexible and brilliant dramatic soprano was heard as Elisabeth de Valois in the revised *Don Carlos* (La Scala, 1868), as Italy's first Leonora in *La Forza del Destino*, and Aida, and as the first soprano in the *Requiem*. She left Mariani and was Verdi's closest female friend after his wife's death. Just how close can best be studied in Frank Walker's definitive, *The Man Verdi*.

STOLZE, GERHARD (1926–   ). German tenor, famous at Bayreuth and Vienna for his Mime, David and Herod since the 1950s, though his Mime has occasionally been criticized for exaggeration. Yet, in *Opera* (June 1969), Greville Rothon, reviewing a Munich performance, gives a majority opinion, 'a bloodcurdling experience: the dramatic intensity of his psychological characterization is ... one of the marvels of today's theatre world.'

STORACE, ANN (1766–1817). English soprano of Italian descent, the creator of Susanna in *Figaro* (1786) and, from 1788, a very popular soubrette in London, despite a notably harsh voice.

STORCHIO, ROSINA (1876–1945). Italian soprano, the creator of Butterfly at its first, disastrous performance (1904). Much admired as a lyric soprano by Toscanini, she also created Mascagni's Lodeletta, Leoncavallo's Musetta and Zazà, and Stefana in Giordano's *Siberia*.

STRACCIARI, RICCARDO (1875–1955). Italian baritone, the finest (Rossini) Figaro in Italy in the 1920s and 1930s, singing the part over 900 times, and a noted Verdian.

STRADA DEL PO, ANNA (dates uncertain). Italian soprano of such unfortunate appearance that she was nicknamed 'Pig' in those ungallant times, but was a most successful Handelian in London in the 1730s.

STREICH, RITA (1920–   ). German soprano, famous, especially in the 1950s (Vienna, Berlin, etc.), for her Queen of the Night, Constanze, Sophie and Zerbinetta, the top of her voice then being astounding.

STREPPONI, GIUSEPPINA (1815–97). Italian soprano, the creator of Abigaille in *Nabucco* (1842), but, more important, Verdi's mistress and, from 1859, his ideally sympathetic, encouraging and intelligent wife. Her voice was both powerful and sweet, and her technique was superb, but ill-health had affected it badly by the time of *Nabucco*, whatever legends say to the contrary: see Frank

Walker's fascinating and definitive, *The Man Verdi*.

STUDHOLME, MARION. English soprano, a delightful actress-singer whose roles at the Wells in the 1950s and 1960s included Blonde, Despina, Adele, Rosina and the perfect Gretel.

SUCHER, ROSA (1849–1927). German soprano, London's first Isolde and Eva (Drury Lane, 1882). At Bayreuth, 1886–94, and Covent Garden's Brünnhilde and Isolde in 1892.

SUPERVIA, CONCHITA (1895–1936). Spanish mezzo-soprano who died in childbirth at the height of her career. She was most famous (and adored) as Rossini's heroines: Rosina, Angelina and Isabella, which she sang in the original keys and in which her bewitching stage personality was seen at its best. Her Carmen divided opinion. Her fame in Rossini roles began at Turin in 1925. As well as Italy and Paris, she also sang in Chicago (1915–16, 1932–3) and Covent Garden (1934–5).

SUTHAUS, LUDWIG (1906–1971). German tenor, a noted Wagnerian (Tristan, etc.), who made his name in Stuttgart (1933–8), then in Berlin (1941–67) and Vienna until his death. He also sang at Bayreuth from 1943. A true Heldentenor at his best (as in the incomparable Furtwängler *Tristan und Isolde*),

though not blessed with a heroic appearance or acting gifts. He had a wide repertoire, including Samson, Florestan, Hermann in *The Queen of Spades*, and the Drum Major in *Wozzeck*.

SUTHERLAND, JOAN (1926–). Australian soprano who made her London début as the First Lady in *The Magic Flute* (Covent Garden, 1952). Early roles included the first Jennifer in Tippett's *Midsummer Marriage*, but it was her Gilda and, especially, her astonishing Israelite Woman in Handel's *Samson* which prepared the knowing for her overnight superstardom as Lucia (1959) (discussed on page 114). The first to realize her potentiality as a dramatic coloratura, born to sing Donizetti and Bellini, was her husband, the conductor, Richard Bonynge (see page 224), later backed by Sir David Webster. Since that epic night, she has triumphed regularly in Italy, at the Met and elsewhere, including Australia with her own company (1965) and in 1974. Her roles include Bellini's Norma, Elvira and Beatrice di Tenda, Violetta and—a most successful foray into comedy—the Daughter of the Regiment. Franco Zeffirelli made her into a considerable actress (by any standards) as Lucia, but she has not always been blessed with such inspirational producers. Except for a period when the projection of words was seriously neglected, her artistry has never wavered. The sound of her voice is unique and the top of it is one of the glories of our age. Soon after stardom came the next accolade, the title 'La Stupenda'.

SVANHOLM, SET (1904–64). Swedish tenor, originally baritone (1930–6), and one of the most reliable and admirable Wagnerians of modern times. No *Heldentenor*, his voice being effective and strong and dry, and not very tall (but slim), his musicianship and dramatic involvement made him the leading Tristan and Siegfried of the immediate post-war period. He had sung Walther and Tannhäuser at Salzburg in 1938, later appearing at Bayreuth. His repertoire in Stockholm included Peter Grimes, Calaf, Don José and Vasco da Gama. He became the Intendant of the Stockholm Opera (1956–63).

SWARTHOUT, GLADYS (1904–69). American mezzo-soprano, beauty and film star (appearing in one movie without singing a note). At the Met from 1929 to 1945, where she was a famous Carmen.

SZÉKELY, MIHÁLY (1901–63). Hungarian bass whose magnificently dark voice was heard in Wagner and (at Glyndebourne, 1957–62) as Sarastro, Rocco, Osmin and Bartolo.

TADDEI, GIUSEPPE (1916–). Italian baritone whose rich voice and dramatic gifts have been heard and seen in Italy and elsewhere since the late 1940s. Especially noted for his Verdi roles, also as Scarpia and Gianni Schicchi, and in Mozart roles.

TAGLIABUE, CARLO (1898–). Italian baritone, at La Scala from 1930 to 1955. He also sang before and after World War Two at Covent Garden and at the Met (1937–9). A Wagnerian of note in Italy, he was best known for his Verdi roles.

TAGLIAVINI, FERRUCCIO (1913–). Italian tenor, superb in *bel canto* roles especially Nemorino and Elvino, and also a famous Cavaradossi and Duke of Mantua. He sang in many leading opera houses, including the Met (1946–54). At his finest, a most beguiling singer with a golden voice.

TAJO, ITALO (1915–). Italian bass, a famous buffo artist in the years after the war (Leporello, Mozart's Figaro, Dulcamara, etc.), though he also sang Boris and King Philip. He was still active in 1973, giving a superb Alcindoro and Benoit in *La Bohème* at Chicago. A vivid personality.

TAMAGNO, FRANCESCO (1850–1905). Italian tenor, the trumpet-toned creator of Otello, his most famous role, even if Verdi had to work hard to stop him acting like a stick (1887). He also sang the role in London and America. His amazingly powerful voice was also heard to advantage as Manrico and Samson. Opinions about him vary sharply, and he was certainly not the most subtle of artists, but there were few who failed to respond to the sheer power of his voice.

TAMBERLIK, ENRICO (1820–89). Italian tenor whose superb voice, looks and acting ability made him famous in London (from 1850), Paris, Russia (where he created Alvaro in *La Forza del Destino* in 1862) and Spain. He was London's first Manrico and Benvenuto Cellini, and excelled as Florestan, Arnold in *William Tell*, and as Rossini's Otello.

TAMBURINI, ANTONIO (1800–76). Italian baritone, renowned in *bel canto* roles, including Riccardo in the first *I Puritani* (1835). He was also the original Malatesta in *Don Pasquale* (1843), and a famous Don Giovanni. London's first Riccardo, Enrico in *Lucia di Lammermoor*, and Malatesta. His technique was compared with the great tenor, Rubini's.

TAUBER, RICHARD (1892–1948). Austrian, later British, tenor, the most admired Mozartian tenor between the two world wars and one of the most popu-

lar operetta arists in history. He also sang Puccini, including the first German Calaf in *Turandot*. Dresden, then Vienna (until 1938), were his chief houses. After the Second World War, during which he was very popular in lighter vein in Britain, he sang once more with the Vienna State Opera on its visit to Covent Garden (1947) as Don Ottavio, dying almost immediately afterwards following a legendary success.

TEAR, ROBERT (1922–). English tenor who joined the English Opera Group in 1964, his roles including leads in Britten's church dramas. A very fine Dov in Tippett's *The Knot Garden* (1970). A superb Lensky in *Eugene Onegin* at Covent Garden (1971–2). Recent successes include Admetus in *Alceste* (Edinburgh, 1974).

TEBALDI, RENATA (1922–). Italian soprano, famous since being chosen by Toscanini for the re-opening of La Scala (1946), and one of the supreme singers of the last thirty years, especially in the 1950s when she and Callas in their different ways bestrode the operatic firmament like shining comets. Her exquisitely beautiful, powerful voice has made her, at her best, a glorious and warm interpreter of Verdi, Puccini, Cilèa and Giordano, though only Italy and America have had their fair share of her in the flesh. The years have diminished her range and steadiness, and the unique quality of her voice, but she still, as in her 1973 Desdemona at the Met, remains a moving, sensitive artist.

TE KANAWA, KIRI (1944–). New Zealand soprano, one of the fastest rising stars of the 1970s, technically superb, an affecting actress and a beautiful woman with a winning personality. Her most famous roles include the Countess at Glyndebourne (1973) and Desdemona at the Met and Covent Garden (1974). Her Micaela in *Carmen* must be the biggest challenge to the star of the evening in the opera's history.

TEMPLETON, JOHN (1802–86). Scottish tenor who was taken in hand by Malibran to make him at least an adequate actor when singing opposite her in *La Sonnambula* (1833). The quality of his singing was never in doubt.

TENDUCCI, GIUSTO (*c* 1736–?). Italian male soprano who yet managed to elope with a councillor's daughter. He adapted Gluck's *Orfeo*, singing in it with Mrs Billington.

TERNINA, MILKA (1863–1941). Croatian soprano, the most famous Isolde of her day and an equally inspired Leonore in *Fidelio*. She was the first London and New York Tosca, and was widely regarded as one of the best operatic actresses of her time, being much admired by Puccini.

TESCHEMACHER, MARGUERITE (1903–). German soprano, creator of the title-role in Strauss's *Daphne* (1938) during her time at Dresden (1935–46). Jenufa, Minnie and the Countess in *Capriccio* were among her noted roles.

TETRAZZINI, LUISA (1871–1940). Italian soprano and ill-favoured non-actress who was forgiven by opera buffs at least for her thrilling high notes and staggering coloratura work. One of the most famous singers of the early years of this century, her Violetta and Lucia were huge successes at Covent Garden in 1907 and later, while she sang with equal acclaim in New York and elsewhere. Lakmé and Amina were other vocal triumphs. Her Covent Garden début as Violetta was played to a heavily papered, apathetic house, which by the end had recognized a phenomenon in their midst. Her sister, Eva (1862–1938), was the first American Desdemona (1888).

TEYTE, (DAME) MAGGIE (1888–). English soprano, a supreme Mélisande, which she studied with Debussy. At the Opéra-Comique, 1907–11, she later sang regularly at Covent Garden and also in Chicago and Boston. An exquisite and attractive actress-singer, her other roles included Cherubino, Butterfly, Thaïs and Hansel; also Belinda to Flagstad's Dido (Purcell) at the Mermaid in London (1951).

THILL, GEORGES (1897–). French tenor, notable at the Paris Opéra (from 1924) as Roméo, Julien in *Louise*, and as Don José. Also sang in Italy, London and New York in the 1920s and 1930s.

THOMAS, JESS. American tenor who, since his Bayreuth début in 1961, has established himself as one of the leading Wagnerians of recent years in Vienna, Munich, the Met, La Scala, Covent Garden, etc. his roles including Parsifal, Walther and Lohengrin. His Tristan at Covent Garden (1971) was vocally and physically almost ideal.

THORBERG, KERSTIN (1896– 1970). Swedish mezzo-soprano, 'the finest Fricka I have ever seèn or hope to see' (Ernest Newman, 1936). During the 1930s, besides being at Covent Garden, she also sang in Berlin, Vienna and Salzburg, and was at the Met from 1936 to 1950.

THORNTON, EDNA (*c* 1880–1964). English contralto, especially fine in Wagner, singing Erda and Waltraute in the English *Ring* at Covent Garden in 1908 under Richter. Sang with Beecham and the British National Opera Company.

TIBBETT, LAWRENCE (1896– 1960). American baritone, at the Met from 1923 to 1950, with occasional guest appearances abroad. A fine actor-singer, he created roles in a number of American operas, including the lead in Gruenberg's *The Emperor Jones* (1933), and at the Met was the first Simon Boccanegra, Balstrode in *Peter Grimes* and Ivan Khovansky in *Khovanshchina*. Iago and Scarpia were other famous roles, both of which he played at Covent Garden (1937).

TICHATSCHEK, JOSEPH (1807– 86). Bohemian tenor, at Dresden 1837–70, and the original Rienzi (1842) and Tannhäuser (1845) for his friend Wagner.

TIETJENS, THERESE (1831–77). German soprano, a thrilling and fine-looking actress-singer until she became exceptionally fat. Sang in London 1858–77, collapsing on stage as Lucrezia Borgia and dying some months later. She was an incomparable Norma, Donna Anna and Agathe, and introduced many roles to London, including Amelia in *Un Ballo in Maschera*, Leonora in *La Forza del Destino* and Marguerite in *Faust*. She also sang in Vienna, New York, etc.

TINSLEY, PAULINE. English soprano of remarkable power and vocal agility, best known for stirring performances in

Verdi, including Leonora in *La Forza del Destino* for the Wells (1968). A striking Queen Elizabeth I in *Maria Stuarda* (1973), and a powerful Santuzza at Covent Garden in 1976.

TÖPPER, HERTHA (1924–). Austrian mezzo-soprano, at Munich from 1952, where she was soon admired in Mozart, Strauss and Wagner. She has also sung at Bayreuth, the Met and Covent Garden, and is now much admired in smaller roles.

TOUREL, JENNIE (1910–). French-Canadian mezzo-soprano, at the Opéra-Comique (1933–40) where her roles included Carmen; also at the Met. She created Baba the Turk in *The Rake's Progress* (1951).

TOZZI, GIORGIO (1923–). American bass-baritone, at the Met and elsewhere since 1955. His notable roles include Sarastro, Figaro, Sachs, Gremin, Oroveso and Arkel.

TRAUBEL, HELEN (1899–1972). American soprano, at the Met from 1934 to 1953 when she fell out with Bing over her night-club singing. When Flagstad left America in 1951, she became the Met's leading Wagnerian soprano, singing Isolde, Brünnhilde, Elisabeth, etc.

TREBELLI, ZELIA (1838–92). French mezzo-soprano, the Met's first Carmen (1884) and frequently in London from the 1860s to the 1880s.

TREPTOW, GÜNTHER (1907–). German tenor, a notable postwar *Heldentenor* in Berlin, Vienna, etc. his roles including Tristan, Siegfried, Otello and Florestan.

TREIGLE, NORMAN (1928–75). American bass, especially associated since the 1950s with the New York City Opera, and especially renowned for his Mefistofele (Boito), also for his portrayal of the Berlioz and Gounod versions of the role. Other roles include Figaro, Handel's Julius Caesar and Boris.

TROYANOS, TATIANA. American mezzo-soprano, the creator of Jeanne in Penderecki's *The Devils of Loudun* (Hamburg, 1969), a triumphant performance. Other notable roles of this attractive actress-singer include Octavian, Carmen and Purcell's Dido.

TUCCI, GABRIELLA. Italian soprano who made her La Scala début in 1959, and has since sung at the Met and Covent Garden, her roles including Tosca, Aida and Desdemona. This fine artist opened the last season at the old Met in *Faust* (1965) and closed it as Mimi.

TUCKER, RICHARD (1914–75). American tenor, at the Met

from 1945, when he made his début as Enzo in *La Gioconda*. His career was one of the most notable in Met history, three decades of stylish, virile and ingratiating singing in Italian and French roles, and a few more, including Lensky. Radamès, Pinkerton, Cavaradossi, Don Carlos and Don José are amongst his many roles.

TURNER, (DAME) EVA (1892–). English soprano, the ideal Turandot, according to Alfano and countless others, including record collectors. After singing with the Carl Rosa, she made her La Scala début under Toscanini as Freia and was a regular visitor to Covent Garden from 1928 to 1948. A superb Wagnerian (including Isolde) and Verdian (Aïda, etc.). Philip Hope-Wallace has written of the 'heroic strength and steadiness of her voice, especially in the upper reach', and it was these matchless assets, plus her ideal timbre for the role, which made her so triumphant a Turandot.

UHDE, HERMANN (1914–65). German bass-baritone and a fine actor-singer, in Munich, Bayreuth, London, New York, etc. His Gunther was superb and other notable performances included Telramund and the Dutchman, also the four parts in *Hoffmann*, which he sang at Covent Garden, in 1954, in English that shamed most British artists.

ULFRUNG, RAGNAR (1927–). Norwegian tenor, a notable actor-singer, at home in Europe and America, his roles including a famous Herod in *Salome*, the painter in Berg's *Lulu*, the title role in Peter Maxwell Davies's *Taverner* at Covent Garden (1973), also his celebrated Gustavus III in *Un Ballo in Maschera*, the King being homosexual as was the historic Gustavus.

UNGER, CAROLINE (1803–77). Austrian contralto who created roles by Donizetti, Bellini, etc. A tribute to her by Rossini is breathtaking: 'The ardour of the south, the energy of the north, brazen lungs, a silver voice, and golden talent.'

UNGER, GEORG (1837–87). German tenor, the creator of Siegfried at Bayreuth in 1876.

UPPMAN, THEODOR (1920–). American baritone, the creator of Britten's Billy Budd at Covent Garden (1951), a splendid assumption vocally and physically. Joined the Met in 1956.

URSULEAC, VIORICA (1899–). Rumanian soprano whom Strauss considered his ideal soprano, an ultimate tribute from the supreme composer-lover of the breed. The wife of the conductor, Clemens Krauss (see page 235), she sang in Berlin (1933–45) and elsewhere, including Salzburg creating Strauss's Arabella, Maria in *Friedenstag* and the Countess in *Capriccio*, in respectively Dresden, Munich and again Munich. She was also a notable Wagnerian and Verdian.

VALDENGO, GIUSEPPE (1914–). Italian baritone, at the Met, 1946–54. His most famous roles were Iago, Amonasro and Falstaff, all recorded for Toscanini. Less happy was his Don Giovanni at Glyndebourne (1955).

VALETTI, CESARE (1922–). Italian tenor whose stylish singing in Rossini, Donizetti, Mozart, etc., was admired at La Scala and the Met during the 1950s and 1960s.

VALLIN, NINON (1886–1961). French soprano, at the Opéra-Comique and elsewhere, famous for her Louise, Charlotte in *Werther*, Manon, etc. She never made a bad record, according to J. B. Steane.

VAN DAM, JOSÉ. Belgian baritone, the superb Figaro in the Solti–Strehler production at Versailles and the Opéra (1973). His Escamillo, heard in many countries, is that rare event in *Carmen*, a total success.

VARNAY, ASTRID (1918–). American soprano, of Austro-Hungarian operatic parentage, at the Met from 1941–56, and a leading Wagner-Strauss singer. She also sang regularly at Bay-

reuth and at Covent Garden in the 1950s, and, having sung the supreme parts, is still a considerable actress-singer as Klytemnestra, the Kostelnička in *Jenufa*, etc. Her technique has never been perfect, but she brings intense excitement into the opera house.

VARESI, FELICE (1813–89). French-Italian baritone, creator of Verdi's Macbeth and Rigoletto, also Germont, which role the foolish fellow thought unworthy of him.

VAUGHAN, ELIZABETH (1937–). Welsh soprano who survived being dubbed 'the pocket Callas' for her—in fact—not entirely convincing Abigaille, in *Nabucco*, with the Welsh National Opera (1961), to become a major actress-singer of exceptional slimness at Covent Garden: Butterfly, Nedda, Musetta, Liu and an underrated Violetta.

VEASEY, JOSEPHINE (1931–). English mezzo-soprano, an actress-singer of fire and personality, who joined Covent Garden in 1955. Her Fricka, Brangäne, Eboli, Dido, etc. have all been much admired; indeed, the first is outstanding, and her comedy roles include a delightful Dorabella. Has sung in Paris and America.

VELLUTI, GIOVANNI BATTISTA (1780–1861). Italian male soprano, the last famous specimen of the breed. After early triumphs, his performance in Meyerbeer's *Il Crociato in Egitto* in London (1825), the first castrato heard there for twenty-five years, thrilled many but allegedly shocked many more.

VERRETT, SHIRLEY. American mezzo-soprano. See page 115 for her performance of Eboli. Since her Carmen at Spoleto (1962), she has rapidly established herself as one of the most exciting actress-singers of modern times, a mistress of every facet of operatic art. She is blessed with personality, looks and fire, which, allied to her technique, disguise the fact that hers is not the most opulent voice. A superstar in Europe and America, her roles include Amneris, Eboli, Dalila, Dido in *The Trojans*, Ulrica (her Covent Garden début, 1966) and Gluck's Orfeo.

VESTRIS, LUCIA ELIZABETH (1787–1856). English contralto, actress and theatre manager, who married into the Vestris family, was London's first Pippa in *La Gazza Ladra* (1821), sang Don Giovanni [*sic*] and Macheath. She later married the actor Charles Mathews II and introduced realism to properties and sets, including the first box set.

VIARDOT-GARCIA, PAULINE (1821–1910). French mezzo-soprano, the younger sister of Malibran but not blessed with her looks. However, her talent was in the best traditions of the incomparable Garcia family, and she also lives on as Turgenev's friend and (perhaps) mistress. Marrying her manager, Louis Viardot of the Théâtre-Italien (1839), she created Fidès in *Le Prophète*, singing it over 200 times. She had many triumphs in London between 1848 and 1856, helping to get *Les Huguenots* staged at Covent Garden, singing Valentine (1848) and London's first Azucena. Her famous Orfeo in Berlioz's version of Gluck's opera (Paris, 1859) had Charles Dickens, amongst others, in ecstasies, and, in 1861, she was magnificent as Alceste. She retired from opera in 1863, though she sang Dalila to Saint-Saëns in private. An artist of exceptional character and gifts, Berlioz adored her.

VICKERS, JON (1926–). Canadian tenor, one of the finest artists of the age, and a notable actor-singer with a rare quality of projecting emotion. A lyric and heroic tenor, he became famous in 1957 as Aeneas in *The Trojans*, having earlier shown his exceptional quality at Covent Garden as Riccardo in *Un Ballo in Maschera*. Since those halcyon days, he has become a major Wagnerian, but has not abandoned his Italian roles, and has added Otello to his repertoire. His Bayreuth début was in 1958, his Met début in 1959. His voice has thickened down the years and there are times when —can it be a fault?—he acts too much with his voice (Peter Grimes); but more perfect tenors of the last decade or more have yet to match his Florestan, Canio Siegmund, or Grimes (*see also* p. 115).

VIEULLE, FÉLIX (1872–1953). French bass, at the Opéra-Comique from 1898 to 1928, creating Arkel in *Pelléas et Mélisande*, and other roles. His bass-baritone son, Jean, sang at the Opéra-Comique, 1928–58).

VINAY, RAMÓN (1914–). Chilian tenor, the finest postwar Otello, for which he was coached by Toscanini. Other tenors have been vocally more magnificent, but as yet no one has matched him as an actor-singer in the role; indeed, the present writer regarded him as the finest Othello or Otello until Olivier played the Shakespearian role in 1964. His baritonal sound was a reminder that he began as a baritone, and he finally returned to the lower voice, singing Iago, Falstaff, Scarpia, and Telramund at Bayreuth (1962).

VISHNEVSKAYA, GALINA (1926–). Russian soprano, married to the great cellist, Rostropovich, and at the Bolshoi from 1952. In the 1960s, she made successful débuts in London

and New York, as Aida, etc. revealing herself as a beautiful woman with an old-fashioned, if effective, acting style, and with a superb voice. A famous Tatyana.

VOELKER, FRANZ (1899–1965) German tenor, outstanding at Bayreuth in the 1920s and 1930s, and elsewhere, as Siegmund and Lohengrin; also successful in Italian roles.

VOGL, HEINRICH (1845–1900). German tenor, creator of Loge and Siegmund at Bayreuth in 1876, singing there until 1897. He was London's first Loge and Siegfried (1882), his wife, Therese Thoma (1845–1921), being the first London Brünnhilde and, for some years, Germany's only Isolde. She was the first Sieglinde.

VON STADE, FREDERICA. American mezzo-soprano whose Cherubino at Versailles and Glyndebourne in 1973 is already a legend. Millions have since marvelled at this role on television. Her Rosina is another delight.

VROONS, FRANS (1911–). Dutch tenor, especially at the Netherlands Opera, where he became assistant director in 1956. His Don José was admired at Covent Garden, and Hoffman and Peter Grimes are among his other roles.

VYVYAN, JENNIFER (1925–74). English soprano, especially

noted for her Britten roles, including the Governess in *Turn of the Screw* (1954), which she created, as she did Penelope Rich in *Gloriana* (1953) and Titania in *A Midsummer Night's Dream* (1960). Mrs Julian in *Owen Wingrave* (1971). She was also a notable Mozart singer.

WÄCHTER, EBERHARD (1929–). Austrian baritone, with the Vienna State Opera from 1954. His Covent Garden début as the Count in *Figaro* (1956) was much admired. This Viennese favourite has a wide range, typically scoring major successes in 1973 within a few days as Dulcamara in *L'Elisir d'Amore* and Jochanaan in *Salome*. A very fine actor-singer.

WAGNER, JOHANNA (1826–94). German soprano, the adopted niece of the great Richard, who created his Elisabeth in *Tannhäuser* (1845). At Berlin 1850–62, she switched to straight acting when her voice left her. However, it returned in the 1870s when she created First Norn at Bayreuth (1876). She was famous as Tancredi, Bellini's *Romeo* and Donizetti's Lucrezia Borgia in the 1850s.

WALKER, EDYTH (1867–1950). American mezzo-soprano who made her name in Vienna and Berlin in the 1890s, then at the Met and in London in Edwardian times. She was London's first Elektra (Beecham, 1910) and a famous Isolde.

WALLACE, IAN (1919–). Scottish bass, a notable buffo at Glyndebourne and elsewhere from 1946, his most famous roles being Bartolo and Don Magnifico in *La Cenerentola*.

WALTERS, JESS (1912–). American baritone, whose rich, warm voice and sympathetic personality made him a favourite at Covent Garden (1948–59), where he was an excellent Papageno and Sharpless. Later at the Netherlands Opera.

WALTZ, GUSTAVUS (died *c* 1753). German bass, and cook for Handel, singing Polypheme in *Acis and Galatea*. The celebrated jibe at Gluck that he knew no more about counterpoint than 'my cook, Waltz' is therefore not so very rude after all.

WARD, DAVID (1922–). Scottish bass, of commanding voice and appearance, who made his name at the Wells in the 1950s, then at Covent Garden, Bayreuth and the Met in the 1960s. One of the finest Wagnerian bass/bass-baritones of the day, his Wotan is especially admired. One of his earliest successes was as the High Priest in *The Pearl Fishers* at the Wells, and another notable non-Wagnerian role was the Commendatore in *Don Giovanni*.

WARREN, LEONARD (1911–60). American baritone, one of the finest Verdians of the post-war years until he died in tragic and dramatic circumstances during a Met performance of *La Forza del Destino*. This powerful and resonant singer made his Met début in 1939.

WATSON, CLAIRE. American soprano, at Munich, Covent Garden, etc. whose notable roles include the Countess in *Capriccio*, the title role in *Ariadne auf Naxos*, the Marschallin and Ellen Orford; also Senta and Sieglinde, this last being a famous interpretation, notably at Munich in 1972 and 1973.

WATSON, LILIAN. English soprano, a rising and enchanting young hopeful of the 1970s who attracts rave notices in *Opera* and elsewhere, even for Barbarina in *The Marriage of Figaro*.

WEATHERS, FELICIA (1937–). American soprano whose début was at Zürich (1961). This fine black singer is best known in America and with Scottish Opera for her Butterfly. Other roles include Salome, Liu and Aida.

WEBER, LUDWIG (1899–1974). Austrian bass, one of the finest Wagnerians of the century, especially famous as Gurnemanz, Daland and Hagen. His majestic career began in 1920 in Vienna, and he was a popular visitor to Covent Garden. Bayreuth 1951–60. His most notable roles included Baron Ochs and Rocco in *Fidelio*.

WEIDT, LUCIE (1879–1940). Austrian soprano, the first Nurse in *Die Frau ohne Schatten* (Vienna, 1919), and Vienna's first Marschallin and Kundry.

WELITSCH, LJUBA (1913–). Bulgarian soprano and voluptuous actress-singer whose exciting career was ruined by illness which destroyed her thrillingly shining voice. Salome was her most famous part, though she was also an exciting Tosca and Donna Anna until the 1950s. Her Salome of the famous 1949 Brook–Dali production caused a scandal *in excelsis* and might even cause a gasp today. A superstar whose comet-like career will never be forgotten by those who experienced part of it.

WHITEHILL, CLARENCE (1871–1932). American baritone, the Wotan of Richter's English *Ring* and a famous Sachs, Golaud and Amfortas. He appeared at Bayreuth in 1904 and 1908–9.

WIDDOP, WALTER (1892–1949). English tenor, with a notably

virile voice, regularly at Covent Garden (1928–38) where his Tristan and Siegmund were much admired.

WILSON, CATHERINE. Scottish-born soprano, a delightful actress-singer in opera and operetta (Rosalinda, *The Merry Widow*) for the Wells, Scottish Opera, etc. Notable in Mozart and Rossini.

WINDGASSEN, WOLFGANG (1914–74). German tenor, the son of leading opera singers, and the most reliable Wagner tenor of the late 1940s and 1950s. A fine artist who really sang the great roles, even though he was not a born *Heldentenor*, skilfully husbanding his voice. Parsifal at Bayreuth in the first post-war festival (1951).

WINKELMANN, HERMANN (1849–1912). German tenor, the creator of Parsifal (1882), and Vienna's first Tristan and Otello. He was London's first Tristan and Walther.

WITTE, ERICH (1911–). German tenor who moved from lighter parts to Florestan and Otello. He made his name in the 1930s, and in the 1950s was a famous Loge at Covent Garden and Bayreuth.

WITTICH, MARIE (1868–1931). German soprano, the first Salome (Dresden, 1905), though the part seems to have baffled and shocked her. A Bayreuth Isolde, Kundry and Sieglinde (1901–10).

WUNDERLICH, FRITZ (1931–66). German tenor who died from injuries sustained in a fall down a staircase when it seemed he was destined to become a supreme lyric tenor. Regularly at Vienna, Munich and Stuttgart, he appeared all over Europe. A renowned Mozartian, he also sang Verdi, Puccini, Lensky in *Eugene Onegin*, and modern roles, including Palestrina (Pfitzner). His Mozart was ardent and elegant, and he had a delightful sense of comedy. His forays into operetta and musical comedy were so successful and enjoyable that the mantle of Richard Tauber could have been his: 'Whom the gods love'.

ZANDT, MARIE VAN (1861–1919). American soprano, for whom Delibes wrote *Lakmé* (1883), which made her dear colleagues so jealous of her that they alleged she was drunk on stage. Drunk she was not.

ZANELLI, RENATO (1892–1935). Chilean tenor who began as a baritone. A great Otello and Italy's chief Wagnerian tenor.

ZEANI, VIRGINIA (1928–). Bulgarian soprano, a famous *bel canto* beauty, at La Scala (1956) and elsewhere. London's first post-war Lucia (1957). Married to Rossi-Lemini, the bass and producer.

ZENATELLO, GIOVANNI (1876–1949). Italian tenor, a very famous and strong singer and the organizer of the Verona Arena Festival (see page 324). He was the creator of Pinker-ton. His first Covent Garden Otello (1908) suffered from over-exuberance in his opening 'Esultate'. He never made that mistake again.

CONDUCTORS

Legendary Interpretations

Listed below are a number of legendary performances of the last quarter of a century. Interpretations can vary quite widely down the years, can become sluggish in old age, but it is even more logical to speak of, say, Knappertsbusch's *Parsifal* than of a singer's Violetta. Physical acting may legitimately vary far more than should a rendering of a score. Great names on both sides of the Atlantic have been omitted, partly for lack of space, partly because their interpretations, arguably, are not legendary. The knowing may complain that Beecham's *Die Meistersinger von Nürnberg* of 1951 has not been included, but he had too little rehearsal time at Covent Garden. He was the legend, not the performances, except, perhaps, the last, and his supreme achievements were earlier.

KARL BÖHM   *Così fan tutte*
The great Austrian conductor is a magnificent Mozartian, and *Così fan tutte* has always inspired him to supreme heights, as a classic recording and also performances at Salzburg in the 1970s have shown. His interpretation is stylish, subtle, exhilarating, mellow but never lacking in passion, and he is totally in control of singers and orchestra. Each tempo is perfectly judged, and the more mature his interpretation becomes, the more it is gloriously satisfying.

COLIN DAVIS   *Les Troyens*
Why Britain should have produced the three supreme Berlioz conductors of the last half-century, Sir Hamilton Harty, Beecham and now Davis, is a mystery. Perhaps British reserve (not always evident in Beecham), cloaking a romantic and passionate nature, can make ideal interpreters of this music, for Berlioz, despite his big effects and aspirations, never publicly wallowed in emotion. Colin Davis has shown his monumental grasp of Berlioz's masterpiece, in concert performances, in the

opera house and on disc. The excitement is intense and always dramatic, the rhythmic vitality successfully projecting the composer's unique, sometimes broken, sometimes lingering, melodies, which often baffle very experienced conductors. Davis always proclaims the rightness of Berlioz's musical ideas, and the moments of sonorous splendour never become empty rhetoric under Davis, but are the equivalent of Shakespeare's inspirational rhetoric in the History plays. He inspires even inexperienced singers of this composer's work with the understanding to interpret Berlioz, and leads those already experienced to new heights.

VICTOR DE SABATA   *Otello*

Toscanini's classic recording of Verdi's *Otello* has clouded the fact that, for sheer electricity and impact, de Sabata's interpretation of the opera can rarely have been equalled by anyone. Admittedly, the conductor who cannot start the masterpiece off like a lightning flash should enter Verdi's home for aged musicians in Milan, but de Sabata unleashed a thunderbolt at Covent Garden with the La Scala orchestra in 1950—and sustained it memorably. There is no reason to suppose that the finest of his *Otellos* in Milan and elsewhere were any less stupendous, less rhythmically vital and dazzling in tone. His retirement because of ill-health in 1953 in his very early sixties was a tragedy.

CARLO MARIA GIULINI   *Don Carlos*

Giulini's standards are so exacting that his reputation as the supreme Verdian conductor of the last two decades has recently been based almost entirely on his definitive account of the *Requiem*. Fortunately, his *Don Carlos* is on disc to prove what operagoers who have heard him in the theatre know: that this is one of the supreme interpretations of an Italian opera. Ever since he first gave it (with Visconti as producer) at Covent Garden in 1958, the opera's greatness has been generally recognized and its popularity has steadily grown. Even allowing for the changing climate of opinion in total favour of Verdi, this was an extraordinary feat. A major occasion was expected, not the revelation that occurred, as the opera, shaped with infinite skill by Giulini, was revealed as a masterpiece. Love scenes ached with tender emotion, ensembles filled the house with waves of glory, the great melodies seized heart and mind, even the allegedly banal 'Friendship' theme of Carlos and Posa. On each occasion this was made to sound like one of Verdi's greatest inspirations; later reprises of it, shaped by the Maestro with controlled rubato, seemed to hang on the air as if they were minted at that moment. These performances were the nonpareil of the art of conducting Italian opera.

REGINALD GOODALL   *The Ring*

After years in the wilderness as a named but rarely heard office holder at Covent Garden, Goodall came to Wagnerian fame in the late 1960s. Those who had heard rare earlier performances of his were not surprised, and a younger generation was awe-struck, instantly making him a much-cheered idol. Even allow-ing for his years of coaching singers and studying, it is almost miraculous that, with so few actual Wagnerian performances behind him, he could in the late 1960s and early 1970s achieve what many eminent conductors never attain, a great *Ring*. True, for Sadler's Wells he had time to prepare his perfor-mances in a way rare at the present time, but how he achieved such 'an indefinable blend of majesty and lyrical radiance' is his own secret. That happy phrase is Peter Heyworth's, writing in the 1970s of performances of *Die Meistersinger von Nürn-berg* in the late 1950s, and it memorably sums up the sound of Goodall's *Ring*, too. It is certainly not achieved by stick technique or obvious personality. Goodall's sometimes slow tempi are quoted against him by detractors, occasionally made frantic by his fame. He forged the Wells orchestra into an instrument capable of playing beyond anyone's expectations, while by inspirational methods he trained his casts to excel themselves, and decisively helped his Brünnhilde (Rita Hunter) and Siegfried (Albert Remedios) to international fame themselves.

HERBERT VON KARAJAN   *Tristan und Isolde*

It is impossible to write of this greatest contemporary inter-preter of *Tristan und Isolde* without mentioning his partnership with the Berlin Philharmonic Orchestra. The result is exquisite beauty, profound spiritual and passionate emotion, tremendous but controlled climaxes, often *bel canto* singing from his casts, and that sound colour which is Karajan's special gift. More-over, the score is really heard by the listener, not obscured at moments by what Joseph Wechsberg has memorably called 'clouds of ecstasy', and some of the score sounds like chamber music with this conductor and orchestra. Karajan's range is exceptional for a jet-age star conductor in his sixties. His *Otello* (Verdi) is for many a legend, and he is one of the finest con-ductors of Puccini. But surely it is *Tristan und Isolde* that is his masterpiece. Other giants have given us even more excitement, more passion, but he and his orchestra penetrate most deeply to the very heart of Wagner's breathtaking transfiguration of a legend, which was already a superb one before the composer brought his genius to it.

ERICH KLEIBER/CARLOS KLEIBER   *Der Rosenkavalier*
It seems only the other day to mere striplings in their mid-forties, who have recently been happily astounded by Carlos Kleiber's performance of Strauss's *Der Rosenkavalier*, that they were responding with joy to his father's classic interpretation. John Higgins was moved to write in *Opera* (Autumn, 1973) that Carlos Kleiber, at Munich, 'lets the score breathe and expand like a man inhaling the air he finds sweetest'. Beautifully put, and applicable to glories long ago. Both father and son became masters of the gaiety and sensuousness of the score, its light and shadows and intoxicating rhythms, and, according to Harold Rosenthal, no conductor since Clemens Krauss has made the waltzes so authentically Viennese as Carlos. Erich Kleiber transfigured the young Covent Garden company in 1950 in this opera and the orchestra rewarded him with their best playing to that date. Carlos, with a much smaller reper-toire than his father, demands particularly long rehearsal periods, which he did not get when he stood in for James Levine at short notice (Covent Garden, 1974), and those who knew this asked themselves just how good he might have been if he had had that extra time.

OTTO KLEMPERER   *Fidelio*
In his Olympian old age, Klemperer made several excursions into the opera house, by far the most successful being Beet-hoven's *Fidelio* at Covent Garden in 1961. The start of the

overture caused a momentary spasm of alarm because of its slow tempo, but seconds later all such thoughts were banished as the most emotionally and artistically satisfying account of the opera many could remember went on its glorious way. It was even (just) possible to forgive the inclusion of the *Leonora No. 3* overture after the Dungeon scene, partly due to the fact that the overwhelming effect of the scene carried the audience safely through the intrusion until the rejoicings and sublimities of the finale. There have been many finer productions of *Fidelio* than this one by Klemperer, which was adequate in the best sense of the word, and there have also been finer casts. Four greater singers were on display: Jurinac, Vickers, Hotter and Frick; but only Vickers and Frick were totally convincing, though Jurinac, in the Dungeon scene, would have melted a heart of steel. There have been more obviously exciting readings of the opera, more lyrical ones, but what set Klemperer's apart was the combination of emotional depth and intensity, and a communicated conviction, through the masterly playing of the orchestra and in every chosen tempo, that this was indeed *Fidelio*. It was Beethoven the great humanist and idealist at his most profound.

HANS KNAPPERTSBUSCH   *Parsifal*

However short the list of legendary interpretations, it would be impossible to leave out Knappertsbusch's *Parsifal*, last heard on August 13, 1964, at Bayreuth, which was also his last appearance in any opera house. *Parsifal* was 'his' opera in the public's mind (though he was never one to speak of 'my' *Tristan, Parsifal*, etc.), and it remains so a decade after his death. Daunting words like 'reverent' have been used to describe his approach to the work, and his tempi were notoriously slow, yet his interpretation was reverent in the true sense of the word because he revered the music and was able to communicate his feeling. As for his tempi, he moulded *Parsifal* so strongly that his long phrases seemed utterly right for the music, and the result was the most moving account, emotionally and intellectually, in living memory. In most of the interpretations chosen for this section the tempi seemed inevitable, the only ones possible. This was particularly so of Knappertsbusch's masterpiece, mercifully preserved on disc for posterity.

GEORG SOLTI   *Die Frau ohne Schatten*

Strauss's opera divides opinion. For hard-line devotees it is an outright masterpiece; for others it is a marathon, a 'pretentious, undramatic, 'long-drawn-out hotch-potch of an opera' (Harold Rosenthal). Solti, that ardent exponent of Strauss, may not share William Mann's opinion that the opera ranks as Strauss's masterpiece, the most moving and beautiful of his operas, but his performances would support such a view of the opera. The composer's immensely rich, kaleidoscopic, sonorous, so well-characterized score can rarely have been more magnificently played than on Solti nights at Covent Garden in the 1960s. The choice of Solti's *Die Frau ohne Schatten* for this section could be controversial, for this performance can never be considered legendary by those who cannot respond to the work. It must be hoped that, despite their reservations, they could recognize a fabulous interpretation executed by an orchestra which, at its finest, is as great as any in the world.

Selected Conductors

ABBADO, CLAUDIO (1933–). The finest of the younger generation of Italian conductors. From the mid-1960s at La Scala and elsewhere, he has made his name as a brilliant, commanding musician, deeply serious in his approach to the score, and completely in tune with his casts. Works he has studied afresh and interpreted memorably include Bellini's *I Capuletti ed i Montecchi* (La Scala and the Holland Festival, 1965), *Don Carlos*, *Simon Boccanegra*) including the Munich Festival, 1971), and *Il Barbiere di Siviglia* and *La Cenerentola*, both with Jean-Pierre Ponnelle as producer. The last was a colossal success in Moscow in 1974 during La Scala's visit. Indeed, Abbado, with Verdi's *Requiem*, *Aida* and *Simon Boccanegra* as well, enjoyed a Russian triumph and an English one at Covent Garden with the same works (less *Aida*) in 1976.

ACKERMANN, OTTO (1909–60). Swiss, his wide-ranging career began when he conducted the Royal Rumanian Opera Company on a tour, aged only 15, and ended with him as General-musikdirektor at Cologne (1953–8) and at Zürich until his death.

ADLER, KURT HERBERT (1905–). Austrian, then American, conductor and manager who, after assisting Toscanini at Salzburg, went to the U.S.A. (see page 312). With the San Francisco Opera since 1943.

ADLER, PETER HERMAN (1899–). A Czech-born American who, after working in his native land, went to the U.S.A. in 1939, helping form the New York Opera Company in 1941. Became Director of N.B.C. Television Opera in 1949.

BALLING, MICHAEL (1866–1925). German. Originally viola player at Bayreuth, he became a conductor in 1896. In charge of many *Tristan und Isolde*, *Parsifal* and *Ring* performances between 1904 and 1924. He also worked at Hallé (East Germany) and Darmstadt.

BARBIROLLI, (SIR) JOHN (1899–1970). English, of Italian parentage, both nations contributing to his unique personality. One of the finest conductors of Italian opera of his day, his famous work with the Hallé Orchestra and his international concert career kept him out of the pit for years at a time, especially after the Second World War. Beginning as a cellist, he joined the British National Opera Company in 1926, and was a regular conductor at Covent Garden (1928–33)—of Italian works and Wagner—being Musical Director of the short-lived Covent Garden English Company, as well as working in the international seasons. He conducted *Tosca* and Turner's *Turandot* in 1937.

After the war, he conducted *Aida* in Vienna (1946–7), and was a guest conductor at Covent Garden (1952–5), conducting Fisher's *Tristan und Isolde* and Ferrier's *Orfeo*, and, as usual, dividing critical opinion, his individual, romantic style sometimes offending the austere. Then, apart from concert versions of opera and some recordings, he vanished from the pit until an *Aida* in Rome with Gwyneth Jones in 1969.

BEECHAM, (SIR) THOMAS (1879–1961). English conductor, manager, wit and one-man ginger group, a native Lancastrian, unlike Barbirolli (above) who was an adopted one. Especially in his early career, he was regularly underrated by some (but not by his players), who could not believe that an amateur and apparently playboyish 'character' could be very good, let alone a genius, which at his best he was. And he was handicapped, like Bernard Shaw, by a talent for publicity which sometimes made him appear a clown. In sober fact, he remains one of the supreme figures in the stormy history of opera in Britain and in the wider field of music in general. That his now legendary company disintegrated after the First World War—though partly reborn as the British National Opera Company—was nothing short of a calamity.

With little musical training and a comparatively modest beginning as a conductor, Beecham became a major figure in 1910 when, backed by his father Sir Joseph (of pills fame), he gave two extraordinary seasons at Covent Garden, which included the first British *Elektra* and *Salome* (Strauss), and the premières of *The Wreckers* (Ethel Smyth) and *A Village Romeo and Juliet* (Delius). Other pre-1914 firsts included Strauss's *Ariadne auf Naxos* and *Der Rosenkavalier*, and he was responsible for the famous Russian seasons at Drury Lane. His legendary Beecham Opera Company began on a permanent basis in 1915 and ended after much glory with the financial collapse of his 1920 international season at Covent Garden. The story of these years can be read in his (much too sober but delightful) *A Mingled Chime*. His remarkable company included Agnes Nicholls, Robert Radford, Frank Mullings, Frederick Ranalow, Norman Allin, Miriam Licette and Frederick Austin.

Away from opera for twelve years, he became the musical and managerial supremo of Covent Garden from 1932 to 1939, also conducting in Germany. During the 1939–45 war, he spent some time conducting opera at the Met, and elsewhere in America, and then was not invited to take part in the birth pangs of the infant Covent Garden Opera Company, which he attacked from time to time, sometimes very irresponsibly. Fortunately, however, he conducted a memorable *Die Meistersinger von Nürnberg* at Covent Garden (1951) and *The Bohemian Girl*, but only three other operas in Britain: *Ariadne auf Naxos* at Edinburgh (1950), *Irmelin* by Delius at Oxford (1953), and *Zémire at Azor* by Grétry at Bath (1955). He also conducted a number of works at the Colón, Buenos Aires (1958).

It is idle to pretend that the impish side of him did not occasionally affect his performances, as when he lost patience with the third act of Siegfried and, as he admitted to Neville Cardus, 'let it rip', to the detriment of composer and singers alike. But he never betrayed his beloved Mozart, or other favourites such as Berlioz, Handel, Delius, Schubert, Haydn and Bizet. Singers were not so universally fond of him as were orchestral players; inevitably, some musicologists —he considered they could read, not hear, music—

blenched at his arrangements; inevitably, his very individual interpretations provoked controversy. He remains unforgotten and unforgettable.

BELLAZZA, VINCENZO (1888–1964). Italian. Regularly at Covent Garden and the Met in the 1920s and 1930s. At Rome and many other Italian houses. Conducted London's first *Turandot* (1927).

BERNSTEIN, LEONARD (1918–). American composer (see page 44) and conductor, who directed the first American *Peter Grimes* at Tanglewood (1946). His operatic career has been limited but spectacular. Apart from conducting his own *Trouble in Tahiti*, his triumphs, some of them controversial, have included a splendid début at La Scala (1953) in Callas's *Medea* and a successful *La Sonnambula* the same year, also with 'La Divina'. His Met début was *Falstaff* (1964), produced by Zeffirelli, and the electric pair enjoyed a triumph to the greater glory of Verdi. With Visconti in Vienna (1966) he had another stunning success with *Falstaff*, but his 1968 *Der Rosenkavalier* there was slow and heavy. (For a good account of it, see Joseph Wechsberg's battlefront report in *Opera*, June 1968.) His Met *Cavalleria Rusticana* (1970) allegedly became dull and showed up Mascagni's 'weaknesses' by obeying his slow tempi, but, doubting much that critics write about '*Cav*', I can only fall back on the motto from Missouri: 'Show me!' However, *Fidelio* in Vienna (1970) was a masterpiece, even subduing one of Bernstein's leading British critics, who not only praised enthusiastically, but used nothing ruder than 'some overheating'. Another contribution by Bernstein to opera has been the operatic chapter in *The Joy of Music,* originally one of his famous telecasts. His musical and theatrical interests are so wide that operagoers can only hope he is lured back more often, perhaps, once again as a composer?

BLECH, LEO (1871–1958). German conductor and composer, particularly associated with Berlin, where he joined the Royal Opera in 1906. Most of his career was spent there until 1937, when his Jewish descent lost him his job. His co-Generalmusikdirektor, Erich Kleiber, had left in 1934. Happily, after seasons in Riga and Stockholm, especially notable for his Wagnerian work, he returned to Berlin in 1949.

BODANSKY, ARTUR (1877–1939). Austrian. After working in Germany and conducting London's first *Parsifal* (1914), he became the Met's chief German conductor (1915–39). Famous, amongst other things, for his pianissimo effects and

for his cuts (shortened versions) in Wagner and others.

BÖHM, KARL (1894–). Austrian. At the time of writing (1974), he has celebrated his 80th birthday with a stunning performance at Salzburg of Strauss's *Die Frau ohne Schatten,* showing 'he can still induce playing of transcendent beauty from ... the largest orchestra' (William Mann). His *Così fan tutte* is discussed on page 215. Engaged by Walter for Munich in 1921, he later served as Generalmusikdirektor at Darmstadt, Hamburg, Dresden (1934–42) and Vienna (1942–4, 1954), resigning after being criticized for spending too much time abroad. Since 1945, he has regularly conducted at Salzburg, in Italy, Bayreuth (from 1963) and at the Met (from 1957). He is particularly renowned for his Mozart and Strauss, giving the premières of Strauss's *Die Schweigsame Frau* (The Silent Woman) in 1935 and *Daphne* in 1938, both in Dresden.

BONYNGE, RICHARD (1929–). Australian. Husband of Joan Sutherland and her chief helper on the way to international fame, not least because he believed that she was born to sing the *bel canto* repertoire at a time when scarcely anyone else shared his belief. He is one of the leading authorities on the period. He made his official conducting début in Rome in

1962, making his Covent Garden début with *I Puritani* (1964). He has lived down a sometimes strong bias against himself as a conductor to become an expert in his field, only failing, perhaps, in *Norma* to satisfy the majority of critics.

BOULEZ, PIERRE (1925–). French composer and conductor who, despite being 'allergic' to Italian opera and actual opera houses, is a magnificent conductor of Wagner at Bayreuth and elsewhere, also of *Pelléas et Mélisande*.

BRAITHWAITE, WARWICK (1898–1971). New Zealander. In opera for almost the whole of his career after joining the O'Mara Company in 1919. He was a key figure at Sadler's Wells, 1933–40, and he returned there in 1960 after four years as Musical Director of the Welsh National Opera. From 1948 to 1952 he was at Covent Garden. A true operatic conductor whose son Nicholas is now rapidly making a similar name for himself.

BÜLOW, HANS VON (1830–94). German conductor and pianist who gave up the law after hearing the première of *Lohengrin* under Liszt. He went to study under Wagner, then with Liszt, whose daughter, Cosima, he married, only to lose her to Wagner. Yet he never wavered in his championship of Wagner

the musician. Before this personal tragedy, he had conducted the première of *Tristan und Isolde* (1865) and *Die Meistersinger von Nürnberg* (1868) as chief conductor of the Royal Opera, Munich. Leaving Munich in 1869, the year Cosima deserted him, he first toured, then conducted in Hanover and Meiningen. This great Wagnerian and first virtuoso conductor also championed Brahms. An admirable man, having disliked Verdi's *Requiem* at first, he later wrote most movingly to the composer about it and the three last operas, recanting *con amore*.

BUSCH, FRITZ (1890–1951). German. His splendid career had two periods of exceptional brilliance and significance. These were from 1922 to 1933, in charge of the Dresden Opera, and at Glyndebourne from 1934 to 1939 and 1950–1 (see page 319). He and Carl Ebert, the great producer, achieved near perfection from the start of the Festival, but, unfortunately, war in 1939 put an end to that. That Busch died so young was tragic, but at least he had helped to re-establish Glyndebourne after the war. A famous Mozartian, it was he who restored *Idomeneo* to the world repertoire, just as he gave Britain Verdi's *Macbeth*. He was also a major Wagnerian and a supremely inspiring rehearser of singers. Also renowned in Stuttgart (1918–22), in Buenos Aires (1933–6), at the Met (1945–9) and elsewhere. This 'uncompromising genius' (John Pritchard) was also a charmer and a tactician. When the mighty Salvatore Baccoloni refused to keep within Mozart's rhythms, Busch finally sent him a telegram of genial protest signed 'Wolfgang Amadeus Mozart'. Conversion was instant.

CAMPANINI, CLEOFONTE (1860–1919). Italian. One of the greatest conductors of his day, whose premières included Cilèa's *Adriana Lecouvreur* and Puccini's *Madame Butterfly*. At Covent Garden (1904–12), where he was much admired, he gave London's first *Butterfly*, *Pelléas et Mélisande* and *La Fanciulla del West* (Puccini). He was Artistic Director of the Manhattan Opera (1906–9) and General Manager at Chicago (1910–19).

CANTELLI, GUIDO (1920–56). Italian. His early death in an air crash deprived the world of an already great conductor, who had just been appointed Music Director of La Scala.

CAPUANA, FRANCO (1894–1969). Italian. In Naples, 1930–7, and La Scala, 1937–40 and 1946–52. He conducted the San Carlo's *La Traviata* at Covent Garden in 1946, the first opera to be heard there after the war, and returned to conduct the resident company in the early

1950s. A noted Wagnerian and a fine conductor of the second rank, liked by his musicians.

CLEVA, FAUSTO (1902–71). Italian conductor, particularly associated with the Met, where, from 1950 until his death, he was in charge of over 650 performances of twenty-seven operas. Previously, he had been chorus-master there.

CLUTYENS, ANDRÉ (1905–67). Belgian. Worked notably in Paris (from 1947) and Bayreuth (1955–8/1965).

COATES, ALBERT (1882–1953). Anglo-Russian composer and conductor, in charge of the St Petersburg Opera (1914–18) after working in Germany. An important figure in London opera in the 1920s and 1930s, he conducted the *Ring* for the British National Opera Company, and Chaliapin in *Boris Godunov*.

COLLINGWOOD, LAURENCE (1887–). English. One of the heroic figures of the young Sadler's Wells Opera, having joined the Old Vic in the 1920s. He was at the Wells from its opening in 1931 as chief conductor and Music Director, 1940–6, most of which time the company was forced to tour. His *Macbeth* was given at the theatre in 1934.

COOPER, EMIL (1877–1960). Russian. Gave the première of

The Golden Cockerel in Moscow (1904) and its British première at Drury Lane (1914). At Chicago, 1929–31, and the Met from 1944 to 1950.

COSTA, (SIR) MICHAEL (1808–84). Italian conductor and composer who settled in Britain in the 1830s. From 1847 to 1869, he was Music Director at Covent Garden, being knighted in 1867. From 1871 to 1879, he was at Her Majesty's.

DAMROSCH, LEOPOLD (1832–85). German. Redeemed the failure of the first Italian opera season at the Met (1883–4) by a German season in which he conducted every performance between November 17, 1884, and February 9, 1885, dying a few days later. His monstrous endurance test included America's first *Die Walküre*. His son, Walter (1862–1950), took over until 1891, his premières including the rest of the *Ring*.

DAVIS, COLIN (1927–). English. Musical Director at Covent Garden (1971–). Had a triumph with his Company at La Scala (1976). At the Wells (1961–5). Best known for his Berlioz (p. 215) and Mozart, also *Peter Grimes*; he has survived a controversial start at the Garden.

DENZLER, ROBERT (1892–). Swiss. Directed the world premières of Berg's *Lulu* (1937) and Hindemith's *Mathis der Maler* (1938) at Zürich, where he was Music Director (1915–27, 1934–47).

DE SABATA, VICTOR (1892–1967). Italian. Second only to Toscanini in his day. At La Scala, 1929–53, finally as Artistic and Music Director. In 1950, he brought his company to London, giving unforgettable performances of Verdi's *Otello* as well as *Falstaff* in a season which saw several older English critics make idiots of themselves in their attacks on the company. Verdi, Wagner and Beethoven found him at his best, while his performance on disc (a form he disliked) of Puccini's *Tosca* (Callas, Gobbi, de Stefano, 1953) remains a gramophone classic.

DESORMIÈRE, ROGER (1898–1963). French. Originally with Diaghilev's Ballet, then at the Opéra-Comique, becoming its director from 1944 to 1946. His local first included Strauss's *Ariadne auf Naxos*.

DOBROWEN, ISSAY (1894–1953). Russian. Made his début at the Bolshoi (1919), then joined Busch at Dresden (1923). At Vienna and Sofia in the 1920s, and Budapest in the 1930s, he later went to Stockholm. He conducted Russian operas at La Scala from 1948 and a fine *Boris Godunov* (Mussorgsky) at Covent Garden in 1952.

DOWNES, EDWARD. English. With the Covent Garden Opera from 1952, and the first Musical Director of Australian Opera, conducting the opening performance in the new Sydney Opera House, Prokofiev's *War and Peace* (1973). A wide-ranging, very reliable conductor he is particularly noted for his Russian performances, including the Western première of Shostakovich's revised *Katerina Ismailova* (1963), which he translated from the original.

EREDE, ALBERTO (1909–). Italian. His career began at Turin in 1935. He conducted at pre-war Glyndebourne, returning in 1946 to become Music Director of the New London Company at the Cambridge. He was at the Met, 1950–5, and the Deutsche Oper am Rhein, 1958–62. A fine teacher who believes in ensemble, he still regularly conducts at Düsseldorf and elsewhere.

FACCIO, FRANCO (1840–91). Italian. Ranks as the first great modern Italian conductor, not least because Verdi approved of him. Faccio went to La Scala in 1871, giving the premières of Verdi's *Aida* and *Otello* and the first Italian Wagner performance, *Lohengrin*. He gave London its first *Otello* (Lyceum, 1889), much impressing Bernard Shaw and others with ears to hear, with his skill.

FAILONI, SERGEI (1890–1948). Italian. Music Director of the Budapest State Opera, 1928–47, and a regular conductor at the Verona Arena.

FRICSAY, FERENC (1914–63). Hungarian. Conductor of the Budapest Opera (1939–45), who became widely known after taking over the première of Einem's *Dantons Tod* at Salzburg (1947) from Klemperer. He also appeared at the San Carlo, Naples, and with Glyndebourne at Edinburgh (1950), but was mainly associated in the 1950s with Berlin and Munich. He was Director of the Berlin Stadtische Opera from 1951 to 1952, but resigned after managerial disputes, and was at the Munich State Opera, 1956–8. He conducted at the rebuilt Deutsches Opernhaus in 1961.

FURTWÄNGLER, WILHELM (1886–1954). German. One of the supreme Wagnerians of this century, his *Tristan und Isolde* recorded with Flagstad proving his greatness for posterity. He built up his reputation with Wagner in Berlin and Paris in the 1920s, and at Bayreuth, La Scala and Covent Garden in the 1930s; however, his interpretations were too individual for some tastes, including the mighty Ernest Newman's, who never accepted his *Ring*. Yet, for most, Furtwängler generated an extraordinary and exciting atmosphere. As Harold

Rosenthal noted when reviewing the 1953 Italian Radio *Ring* (*Opera*, January 1973): 'an oustanding conductor, who just knows how to let the music ebb and flow, and whose broad, expansive reading convinces the listener of the inevitability of fate'. His equivocal position in Nazi Germany created storms of non-musical controversy, and he was not allowed to conduct in America after the war, though, happily, the British let him do so. A film of his Salzburg *Don Giovanni* is with us.

GAVAZZENI, GIANANDREA (1909–). Italian. Noted for his 'drive and effective communications' (Alessandro Camuto) and 'brassy attack' (Peter Hoffer). Also a composer and writer, he has been a regular conductor at La Scala and elsewhere since 1948. He is highly regarded in Italy. In the notable 1972 revival of *I Masnadieri* at Rome, 'his fine balancing of the vocal parts was worthy of Toscanini' (Luigi Bellingardi).

GIBSON, ALEXANDER (1926–). Scottish. Artistic Director of Scottish Opera, which he founded in 1962 (see page 292). By the mid-1960s, he and his brilliant team had raised it to world class. Has had personal triumphs with *Les Troyens*, *The Ring,* Verdi, Puccini, operetta, etc. Before this, he had worked at the Wells, including a period as Musical Director

(1957–9). In a time of financial crisis, his achievements include the première of Gardner's *The Moon and Sixpence* and the famous *Merry Widow* production which established operetta as a regular feature of the Wells repertoire.

GIULINI, CARLO MARIA (1914–). Italian. One of the supreme conductors of our day, whose high standards and suspicion of producers make him, sadly, limit his appearances in the pit. That the greatest living Verdian should confine his activities to the *Requiem* is an eternal frustration, and that neither the 1972 nor the 1973 indices of *Opera* contain references to him, speaks for itself. His incomparable 1958 *Don Carlos* with Visconti is discussed on page 216. Before that, they had collaborated at La Scala, notably in the now legendary productions with Callas of *Alceste* and *La Traviata*. He gave a scintillating account of *Il Barbiere di Siviglia* at Covent Garden (1960), and followed it with his vivacious, authoritative and magical *Falstaff* (1961), with Zeffirelli as producer. His *Don Carlos* in Rome (1965) was summed up by Ireneo Bremini as 'beyond praise', which was a fair description of his Covent Garden *Il Trovatore* earlier in the year. 1965 was the crucial year in Giulini's operatic career, for he refused to accept a Holland Festival production, the designs included, of *Don*

Giovanni, offering to resign rather than conduct. Peter Diamond sided with him. After a compromise of sorts in Holland, the opera reached Edinburgh with an almost bare stage, atmospheric lighting, and simple moves given by Giulini himself. The point should be stressed that Giulini was not advocating Conductor's Opera, but Composer's Opera.

Fortunately, Giulini felt able to collaborate with the great de Fillipo in *Rigoletto* (Rome, 1966), and again with Visconti in a reading of *La Traviata*, which was great in the strictest sense of the word (Covent Garden, 1967), and in *Figaro* at the Met (1968).

GOODALL, REGINALD (1905–). English. Known for years to be a major Wagnerian by the discerning, or lucky (to be at rare performances) few, but seemingly doomed to end his days as a back-room coach at Covent Garden. After minor appointments in the 1930s, he joined the Wells in 1944, conducting the première of *Peter Grimes* (1945), the next year joining the new Covent Garden Company as a conductor. For twenty years he conducted either Italian works for which he was not suited (though he loves Verdi), or occasional Britten or *Boris Godunov* (Mussorgsky) performances and fine *Wozzecks* (Berg), but no Wagner except on tour. Suddenly, in the 1950s, he was

allowed some performances of *Die Meistersinger von Nürnberg*, then appeared to become a non-conductor despite his name on the advance programmes. In fact, partly because of eye trouble, he became a coach. Fortunately, the Wells, via Edmund Tracey backed by Stephen Arlen, chose him for *Die Meistersinger* and, in 1968, aged 62, a great Wagnerian was revealed, with a beat almost as indecisive as that of Furtwängler, his idol. There are some who find his tempi too staid, but, for most, his Wagner is spacious, majestic, weighty, poetic and deeply felt. In 1971, he returned to Covent Garden for *Parsifal,* after less rehearsals than he gets with the Wells, but it gradually became a typically sustained and glorious account of the score. As for his *Ring*, which has made him a household name, operatically speaking, it has been featured on page 217. The first *Evening Standard* Opera Award naturally went to him (1973).

GOOSSENS family. Eugène (1845–1906) was English but born in Belgium, and gave the first English *Tannhäuser* (1882) with the Carl Rosa. Eugène II (1867–1958) also conducted for Carl Rosa, and other companies, including Beecham's from 1917. Eugène III (1892–1962) began with Beecham, then conducted for the British National Opera

Company. Later, he changed to concert work. His two operas, *Judith* (1929) and *Don Juan de Mañara* (1937), had librettos by Arnold Bennett.

GUI, VITTORIO (1885–1975). Italian. Chiefly responsible for founding the Maggio Musicale in Florence, an annual event since 1938. He had started the Florence Orchestra ten years earlier. Formerly the doyen of Italian conductors, his magnificent career included working with Toscanini at La Scala in the 1920s and 1930s, notable successes at Covent Garden (1938–9, 1952), and a long reign at Glyndebourne from 1952, beginning with a sparkling *La Cenerentola* (Rossini). It was Gui who was mainly responsible for the Rossini revival in Italy in the 1920s and 30s. Not the least of his triumphs at Glyndebourne, apart from Mozart, Rossini, Gluck, Bellini and Verdi, was his *Pelléas et Mélisande* (Debussy), 'authoritative and affectionate', according to Spike Hughes. In Florence his revivals have included Spontini and Cherubini and contemporary operas, also an historic *Khovanshchina* (Mussorgsky) in 1948. As late as 1972, he walked out before a Rome *La Traviata* when given singers and a production of which he did not approve.

HALASZ, LÁSZLÓ (1905–). Hungarian, then American, conductor at Budapest, Prague, Vienna and Salzburg in the 1920s and 30s; also the U.S.A., where he became Director of the City Center, New York (1943–51). After being dismissed somewhat drastically, he returned to Europe.

HEGER, ROBERT (1886–). German. Worked in Berlin (1933–50) and elsewhere, including Covent Garden (1925–35) to which he returned with the Munich Company (1953), conducting London's first *Capriccio* as part of an excellent, but shamefully ill-attended, Strauss Festival.

JOCHUM, EUGENE (1902–). German. His early posts included Hanover (1934–9) and, since 1945, he has appeared regularly in leading German houses and at Bayreuth, where, unlike some of the 1970s conductors, he has maintained an international standard, notably his 1972 *Parsifal*.

JULLIEN, LOUIS (1812–60). French. Conductor of concerts and opera who tried to found a national English Opera at Drury Lane, with native works included, and with Berlioz as conductor. He went bankrupt.

KARAJAN, HERBERT VON (1908–). Austrian. His *Tristan und Isolde* is featured on page 217. One of the finest post-war (1945) conductors, not the least of his virtues is a wide-ranging taste, extending to

Italian *verismo*. His *Tosca*, passionate, dramatic, warm and totally committed, should be forcibly fed to Joseph ('Shabby little shocker') Kerman and his disciples. Von Karajan excels in *bel canto* operas and Verdi as well as Wagner and Strauss. His classical interpretations divide opinion, especially his *Fidelio*, which at times down the years has been accused by some of lacking heart and the profundity of other great conductors. Making his début at Ulm in 1928, he was in Berlin throughout the war, becoming internationally famous soon after. He was artistic director of the Vienna State Opera from 1956 to 1964; is well-known at La Scala, not least for his incomparable *La Bohème* with Zeffirelli (1963); has appeared at Bayreuth; and has been artistic director at Salzburg, 1958–60, and from 1964. In 1966 he inaugurated an Easter Festival there. His Wagnerian performances at these Easter seasons with the Berlin Philharmonic, if anything becoming more lyrical down the years, are for many one of the great events of each year, while amongst his finest summer successes have been his 1970 and 1971 performances of Verdi's *Otello* (Vickers, Freni, Glossop). More often than not now he is his own producer, a fervent user of lighting and dark shadows, and a believer in singers who can act and look their parts. In his huge Salz-burg theatre, and with the orchestra unconcealed, unlike Bayreuth's, this can sometimes lead to inadequate volume from his hand-picked casts. Down the years, he has been given much jet-set publicity, and, indeed, he is a glamorous figure. But his dedication to opera is total, and often the results of that dedication are stupendous. His decision to give *Die Meistersinger von Nürnberg* in two parts at Salzburg (1975) resulted in an unforgettable last act given by uniquely fresh singers.

KEILBERTH, JOSEPH (1908–68). German. Died while conducting *Tristan und Isolde* in Munich during the Festival. After holding posts at Karlsruhe and Dresden, he went to the Munich State Opera in 1951, remaining there until his death, also conducting at Bayreuth and elsewhere. He was best known for his Strauss performances, though his repertoire was wide. His performances of Pfitzner's *Palestrina* were famous, and he was a noted Wagnerian and Mozartian.

KEMPE, RUDOLF (1910–76). German. Greatly admired in Britain as well as Germany, and a favourite of orchestral players, whom he inspired to play with maximum beauty. Though best known for his Wagner and Strauss, he was also a fine Verdian and Puccinian, and expressed regret that he was too rarely asked to conduct Italian opera. His 1957 *Madame Butterfly* at Covent Garden (with de los Angeles) remains a treasured memory. His 'chamber-music' *Ring* created controversy after the first delighted impact, but for all except those who can only listen to one interpretation, it was as fascinating as another's fire and drive—in London's case being the next in the Covent Garden pit, Georg Solti. Kempe not only trained orchestras and singers to rare heights, he instructed audiences; witness the clarity of texture of his memorable 1973 *Elektra* (Strauss) at Covent Garden, and the equal clarity of the singers. A musicians' musician, whom the public adored.

KLEIBER, ERICH (1890–1956). Austrian, then Argentinian conductor, whose *Der Rosenkavalier* is featured on page 218. His son Carlos has astounded Vienna (*Tristan und Isolde*, 1973) and Covent Garden (*Der Rosenkavalier*, 1974) by proving to be as great a conductor in the strictest sense of the word, as was his father. Munich and other German cities already knew this, not least from stunning *Wozzeck* performances. Carlos is a perfectionist who demands as many rehearsals as possible.

His father made his name as the Generalmusikdirektor of the Berlin State Opera (1923–33), giving the house one of the supreme periods of its history. The première of Berg's *Wozzeck* (1924) was only one major event. He left Berlin and Germany over Hindemith's *Mathis der Maler* (see Hindemith, page 60), going to Amsterdam, then, during the Second World War, to the Teatro Colón, Buenos Aires. It was the great good fortune of the infant Covent Garden Opera Company, under constant attack from critics and many operagoers, to get the services of Kleiber from 1950 to 1953. The orchestra became a great one on Kleiber nights, and, if even he could not turn the resident company into great singers, he helped eradicate part of the inferiority complexes that afflicted many of them, and frequently got them to excel themselves. His repertoire included Tchaikovsky's *The Queen of Spades*, *Le Nozze di Figaro, Carmen* and, most notably, *Der Rosenkavalier* and Britain's first *Wozzeck*. He became chief of the Berlin State Opera again in 1954, but interference forced him to resign.

KLEMPERER, OTTO (1885–1973). German. His *Fidelio* is featured on page 218. Younger concert and operagoers, who regarded him with awe as the ultimate authority on Beethoven, and as a magnificent-looking old man whose private afflictions only increasee his majestic image, often failed to appreciate how wide-ranging his career had been. Mahler recommended him to the Prague National Theatre (1907–10), after which he went to Hamburg and other German houses, culminating in Berlin (1927–33), where he first conducted at the Kroll Opera, then the State Opera. This rich period in the capital included many premières, among them Hindemith's *Cardillac*, Schoenberg's *Erwartung*, Janáček's *From the House of the Dead* and Stravinsky's *Mavra*, and he also conducted many repertoire works, Italian ones included: Puccini's *Il Trittico*, Verdi's *Luisa Miller*, etc. He later revealed something of his musical nature by stomping out of Bellini's *La Sonnambula* at Covent Garden, but publicly hailing *Norma*.

Forced to leave Germany by the Nazis, he went to the U.S.A. and, apart from a spell in Budapest (1947–50), was essentially a concert conductor for the rest of his life. Fortunately, Covent Garden persuaded him to conduct—and produce—*Fidelio* in 1961, and he also conducted and produced *The Magic Flute* (1962) and *Lohengrin* (1963). The former was disappointing, often dull and slow to listen to, and visually unfortunate; the latter was a musical triumph, slow perhaps, but majestic and glorious and mainly well sung. The rest is silence. It is better to end this entry with the word *Fidelio*.

KNAPPERTSBUSCH, HANS (1888–1965). German. His *Parsifal* is featured on page 219. This was his most famous interpretation, and Wagner's works generally, and Strauss, saw him at his peak of achievement. Generalmusikdirektor of the Munich Opera (1922–36), his criticism of the Nazis forced him to go to the Vienna State Opera (1936–50). He conducted at Bayreuth from 1951, and in Milan, Rome, Paris and Zürich. Covent Garden only heard him— memorably — in Strauss's *Salome* (1937), where his custom of not taking a curtain call was noted. For a personal account of this very great conductor, see *Opera*, January, 1966, where Hans Hotter paid him tribute. Knappertsbusch's authority, devotion to the composer and personality remain unforgotten.

KONWITSCHNY, FRANZ (1901–62). German. Posts included Frankfurt (1938–45), Hanover (1946–9), conductor of the Leipzig Gewandhaus Orchestra from 1949, Dresden (1953–5), then Generalmusikdirektor of the (East) Berlin State Opera from 1955. He conducted at Covent Garden (*The Ring*, 1959), in East Europe and in Italy, being best known for his performances of Wagner, Strauss, Mozart and Russian composers.

KOUSSEVITSKY, SERGE (1874–1951). Russian but later settled

in America. He commissioned Britten's *Peter Grimes* for the Berkshire Festival, though Sadler's Wells gave the opera its première (1945). Though best known for his concert hall work, he helped popularize Russian opera in the West, notably in Paris in 1921.

KRAUSS, CLEMENS (1893–1954). Austrian. Friend, and a famous interpreter of Richard Strauss. After making his name at Frankfurt (1924–9), he went to Vienna (1929–35), Berlin (1935–7), and Munich as General-musikdirektor (1937–42). He conducted the first *Arabella* (Dresden, 1933), *Friedenstag* (Munich, 1938), *Capriccio* (Munich, 1942), for which he wrote the libretto, and *Die Liebe der Danae* (Salzburg, 1952), all operas by Strauss. A favourite with singers, three of his most famous were with him in Vienna, Berlin and Munich: Adele Kern, Julius Patzak and Viorica Ursuleac, who became his wife. Covent Garden enjoyed him in several capacities, giving the London premières of *Arabella* and Weinberger's *Schwanda the Bagpiper* in 1934, *Salome* and *Fidelio* with the Vienna State Opera in their legendary 1947 season, and conducting *Tristan und Isolde*, *Fidelio* and *Die Meistersinger von Nürnberg* (1951–3) with the resident company. He was a magnificent builder of ensembles in an age when it could be done.

KRIPS, JOSEF (1902–74). Austrian. A great Mozartian, for whom orchestras often played ravishingly. At the Vienna State Opera from 1933 to 1938, when he fell foul of the Nazis. He conducted the first post-war performance in Vienna and soon restored the Vienna Opera to its former glory, and helped restore the Salzburg Festival as well. The sight of this benign, bald-headed veteran inspired confidence in any discerning audience, confidence based on previous performances of *Der Rosenkavalier* which were essentially Viennese, and stirring ones of *Fidelio*. He conducted both these at Covent Garden, where he made his début in the 1947 visit by the Vienna State Opera (*Don Giovanni, Figaro, Così fan tutte*).

KROMBHOLC, JAROSLAV (1918–). Czech. A notable personality at the Prague National Theatre since the 1940s. Perhaps the most authoritative interpreter of Janáček.

KUBELIK, RAFAEL (1914–). Czech. Made his name with the Czech Philharmonic and at Brno, then left Czechoslovakia in 1948. In Britain, he conducted memorable performances of Janáček's *Katya Kabanova* at the Wells (1954), and was Musical Director of Covent Garden, 1955–8, highlights of his reign being his opening production, Verdi's *Otello*, and Berlioz's *Les*

Troyens. Though fuller and better performances of the latter have been given since, this production of *Les Troyens* was the most important Berlioz event of the century, paving the way for the composer's secure, if controversial position as a great master. Appointed Musical Director of the Met in 1973, after years of concert work, he had the misfortune to lose his brilliant new Director of Productions, Goran Gentele, before their first season together began, and his short reign, which included *Les Troyens*, was ill-starred.

LACHNER, FRANZ (1803–90). German. He made the Munich Opera world-famous, first appearing there in 1836, and becoming Generalmusikdirektor from 1852 until he died. Anti-Wagnerian, he was 'converted' and produced *Tannhäuser* (1855) and *Lohengrin* (1858).

LEINSDORF, ERICH (1912–). Austrian-born American. Having assisted Bruno Walter and Toscanini at Salzburg in the 1930s, he made his Met début with *Die Walküre* in 1938. He stayed until 1943, then returned in 1962. Following a triumphant return to the Met in late 1971 with *Tristan und Isolde*, his 1972 *Ring* at the Met, robust, no-nonsense and traditional in the best possible way, was much admired. *Tannhäuser* at Bayreuth (1972).

LEITNER, FERDINAND (1912–). German. He became Musical Director of Stuttgart in 1947, taking up the equivalent post in Zürich in 1969. A thoroughly reliable conductor, he is particularly admired for his Strauss performances. 1972 found him conducting memorable performances of *Capriccio* in London (with the Bavarian State Opera) and Munich. He has made many guest performances in Europe and South America.

LEVINE, JAMES (1943–). American. A major figure at the Met, where he is now Musical Director. He is especially noted for his Verdi.

LUDWIG, LEOPOLD (1908–). Austrian. His many posts have included Generalmusikdirektor at Hamburg State Opera, 1950–71. His *Ring* in Stuttgart in 1971 was much admired.

MAAZEL, LORIN (1930–). American. A former boy prodigy, who became Music Director of the Deutsche Opera, West Berlin, in 1964. He has made its orchestra a marvellous instrument. A renowned interpreter of Russian music, also of Wagner and Strauss, Verdi and Puccini.

MACKERRAS, CHARLES (1925–). American-born Australian. Musical Director of Sadler's Wells/ English National Opera since 1970. Three years' study in Prague made him a passionate champion of Janáček, not only as a brilliant conductor of the composer, but as the leader of the uphill struggle to get him accepted. Long engagements at the Wells in the 1950s and 1960s included memorable performances of Janáček's *Katya Kabanova*, *The Makropoulos Case* and *From the House of the Dead*. For the three years before his present post, he was First Conductor of the Hamburg State Opera. His repertoire is enormous and he is quite simply one of the best operatic conductors in the world, of Verdi, Wagner and Puccini. A regular guest at Covent Garden.

MAHLER, GUSTAV (1860–1911). Austrian composer (but not of operas, except for two early, unpublished ones) and one of the greatest of all operatic conductors. After early appointments in Prague and Hamburg, he became, in the space of a year—1897—conductor, Director and Aristic Director of the Vienna Opera, remaining there until 1907. He coined the immortal phrase, 'Tradition is Schlamperei' (Tradition is slovenliness), built up a legendary ensemble, proved a magnificent producer of Mozart, Wagner and Verdi, as well as a superlative conductor. He spent fortunes, but wiped out the Opera's deficit, and for the first and last time made Vienna's Opera the greatest in the world. An artistic dictator and a

Jew, he invitably made enemies. He conducted Covent Garden's first *Ring* cycle (1892) and was at the Met from 1907 to 1910.

MANCINELLI, LUIGI (1848–1921). Italian. His positions included Covent Garden (1888–1905), where he conducted the first British *Falstaff* (Verdi) and *Tosca* (Puccini); also the Theatre Royal, Madrid (1888–95), and the Met (1893–1903), where his many American premières included Verdi's *Ernani* and *Falstaff*, Saint-Saëns' *Samson et Dalila*, and Puccini's *La Bohème* and *Tosca*. He wrote a number of operas.

MASCHERONI, EDOARDO (1852–1941). Italian. Admired by Verdi, for whom he conducted the first *Falstaff* (1893). Earlier, he had conducted the first Italian *Fidelio* (Beethoven) in Rome and the première of Catalini's *La Wally* at La Scala (1892), where he also gave a number of Wagner performances, including La Scala firsts: *Tannhäuser, Der fliegende Holländer*, and *Die Walküre*.

MATAČIĆ, LOVRO VON (1899–). Yugoslav. Held major appointments in Dresden and Berlin in the 1950s and succeeded Solti at Frankfurt in 1961.

MEHTA, ZUBIN (1936–). Indian. At La Scala, Vienna and Salzburg, from the early 1960s, and the Met from 1965. One of the most fiery conductors in opera, and none the worse for that. His Rome *Tristan und Isolde* (1972) was conducted 'with a vehemence and nerve-wracking lucidity which was almost hallucinatory' (Luigi Bellingardi, *Opera*), and many of those who have not had the chance to hear a performance conducted by him in the flesh will know his thrilling, totally Puccinian, *Turandot* recording with Sutherland.

MITROPOULOS, DIMITRI (1896–1960). Greek. Conductor and composer, best known for his concerts, but occasionally in opera, notably at the Met, 1954–60, where, in 1958, he conducted the first *Vanessa* (Barber). He also gave Berg's *Wozzeck* at La Scala and Strauss's *Elektra* at the Florence Festival.

MOLINARI-PRADELLI, FRANCESCO (1911–　). Italian. Has worked in many leading houses in Italy, also in San Francisco (from 1957), Vienna and Covent Garden.

MONTEUX, PIERRE (1874–1964). French. He made occasional and welcome visits to conduct opera in Paris and New York, most notably at the latter, 1953–6, when he gave superb performances of *Manon*, *Faust* and *Hoffmann*.

MOTTL, FELIX (1856–1911). Austrian conductor who assisted Wagner at the first Bayreuth Festival (1876) and later conducted there. At Karlsruhe in 1890, he gave the first complete *Les Troyens*, on two nights. Later, he conducted in London and New York, and was at Munich, 1903–11, as Director from 1907. His wife was the soprano, Zdenka Fassbänder (see page 143).

MUCK, KARL (1859–1940). German conductor, in charge of Moscow's and St Petersburg's first performances of *The Ring* (1889). Much of his career was spent in Berlin (1892–1912) where he was Generalmusik-direktor from 1908. He conducted 1,071 performances of 103 operas there, thirty-five of them novelties. At Bayreuth, 1901–30, where his *Parsifal* was regarded as the finest of his period.

MUDIE, MICHAEL (1914–62). English conductor of the Carl Rosa (1935–9) and Sadler's Wells (1946–53), where he showed himself to be a brilliant interpreter of Italian opera.

MUGNONE, LEOPOLDO (1858–1941). Italian conductor and composer of almost Mozartian precocity, his first opera, *Il Dottore Bartolo Salaspariglia* being produced when he was 12. At 16 he was conducting a season of comic operas at La Fenice. In 1890 he conducted the first *Cavalleria Rusticana*, and *Tosca* in 1900, both in Rome, then appeared regularly at La Scala and Covent Garden, his London premières included Cilèa's *Adriana Lecouvreur* (1904). An excellent conductor.

NAPRAVNIK, EDUARD (1839–1916). Russian. He succeeded Lyadov as Chief Conductor of the Imperial Theatres in 1869. His more than 4,000 performances included the premières of Mussorgsky's *Borus Godunov* and Tchaikovsky's *The Maid of Orleans*, which was dedicated to him.

NIKISCH, ARTUR (1855–1922). Hungarian. Originally a violinist. At Leipzig, 1878–89, and Director of the Budapest Opera, 1893–95, he became best known as a concert conductor, occasionally appearing as a guest in opera houses. His *Ring* cycles in 1913 and 1914 at Covent Garden were hugely admired.

PANIZZA, ETTORE (1875–1967). Argentinian. At Covent Garden, 1907–14, La Scala for many seasons between 1921 and 1948, the Met, 1934–42, and the Colón, Buenos Aires, 1921–67. His La Scala premières included Puccini's *Il Trittico*, and the first Italian *Khovanschchina* (Mussorgsky). He also composed operas.

PERLEA, JUNEL (1900–70). Rumanian. Much of his early career was at the Bucharest Opera, where he was Director 1934–44. His local premières

included *Der Rosenkavalier*, *Falstaff* and *Die Meistersinger von Nürnberg*. From 1946, he appeared regularly in Italy, including La Scala. At the Met, 1949–50.

PITT, PERCY (1870–1932). English. Trained in Germany, and spent much of his career at Covent Garden from 1902. He became Music Director of the Grand Opera Syndicate (1907–24), conducted with the Beecham Opera Company (1915–18), and became Artistic Director of the British National Opera Company (1920–24).

POLACCO, GIORGIO (1875–60). Italian. His early career included the première of Leoncavallo's *Zaza* (Milan, 1900), and much of his later work was in South and North America, including seven seasons in Rio de Janeiro, a spell at the Met (1912–17), and a famous period at Chicago, 1918–1930, as chief conductor from 1921.

PRÊTRE, GEORGES (1924–). French. Well known in Europe and America, and often controversial except in French opera, though his *Carmen* sometimes divides opinion. At his finest, he generates much excitement.

PREVITALI, FERNANDO (1907–). Italian. Helped Gui found the Florence Orchestra and Festival (1928–36), then became the influential Director of the Radio Italiana Orchestra.

He was regularly at La Scala in the 1940s. A distinguished Verdian, he has also conducted many modern works, including the première of Dallapiccola's *Volo di Notte* at Florence (1940).

PRITCHARD, JOHN (1921–). English. He has been closely associated with Glyndebourne since 1947. He has also conducted regularly at Covent Garden since 1952, and abroad, including seasons at the Vienna State Opera in the 1950s and 1960s. His repertoire is immense, and he has conducted some important premières: at Glyndebourne, Henze's *Elegy for Young Lovers* (1961), an English first, and at Covent Garden, Britten's *Gloriana* (1953), and Tippett's *The Midsummer Marriage* (1955) and *King Priam* (1962). At his best, a magnificent Mozartian.

QUADRI, ARGEO (1911–). Italian. Especially well known in Italy and at the Vienna Volksoper, where he has often conducted Verdi's *Nabucco* and Rossini's *William Tell* (since 1957).

RANKL, KARL (1898–1968). Austrian, then British. Widely experienced in Germany before the war (1939), after which he became Musical Director of the new Covent Garden Company in 1946. He left in 1951 after a stormy reign, almost inevitable when a company had to be built up from nothing. Yet by the time he left, it was beginning to find its feet in a modest way (not least because of Kleiber's first spell with the company). Not a great conductor, though his Strauss was generally admired, and his personality grated. His partnership with the young Peter Brook was unhappy, yet the foundations were laid. From 1958 to 1960, he was Music Director of the Elizabethan Opera Trust in Australia.

REINER, FRITZ (1888–1963). Hungarian, then American. He gave the first German *Die Frau ohne Schatten* (Strauss) at Dresden in 1919. He conducted at San Francisco (1936–8) and at the Met (1948–52), being best known for his Mozart, Wagner and Strauss performances. In the pit for Flagstad's London début as Isolde in 1936.

RICHTER, HANS (1843–1916). German. Originally a horn player, from 1866 he was closely associated with Wagner, which culminated in his conducting the first *Ring* at Bayreuth (1876) and in his working there until 1912. Gave the first English *Tristan und Isolde* and *Die Meistersinger* at Drury Lane (1882), and the first English *Ring* (Covent Garden, 1908), but he failed to found a permanent English National Opera owing to the hostility of the Covent Garden management of the day. A renowned conductor, his career was a glorious one.

ROBERTSON, JAMES (1912–). English. Music Director of Sadler's Wells Opera in a very fine period, 1946–54, his company being a strong one, and the standard of productions usually light-years ahead of Covent Garden at that time.

ROSBAUD, HANS (1895–1962). Austrian. After holding various posts in Germany between the wars, he became Chief Conductor of the Aix-en-Provence Festival (1947–59). A brilliant conductor of modern music, he gave the première of *Moses und Aron* in Zürich (1957), and famous performances of two other Schoenberg works, *Erwartung* and *Von Heute auf Morgen*, at the 1958 Holland Festival.

ROSENSTOCK, JOSEPH (1895–). Polish. Conducted mainly in Germany until 1936. At the New York City Centre, 1948–55; Cologne, 1958–9; at the Met in the 1960s.

ROZHDESTVENSKY, GENNADI (1930–). Russian. His appointment as Chief Conductor at the Bolshoi, Moscow, in 1965 made him the youngest ever to hold the post. He retired in 1970 to devote more time to concerts, having proved himself an admirable and brilliant interpreter of Russian and other opera.

RUDEL, JULIUS (1921–). Austrian, later American, conductor who has been Artistic Director of the New York City Opera since 1957. A very fine musician and a superb administrator, he has made the company the most adventurous in America, with a repertoire which includes Handel, Henze and Monteverdi, as well as the obvious giants. One of his greatest triumphs was Boito's *Mefistofele* with Treigle (1969), and he has greatly assisted the career of Beverly Sills. Recent overseas successes have included *Figaro* and *Il Trovatore* in Paris, and Strauss's *Capriccio* in Hamburg.

SALMHOFFER, FRANZ (1900–). Austrian conductor and composer whose career has been mainly in Vienna. He became Director of the Volksoper in 1955. His operas have had some local success.

SANTINI, GABRIELE (1886–1965). Italian. He assisted Toscanini at La Scala (1925–9), then went to Rome (1929–32), where he became Music Director (1944–62). He also conducted in London, Chicago and Buenos Aires.

SANZOGNO, NINO (1911–). Italian conductor and composer who has worked at La Scala from 1941, where he rapidly made his name as an expert on contemporary works, including

Oedius Rex (Stravinsky) *The Consul* (Menotti), *Troilus and Cressida* (Walton), *The Fiery Angel* (Prokofiev) and *Les Dialogues des Carmélites* (Poulenc). At La Piccola Scala, he proved a brilliant interpreter of 18th-century Italian works. Though a notable middle and late Verdian, he is least noted for his interpretations of 19th-century music. A typically fine Verdi performance was his *Simon Boccanegra* at the Verona Arena (1973).

SAWALLISCH, WOLFGANG (1923–). German. One of the finest conductors to appear in Germany since 1945. His posts from 1953 have included Aachen, Wiesbaden and Cologne (1959–63), and he conducted at Bayreuth from 1957 to 1961, including *Tristan und Isolde, Der Fliegende Holländer,* and *Tannhäuser*. Since 1971, Generalmusikdirektor of the Bavarian State Opera, Munich. An excellent musician, technically superb, but not, it appears, one who reaches the supreme heights.

SCHALK, FRANZ (1863–1931). Austrian. Worked notably at Vienna from 1900 until his death, sharing the first conductorship with Strauss from 1919, until the two fell out in 1924. He helped found the Salzburg Festival. His *Ring* performances at Covent Garden before the First World War were greatly admired.

SCHERCHEN, HERMANN (1891–1966). German conductor, most of whose appearances, in opera were with contemporary works. These included Dallapiccola's *Il Prigioniero* at Florence (1950) Henze's *König Hirsch* in Berlin (1956), and Prokofiev's *The Gambler* in Naples, the first two being premières.

SCHIPPERS, THOMAS (1930–). American. In charge of the première of Menotti's *The Consul* (1950) and, since then, a regular conductor of that composer in New York, at Spoleto and elsewhere. He has also conducted Puccini memorably at Spoleto, including a superb *Manon Lescaut* in 1973. He has become one of the finest Verdians of the day, 'faithful to the example of Toscanini', said Alessandro Camuto of his brilliant *La Traviata* at La Fenice (1972). In 1966, a year in which he conducted an excellent *L'Elisir d'Amore* (Donizetti) at the old Met, he opened the new building in Lincoln Center with Barber's *Antony and Cleopatra*, conducting an all-American cast.

SCHMIDT-ISSERSTEDT, HANS (1900–73). German. His career began in the 1920s and he became first conductor of the Hamburg State Opera in 1935, going to Berlin to the German Opera in 1943. Though he later became best known as the conductor of the North German Radio Symphony Orchestra (not least to British listeners), he conducted opera in Hamburg, Munich, Glyndebourne and Covent Garden. In the last house, his *Tristan und Isolde* (1962) was widely admired, except for those who wanted more intensity, while his 1972 *Der fliegende Holländer* was inspired.

SCHUCH, ERNST VON (1846–1914). Austrian. At Dresden from 1872 to 1914, becoming Generalmusikdirektor from 1882. He gave the premières of Strauss's *Der Feuersnot, Salome, Elektra and Der Rosenkavalier*, and was a major Wagnerian, also introducing Puccini to Dresden.

SCHÜLER, JOHANNES (1894–1966). German. At the Berlin State Opera (1936–49) and Generalmusikdirektor at Hanover (1949–60).

SEBASTIAN, GEORGE (1903–). Hungarian. In Germany between the wars, then at San Francisco (1944–7) and the Paris Opéra from 1947 until the reforms of the early 1970s.

SEIDL, ANTON (1850–98). Hungarian conductor who helped Wagner prepare the score of *The Ring*, the composer then recommending him to Leipzig. Later, at the Met (1885–9), he gave the first American performance of *Die Meistersinger von Nürnberg, Tristan und Isolde*, and all *The Ring* except

Die Walküre. He conducted London's first *Ring* at Her Majesty's (1882), later making a good impression at Covent Garden (1897), and at Bayreuth with *Parsifal* (1897).

SERAFIN, TULLIO (1878–1968). Italian, for many years the doyen of his nation's conductors. At his finest, a great conductor, but even more remarkable perhaps was his guidance of singers, especially at vital moments early in their careers. Ponselle, Gobbi, Callas and Sutherland are only some of those whose rise to fame was blessed with his help and inspiration. Beginning as a violinist at La Scala, he first conducted there in 1909 two years after his Covent Garden début. He was chief conductor and artistic director in Rome from 1934 to 1943 and again in 1962, his first spell seeing the local première of Berg's *Wozzeck* with Tito Gobbi; while at the Met (1924–34), apart from numerous Italian repertory performances, he conducted world premières of several native operas, including Gruenberg's *The Emperor Jones* and Taylor's *Peter Ibbetson*. His La Scala premières included the first Italian *Der Rosenkavalier* (1911), the first *Oberon* (Weber, 1913) and the first *Peter Grimes* (Britten, 1947), and he conducted Callas on many glorious occasions in the 1950s. In 1959, having coached Joan Sutherland as

Donizetti's Lucia, he was in the pit for her legendary first night.

SOLTI, (SIR) GEORG (1912–   ). Hungarian, then British, conductor, knighted in 1971. At Budapest (1933–9) and Salzburg (1937–8) assisting Toscanini, after which, being Jewish, he was forced into exile in Switzerland. He made his name at Munich (1947–52) and, especially, at Frankfurt (1952–61), and elsewhere, before becoming Music Director of Covent Garden in 1961. He had conducted a superb *Der Rosenkavalier* there in 1959.

His ten-year reign in London aimed at making Covent Garden the world's finest opera house, and judged as a house where opera is (rightly) music and drama, the Company achieved his ideal on a number of occasions and never descended to the dramatic depths often plumbed by most other great companies. His own special glories were Wagner, Strauss and Verdi, though it should be stressed that his dynamic, often electrifying readings sometimes triggered off over-tension on first nights. By the third performances, when there were no critics officially present to record for posterity, there was often greatness, notably when he conducted Verdi's *Otello*. Particularly fine were the British première of Schoenberg's *Moses und Aron*, produced by Peter Hall (1965), Strauss's *Arabella*,

and all his Wagner, because, however much opinion varied on interpretation, no one could deny the excitement he generated. His finest Mozart was perhaps his *Don Giovanni* (1962, with Zeffirelli) as darkly romantic as it was fiery and dramatic. (See also *Covent Garden*, page 288.) Solti finished his reign with magnificent performances of Wagner's *Tristan und Isolde* and Tchaikovsky's *Eugene Onegin*. He had not created a genuine ensemble and he (probably rightly) says it is impossible in the jet age. In 1973, with Strehler, he opened the Liebermann reign at the Paris Opéra with a powerful account of *Le Nozze di Figaro* at Versailles, returning to Covent Garden for Bizet's *Carmen*, as relaxed as his first return the previous year had been sensuous and warmly dramatic in Strauss's *Elektra*. His 1975 performance of Strauss's *Die Frau ohne Schatten* at Covent Garden was as thrillingly satisfying as earlier performances.

STEINBERG, WILLIAM (1899–   ). German, then American conductor, Generalmusikdirektor at Frankfurt (1929–33) until the Nazis sacked him. He had conducted the première of Schoenberg's *Von Heute auf Morgen* there (1930). Since the war, his performances of Wagner, Verdi and Strauss in San Francisco, the Met, and elsewhere have been much admired.

STIEDRY, FRITZ (1883–1968). Austrian, he succeeded Bruno Walter as Chief Conductor of the Berlin Stadtische Opera in 1929 after spells (from 1907) at Dresden, Berlin and Vienna Volksoper, returning to Berlin in 1928. With Carl Ebert he gave a superb *Macbeth* and an equally famous *Simon Boccanegra*. Exiled in 1933, he conducted in Russia until 1937. From 1941, he became a regular conductor in America, especially at the Met (1946–58).

SZÉLL, GEORG (1897–1970). Hungarian, then American, conductor, who began as a child pianist. His posts between the two world wars included Generalmusikdirektor of the Prague German Opera (1929–37). Noted for his performances of Wagner and Strauss at the Met (1942–6). At Salzburg in 1949, he conducted *Der Rosenkavalier*, later conducting Mozart and a number of premières, including Liebermann's *Penelope* (1954).

TALICH, VÁCLAV (1883–1961). Czech, who had a stormy yet important career at the National Opera, Prague, running and reforming it from 1935 to 1945, being removed until 1947, and finally ejected from it and other posts in 1948.

TIETJEN, HEINZ (1881–1967). German conductor and producer, much of whose long career was spent in Berlin and at Bayreuth where he was Artistic Director of the festival, 1931–44, conducting there again in 1959. His Berlin posts included General Intendant of the Preussisches Staatstheater (1927–45), and Intendant of the Stadtische Oper (1948–54), after which he went to Hamburg for five years. His productions were decently traditional, including Wagner's *Der fliegende Holländer*, *Parsifal* and *Die Meistersinger* in the early 1950s at Covent Garden.

TOSCANINI, ARTURO (1867–1957). Italian. If there was a Mount Rushmore of opera conductors and only three could be sculpted on the mountain side, one would have to be Toscanini, for his stupendous achievements and for his ferocious dedication to music. So fierce was his devotion that it could cause volcanic outbursts against singers, musicians, indeed against anyone who stood in the way of his vision.

Originally a cellist [he was in the pit for the first *Otello* (Verdi) in 1887], he sprang to fame in Rio de Janeiro by taking over from an unpopular conductor at a moment's notice (1886), conducting Verdi's *Aida* from memory. He conducted the première of Leoncavallo's *Pagliacci* (Milan, 1892) and Puccini's *La Bohème* (Turin, 1896), becoming chief conductor at La Scala in 1898, where he played Wagner and introduced Strauss's *Salome* and Debussy's *Pelléas et Méli-*

sande, as well as giving his beloved Italian repertoire. He left in 1902 after refusing to allow a baying audience a Zenatello encore, but returned from 1906 to 1908. At the Met (1908–15), his premières included Puccini's *La Fanciulla del West*, while his third La Scala period (1921–9) was one of the greatest in the theatre's history. Premières included Boito's *Nerone* and Puccini's *Turandot*, and he gave many legendary performances, including Verdi's *Falstaff* and Donizetti's *Lucia di Lammermoor*. His company included Del Monte, Dalla Rizza, Raisa, Supervia, Pertile, Stabile and Journet. Then he left after falling out with the Fascists, not returning until the theatre was reopened in 1946 after being bombed during the war.

He conducted in pre-Nazi Bayreuth (1930–1) and at Salzburg (1934–7), where his *Falstaff* and *Fidelio* are cherished to this day as two of the supreme performances of the century. These were his last operatic performances in the theatre, though he gave concert performances of Italian opera for the N.B.C. in New York which are widely known from recordings. His *Otello* and *Requiem* will remind posterity of his incomparable stature as a Verdian, and other recordings, even the controversial *La Traviata*, are almost equally valuable. His championship of Italian opera was especially valuable between the two world wars when many reputable critics were so besotted by all things Germanic in music that they grossly underrated all things Italian.

WALTER, BRUNO (1876–1962). German, then American, conductor who, after various posts, became Mahler's assistant at the Vienna State Opera in 1901. Remaining in Vienna until 1912, he became Generalmusikdirektor at Munich (1913–22) was at the Berlin Stadtische Oper, 1925–9, and Generalmusikdirektor at Vienna, 1936–8, having conducted at Salzburg from 1922 to 1937. He conducted at the Met—after been forced to flee the Nazis—for many seasons between 1941 and 1959. He also conducted in Italy, Chicago and at Covent Garden (1910 and 1924–31). The 1924 season at Covent Garden can never be forgotten by older operagoers, being the first international season since 1914 and including the first German-Austrian *Ring* since then, conducted by Walter, and the classic *Der Rosenkavalier* (Strauss), again with Walter in the pit, as he was to be on many other legendary occasions. This great, esteemed conductor, renowned for his warmly lyrical approach, excelled in Wagner, both Richard and Johann Strauss, Mozart and Beethoven in the opera house. He inspired singers and audiences alike—which perhaps is a cold way of describing the love he generated for music and himself.

WEINGARTNER, FELIX (1863–1942). Austrian, one of the greatest and most influential conductors of his time, whose operatic career began when his own opera, *Sakuntala*, was produced at Weimar in 1884. Before the First World War, his appointments included Berlin, 1891–8, and Vienna as Mahler's successor, 1908–10, and, between the two world wars, much of his career was in Vienna, at the Volksoper (1919–24) and the State Opera (1935–6).

WOLFF, ALBERT (1884–1970). French conductor, mainly associated with the Opéra-Comique (1908–46), though he also conducted at the Met, Covent Garden and Buenos Aires.

ZUMPE, HERMANN (1850–1903). German conductor who helped Wagner prepare the first *Ring* at Bayreuth, then held posts including Munich (1900–3), where he conducted Wagner in the new Prinzregententheater. His *Tristan und Isolde* at Covent Garden (1898) was superb.

PRODUCERS

Famous Productions

The time span of this selection is 1958–73. Despite wise advice from theatrically minded and well-travelled experts, it has not been easy to decide what to feature partly because of a lurking suspicion that some superb productions even over such a short period, are either unknown to the author or unreported in Britain. Scanning a *Scala International* of 1974, the reader could discover that there are fifty-nine opera houses in West Germany, including ones at Hof and Pforzheim, neither of which has 100,000 inhabitants, and Rendsburg, which, according to *Pears*, has only 35,000. It would be insulting to suggest that the work of such theatres has been taken into account; while, behind the Iron Curtain, how is one to evaluate the standard of performance at the Dracula Theatre, Transylvania, or wherever?

So it must be understood that the following list is partly legendary (Felsenstein's *Otello*, Hall's *Figaro*) and partly selective (Besch's superb *Così fan tutte*, which the author knows well). If the book were British-based, it would have been pleasant to dwell on local productions of the 1940s, 1950s and 1960s which dragged opera kicking and screaming into modern times: Brook's *Salome* (1949), Geliot's *Mahagonny* (1963), Wanamaker's much-abused *La Forza del Destino* (1962–). It should be noted that the last producer has not been given an entry (despite *King Priam*) in the *Who's Who* section because he has not been regularly associated with opera, and this applies to other producers. On a personal note, it is hard to leave out various British producers who have given so much pleasure to all operagoers in their forties or over, but overseas readers would rightly rage if this section suggested that Britannia rules the stage.

LUCHINO VISCONTI   *Don Carlos* (1958)
Even without Maria Callas to inspire him to the extraordinary

heights of his work at La Scala earlier in the 1950s, this production at Covent Garden was, and remains, Visconti's masterpiece. The opera itself, as was noted when discussing Giulini's awe-inspiring contribution (page 216), became popular overnight in London and has grown more so down the years. Even with the tide running so strongly in Verdi's favour by 1958, Visconti gave the opera the totally committed and truthful romantic realism needed to show a hopeful Covent Garden public that it was an outright masterpiece, so banishing memories of a 1933 production which had been badly performed and in consequence provoked (now) fatuous attacks on the work itself. (It was given at the Wells in the 1930s and 1950s.)

There was no chorus in this 1958 production, only Spaniards, French and men from Flanders. The settings opened in the Forest of Fontainebleau with a chateau which seemed a mile away, and continued in the Monastery of San Giusto, where it was difficult at first to detect which were monks and which were statues kneeling beneath the grey walls. And so the glory continued, only the Auto-da-Fé scene slightly lowering the tension, partly because of lack of numbers on stage.

Under Visconti's sensitive, inspired guidance, the cast excelled itself, and though it seems invidious to pick out individuals, it is hardly possible not to recall that Christoff's Philip was a masterpiece to match the production, Brouwenstijn's Elisabeth the most sympathetic interpretation of the role seen in Britain, and Jon Vickers the best-acted Carlos. Only a year before he had been a bluff, heroic Aeneas; now, in a more difficult part to act, he showed us boyish eagerness, rashness, affectionate idealism and despair.

This fabulous recreation of an era, of controlled but passionate Spanish pride, has become a noble skeleton of former greatness down the years. Inevitably it is hard to prove now that it was once the greatest production of an Italian opera—some would say of any opera—ever seen in Britain.

Cast included Gré Brouwenstijn as Elisabeth de Valois, Jon Vickers as Don Carlos, Tito Gobbi as Rodrigo, Boris Christoff as King Philip II, Fedora Barbieri as Eboli, and Marco Stefanoni as the Grand Inquisitor. Conductor, Carlo Maria Giulini. Producer and designer, Luchino Visconti.

WALTER FELSENSTEIN   *Otello* (1959)

This production was the most famous operatic occasion of the year in Germany, some might say the most notorious. It is possible to accept at a distance that theatrically this was the most remarkable *Otello*—or *Othello*—seen in the 1950s. Britain has not been overblessed with great productions of the play, and even Olivier's *Othello*, matchless for many including this author, was very controversial. Felsenstein, given long rehearsals, and the arch champion of realism in depth, was already a legend by 1959, having made the Berlin Komische Oper the theatrical Mecca of operatic art. But his artists have rarely been in the top flight as singers, and quite often have not even been in the second. This production had an Otello (Hanns Nocker) whose intensity and detailed subtlety as an actor was, we are told, unrivalled in Europe, but, according to *Opera's* distinguished correspondent, Horst Koegler (February, 1960), 'he is hardly to be heard'. The other principals, without embracing the art of silence, were hardly ideal vocally, and the conducting was below par, though with the pit partly covered over to bring the action forward, the over-thin sound that emerged can hardly be blamed on the players. Yet Mr Koegler was not alone in hailing this *Otello* as his supreme operatic experience in twenty years.

Such was Felsenstein's triumph, which was complete enough to challenge the conventions of opera. Men do not sing at their death and neither, it seems, did Mr Nocker.

The opening of the opera was visual thunder and lightning, with the chorus possessed by the fury of the waves until they lay flat on their faces—and the tension *increased*. Every word of the ensembles was heard(!), every character was presented in theatrical depth, the settings were superb. But was this Verdi's *Otello*? Can an inadequately sung opera achieve maximum effect? The answer appears to be that it can and did, but not for those who could not accept 'un-singing'. The Callas Tosca of 1964? But her art was then greater than ever and, though she cut corners vocally, this is not so serious with *Tosca*; and it was, even her enemies will allow, sung. But *Otello*? Opera is the most compromise-ridden of the arts because it is so damnably difficult to get anywhere near perfection. All one can say about this *Otello* is that it stirred many to the very soul. Clearly it was not true opera.

Cast included Hanns Nocker as Otello, Ernst Gutstein as Iago, Anny Schlemm as Desdemona, Hanna Schmoock as Emilia and Hermin Esser as Cassio. Conductor, Vaclav Neumann; Producer, Walter Felsenstein; Designer, Rudolf Heinrich.

FRANCO ZEFFIRELLI   *Cavalleria Rusticana* (1959)

After the romance of his *Lucia* and before the steely realism of his Shakespearean *Romeo and Juliet* at the Old Vic, Zeffirelli gave Covent Garden an electrifying *Pagliacci* and a history-making *Cav*, the ultimate in *verismo* production. From the dawn slowly breaking over a Sicilian town to the shattering ending, this was the genuine article, not least because for the first and last time at Covent Garden, except in Visconti's *Don Carlos* and Zeffirelli's *Pag*, every member of the cast appeared to be a genuine native of the locality on view. Others have striven for this, some have even come near it, but this, even at close range, was *it*. Incredibly, and though Zeffirelli finally disowned the production after a decade or so because of inevitable mutations, much of its former glory can be glimpsed, not least because the chorus still excels itself. Naturally, only the original principals, listed below, and their immediate successors were totally part of the production.

Cast: Amy Shuard as Santuzza, Janet Coster as Lola, Edith Coates as Mamma Lucia, Charles Craig as Turiddu, and Otakar Kraus as Alfio. Conductor, Edward Downes; Producer and Designer, Franco Zeffirelli.

CARL EBERT   *Pelléas et Mélisande* (1962)

Ebert's glorious and long career was full of legendary productions, and it is sheer good fortune that the one considered by many to be the finest of all, fits in the time span of this section. Certainly Glyndebourne's historian, Spike Hughes, considered *Pelléas* Ebert's masterpiece. Indeed, everything conspired to make the whole experience unique; not simply the producer's matchless way with the elusive work, but Gui's conducting of it, Montresor's designs, and a fine cast. The revival in 1963 was, if anything, even finer. The production was powerful and impassioned, yet sensitive to a degree to the symbols and understatements of this strange twilight world, pierced from time to time with light.

Cast: Henri Gui as Pelléas, Denise Duval as Mélisande, Michel Roux as Golaud, Kerstin Meyer as Geneviève, Guus Hoekman as Arkel, Rosine Brédy as Yniold, and John Shirley-Quirk as the Doctor. Conductor, Vittorio Gui; Producer Carl Ebert; Designer, Beni Montrésor.

WIELAND WAGNER   *Salome* (1962)
It may seem capricious to choose a non-Wagnerian production with which to praise Wieland Wagner, but one of the two most obvious choices, the 1951 *Ring*, lies outside the time limits of this section, and the other—his sublime *Parsifal*—was originally produced before the period chosen, and developed and changed down the years. One of his most thrilling and famous productions was his Stuttgart *Salome*, which followed a controversial *Elektra* of a few weeks earlier. The *Salome* was not controversial, merely sensationally successful. A great cistern on a raked platform dominated the proceedings. Herod's palace was an ominous, doom-laden spot though not strongly defined, and only the costumes set the scene in Judea. Salome—Anja Silja in one of her supreme performances—was totally and obsessively riveted by the huge cistern and its contents, spending much of the time lying serpent-like on the ground facing it. Her dance was a dance of the single veil and her figure when it dropped was a national glory. Wagner had his Baptist moving purposefully about the stage, a change for a part in which the singer normally has next to no moves to remember. By contrast, the usually volatile Jews sang their quintet as statically as guardsmen on sentry duty. As in all Wieland Wagner's casts, the standard of acting was high throughout, but it was his protégée's evening, especially as her voice was at its finest in the finale. Her dance began with only her hands above her cloaking red veil, which she later dropped in a single electric movement, continuing to stare at the cistern, her back to the audience. Herod had every reason to be beside himself, and Wieland Wagner proved, like Visconti with Callas, that a great producer with the right actress-singer can reach heights of visual dramatic truth as unforgettable and tremendous as anything the straight theatre can offer.

Cast included Anja Silja as Salome, Gerhard Stolze as Herod, Carlos Alexander as John the Baptist, Grace Hoffman as

Herodias, and Jess Thomas as Narraboth. Conductor, Ferdinand Leitner; Producer and Designer, Wieland Wagner.

GIORGIO STREHLER
Die Entführung aus dem Serail (1965)
This has been (from 1965 to 1974) one of the most famous productions of Mozart or anyone else in operatic history, and will remain a legend. Almost universally admired (except by one critic whose other contributions included an attack on Callas's acting as Tosca), it was the most successful staging people could remember of an opera which is as much a sublime hotch-potch as *Cymbeline*. With a marvel of a score which embraces jolly and intoxicating *Singspiel* and *opera seria*, a production must range from simple, natural, sincere acting, to formal stylization with no pretence at reality. The warmth and gaiety of the opera must be played without farce, or at least with farcical moments kept under iron control, otherwise little can be got from the piece except a merry evening out, interspersed with sublime moments. It may be some of Mozart's freshest and most enchanting music, but as an opera it can appear trivial.

Strehler, in his first Salzburg production, triumphantly solved the problem with the utmost taste, wit and theatrical cunning. His inspirations included the silhouetting of his actors as they appeared, and, among small delights, were Pedrillo's two wine bottles carried on in a sedan chair. No doubt his experience in *commedia dell'arte*, especially *The Servant of Two Masters* at his Milan theatre, enabled him to achieve unreality *and* depth of feeling, not least in the serious playing of the Pasha Selim and the visual charm of Luciano Damiani's sets. These, allied to the frequent use of silhouette, totally fulfilled a conception carried out perfectly by his actors and complemented by the splendid playing of the Vienna Philharmonic under Mehta.

Cast: Anneliese Rothenberger as Constanze, Reri Grist as Blonde, Fritz Wunderlich as Belmonte, Gerhard Unger as Pedrillo, Fernando Corena as Osmin. Conductor, Zubin Mehta; Producer, Giorgio Strehler; Designer, Luciano Damiani.

ANTHONY BESCH   *Così fan tutte* (1967)
By some happy stroke of genius, when Anthony Besch and his

designer, John Stoddart, were asked to stage *Così* for Scottish Opera, they conceived an idea which sounded and sounds contrived but which was sheer inspiration. The opera began with black and white sets and costumes as properly formal as Fiordiligi and Dorabella in Act I, but gradually colour crept in as feeling mounted in the music, to vanish at the end, returning to all black and white, passionless respectability. There was none of that curse of Mozartian production, posturing archness, but true comedy, never overdone, the actors totally relaxed and working as an inspired team. Happy production touches were a first scene set in a Turkish Bath, and a second with the ladies rising from confections of beds. If the ladies were the stars (with clever Scottish Opera giving Janet Baker a chance to prove herself a delicious comedienne), all Besch's cast acted excellently for him. With superb playing by the Scottish National Orchestra under Alexander Gibson, the whole became totally magical and truthful. For the record, Ruth and Thomas Martin's translation was used, not Rev. Marmaduke Browne's antique one with its immortal statement: 'Ladies have such variations, permutations, combinations.'

Cast: Elizabeth Harwood as Fiordiligi, Janet Baker as Dorabella, Jennifer Eddy as Despina, Ryland Davies as Ferrando, Peter van der Bilt as Guglielmo, and Inia te Wiata as Alfonso. Conductor, Alexander Gibson; Producer, Anthony Besch; Designer, John Stoddart.

GUNTHER RENNERT   *Fidelio* (1970)
Fidelio, with which he reopened the Staatsoper in Munich in 1945, has played a key part in Rennert's distinguished career. It introduced him to Glyndebourne in 1959, where his designer was Ita Maximowna and the conductor was Vittorio Gui. It was the outstanding feature of the theatre's silver jubilee season.

At Salzburg in 1970, he was in charge of the Beethoven bi-centenary production only two years after a truthful and simple account of the work at the Festival. Somewhat sensationally, the new production was a rare case of opera-in-the-round, for as the Festspielhaus was being used by Karajan for rehearsals of *Otello*, the Felsenteitschule was commandeered, and the galleries, carved from stone cliffs from which privileged spectators once watched horses, were filled with operagoers.

Fidelio was, of course, played mainly forward towards conductor and orchestra, so the 'round' was less than ideal for those up in the galleries. However, the noblest of operas was certainly played 'among mankind' as it was claimed in the programme—or was it? No matter, after Böhm had begun with *Leonora No. 3*, which is certainly far less sinful than playing it later in the opera, Rennert directed an urgent, exciting, sometimes violent, performance *played without an interval*. The singers were exposed on ramps and platforms without benefit of scenery, but under Rennert's direction the acting was mainly excellent, even the weather contributing a clap of thunder at one performance on Pizarro's entrance. This was fine music-theatre, a highly charged evening which was perhaps a portent of things to come when Pierre Boulez gets his wish and all opera houses are blown up.

Cast included Ingrid Bjoner as Leonore, Edith Mathis as Marzelline, James King as Florestan, Donald Grobe as Jacquino, Theo Adam (and later Franz Mazura, who got the thunderclap) as Pizarro, Franz Crass as Rocco, Tom Krause as Don Fernando. Conductor, Karl Böhm; Producer, Gunther Rennert; Designer, Rudolf Heinrich.

PETER HALL   *Le Nozze di Figaro* (1973)
It is opera's good fortune that Peter Hall, one of the half-dozen supreme theatre directors of the age, is fascinated by all its problems and is genuinely musical. He has called Mozart the most erotic composer in musical history and *Figaro* the first absolutely realistic opera, and, at Glyndebourne, he and John Pritchard searched for and found the real meaning of the music. The result was a production worlds away from the admittedly often enjoyable excesses of the buffo tradition, a deeply serious, superbly acted, sensuous interpretation, yet full of humour springing from the situations. It was indeed erotic, with the Countess undoubtedly drawn to the highly sexed Cherubino for all that her 'Porgi amor' had been genuinely tear-laden for the loss of her husband's love; and so intense was the staging that we knew, as Andrew Porter happily put it, that 'if Cherubino, not Susanna, had emerged from the Countess's dressing-room, he would after all have been killed'. Cherubino was not dressed up, as the producer did not discover a demand

for it in the stage directions, the recitatives were as natural as speech; Bartolo was a rather seedy, non-buffo human being; and the final proof that Hall found the reality he sought was the total success of the production when it was transferred to television. Every opera-lover knows that sinking feeling brought on by a visual absurdity when watching televised opera, which, while not worrying him, will alienate millions. Not for a split second could any have been alienated by this masterpiece.

Cast included Elizabeth Harwood as the Countess, Ileana Cotrubas as Susanna, Frederica von Stade as Cherubino, Nucci Condo as Marcellina, Elizabeth Gale as Barbarina, Benjamin Luxon as the Count, Knut Skram as Figaro, Marius Rintzler as Bartolo, John Fryatt as Basilio, Bernard Dickerson as Curzio and Thomas Lawlor as Antonio. Conductor, John Pritchard; Producer, Peter Hall; Designer, John Bury. The very gifted John Cox has kept the production up to standard, even the exacting Peter Hall being satisfied.

Selected Producers

ARUNDELL, DENNIS (1898–). English producer, also actor, composer and author. From 1946 to 1958, he regularly produced at Sadler's Wells, his productions usually being realistic and straightforward but never dull, and well-acted. The most notable were: Wolf-Ferrari's *The School for Fathers* (*I Quatro Rusteghi*) (1946), Janáček's *Katya Kabanova* (1951), Menotti's *The Consul* (1954), and *The Flying Dutchman* (1958).

BESCH, ANTHONY (1924–). English. An excellent and now international producer whose famous *Così fan tutte* for Scottish Opera is discussed on page 254. Other notable productions include *Count Ory* for the Wells (1963). His *Magic Flute*, with John Stoddart's designs, is currently a huge success at the Coliseum (1975). He and Stoddart also staged Covent Garden's stirring *La Clemenza di Tito* (1914), and a very successful *Don Giovanni* at the Coliseum (1976).

BROOK, PETER (1925–). English. His brief reign as Director of Productions at Covent Garden (1949–50), at a time when the infant company was under constant attack,

should have happened a decade later. As it was, his mixture of inexperience, daring and blazing talent clashed with the Musical Director, Karl Rankl, and the stone age attitudes of many senior critics. Bliss's *The Olympians* was a success for him, *Boris Godunov* had moments of glory, and *Salome* (designed by Dali, realized by Welitsch) was a grand scandal, light years ahead of its time. He had happier experiences at the Met: *Faust* (1953), *Eugene Onegin* (1957). Now he distrusts most theatre and is grossly critical of opera.

COPLEY, JOHN (1933–). English. After stage-managing at the Wells, he became deputy stage manager at Covent Garden, then, with the gifted Ande Anderson, a resident producer; over the last decade, he has established himself nationally and internationally as a producer in his own considerable right. An admirable blend of musician and man-of-the-theatre, his Mozartian productions at Covent Garden and splendid *La Bohème* (1974), with stunning sets by Julia Trevelyan Oman, have been admired even by those who think he allows too much 'business' on occasion. His

Wells' *Carmen* is the best seen in Britain, while overseas (Holland, Belgium, Australia and Greece) he made a magnificent traditionally American début with *Lucia di Lammermoor* at Dallas (1973), with Henry Bardon as designer. A good *Faust* (1974) at Covent Garden has been followed by a brilliant *Der Rosenkavalier* for the English National Opera.

DE FILIPPO, EDUARDO (1900–   ). Italian producer, his country's leading dramatist and a magnificent actor. In opera he is best known for his *opera buffa* productions, but his *Rigoletto* (Rome, 1966) was greatly admired.

DEXTER, JOHN (1925–   ). English producer and leading theatre director, now Director of Productions at the Met. After a *Benvenuto Cellini* at Covent Garden (1966), which suffered from lack of rehearsal time and experience, he made his name in opera at Hamburg, most notably with Verdi's *I Vespri Siciliani*, which opera was his Met début in 1974. Too stark (with Svoboda as designer) for local taste, and suffering in New York from cast changes, it is yet a most notable conception. His other Hamburg productions included a very fine *From the House of the Dead* (Janáček) 1972, while his *The Devils of Loudun* (Penderecki) for Sadler's Wells (1973) was a magnificent piece of musical theatre.

EBERT, CARL (1887–   ). German producer and manager, an ex-actor who was one of the first and greatest producers of opera. He became famous at the Stadtische Opera, Berlin (1931–3), leaving Germany after refusing to collaborate with Hitler, though he returned to Berlin from 1956 to 1961. His wide-ranging career included organizing the Turkish National Theatre and Opera (1936–47), and working at the Met (1959–62), but it is not chauvinistic to claim that his supreme achievement was the founding, with Fritz Busch, of the Glyndebourne Festival (1934), which set new standards of opera production not merely in Britain but everywhere. A matchless trainer of singers as actors, his most famous productions were of Mozart and Verdi opera (especially *Macbeth*, which he and Busch introduced so memorably to Britain in 1938), also his masterpiece, *Pélleas et Mélisande* (see page 252). Given the opportunity for long periods of rehearsal, his flair for detail and ensemble was widely admired. His son, Peter Ebert, having worked at Glyndebourne, and in Europe and America, in 1965 became Director of Productions for Scottish Opera, where his many striking achievements have included *The Ring* and *The Trojans*.

ERHARDT, OTTO (1888–1971). German. He became chief producer at Dresden in 1927, leaving under Nazi pressure in 1933. After working for Beecham at Covent Garden, he became producer at the Colón, Buenos Aires (1938–60), also working at La Scala, Vienna, Munich and for the New York City Opera. His premières included Strauss's *Die Aegyptische Helena* (Dresden, 1928).

FELSENSTEIN, WALTER (1901–75). German, even approved of by Brecht (who wrote off most opera performances as bourgeois 'culinary' art). After working as an actor and producer in Germany and Switzerland, he became producer and intendant of the Berlin Komische Opera in 1947. Blessed with extensive rehearsals, and using his laser-like intelligence to grasp the essentials of an opera, his most famous productions, some controversial, others not, have included *The Cunning Little Vixen*, *Contes d'Hoffmann*, *The Magic Flute* and *Otello* (see page 251). A particular success of the 1970s was his *Carmen* in Berlin (1972) with the Russian, Emma Sarkissjan, who had also sung the title-role for him in Moscow.

FORZANO, GIOVACCHINO (1883–1970). Italian producer and librettist (of *Gianni Schicchi*, Leoncavallo's *Oedipus Rex*, etc.). Originally a baritone, he began producing in 1904, staging works in Italy, Vienna and at Covent Garden, and the premières of *Nerone* (1924) and *Turandot* (1926), both at La Scala.

FRIEDRICH, GÖTZ (1930–). German. Worked with Felsenstein in East Berlin in the 1950s, then in West Germany, Holland, etc. Currently the producer of Covent Garden's exciting, controversial *Ring* and appointed principal producer (1976).

GENTELE, GORAN (1917–72). Swedish. Regularly produced at Stockholm's Royal Opera (1952–62), after which he became Director. His historically authentic *Un Ballo in Maschera* was much admired at home and abroad. Appointed General Manager of the Met in 1970 he was tragically killed in a car smash before taking up his key post.

GRAF, HERBERT (1904–73). Austrian, then American, producer, who left Germany because of Hitler. At the Met (1936–60), Salzburg and La Scala, and Director of Zürich Opera (1960–3). He produced Toscanini's famous *Die Meistersinger* and *The Magic Flute* at Salzburg in the late 1930s, returning in 1951 with *Otello*, conducted by Furtwängler, and was in charge of the *Ernani*, in the Verona Arena, which celebrated the Festival's 50th season (1972). At Geneva,

1965–72. One of the first to establish the producer as a leading figure in the opera house.

GRAHAM, COLIN. English producer and director of plays, particularly associated with the English Opera Group and Sadler's Wells. He has produced all Britten's chamber operas and church parables, also several premières of *Owen Wingrave*, including the original on television. For the Wells, his most notable productions have included *Gloriana* (1966) and Prokofiev's *War and Peace* (1972). Director, with Steuart Bedford, of the English Music Theatre Company.

GUTHRIE, (SIR) TYRONE (1900–71). Anglo-Irish producer and one of the most exciting and influential directors of plays of the century. Director of the entire Vic–Wells organization for most of the war, producing *Figaro*, *La Bohème*, and *La Traviata*, he later produced an exciting *Carmen*, which starred Anna Pollak and startled some people, and *The Barber of Seville* which startled far more. He staged *Peter Grimes* at Covent Garden (1947) and *Carmen* and *La Traviata* at the Met in the 1950s. He could be cavalier with Shakespeare and, not surprisingly, even more with opera; but he handled singers and crowds splendidly and brought truth to his productions, even if the music sometimes suffered. All complacent opera buffs and singers should be force-fed his chapters on opera in *A Life in the Theatre*.

HARTMANN, RUDOLF (1900–). German, a producer from the mid-1920s, joining the Berlin State Opera in 1934, where he collaborated with Clemens Krauss (see page 235). He left there for Munich (1938–44), becoming Staatsintendant there (1953–67). A thoroughly professional, unrevolutionary producer, he is best known for his many Strauss productions, including the premières of *Friedenstag* and *Capriccio* at Munich, and *Die Liebe der Danae* at Salzburg (1952). His most admired Covent Garden staging has been *Arabella* (1965).

HALL, PETER (1930–). English. Director of the National Theatre, and for a few brief weeks in 1971 destined, it seemed, to be Director of Productions at Covent Garden. As he is the most musical of all British 'straight' directors, his loss was a tragedy, as his work at Glyndebourne has proved. After Gardner's *The Moon and Sixpence* (1957), his next operatic production was the historic *Moses und Aron* (1965), which was followed by Tippett's *The Knot Garden* (1970), with Timothy O'Brien's designs, modern and imaginative staging at its best. Meanwhile, at Glyndebourne, he and the designer John Bury found a modern solution to the spectacular and magic-laden problems of Venetian opera, demonstrating their success with Cavalli's *La Calisto* (1971), fortunately also seen on television, which was theatrical perfection, moving, funny and sensuous. Some would say that their *Il Ritorno d'Ulisse in Patria* (1972) was equally stunning, with its mechanical marvels (gods descending from heaven), and some of the most beautiful stage groupings even Glyndebourne has ever seen. As in all Peter Hall productions, singers are led to visually truthful performances, though in none more so than in *Figaro* (see page 256).

PONNELLE, JEAN-PIERRE. French producer and designer who first made his name in the latter capacity, becoming internationally known as a producer at Salzburg with *Il Barbiere* (1968). His *Pelléas et Mélisande* (Munich, 1973) was a masterpiece of poetry and symbolism, and arguably his finest production to date, though he is best known for his Mozart, Rossini and Donizetti. He is a master of operatic characterization, his ideas being sometimes controversial but always carried out with total conviction.

REINHARDT, MAX (1873–1943). Austrian producer, manager and actor who helped found the Salzburg Festival. He made Berlin Europe's theatre capital, before Hitler's coming forced him to leave, and was the most influential man of the theatre in his day, particularly famous for his spectacular productions and use of crowds. He was only once directly concerned with opera, being the actual, though not the named, producer of the first *Der Rosenkavalier* (1911). *Ariadne auf Naxos* was written by Strauss as a thanks offering to him.

RENNERT, GUNTHER (1911–). German. An international reputation since being Intendant at Hamburg (1946–56), including spells at Glyndebourne, Covent Garden, the Met, etc. *See* p. 255.

SCHENK, OTTO. Austrian. Since the early 1960s one of Europe's busiest opera producers, also a notable theatre director. He has produced *Fidelio* in Vienna and at the Met, and his *Der Rosenkavalier* for Munich (1972), with designs by Jürgen Rose, was much admired. The two were responsible for *Un Ballo in Maschera* at Covent Garden (1975).

SCHUH, OSCAR FRITZ (1904–). German producer whose productions of Mozart and Berg's *Wozzeck* were famous in Vienna between the wars. From 1959 to 1962, the administrator of the Cologne Opera.

SHAW, GLEN BYAM (1904–). English producer, director of

plays and ex-actor, Director of Productions at Sadler's Wells/ English National Opera since 1962. As befits a distinguished ex-Director of Stratford, he is notably good at turning singers into actors. His many productions include excellent stagings of *The Rake's Progress*, *Idomeneo* and the historic Goodall *Ring* with John Blatchley. The latter's simple, almost bare-staged productions of *Cav* and *Pag* (1971), which concentrate almost entirely on character as opposed to traditional *verismo*—romantic realism—are viable theatrically. With the right casts, this modern approach is admirable.

STREHLER, GIORGIO. Italian producer and manager, founder of the Piccolo Teatro di Milano (1947) and now increasingly involved in opera. His operatic fame dates from his Salzburg production of *Die Entführung* (1965), discussed on page 254. Since then, his productions have included an apparently Brechtian *Cav* and *Pag* at La Scala, and a much acclaimed *Fidelio* at Salzburg, where he became artistic consultant to von Karajan in 1972. His *Simon Boccanegra* at La Scala (1971), brought out brilliantly the political topicality of the plot, 'Establishment versus People', as Peter Hoffer noted in *Opera*; while his beautifully acted, passionate and amusing *Figaro*, at Versailles and Paris (1973) with Solti, was musical

theatre at its best. Other productions have included Dessau's opera of Brecht's *Verurteilung des Lukullus* at the Teatro Lirico (1973), and a much-abused *Magic Flute* at Salzburg (1974), which was under-rehearsed, perhaps, and apparently improved rapidly. Strehler's commitment to theatrical truth and his ability to inspire singers to act, allied to his feeling for music, has raised performing standards wherever he has worked.

VISCONTI, LUCHINO (1906–1976). Italian producer, designer and director of films and plays. His family having been connected with La Scala down the centuries, he became personally involved after noting the extreme dramatic potential of Callas, with whom he had worked in *La Vestale* (1954), and subsequently in *La Sonnambula*, *La Traviata*, *Anna Bolena* and *Iphigénie en Tauride*. These legendary productions, which saw the emergence, via native talent and the guidance of Visconti, of a great actress-singer in Callas—great in the narrowest sense of the word— made Visconti's name as well as that of his superstar. His belief in opera, together with a wonderful eye, mastery of detail, and ability to project operatic realism, did not prevent criticism as well as loud praise, especially in *La Traviata*, updated to the 1880s; but what can one say of critics who allege that the composer was abused by Visconti's Violetta, who sat on a table and threw away her shoes before 'Sempre libera'? His *Don Carlos* at Covent Garden is discussed on page 249. Less universally acclaimed were his *Der Rosenkavalier*, *Il Trovatore* and *La Traviata*, though the last at least, updated to the 1890s at Covent Garden, was a stunning production, totally obsessed with the musical drama, despite a strange Act II, grey, black and white and set in a dark, wintry garden. His productions at Spoleto have included *Macbeth*, Donizetti's *Duca d'Alba*, and *Manon Lescaut* (1973). With Bernstein, he gave Vienna one of the greatest productions of *Falstaff* in the opera's history (1966).

WAGNER, WIELAND (1917–66). German producer and designer, the grandson of Richard and son of Siegfried Wagner. With his brother Wolfgang (1919–), he ran the Bayreuth Festival from 1951 until his death, when Wolfgang took over sole charge. At Bayreuth, Wieland, especially, transformed Wagnerian production, though not as completely as is supposed; for, before the war, Emil Preetorius began to abandon realism for symbolism. The brothers opted strongly for symbolism and universality, simplifying the look of the operas and abandoning naturalism. They were in the forefront of European drama, as well as opera, not least in their use of lighting; but this true revolution, when copied by lesser men, has often had disastrous results elsewhere.

Wieland did not eschew extreme romantic beauty (*Die Meistersinger*, Act II, 1856), while his epic moments—Brünnhilde in a sea of fire on the very roof of the world—were unequalled. Indeed, the early post-war festival both stunned and excited, and caused little controversy; but, for some, the personalities of the characters were lost down the years to noble formalism, with unsatisfactory and sometimes downright ugly costuming doing little to help. Yet until Wieland's final *Ring* (1965)—in which too many of the facts of the story were abandoned (from Alberich's making no effort to get the gold in the opening scene of *Rheingold*, onwards)—his handling of sparse movement, lighting and design had provided the most vivid and truthful accounts of the operas in living memory. And even this 1965 *Ring* would doubtless have developed.

Wieland also staged Verdi, Beethoven, Bizet, Strauss, Orff, Gluck and Berg, often at Stuttgart (see page 253), finding a supreme exponent of his ideals in Anja Silja (Salome, Marie in *Wozzeck*, Lulu, etc.); his ideal Bayreuth soprano was Varnay.

Wolfgang, without his

brother's genius, has a formidable talent, and, if his second *Ring* (1970–   ) is considered, remains closer to his grandfather's wishes. Overdark, it used his earlier (1960) saucer, which could be tilted and split into pieces, and the interpretation was both logical and epic, though disappointingly prosaic and ugly, for some, and 'lacking in human emotion' (William Mann).

WALLERSTEIN, LOTHAR (1882–1949). Czech, then American, conductor and producer who staged sixty-five operas at Vienna (1927–38) and regularly worked at Salzburg in the same period. At the Met (1941–6).

WALLMANN, MARGHERITA (1904–   ). Austrian. Originally a dancer until forced to retire after an accident. She has produced operas in many countries, especially in Italy, at La Scala, since the 1950s. Her premières there have included Milhaud's *David* (1955) and Poulenc's *Les Dialogues des Carmélites* (1957), and she has also produced many 19th-century operas. At her best she handles crowds and individual singers notably well. One of her more recent successes was an excellent staging of Rossellini's *La Reine Morte* at Monte Carlo (1973).

ZEFFIRELLI, FRANCO (1923–   ). Italian producer, director of plays and films and designer. He first became widely known in opera producing Callas in *Il Turco in Italia*, but it was his *Lucia* with Sutherland at Covent Garden in 1959 which made him famous. This beautiful modern evocation of the age of *bel canto* also proved his genius for inspiring singers to act. In this role, Sutherland became in his hands a genuine tragic actress, and he saw to it that she looked beautiful. There followed *Cav* (see page 252) and *Pag*, and it became clear in these and in *Falstaff* that he had a genius for getting singers to act, relax and look as if they belonged on a stage, and even carry off the most inventive 'business' with aplomb. Already under attack for fussiness and for distracting from the music (not only from those who want opera to be a glorified concert in costume), he then divided Covent Garden yet again with a warmly romantic *Don Giovanni*. This production abandoned previous realism in favour of clashing styles of décor and costume, and a suggestion of a timelessness. His other productions in Britain have included a scintillating *L'Elisir d'Amore* at Glyndebourne, better in its second season (1961) with a stronger cast, but still too fussy for some; and the Callas–Gobbi *Tosca* of 1964, which was *verismo* at its best, and which provided an Act II that must surely rank as the greatest single scene in the history of opera in Great Britain.

He has produced at the Met and in Dallas, Chicago and San Francisco. His Met *Falstaff* (1964), with a straightforward last act and no rising tree, as in London, was a triumph, but his *Otello* (1972), though it looked gorgeous, apparently lacked the heart of the matter and overdid the epilepsy. Zeffirelli also produced the opera chosen to open the new Met in 1966, Barber's *Antony and Cleopatra*, in which the stage machinery was a prominent feature of the evening, along with human movement.

Zeffirelli's supreme achievement in Italy, some would say anywhere, was his *La Bohème* (with von Karajan) at La Scala in 1963, brilliantly solving all the problems of Act II and providing a rare example of total stage reality. This production, an adaptation of which was seen at Salzburg in 1975, was hailed by many as definitive, a milestone in the history of opera. Detractors of Zeffirelli, who regard him as a showman, a latter-day Barnum, should read reports of it and ponder.

LIBRETTISTS

A Cautionary Tale

Watched by millions on television, André Previn, while interviewing Peter Hall, mocked the libretto of *Il Trovatore* and, by obvious implication, the opera itself. He even revealed that he had once had a merry evening with a famous Met baritone when they had fallen about with amusement at the obscurities of the plot. Hall quietly defended opera, made the obvious comparison with Shakespeare's plots, won on logic and truth, but lost the battle (surely) as far as the viewers were concerned.

Earlier that year (1974), Franco Zeffirelli had selected his own choice of records for the excellent radio programme, *Man of Action* (whose title, however is odd: a philosopher contemplating his navel for a decade would be a man of action by the B.B.C.'s reckoning). As well as glorying in dramatic recitative, Zeffirelli publicly extolled the virtues of the libretto of *Il Trovatore*. Who was right?

Every true operagoer knows the answer. *Il Trovatore*'s libretto, though obviously not to be compared with, say, the admirably constructed *La Traviata* as a piece of story-telling, is admirable because of its straightforward but vivid characterizations and, especially, the very strong dramatic situations. Coincidences? Meat and drink to Shakespeare, Dickens ... So why does *Euryanthe* fail despite Weber's genius? Because it is impossible to identify with plot or people.

Of course, it is not as simple as that, or the battle between words and music would not have lasted so long. There was no battle during opera's golden dawn, when Monteverdi in particular created unequalled dramatic recitative: the battle began with the coming of formality, the recitative, the aria and chorus of the late 17th and the 18th centuries. And let it be noted that over-literary librettos (too many British operas) are as much a handicap as 'illiterate' ones. Ultimately, it is dramatic power (including characterization) that matters, plus the ability to please and excite the composer. The job of the librettist has always been one of compromise and frustration, but there are enough good librettos for the operagoer not to give way to doubt when the Previns of this world imply that libretto equals rubbish.

Selected Librettists

AUDEN, W. H. (1907–75). Anglo-American poet who, with Chester Kallman, wrote the librettos for Stravinsky's *The Rake's Progress* (1951), and for *Elegy for Young Lovers* (1960) and *The Bassarids* (1966); both by Henze.

BERLIOZ, HECTOR (1803–69). French. The great composer acted as his own librettist. *Béatrice et Bénédict* is a mainly successful merger of Shakespeare's *Much Ado About Nothing* and Berlioz himself; while *Les Troyens*, his tribute to Virgil, is for those who, like the author of this book, swallow the work whole, a masterly libretto. Others condemn or criticize parts of its architecture.

BOITO, ARRIGO (1842–1918). Italian. Also see page 46. Neither of his own operas, *Mefistofele* and *Nerone*, have remarkable librettos, but, as Tobia Gorrio, an anagram of his own name, he provided a serviceable one for Ponchielli's *La Gioconda*. His reputation as a librettist rests on his collaboration with Verdi, first on the revised *Simon Boccanegra*, and then the two Shakespearean masterpieces. *Otello* is a miraculous libretto, truly Shakespearean, poetically magnificent in its own right, and opening with the Landing at Cyprus (i.e. without Shakespeare's Act I), structurally beyond praise throughout. *Falstaff*, based on *The Merry Wives*, actually improves on Shakespeare, not only in bringing the fat knight closer to the great creation of the *Henry IV* plays, but also incorporating parts of those plays into the opera, most notably the Honour speech from *Part I*. To read of the collaboration of the two giants, after early misunderstandings and hostility, is as fascinating as it is moving.

CALZABIGI, RANIERI (1714–95). Italian. Interesting as his early life was (including running a lottery with Casanova under La Pompadour's protection), his operatic importance lies in his collaboration with Gluck in reforming opera: *Orfeo, Alceste, Iphigénie en Aulide*. (See Gluck, page 55.)

CAMMARANO, SALVATORE (1801–52). Italian. His librettos include *Lucia di Lammermoor* and Verdi's *Alzira, Battaglia di Legnano, Luisa Miller* and *Il Trovatore*. The last is discussed at the beginning of this section.

CROZIER, ERIC (1914–). English. The librettist of Britten's *Albert Herring, Let's Make an Opera* and *Billy Budd* (co-author with E. M. Forster), also of Berkeley's *Ruth*. Producer of the first *Peter Grimes* and co-founder (with Britten and Pears) of the English Opera Group (1946).

GIACOSA, GIUSEPPE (1847–1906). Italian.
ILLICA, LUIGI (1857–1919). Italian. Both these playwrights collaborated with Puccini in *Manon Lescaut, La Bohème, Madame Butterfly* and *Tosca,* difficult but triumphant assignments, Giacosa was the more poetic of the two, but Illica was a fine and imaginative craftsman, whose other librettos included *La Wally* (Catalani) and *Andrea Chénier* (Giordano).

GILBERT, (SIR) W. S. (1836–1911). Also see *Sullivan* (page 92). The fact that the Savoy Operas are also called Gilbert and Sullivan is indicative of the rare importance of this particular librettist: British to the backbone, an extraordinary contriver of situations, and of outstanding wit. His flair for words made him a master of comic verse, a lyric writer unmatched in Britain until the appearance of Noël Coward. The fact that some of his barbs are now unintelligible, outdated or even to modern ears unfunny, should not obscure his prowess. His unpleasant gibes at ageing spinsters (alas, poor contraltos) border on the sadistic, and his often sickly sentiment is too much for some today; but he was a master-craftsman and also a brilliant producer, one of the first the theatre had known.

HALÉVY, LUDOVIC (1834–1908). French. The nephew of the composer Halévy, he collaborated with Henry Meilhac in writing librettos for Offenbach, Bizet (*Carmen*) and Delibes.

HOFMANNSTHAL, HUGO VON (1874–1929). Austrian. A notable poet and playwright, he is best remembered as Richard Strauss's incomparable librettist: *Elektra, Der Rosenkavalier, Ariadne auf Naxos, Die Aegyptische Helena, Arabella, Die Frau ohne Schatten.* The last, the controversial *Frau,* meant most to him (and to an ardent minority of opera-lovers). Anyone wondering about the nature of composer-librettist collaboration cannot do better than read his published correspondence with Strauss, and William Mann's *Richard Strauss,* a critical study of the operas.

MENOTTI, GIAN CARLO (1911–). American, of Italian birth. See also page 67. Menotti's chief strength (and this author is the last person to sneer at his much-derided music) is as a librettist; though so strong is his theatrical imagination that playwright might be a better word for him, certainly when referring to *The Medium, The Telephone* and, in particular, *The Consul*. Greater literary talents have tried their hand at librettos in Britain, but none has solved the problems of operatic English as well as Menotti at his best.

METASTASIO, PIETRO (1698–1782). Italian. Statistically, if in no other way, he was the greatest of librettists, twenty-seven of his works being used by fifty composers to write 1,000 operas. *Artaserse* enjoyed forty settings in 100 years. Opera was going through its most formal period and his pleasant and skilful verse fitted the formula like a glove. Gluck's revolution was against Metastasian opera, the corruption of the dramatic side of the art which led to already fossilized plots and emotions being constantly interrupted by flights of brilliant vocal acrobatics.

PONTE, LORENZO DA (1749–1838). Italian. With Boito and Hofmannsthal, one of the trinity of great librettists. He also managed to fit in a lot of living, as related in his gusto-laden autobiography. He wrote three immortal librettos: *Figaro Don Giovanni* and *Così fan tutte*, all inspiring Mozart to surpass even himself. The first is perfection; the second, written in haste, is less perfect but endlessly fascinating and argument-provoking; the third is at last recognized as the setting for one of the most sensuous and serious of all comedies. Da Ponte lived in America from 1805 until his death, helping establish Italian opera in New York in the 1820s and 1830s.

QUINAULT, PHILLIPE (1635–88). French. This playwright and poet collaborated with Lully on twenty operas, formally constructed but on a wide range of subjects.

ROMANI, FELICE (1788–1865). Italian. He wrote over 100 librettos and was, after Boito, the finest Italian librettist of the 19th century, a notable poet whose only fault was alarming composers by his late delivery (presumably partly because he was doing too much). The fortunate Bellini had *Norma* and *La Sonnambula*, but not, alas, *I Puritani* from him; while his works for Donizetti included the delightful book for the enchanting, joyous *L'Elisir d'Amore*, taken from an earlier work by Scribe.

SCRIBE, EUGÈNE (1791–1861). French. He apparently wrote 374 works in all, including 114 librettos, hence snide references to the 'Scribe factory'. The jibe suggests sour grapes, for the great composers of the day flocked to him. Auber used him thirty-eight times, Meyerbeer for *Les Huguenots*, *Le Prophète*, etc. Rossini for the irresistible *Comte Ory*,

Verdi for *Vêpres Siciliennes* and, indirectly, *Un Ballo in Maschera*—to name but a few.

WAGNER, RICHARD (1813–83). A questionnaire amongst Wagnerians once revealed that the story of the *Ring* was almost as big an attraction as its music. How the Master would have approved, for he was a mighty story-teller. Westerman claims that the language of the *Ring* has 'rare charm', and defends the composer's fondness for alliteration. The libretto of *Die Meistersinger* excellently depicts both environment and characters. Wagner found himself as a librettist with *Der fliegende Holländer*, while for perfect mixing of music and text, *Tristan und Isolde* was his masterpiece. He had a fixation about redemption through love, even in death, but what Wagnerian would complain about that gateway to sublimity? Wagner's genius as a composer-librettist was steadily unique, and genius on such a level can know no duplication.

OPERA ROUND
THE WORLD

A Lyric Gazetteer

A short guide to operatic countries, centres and theatres which provide or have provided seasons down the centuries

ARGENTINA. The capital, Buenos Aires, has had opera since the 1750s, the first complete Italian opera given being *Il Barbiere* in 1825. Interest grew, especially with visiting touring companies playing fairly regularly. The Teatro de la Opera opened in 1872 and it was there that Toscanini established Wagner in Argentina between 1901 and 1906, also giving superb performances of Italian works.

The city's best-known opera house, the Colón, dates from 1857, the present Colón being opened in 1908. It has an international season every year.

AUSTRALIA. Until the opening of the Sydney Opera House (1973), the Australians were best known operatically for their singers. Well-organized competitions, a good climate, a love of singing, fine physiques, and resonance increased by a remarkable number of jutting chins, have all presumably helped to account for the abundance of fine singers, and so has the influence of Nellie Melba (see page 171), in whom even tone-deaf Aussies took pride. But until after the Second World War, Australia depended mainly on touring companies from abroad. Famous singers visited Australia to sing with the Williamson and Quinlan companies early in the century, and Melba's farewell company in 1924 included Toti dal Monte and Dino Borgioli.

The Elizabethan Trust united native companies in 1954 at a time when Australia's most famous singer abroad was Joan Hammond, and Marie Collier, Ronald Dowd and others were rapidly making their name. The long, stormy saga of the Sydney

Opera House began when the New South Wales government held the international competition in 1955 which Joern Ultzon (who later left in controversial circumstances) won. The Trust became the Australian Opera Company in 1969, a decade after Joan Sutherland inherited the mantle of Melba with her Covent Garden *Lucia*. She, her husband, Richard Bonynge, and a good company made a first return home in 1965. Edward Downes became Music Director of the Australian Opera in 1972 and conducted the opening opera, *War and Peace*, produced by Sam Wanamaker. Alas, the Opera House has in the event become a concert hall, with the smaller hall given to opera and ballet. But at least it exists, the building is a marvel, Sutherland has returned, and the flow of Australian singers to astound the 'Poms' and others is never ending. The future is bright.

Footnote: In February, 1975, the English National Opera's *Magic Flute* had six Australian principals.

AUSTRIA. Noting that Graz has had an opera house since 1899, that Innsbruck has a flourishing company, and that Bergenz and Salzburg are discussed in the next section (pages 317 and 322), concentration can focus on Vienna, one of the half-dozen supreme operatic centres. Opera there dates back to the 1640s. Operatic activity was immense in the 18th century. Gluck was appointed court Kapellmeister in 1754, six years after his *Semiramide Riconosciuta* had opened the Theater bei der Hofburg, and no less than ten of his operas had Viennese premières. The Burgtheater's premières included Mozart's *Die Entführung, Figaro* and *Così fan tutte*, and Cimarosa's *Il Matrimonio Segreto*. At the Theater auf der Wieden, *Die Zauberflöte* (1791) was staged by Emanuel Schikaneder, challenging the royal monopoly. He also produced *Fidelio* (1805), at the Theater an der Wien, opened in 1801.

Rossini had a huge following in Vienna, and so did Donizetti, court composer from 1842 until his health failed. Later highlights included performances of Verdi, Wagner conducting—and hearing—*Lohengrin* for the first time (1861), and the opening of Die Oper am Ring with *Don Giovanni* (1869). Richter conducted the *Ring* during the Franz Jauner regime (1875–80), then ruled Viennese opera with Jauner's successor, William Jahn (1880–96), a glorious period eclipsed by the supreme glory of Mahler's reign, 1897–1907 (see page 237).

Vienna remained one of the world's supreme operatic centres (with the Hofoper becoming the Staatsoper in 1918) until 1938. Between the wars, Schalk (with Strauss from 1920 to 1924), Krauss, Weingartner and Walter were successively the musical and artistic directors, and singers included Piccaver, Jeritza, Lehmann, Schumann, Mayr, Tauber, Schorr, Olszewska, Ursuleac, etc. The coming of the Nazis saw the departure of Walter, Schumann, Lehmann, Tauber, Piccaver, Schorr, Kipnis and List, and not until 1943 was order partly re-established under Böhm, who gave *Capriccio* for Strauss's 80th birthday. The house was destroyed by bombs in 1945, but the same year opera was reborn at the Volksoper under Krips and at the Theater an der Wien, the Vienna State Opera playing at these two theatres until the reopening of the new State Opera in 1955.

Under Böhm, Krips and Kraus, the post-1945 period was a particularly glorious one, not least because of the singers, who included Gueden, Jurinac, Schwarzkopf, Seefried, Welitsch, Hotter, Kunz and Patzak. The new house, under Böhm (1954–6) and von Karajan (1956–64), has had a more controversial time, though helped by exchange productions with La Scala and many Italian singers singing in their own language. Performances have varied from sublime (especially at festival time) to dismal, with too little use of very modern theatrical facilities. The Volksoper became independent again in 1955 under Salmhofer, and gives many operettas plus some operas, one of which, *Nabucco*, has been a Viennese favourite for many years.

Recent Opera Directors have included Egon Hilbert (died 1968), Heinrich Reif-Gintl, a unique man without enemies who was at the State Opera a record forty-nine years, and, since 1972, Rudolf Gamsjager, who has also taken over management of the Volksoper. Down the years the Viennese have been dubbed musically conservative, and the city gets more than its share of operatic crises. But it remains one of the most operatic spots on earth—and the Vienna Philharmonic Orchestra, which serves the Opera, is one of the world's supreme instruments.

BELGIUM. The four main centres of Belgian opera are Antwerp, Brussels, Ghent and Liège. **Brussels'** opera house is the famous Théâtre Royale de la Monnaie where Melba made her début. Today's theatre dates from 1856 and its golden age was from

1875 to 1889 under Lapissida, when the company included Calvé, Rose Caron and Melba, and Dupont was the chief conductor. In the 1950s, singers included Rita Gorr at the height of her powers. A total policy switch occurred in 1859 when Maurice Huismann ended the permanent ensemble and instead engaged foreign companies and groups for the Monnaie, along with French and Belgian singers for certain operas. Standards have varied, but the theatre remains an important one and, on occasion, a major centre: Béjart's hugely controversial, totally riveting *La Traviata* in 1973 was one such occasion. **Antwerp** is the home of the Royal Flemish Opera and its big and imaginative repertoire is sung in Flemish. **Ghent's** repertoire is even larger than Antwerp's. French, German and Flemish are the languages used, and many foreign singers appear with the company. **Liège's** opera is of first-rate French provincial standard, achieved after the tenor, André d'Arkor, took over its direction in 1945.

BRAZIL. The Brazilian operatic headquarters is the Teatro Municipal at Rio de Janeiro, and opera is also given in São Paolo, but there is no strong lyric tradition in the country. Bidu Sayão is probably the best-known Brazilian singer (see page 191), and Carlos Gomez and Villa Lobos the most famous operatic composers.

BRITAIN. See Great Britain.

BULGARIA. The first opera (and drama) company was founded in 1880, two years after independence from Turkey was achieved, and a National Opera was formed in Sofia in 1908. There are now a number of large opera companies, the National Opera sharing the theatre with the Ballet. Apart from Georgi Atanasov (1881–1931), the founder of Bulgarian opera, there have been a number of native composers, mainly known locally; while the two most famous living singers are the two most famous Boris Godunovs; Christoff and Giaurov.

CANADA. Opera in Canada consisted of visits from touring companies until 1946 when the influential Royal Conservatory Opera School was founded in Toronto, and not until the late 1960s did opera begin to gain the prestige of ballet. Toronto's first Opera Festival was in 1950, and its company became the Canadian Opera Company in 1959, being based at the new O'Keefe Centre from 1961. Touring has been very much a feature of the company, which made history in 1967 with Harry Somers's *Louis Riel*, an epic about a still controversial French-Canadian Indian figure, who led two rebellions in 1870 and 1885. This splendid national work was acclaimed by Canadians and visitors alike. L'Opéra de Quebec is French Canada's leading organization, based on Montreal and Quebec, taking over from the Théâtre Lyrique de Quebec of the 1960s. The present company's 1974–5 season was Italian and German with *Tristan und Isolde* a huge success (Vickers, Knie, Mehta). The West has its opera seasons: at Edmonton, Winnipeg, now Calgary, and, most notably, Vancouver, where there has been regular opera since 1951 and, from 1958, an International Festival, Joan Sutherland being only one of many famous singers who have appeared. Irving Guttman directed the seasons from 1960 to 1974. In the 1950s and 1960s, opera played a subsidiary but important role in the Stratford, Ontario, Festival. The increased opportunities at home are leading even the most celebrated Canadian singers (including Jon Vickers) to return from time to time.

CZECHOSLOVAKIA. This is one of the most operatic nations in Europe, and Prague remains one of the most musical capitals, as it was in Mozart's day: *Don Giovanni* and *La Clemenza di Tito* were both premièred there. Previously the capital of Bohemia, Prague has an operatic tradition dating back to the early 17th century. Weber was musical director of the German Opera House, 1813–17. Smetana was director of the Provisional Theatre, 1866–74, during which time six of his national operas were produced, including *The Bartered Bride;* and his *Libuse* opened the National Theatre in 1881, by which time Czech opera was well-established. The German Opera under Neumann continued to flourish, becoming the Smetana Theatre, part of the National Opera, in 1948. Brno is one of a dozen or so notable provincial houses. Its *Lulu* (1972) was the first in Eastern Europe and a notable success, with Jaroslava Janská in the lead. Janáček, hugely popular in his native land, had his *Jenufa* and later works first given there. Destinn is perhaps the most famous of all Czech singers, and one of the most notable of today's is Dvorakova. The 150th anniversary of Smetana's birth was splendidly celebrated in 1974, not least by a notable performance of his last opera, *Devil's Wall*, designed by Svoboda.

DENMARK. Opera has never been as much a feature of Danish life as ballet, even though it was not a dancer but the singer Jenny Lind that Hans Andersen fell for (he was also a librettist). Companies from abroad have visited Copenhagen since the 18th century. The city's present Royal Theatre opened in 1874 and it was there that Melchior, amongst others, began his career. There have been a number of Danish operas, but none can be claimed as *the* national opera. A very fine one is Kunzen's *Holger Danske* (1789) on the Oberon theme. There is an annual festival in Copenhagen, with visits from foreign companies.

EIRE. The Irish currently provide the world with the most enjoyable of festivals—Wexford (see page 324). They take to opera almost as readily as the Welsh, first experiencing it in 1711 (Handel's *Rinaldo* in Dublin). Only in the 19th century was Dublin allowed to hear seasons, on occasion of great splendour, direct from the Italian houses in London. Leading and lesser touring companies played at the Gaiety, Dublin, while from 1908 to 1910, the Dublin Opera Company's performances included McCormack as Faust. Since 1941, regular seasons have been given by the Dublin Grand Opera Society, using Radio Eireann's orchestra and employing a local chorus and guests from abroad. Limited rehearsal time and lack of a regular company has not prevented many successful performances, and, though Italian opera is especially popular, many other works are given.

FINLAND. Touring German companies brought opera to Helsinki in the early 19th century, the first Finnish opera being *Kung Carls Jakt* (King Charles's Hunt), 1852. However, the composer was German and it was sung in Swedish. The first opera to a Finnish text was Merikanto's *Pohjan Neito* (The Maid of Bothnia), first staged in 1908. The most popular native work has been Madetoja's *Pohjalaisia* (The East Bothnians), produced in 1924. Finland's first permanent company began in 1873, but it closed in 1911, the year in which Edward Frazer and Aino Ackté (the first Salome) founded a company that in 1914 became Finland's National Opera, the Suomalainen Ooppera. Several native operas were given in 1973 to celebrate the centenary of the first permanent company (which had opened with *Lucia*).

FRANCE. Opera in Paris dates back to 1645, the first French work being given in 1650, Dassoucy's *Andromède*, at the Petit Bourbon. For 140 years, from 1660, opera was given at more than twenty theatres in the city at various times; from 1800 until 1918 at some thirty theatres. The most famous was the Académie de Musique, later the Opéra, which was opened in 1671, and which saw the works of, among others, Lully and Rameau. Various theatres housed France's premier company, with Spontini and Cherubini active in Napoleon's time, and the operas of Rossini, Mozart, Donizetti and Weber performed after a move to the Rue Lepeletier in 1822. Then came the sumptuous period of Meyerbeer, Auber, *Guillaume Tell*, Verdi's Parisian operas, etc., with magnificent casts. Today's **Opéra** opened in 1875, a most notable period being 1885–1906 when Pierre Gailhard and others ran the great theatre. Even Francophiles will admit that the Opéra went into a slow decline, losing its status as one of the handful of supreme houses; but the regime of Rolf Liebermann, who left Hamburg for Paris in 1972, and who had Georg Solti as musical adviser, has re-established the international prestige it once enjoyed.

The **Opéra-Comique**'s long history dates back to 1715, its move to the Rue Favart coming in 1783, and an amalgamation with a rival in 1801. During the 19th century it played a major role in French opera, with premières by Auber, Méhul, Donizetti (*La Fille du Régiment*, 1840), and Thomas (*Mignon*, 1866). Then, under Léon Carvalho (who had been Director of the Théatre Lyrique), it gave the first *Hoffmann, Carmen*, Delibes' *Lakmé* and Massenet's *Manon*. Albert Carré took over in 1898 and his premières included a legendary one, *Pelléas et Mélisande* (1902). The Opéra and Opéra-Comique were merged in 1939, and A. M. Julien became their joint administrator in 1959. The de Gaulle regime stole *Carmen* from the Comique to give to the Opéra, a portent of its doom, for, sadly, it closed in 1972, to reopen as an opera studio.

Offenbach's immortal little Bouffes-Parisiens opened in 1855, and other famous Parisian theatres include the Théâtre-Lyrique (1852–   ), now the Théâtre Sarah Bernhardt. Premières have included *Faust* (1859) and Berlioz's *Les Troyens à Carthage* (1863). It housed the Opéra-Comique for a time. The Théâtre-Italien lasted from the 1820s to the 1880s, and saw many fabulous golden age performances by Grisi, Mario, Lablache, etc. Its most famous première was *Don Pasquale* (1843). Mention must also be made of the Théâtre des Champs-Élysées (1913–   ) which has housed famous foreign troupes from Diaghilev's day onwards.

Other French operatic centres include Bordeaux, Lyons, Mulhouse, Marseilles and Strasbourg. The Aix-en-Provence Festival is discussed on page 315.

GERMANY. In a book of this size, scant justice can be done to the most seriously operatic of all countries. Divided into kingdoms, etc., for much of its history, and, since 1949, into two nations, only some cities can be sampled. There are almost sixty opera companies in West Germany alone. With subsidies a long-established tradition, and with many modern theatres—a rare blessing of wartime destruction—the scene is not so much remarkable (except at the great houses) as secure and part of everyday life. Yet, in 1976 even West Germany's opera is threatened by inflation. For convenience, as so many towns are to be mentioned, alphabetical order will be adopted; also W for West Germany, E for East.

Bayreuth (W). See Festivals, page 316.

Berlin. The Deutsche Staatsoper Unter den Linden (E), Komische Oper (E) and the Deutsche Oper (W) are today's three houses. Opera in the city dates back to 1688, and an opera house, the Hofoper, to 1742. Spontini was its musical director from 1819 to 1842, being succeeded by Meyerbeer. Meanwhile, German Romantic opera was born at the Schauspielhaus with Weber's *Der Freischütz* (1821). Weingartner, Karl Muck and Strauss ruled the Hofoper from 1891–1918, creating a fine ensemble. The Krolls Theatre (1924) became a world famous experimental house under Klemperer (1927–31), Hindemith's *Cardillac*, Schoenberg's *Erwartung* and Stravinsky's *Oedipus Rex* being among the works staged. Meanwhile the Staatsoper (1918–43) enjoyed major talents such as Kleiber

(1924–34), Furtwängler and Krauss, the first giving the première of *Wozzeck* (1925). There was a superb roster of singers, many of whom have entries in the section in this book on *Singers*. The theatre was bombed in 1943, returning to its site at the Unter den Linden in 1955. The Stadtische Oper opened in 1912 and was bombed in 1944, reopening in the Theater des Westens, where its casts have included Fischer-Dieskau. Carl Ebert was its Director General and producer from 1956 to 1961, having previously held the post 1931–3, and its Music Director was Lorin Maazel (1965–71). The Komische Opera (1947–) has become internationally famous through its producer, Felsenstein (see pages 251 and 260).

Brunswick (W). An operatic town since the 17th century, its Landestheater was bombed, the present Staatstheater opening with *Don Giovanni* in 1948.

Bremen (W). An operatic centre since the 18th century, it lost its opera house in the war, the Theater am Goetheplatz opening in 1950.

Cassel. See **Kassel.**

Cologne (W). Major German house, particularly under Klemperer (1917–24). His premières included Korngold's *Die Tote Stadt* (1920). Here also bombs destroyed the opera house, today's being opened in 1957. Distinguished music directors have included Wolfgang Sawallisch and Istvan Kertesz. Recent major successes have included a splendid *La Fanciulla del West* (1972), conducted by Santi and produced by Hans Neugebauer, excellent for the morale of those who resent the neglect of this superb opera.

Dessau (E). The house has had strong Wagnerian traditions ever since staging *Die Meistersinger* soon after its Munich première (1869). Knappertsbusch was amongst its conductors.

Dresden (E). A major operatic centre since the 18th century, though Italian-orientated until Weber's day. *Rienzi, Tannhäuser* and *Der Fliegende Holländer* were premièred there in the 1840s, since when particularly famous periods have included that of the conductor von Schuch (1882–1914) who, with a stellar ensemble, gave the premières of *Elektra* and *Salome*, and the reign of Fritz Busch (1922–33), who was succeeded by Böhm (1934–42). Strauss's *Arabella* was one of a number of premières (1933), and casts included Rethberg, Tauber and Cebotari. The opera house was bombed in the notorious 1945 raid and rebuilt in 1948, and has had amongst its music directors Kempe and von Matacic.

Düsseldorf-Duisburg (W) houses the Deutsche Opera am Rhein, a very strong ensemble, one of whose most recent triumphs (1974) was *Wozzeck*, conducted by Günther Wich, with Guillermo Sarabia in the title-role and Hildegard Behrens as an exceptionally fine Marie. Düsseldorf's theatre dates from 1956, replacing one of 1875; Duisberg's dates from 1950, replacing a 1912 building.

Frankfurt-am-Main (W). A famous centre since the 1880s, its earlier conductors included Weingartner and Krauss. Postwar music directors have included Solti and von Matacic. Orff's *Carmina Burana* is among many local premières (1937). Christoph von Dohnanyi is currently in charge.

Halle (E). See page 321 for the Halle Festival.

Hamburg (W). Germany's oldest-established opera (1678), and one of the leading European companies. Handel's *Almira* (1705) was premièred at an early theatre, and the first German *Otello* and *Eugene Onegin* were given in the city. Music directors of the Stadttheater have included Mahler, Klemperer and Böhm. Despite bombing, opera continued on the stage of the old house until the new opera opened in 1955 with *Die Zauberflöte* produced by Rennert, the Intendant, 1946–56. He was succeeded by Tietjen, then Liebermann, who left to take over the Opéra, Paris in 1972, being replaced by August Everding. This major repertoire theatre has had Jenny Lind, Lilli and Lotte Lehmann, Melchior and Hotter amongst its stars. Renowned for its contemporary opera productions, many classical works are also given, notably John Dexter's production of Verdi's *Sicilian Vespers*. *Moses und Aron*, premièred in a concert in 1954, was produced by Bohumil Herlischka in 1974 to a mixed reception as is usual with this opera.

Hanover (W). An operatic city since the 1640s, the present opera house was built in 1845, rebuilt in 1950. Henze's *Boulevard Solitude* (1952) is among its premières, and recent productions have included Kodály's *Harry Janos* (1974).

Karlsruhe (W). The first complete *Les Troyens* was given here in 1890 under Mottl.

Kassel (W). A notable centre since the 1820s, Spohr being in charge from 1822 to 1857 and Mahler from 1883 to 1885. A recent success was Berg's *Lulu* (1974), conducted by James Lockhart and with Hildegard Uhrmacher as a highly effective Lulu in Michael Geliot's production.

Mannheim (W). Many famous conductors have served the city's opera, including Weingartner (1889–91), Furtwängler (1915–20) and Kleiber (1922–3). Wellesz's *Alkestis* had its première there in 1923. The 1779 National Theatre was destroyed in 1943 and rebuilt in 1957. Horst Stein became Generalmusikdirektor in 1963. In 1975 Hans Wallat was music director, and the wide-ranging repertoire including Tchaikovsky's *Maid of Orleans*, Leoncavallo's *Edipo Re*, and all Wagner's supreme works.

Munich (W). The city is one of the most operatic spots on earth, and since the 1850s has been one of the greatest centres of opera. If London's opera houses ever collapse from inflation and philistinism, the desperate operagoer might well emigrate to Munich to enjoy constant, first-rate performances, and to be within striking distance of other main centres. The Residenztheater, a rococo delight by Cuviliès, opened in 1753. Its auditorium was rebuilt elsewhere in 1958 during modernization of the rest of the building. Its premières have included *Idomeneo* (1781). The Hof und Nationaltheater was opened in 1818, burned down and rebuilt in the 1820s, then bombed in 1943, and reopened in 1963. The Prinzregententheater, originally intended only for Wagner, opened in 1901. It housed the Bavarian State Opera, 1945–63.

Munich's greatness dates from Lachner's regime (see page 236). He was director of the Opera from 1852 to 1890, and premières included *Tristan und Isolde*, *Die Meistersinger*, *Rheingold* and *Walküre*. Musical directors have included Bülow, Walter, Knappertsbusch, Solti and Kempe, and, from 1971, Sawallisch. The summer festival is included in the next section (page 321). The city has been a Straussian paradise since 1919, premières being *Friedenstag* and *Capriccio*. Other premières have included Pfitzner's *Palestrina* and Orff's *Der Mond*. It is pointless mentioning singers: nearly every famous German artist has been with the company.

Nuremberg (W). The first German opera, *Seelewig*, was given in the city in 1644. Today's opera house was built in 1905, damaged in the war, and reopened in 1945. Hans Gierster is the Music Director, previous ones including Fritz Stiedry.

Stuttgart (W). Opera has been given in the city since the 17th century. Today's house was opened in 1912 and saw the première of the first version of *Ariadne auf Naxos*. It has been a notable operatic centre ever since and has toured abroad. The first German *Mathis der Maler* (Hindemith) was given in 1946, and from 1947 to 1969 Ferdinand Leitner was Generalmusik-direktor. His singers included Modl, Windgassen and—regularly—Borkh, Varnay, Rysanek and London, and Wieland Wagner and Gunther Rennert both directed for him. The repertoire has always been vast at the theatre, which is officially the Württemberg State Opera. Currently, Silvio Varviso is Music Director.

Weimar (E). Though still an operatic centre, Weimar's importance is historical. Immortalized by Goethe, it became operatically great under Liszt, chief Kapellmeister, 1847–58, with Bülow as another conductor. Premières have included *Lohengrin*, Schubert's *Alfonso und Estrella* and *Der Barbier von Bagdad* (Cornelius), and the admirable Liszt also gave the second productions of *Benvenuto Cellini* and Schumann's *Genoveva*. His successor, Lassen, produced the first *Samson et Dalila* (1877) and the second *Tristan und Isolde* was given under him. Other key events included the première of *Hansel und Gretel* (1893), and also the first *Guntram* (1894), composed by the company's first conductor, Richard Strauss.

Wiesbaden (W). This spa and wine centre has been a leading opera house since the 1950s, under Friedrich Schramm (1952–62), with Wolfgang Sawallisch and Heinz Walberg as Music Directors. There is an annual festival.

Wuppertal (W). In the small opera house, opened in 1956, a progressive regime has made the town one of the most admirable minor operatic centres in Germany, a fine place to end this all-too-short visit. Though it has made a reputation for its Monteverdi productions, its championing of modern opera is also notable. The 1973–4 season included the première of Blacher's *Yvonne*, a 'black operetta' (Horst Koegler), Rossini's *Il Turco in Italia*, Humperdinck's *Königskinder, Hoffmann, Nabucco, Lulu* (Berg) and *Iphigénie en Tauride* (Gluck). There's riches.

GREAT BRITAIN. Until the end of the Second World War, opera in Britain had a slender but limpet-like place in the artistic life of the nation, surviving crisis after crisis, and possessing a starry international season at Covent Garden which gave a false impression that the country as a whole cared a damn. Firmer roots were already established at Sadler's Wells and Glyndebourne and by the Carl Rosa on tour; but the position was far worse than in the 19th and early 20th centuries when there was more touring opera and more London-based opera. Now only inflation can hold Britain back operatically, even though the operatic public is even smaller than the minority that patronizes the theatre. There follows an alphabetical list of some British institutions and operatic centres, Aldeburgh, Glyndebourne and the Edinburgh Festival being omitted because they feature in the next section.

Arts Council. Formed in 1940 as the Council for the Encouragement of Music and the Arts, its function is to get as much money as possible from the Treasury, via the Government, to subsidize the Arts in Britain. It is regularly abused, but rarely by operagoers, who know that without its sympathy, opera in Britain is dead. Subsidies are never more than barely adequate, but that is no fault of the Arts Council.

Beecham Opera Company. See page 222.

Birmingham. The greatest figure in the history of British Rep., Sir Barry Jackson, also loved opera, and in the 1920s regularly mounted productions at his world-famous Birmingham Rep., of Mozart, Cimarosa, etc. and the now legendary production of Boughton's *The Immortal Hour*, which later had a long London run. As he was using his private money, Sir Barry finally had to abandon opera. The Midland Music Makers have put on a number of ambitious productions since the war.

British Broadcasting Corporation. The B.B.C., which started relaying opera in the 1920s, has been one of the greatest impresarios in the history of the art. A reasonable number of televised operas are given, including direct transmissions from theatres, in between money disputes.

British National Opera Company. When the Beecham Company collapsed (see *Beecham*, page 222), in 1920, a new company was formed by some of its stars and musicians, including Percy Pitt (the first director), Robert Radford, Walter Hyde, Norman Allin, Aylmer Buesst and Agnes Nicholls. It toured extensively and played annually in London,

first at Covent Garden, then at His Majesty's, where the première of Vaughan Williams' *Hugh the Drover* took place (1924).
The *Ring* was in the company's repertoire, guests included
Melba, young conductors included Barbirolli—and then the
money ran out in 1928. The Covent Garden English Company,
which took over, survived three seasons.

Cambridge. The University has had a fine operatic tradition,
in large part due to Professor Edward Dent (1876–1957). Even
if he had never translated an opera, his influence would still
have been immense. Purcell, Handel, Honegger and Vaughan
Williams were given in the 1920s and 1930s and, since his
death, the tradition of Cambridge opera has continued. The
Cambridge University Opera Group has performed an astonishing variety of works, and nurtured the New Opera Company
(see page 294). Cambridge's supreme achievement was *The
Magic Flute* (1911) which restored the opera to Britain.

Carl Rosa Company. Like Donald Wolfit's Shakespeare
Company, the Carl Rosa endured the stigma of being 'tat' in
its final years, yet both contributed nobly to the artistic health
of the nation, bringing Shakespeare and opera to hundreds of
thousands outside London until the 1950s. Karl Rose (1842–
89) settled in Britain in 1866 and was inspired to present opera
in English, founding his company in 1875, having previously
changed his name to Carl Rosa. Not until 1889 did the Carl
Rosa become a touring company, after regular London
seasons. In the 1920s, there were sometimes three companies on
the road. In 1950, following the death of H. B. Phillips, his
widow ran the company, with Arthur Hammond as Music
Director. Despite grants, the enterprise foundered in 1958.
An attempted revival failed.

The Rosa style in its later days was 'stand up and deliver',
and its singers (who down the years included Turner and
Craig) sang sturdily and sometimes thrillingly.

Covent Garden. There have been three theatres in Bow
Street, the first, mainly devoted to drama, opening in 1732 and
being burnt down in 1808. Handel's *Alcina* (1735) *Atalanta*
(1736) and *Berenice* (1737) had their premières there. In 1809,
the second Covent Garden opened, and in 1826, Charles
Kemble asked Weber for an opera, which resulted in *Oberon*.
In 1847, the theatre became the Royal Italian Opera, its
company including singers who had broken away from Her

Majesty's with the conductor Michael Costa. The regime opened with Rossini's *Semiramide* (Grisi, Alboni, Tamburini, etc.). In 1849, Frederick Gye became manager (until 1877), and in 1856, the theatre was burnt down, today's building opening in 1858. Until 1939, except during the First World War, there was an international season each summer from late April to late July (and occasional autumn and winter seasons), and nearly every great singer of each age appeared. Opera was a Society pet, though as soon as such a statement is made, the qualification is needed that there were by all accounts many opera-lovers present.

Until the reign of Augustus Harris from 1888 to 1896, all operas were given in Italian in this third house. Harris (1852–96), the son of a stage manager, had worked with Mapleson and also had a lease of Drury Lane. His stars included the de Reszkes and Melba, and he not only brought in opera in the original, but also introduced Wagner. The famous pre-war Beecham seasons, which began in 1910 with the first British *Elektra*, were winter ones.

Opera resumed in 1919 with *La Bohème*, starring Melba and conducted by Beecham. The chief conductor from 1924 to 1931 was Bruno Walter, Beecham then taking over until 1939. Owing to the current taste, Italian opera, Puccini apart, tended to be neglected between the wars. Not a note of Verdi was heard in the International seasons of 1929 and 1935.

During the Second World War, as if to prove how little hold opera had in Britain, the theatre became a dance hall. In 1946, the Covent Garden Opera Company, subsidized by the Arts Council, was formed, but, inevitably, there was precious little operatic know-how at the Garden in any department. The first Music Director, Karl Rankl (1946–51—see page 240), hardly helped, though he deserved some credit for keeping things going. Fortunately, David Webster (1903–71), later Sir David, was a good manager who got steadily better, and was finally a superb general administrator. Rankl and his young potential genius, Peter Brook, director of productions for a time, did not get on. Inexperience and a cavalier attitude, also the traditions of the day, handicapped Brook, who yet made controversial history with *Salome*, designed by Dali and starring Welitsch. Morale was generally low among British artists until Kleiber (whom the fast-improving orchestra adored) came in

1950. His *Der Rosenkavalier* and *Wozzeck* were the first *company* successes, though there was much fine Wagner to be heard, with Flagstad, Hotter, etc. Other foreign stars appeared, including Schwartzkopf and Silveri, but the Italian repertoire was in poor shape. Some tenors still haunt the imagination. Other highlights of the pre-Kubelik years included *Billy Budd* (1951), Callas as Norma (1952), Ferrier as Orpheus (1953), and the much-maligned *Gloriana* (1953). Something of an ensemble was growing, opera for better or worse was still mainly in English, Douglas Robinson's chorus had been splendid from the beginning, and young singers such as Geraint Evans, Shacklock and Fisher, were making their names. But generally the company had an inferiority complex, and audience reaction, except on rare occasions, was by today's standards very muted.

Kubelik took over in 1955 and, from the opening production of his reign—*Otello* with Brouwenstijn, Vinay and Kraus—things began to go right. The peaks of his period (1955–8) were twin Everests: *Les Troyens* (1957) and *Don Carlos* (1958). Solti (1961–71) announced his intention of turning Covent Garden into the world's greatest opera house and almost succeeded. But the Kubelik era, then the interregnum, which included Zeffirelli's *Lucia* (Sutherland/Serafin) and his *Cav* and *Pag*, began the process, as did incomparable Callas performances. The standard of singing, native and foreign, had soared, and there was no longer a tenor famine, especially after Webster signed up Vickers. Now production standards were usually adequate, often very fine, sometimes great, whereas earlier the Wells had dominated this side of opera.

The Solti era saw a change to *stagione* (see page 339), which obtains today, productions being given a number of performances over a short period, perhaps to reappear later, or in the next season, and most operas are in the original. For most patrons, this has been the right policy, but it has lessened the impact of Mozart, *Der Rosenkavalier* and certain other works, for all the full houses. Deprived of the sort of funds to draw galaxies of superstars, most famous singers appeared, sometimes very briefly, in the Kubelik and Solti eras. High peaks of Solti's decade included Klemperer's *Fidelio*, the Callas, Gobbi, Zeffirelli *Tosca* (1964), memorable Strauss nights under Solti, and magnificent revivals of *Don Carlos*; also Nilsson's Isolde, and other Wagnerian triumphs (if not of staging).

Moses und Aron (1965) was a triumph also, for Solti, Peter Hall, the now superb orchestra and everyone involved. Colin Davis took over from 1971 and, after a controversial start and a continuing policy of too many conductors, is settling in to one of opera's toughest jobs. (See *Programme Notes* at the beginning of this book.) But he was cruelly handicapped at the beginning when his director of productions, Peter Hall, who had staged a *Tristan und Isolde* which boded infinitely well for the future (for all its detractors), resigned before Davis had begun working in his new post. Many of the more recent happenings at the Garden, and those who have sung there, appear elsewhere.

Denhof Opera Company. Founded by Ernst Denhof in 1910 to present the *Ring* outside London, it added other operas, including *Orfeo, Pelléas et Mélisande* and *Elektra*, before collapsing in 1913. Beecham, who had been a conductor with the company, took over, and two years later his own company was born.

Edinburgh. Apart from touring companies, its operatic history really began with the Festival (see page 318).

English National Opera. See Sadler's Wells Opera, page 291

English Opera Group. See Aldeburgh Festival, page 315.

Glasgow. Scottish Opera has a separate entry below. In the 19th century and well into the 20th, Glasgow depended on touring companies. The Glasgow Grand Opera Society, founded in 1905, has a knack of making history every few years, especially when it gave the British première of *Les Troyens* (1935), conducted by Erik Chisholm.

Glyndebourne. See page 319.

London. Covent Garden and Sadler's Wells have separate entries in this section. The capital has been the major operatic centre of Britain from the 17th century, when Dorset Garden Theatre and Drury Lane staged musical works. The first Italian opera heard in Britain was at the Queen's Theatre, later the King's, in the Haymarket—Greber's *Gli Amori d'Ergasto*. From Handel's day onwards, this was the home of Italian opera in London, and not until the 1830s was its supremacy challenged, by Alfred Bunn at Drury Lane. Many Mozart and Rossini operas were premièred at the King's, where casts were often stellar. In 1837, the theatre became Her Majesty's and, under two great managers, Benjamin Lumley (1811–75) and J. H. Mapleson (1830–1901), much operatic history was made.

Lumley's reign (1841–52, 1856–59) saw many major British premières of Donizetti and Verdi operas, including *Masnadieri*, with Verdi conducting Jenny Lind. The break in his management was due to a quarrel with Grisi, Mario, Persiani and Tamburini, who all left for Covent Garden and forced him to close. Mapleson, known as 'The Colonel', gave premières of *Faust, Carmen*, Verdi, etc., in seasons at Her Majesty's, Drury Lane and Covent Garden, also touring America with his stars.

Drury Lane has had occasional seasons of opera. Alfred Bunn (1806–60), mean, deplorable but fascinating, gave London bad librettos and translations, and his casts as little as possible, but he did give London Malibran and Schröder-Devrient. Drury Lane presented the first Wagner in Britain: *Der fliegende Holländer* in 1870; Richter gave the first *Die Meistersinger* and *Tristan und Isolde* in 1882. Other highlights have included the Russian seasons of Diaghilev with Beecham in 1913 and 1914, including Chaliapin as Boris, also Beecham's seasons in the First World War.

Other London theatres associated occasionally with opera have been the Lincoln's Inn Theatre, where *The Beggar's Opera* was first produced (1728), and the London Opera House (later the Stoll), which Oscar Hammerstein (1846–1919) hoped to make a rival to Covent Garden when it opened in 1911. It was occasionally and enjoyably used by other companies until it was pulled down in the 1950s. The Lyceum saw the first local *Otello* in 1889. Chaliapin sang there in 1931. A brief mention must be made of Sir Bernard Miles's Mermaid, where Flagstad opened the proceedings in 1951, when the theatre was still in Miles's back garden, singing Dido for a pint of stout per performance. For the Old Vic, see *Sadler's Wells*, page 291. See also *Camden Festival*, page 317.

Manchester. Hallé gave a season of opera in 1855, before and after which much of the city's operatic life depended on tours. Famous Beecham seasons from 1916 to 1919 are still recalled with awe. Other notable events there have included the death of Malibran (1836) and the first British *La Bohème* (1897).

Moody-Manners Company. Formed by Charles Manners and his wife Fanny (see page 169), it toured from 1898 to 1916, having two companies at one time. Florence Easton and John Coates were among the singers.

Oxford. The university Opera Club was founded after a famous performance of Monteverdi's *Orfeo* in 1925, realized by J. A., later Sir Jack Westrup (1904–75), and ever since, except in the war years, there has been a continuous series of annual productions covering the whole of operatic history.

Sadler's Wells Opera (from 1973 the English National Opera). The most important company in the whole chequered history of opera in Britain. It came into being because of an eccentric glorious, God-intoxicated, impossible woman of genius, Lilian Baylis (1874–1937), who also founded the Old Vic and the Sadler's Wells (now the Royal) Ballet. Manager of the Old Vic from 1898, under her aunt Emma Cons, and sole manager from 1912, she believed in opera and Shakespeare for the people, and by 1914 she was providing this for the people, with Charles Corri cutting down music scores to suit the small theatre orchestra. Everything had to be done cheaply; singers (and actors) were paid next to nothing, but the company prospered. Key figures included Edward Dent (translator of Mozart), Clive Carey, a singer turned producer of Mozart and other works, the conductor Lawrence Collingwood, and Miss Baylis herself, who controlled her singers and actors by native shrewdness and divine inspiration, and by choosing the right helpers. Her casts included Joan Cross, Edith Coates, Tudor Davies, Henry Wendon and many other fine artists, who were expected to act as well as sing, even those who were not naturally gifted.

In 1931, Lilian Baylis, having miraculously raised enough money, opened a new theatre on the site of Sadler's Wells, and the actors and singers commuted between the Old Vic and the new theatre until common sense dictated a split, the opera and infant ballet sticking to the Wells. Miss Baylis died honoured but unsubsidized, her Sadler's Wells Opera Company, if less fashionable than the ballet, going from strength to strength. Many singers not listed in this book did magnificent work for the company in the 1930s and 1940s, including Janet Hamilton-Smith, Redvers Llewellyn and Ruth Naylor. The company toured during the war led by Tyrone Guthrie. Its greatest singer at that time, Joan Cross, then returned to the Sadler's Wells Theatre for the legendary first night of *Peter Grimes*.

The period 1948–66 was under Norman Tucker, and it was in

many ways a great one. In the 1950s in particular, a real ensemble was built up and the theatrical standard was far ahead of Covent Garden's at the time (that is, until *Don Carlos*, 1958, and later happenings). James Robertson, Alexander Gibson and Colin Davis were the music directors, appalling financial crises were just surmounted; Janáček was discovered, *Simon Boccanegra* was given an historic production in 1948, and operetta was introduced a decade later with great success (though the inevitable *Die Fledermaus* had, of course, been there all the time). Many fine singers made their names and a few new operas were given, though lack of funds kept the number low and cut down touring to a minimum. The most notable producer of the period was Denis Arundell, though Basil Coleman, George Devine, Wendy Toye and others did fine work. Glen Byam Shaw became Director of Productions in 1962, a perfect choice for an ensemble theatre. Some Wells stars, including Shuard, Ward, Glossop and Craig, left to become internationally famous. Of those who remained, four may be said to typify the company at its best: Anna Pollak, Marion Studholme, Denis Dowling (still with the company) and Frederick Sharp.

The Company went to the Coliseum in 1968. This move was a triumph for Stephen Arlen, in charge from 1966 to 1972. Though not ideal, the Coliseum has proved superb for Wagner and such big productions as *La Forza del Destino*, *Damnation of Faust*, etc. if not so happy for Mozart. Lord Harewood succeeded to Arlen's post on the latter's death. Among present-day singers who cannot be left out of this short account, are Francis Egerton, Elizabeth Connell, Anne Evans and John Brecknock; among conductors, Bryan Balkwill. And happy the theatre which can call upon designers of the calibre of Ralph Koltai, Desmond Healey, Peter Rice, and which has a founder member of the firm of Motley as head of design, and Charles Bristow to light those designs. Without the publicity of another House in London, the Wells/English National Opera remains, under Harewood, as it always has been—a national treasure.

Scottish Opera. Founded in 1962 by Alexander Gibson, conductor of the Scottish National Orchestra, and based at Glasgow, the most musical city in Scotland. It began with a week's season: *Pelléas et Mélisande* and *Madame Butterfly*, and within five years had an international reputation. This was due (i) to Gibson and his use of the orchestra, and to his decision to aim from the start at the highest standards; (ii) to his enlightened board and, in particular, to Peter Hemmings who joined Scottish Opera as Administrative Director in 1966; (iii) to the build-up of such a strong company spirit that fine singers were, and are, that much easier to obtain; and (iv) to the result of all this—the extraordinary standard of musical and theatrical performance. A turning point was the now legendary production of *Così fan tutte* in 1967 (see page 255), and another was *Les Troyens* with Janet Baker as Dido (1969). Meanwhile, a remarkable *Ring* was being built up, produced by Peter Ebert, Director of Productions, and designed by Michael Knight. Other note-worthy points: a wide-ranging repertoire; extensive coverage of Scotland; forays into England and successes abroad; its own Opera-for-All group by the mid-1960s, taking opera to smaller communities; fifty-two week contracts being issued in 1973 to twenty-four choristers and ten young principals; and the purchase from Scottish Television in 1974 of the Theatre Royal, Glasgow, which became a permanent opera house in October 1975. The future, national crises permitting, seems thrilling. The theatre will be available for other companies.

The above may seem over-rosy to those who do not know the company's work, and, naturally, it has had visual and vocal failures. But the spirit of the organization, an ensemble on and off stage, has a warmly electric effect on everyone, not least on audiences.

Welsh National Opera. Love of singing is an evident characteristic of the Welsh, so it is hardly surprising that the number of opera singers produced by the Principality is out of all proportion to its size. A working-class Welsh boy with a voice has far more chance of being discovered than his English, Scottish or Irish equivalent, and it is this, rather than innate Welsh vocal superiority, that has made Welsh singing famous—and now internationally famous: Sir Geraint Evans, Gwyneth Jones, etc.

Yet Welsh opera was essentially amateur, or dependent on touring companies, until the founding of the Welsh National Opera in Cardiff in 1946, the main architect being W. H. Smith, and, indeed, the chorus remained amateur for many years. Amateur? It was inevitably one of the best in the world, many of the young company's greatest successes being in works which gave it maximum opportunity: *Nabucco, I Lombardi, Mefistofele,* etc. 'Va pensiero' sung by this chorus is unforgettable. Originally, finance compelled simple production standards, and the Welsh, unlike the Scots, did not have an orchestra to hand. The Bournemouth Symphony Orchestra regularly became honorary Welshmen. Music directors since the early 1960s have been Charles Groves, Bryan Balkwill, James Lockhart, and now Richard Armstrong. The Artistic Director is the very gifted and forward-looking Michael Geliot, working in conditions far more conducive to art than faced John Moody in the early days. Famous Welsh and other singers strengthen what is now a very strong company; the Welsh Philharmonia, at its best, is a fine opera orchestra; audience support is legendary. And the company tours far beyond Wales. In 1974, after June in Llandudno, it set off on an autumn tour of Cardiff, Swansea, Birmingham, Manchester, Oxford and Norwich, with new productions of *The Flying Dutchman, Simon Boccanegra, L'Elisir d'Amore, La Bohème, Don Carlos* and *The Barber.* The *Don Carlos* was the best to be heard and seen in Britain for some time. John Mauceri, an American, was making his British début, Geliot's fine production was rehearsed by Julian Hope, and Annena Stubbs's designs were much admired. An excellent cast included Forbes Robinson as Philip, Terence Sharpe as Posa, Janet Coster as Eboli, Anne Edwards as Elisabeth, Keith Erwen as Carlos, and Richard van Allan as the Inquisitor. Guest artists (as in Scotland) often excel their London performances, while the company has a fine record for bringing on young singers. As everywhere else in Britain, only money problems can spoil matters.

Many smaller groups exist in Britain, including the New London Opera Co. (1960–), with a splendid record of modern productions, including Prokofiev's *The Fiery Angel* (1965) with Collier; Kent Opera; Phoenix Opera; The Hammersmith Municipal Opera, where companies have given rarities such as Mascagni's *Iris,* Puccini's *La Rondine* and *Edgar,* and Smyth's *The Wreckers.* Camden Festival is in the next section (page 317).

GREECE. Though opera goes back to the 18th century in Greece, or, more accurately, in Corfu, where there were Venetian rulers, the mainland did not hear any until the 1840s, and a Greek company was not formed until 1887. Touring companies provided much of the opera. The National Lyric Theatre (1940) became the National Opera in 1944, and Greece has provided a few international singers, including the dominating figure of our generation, Callas, and also Arda Mandikian and Nicola Zaccaria. As opera was invented to try and capture something of ancient Greek drama, it is right that pinnacles of Greek operatic experiences were *Norma* and Cherubini's *Medea* at Epidaurus with Callas.

HOLLAND. Despite a high mortality rate amongst early Dutch national companies, Netherlanders have been able to enjoy a reasonable amount of opera down the years, Amsterdam and the Hague sharing local and foreign companies. From 1897 to 1942, visiting Italians were very successful, and from 1893 to 1939, the Wagnervereeniging gave regular Wagnerian seasons, with leading singers and with conductors of the calibre of Strauss and Kleiber. It was revived for a time after the war. There has been continuity in opera since 1941 when the Amsterdam Opera Class developed into the Municipal Theatre Enterprise, and was then succeeded by the Nederlandse Opera (originally started in 1886). This performed in all leading Dutch cities, becoming in 1965 the Nieuwe Nederlandse Opera, and collaborating with the Monnaie in Brussels. Now the Nederlandse Operastichting, it has been run by Hans de Roo since 1971, who succeeded Maurice Huisman, now in charge of La Monnaie's Belgian National Opera. See also Holland Festival, page 321.

HUNGARY. Opera in Hungary dates back to the 17th century, when fine performances were staged in stately homes. Haydn had an opera house at Eszterhazy. The capital, Budapest, got its first company as part of the National Theatre, opened in 1837, though only two performances a week were given at first. In 1884, a new opera house was opened, a splendid theatre which still flourishes. The city now has two houses, giving some 600 performances a year, while between 1938 and

1955, a Rolling Opera company toured the country by special train. Budapest has attracted many great names, including Mahler and Klemperer as resident conductors, and Strauss, Furtwängler, Walter, Kleiber and others as guests. Only a few Hungarian singers have been internationally famous, but many great singers have sung in Budapest. There are also several opera companies outside the capital.

IRELAND, REPUBLIC OF, *see* EIRE.

ITALY. The birthplace of opera and, for the majority of opera-goers, the Land of Heart's desire. From the second decade of the 19th century, when Rossini shot to fame, to the death of Puccini in 1924, Italy was the scene of a unique phenomenon in history, the hearts and minds of a people gripped by an art form—opera. Only Elizabethan London can be compared with it: a succession of new, vibrant works, interspersed with masterpieces, and given before audiences of all classes, who were ravished by these operas; works which were sometimes above their heads but never above their hearts. Even those with only the slightest acquaintance with operatic history know Verdi's unique place in Italian hearts, more than simply a musical one. This was the perfect situation: composer, singers, audiences working as one, just as playwrights, actors and audiences did in Shakespeare's day. By Puccini's time, the immediate electricity of Risorgimento Italy had vanished, but the intense passion remained. Now football is Italy's most popular pastime, but there is still a huge public for opera, even if it is now a museum art, and the magic remains on occasion. Once it blazed.

There follows a short tour of some Italian houses, not taking into account the financial/political crises of 1974–5 that affected all but La Scala, Turin, Parma, Palermo and Bologna, and even forced these to reduce their programmes.

Bari. Opera is given in a winter season at the Teatro Petruzzelli, which seats 4,000, and at the Teatro Piccinni.

Bergamo. The autumn seasons at the Teatro Donizetti are famous, the audience being among the toughest in Italy, second only to Parma, but highly appreciative of merit. As well as Donizetti revivals—he was born and died in Bergamo—an astonishing number of premières have been given in the last four decades, though none of the operas has conquered the operatic world.

Bologna. At its famous Teatro Communale (opened 1763), Wagner was promoted by Mariani (1871–7), and its reputation for daring has continued into modern times, with a season opened by Berg's *Wozzeck*, and Britten's *Billy Budd* added to the repertoire in 1973. Even more significantly, *Billy Budd* was announced for the 1973–4 season as well, a four-month season. Few Italian houses offer a more wide-ranging repertoire.

Brescia. Devout Puccinians treasure the first successful *Madame Butterfly* at the Teatro Grande (1904), after being revised following its disastrous La Scala première. Previously Toscanini had conducted there in 1894, the year after the theatre opened, and Eva Turner sang her first Italian Turandot in the theatre (1926).

Catania. Bellini was born in the city and the 150th anniversary of his birth was celebrated at the Teatro Massimo Bellini (opened in 1890) in 1951 with his three masterpieces, *Norma, La Sonnambula* and *Il Puritani*, and also *Il Pirata*. The four-month Spring season in 1973 included Stravinsky's *The Rake's Progress* and a new Rossellini opera, as well as more traditional fare.

Florence. Opera was born here in 1597, and the 17th-century Teatro della Pergola still survives. It housed the first Italian *Figaro* (1788) and *Die Entführung* (1935), and its premières included Verdi's *Macbeth*. The Teatro Communale dates from 1862 and is one of Italy's leading houses, with casts to match. For the Florence May Festival, see page 319.

Genoa. Opera has been given in the city since the 1640s, though not until 1821 was there a worthy theatre, the Teatro Carlo Felice, later destroyed by bombs, but partly rebuilt. The young Toscanini excelled himself here in the 1890s, and later Wagner and Strauss became remarkably popular in the city, especially the former. The repertoire remains adventurous: in 1973 it included Prokofiev's *The Fiery Angel*, Verdi's *I Lombardi*, and a new work by Bussotti.

Milan. La Scala, built in 1778, is the most famous opera house in the world and the supreme Italian composers all wrote works for it, notably Bellini (*Norma*), Verdi (*Otello, Falstaff*), and Puccini (*Butterfly, Turandot*). At its finest, no other theatre can excel its standards, though some may on occasion equal it. The ages of greatest glory were those when Toscanini was in charge (1898–1903, 1906–8, 1921–9), the Maestro not only providing classic Italian performances, but introducing Wagner, Strauss, Debussy, etc. into the repertoire. His singers included Toti dal Monte, Dalla Rizza, Supervia, Raisa, Stabile, Journet and Pertile. Not until 1931, with the coming of Victor de Sabata, did the theatre regain its stellar form, and it remained supreme, though Mussolini had dreams of making Rome the operatic capital. In 1943 it was badly bombed.

It reopened in 1946 with Toscanini conducting a concert. De Sabata's health forced him to retire in 1954. Carlo Giulini was at La Scala from 1951 to 1956, but this greatest of living Italian conductors has virtually abandoned opera. Fortunately, the theatre has the services of Claudio Abbado, a thrilling conductor of almost equal stature. Other conductors since the mid-1950s have included Gavazzeni, Votto and Sanzogno.

The years 1952 to 1958 saw Callas as 'La Regina della Scala', the greatest period of her career, when *Anna Bolena* (Donizetti) *Medea* (Cherubini) and *Il Pirata* (Bellini) were revived for her, and Visconti, who turned her from a good actress to a great one, produced her in *La Vestale* (Spontini), *La Traviata* and *La Sonnambula*. It goes without saying that she was merely the greatest of a galaxy of stars, including Tebaldi in her glorious prime. La Scala visited Moscow (in 1964 and 1974) and other capitals, including London in 1950 and 1976. Financial and other crises are now (1976) threatening its existence.

In 1955 La Piccola Scala, a theatre for smaller works, opened within La Scala, seating some 600, and proving ideal for Mozart, Cimarosa, Rossini, etc. There is also a major museum attached to the theatre. Strangely, except in the upper regions, the main auditorium houses one of the least demonstrative Italian audiences of the day, certainly for the average performance. It was not always so. In the Callas era, the atmosphere was sometimes akin to the Roman Arena.

Milan has, and has had, other opera houses. The Teatro della Cannobiana (1779–1894) saw the première of Donizetti's *L'Elisir d'Amore* (1832) and many other works, and was replaced by the Teatro Lirico, where Caruso made his local début (1897) and premières included Cilèa's *Adriana Lecouvreur*. After serving the bombed-out La Scala Company, it later became a cinema.

The Carcano, opened in 1803, staged the first Milanese performance of Verdi's *La Battaglia di Legnano* (1859), while the Dal Verme (1872) housed the first *Pagliacci* (1892). It, too, became a cinema.

Naples. Opera has been heard in the city since the 1650s and, 150 years later, Naples was Italy's operatic capital, by which time *opera buffa* was a firmly entrenched local speciality. The leading theatre was, and remains, the San Carlo (1737), the present building dating from 1816. From 1809 to 1824, Domenico Barbaia was the impresario, giving Rossini's operas specially written for the house (including *Mosè* and *Otello*), and commissioning Bellini's early successes. His mistress, Colbran, deserted him for Rossini whom she later married. Verdi was not so happy in Naples, partly because of local censorship difficulties. In the Second World War, thousands of British troops discovered opera at the San Carlo, which the British army restarted and ran. It is the second opera house in Italy, with a notably warmer audience than La Scala, Neapolitans making a family outing of opera, complete with delighted chatter.

Palermo. Opera dates back to the 1650s in the Sicilian town, being given in several theatres before the Teatro Politeama Garibaldi (1874) became the leading house, then being supplanted by the Teatro Massimo (1897). Many leading singers have appeared on its huge stage, and the policy in modern times has been quite adventurous: for instance, the 1972–3 season included works by Auber, Menotti and Cimarosa, also *Elektra*.

Parma. The operatic equivalent of Abilene and Dodge City in the 1870s, or so some timid singers might say. Its operatic history dates back to the early 17th century. Verdi was born nearby and Toscanini was born in the city, so the locals fancy themselves as judges of singing, with reason. To succeed there in the Teatro Regio (1829) is very heaven, to fail may result in execration from the auditorium, porters refusing to handle baggage on artistic grounds, and other extreme manifestations. For during the winter season, Parma is the most operatic spot on earth, and Verdi still lives in the hearts of people of all classes. As the town is a delight and the food world-famous, to add to the operatic joys, Parma must rank as paradise.

Rome. Private, then public, opera in Rome dates from the 17th century. Of a number of theatres, two stand out, the Argentina and the Costanzi. The Argentina saw the notorious première of *Il Barbiere* in 1816, also Verdi's *I Due Foscari* (1844) and *La Battaglia di Legnano* (1849), which latter helped start a revolution. The Teatro Costanzi was opened in 1880, later rebuilt and reopened as the Teatro Reale dell'Opera in 1928. In 1946 it became the Teatro dell'Opera. Its premières have included *Tosca* in 1900. In the mid-1960s, after lagging behind the other great Italian houses, the repertoire was greatly expanded, producers included Visconti and de Fillipo, conductors Giulini, Abbado and Mehta, also the designer, Kokoschka. The new found standards were not always sustained, though the latter part of the 1973–4 season suggested good times were around the corner, inflation permitting. Both *Pelléas et Mélisande* and *Don Carlos* were triumphs.

Siena. Since the 1930s, when Count Chigi-Saracini founded the Accademia Chigiana, there have been performances of early operas at the Teatro dei Rozzi and Teatro dei Rinnovati, including works by Galuppi, Vivaldi and Scarlatti, as well as Cherubini and Donizetti.

Turin. The Teatro Regio opened in 1741, burned down in 1936 and at last reopened (with the controversial *I Vespri Siciliani* (Verdi), produced by Callas and Di Stefano) in 1974. Other theatres in the city include the Teatro Lirico, the Alfieri, the splendid Carignano (1753) and the Teatro Nuovo. Turin has been a very influential opera centre since the 1870s when, during the régime of Carlo Pedrotti, famous productions of *Mefistofele* (1876) and *Lohengrin* (1877) were given, the last 'marking the awakening of Italy to the genius of Wagner' (Giuseppe Depanis). Premières of Catalani's *Loreley* (1880), and Puccini's *Manon Lescaut* (1893) and *La Bohème* (1896) followed, the last conducted by Toscanini, who was at the Regio in 1886, 1889–91 and 1895–8. Other premières included Alfano's *Risurrezione* (1904). As well as many Italian firsts, including *Ariadne auf Naxos*, the modern Rossini revival began in the city in 1925 under Vittorio Gui. Recent successes have included a brilliant *Francesca da Rimini* (Zandonai) in 1974, with Raina Kabaivanska superb in the title-role.

Venice. The city's Teatro San Cassiano (1637–1800) was the world's first public opera house, and by 1678 there were ten of them. It was a question of supply and demand, for Venice played a key role in the early development of opera, not least on the spectacular side. Rossini had five Venetian premières at the Teatro San Moise, and Malibran was later welcomed to the city with trumpets and a theatre was named after her. The lovely La Fenice dates from 1792 and its many premières included Rossini's *Tancredi* and *L'Italiana in Algeri*, and Bellini's *I Capuletti ed i Montecchi*, also five of Verdi's operas, *Ernani, Attila, Rigoletto, La Traviata* and *Simon Boccanegra*, and Stravinsky's *The Rake's Progress* (1951). Though the city is no longer an operatic paradise, it has a famous two month winter season (except 1974–5), and no operagoer could do better than expire there, at an advanced age, in its most beautiful auditorium.

Verona. See Verona Festival, page 324.

MEXICO. Though operatic performances in Mexico began in 1806, it was the tour of the Garcia family in 1830 which gave Italian opera a popularity that survives to this day. And a number of native composers wrote works. The 1910 revolution saw the end of foreign touring companies, apart from occasional bull-ring performances by Caruso and others, and not until the 1940s was a permanent company of Mexican and European singers established, Kleiber and Beecham being among the conductors.

NORWAY. Opera reached Norway in the 18th century, the first national work, Thrane's *Fjeldeventyret* (Mountain Adventures) being staged in 1840. Occasional operas were given in Oslo before the Norwegian State Opera House opened in 1900, while the Norwegian National Opera, based in the capital but touring other leading cities, opened in 1959 with Flagstad as Intendant. She resigned because of illness in 1960. Many Norwegian singers take part in the wide-ranging seasons, Flagstad's most notable successor being Aase Nordmo-Løvberg.

POLAND. Opera has been given since 1613 in Poland, national opera beginning in the 1770s and the most famous of them, *Halka*, being produced in 1848. Its composer, Moniuszko, was director of the Warsaw opera for thirty-nine years and encouraged native works. Between the two world wars, opera flourished greatly but very traditionally, thus driving many ambitious artists to Paris. In the Second World War, every theatre was damaged or destroyed. Yet there was a resurgence of opera, even in makeshift conditions, after 1945, not only in Warsaw, but in nine other cities, the most significant theatre being at Poznan, where a superb *La Gioconda* (Ponchielli) was given in 1974. Polish opera covers a wide range, and famous singers from the West appear from time to time, including Sir Geraint Evans as Falstaff in 1975, directed by Regina Resnik. Modern works heard there include Britten's. The National Theatre in Warsaw, destroyed in 1939, reopened in 1965.

PORTUGAL. For Portugal read Lisbon, where the San Carlos, opened in 1793, and based on Naples' San Carlo, is one of Europe's main Italian houses outside Italy, though other works are sometimes given. Notable events in 1974 included Sutherland as Lucia and Resnik in the title role of Menotti's *The Medium,* and down the years few great singers have not appeared at the theatre.

RUMANIA. Opera dates back to the 1720s and there are now opera houses in eight cities, including the capital Bucharest, the leading ones being at Cluj, Iaşi and Timişoara. There are many native operas and operettas, though few are known elsewhere. Opera in Bucharest dates from 1787, and when the National Theatre opened in 1853, a Rumanian company alternated with an Italian one. Unfortunately, native singers were paid less and many emigrated; indeed, much of the capital's operatic history has seen Rumanians struggling for their rights, even after a Rumanian Lyric Society was formed in 1919. They survived everything, including an earthquake and bombing. A new Opera was opened in 1953.

RUSSIA. Italian opera reached Russia in 1731 and, twenty-four years later, the Italian composer, Araia, wrote *Cephalus and Procris* to a native text, sung by Russians. French influence came in in the 1760s and was only removed by another sort of influence, Napoleon's. Meanwhile, Russian composers were studying in Italy and, at last (1773), a Russian, Berezovsky, wrote an opera, *Demofoonte.* Catherine the Great used opera for political and propaganda purposes, herself providing librettos. The success of Weber's *Der Freischütz* (1824) inspired Russian composers until the father of Russian opera, Glinka, appeared (see page 55). His mighty successors are all in Part I, *Composers*.

Many of the Soviet Union's forty or so opera houses give works which are essentially oriental in nature, as well as standard Western classics. Some of the finest singers are from the Ukraine, whose chief house is the Shevchenko Opera House at Kiev, and even a short account cannot leave out Riga, once capital of Latvia, where Wagner worked, then fled his creditors. But the two most important centres remain Moscow and Leningrad (once St Petersburg and the Russian capital).

Moscow. The first public theatre, built by an Englishman named Maddox, was the Petrovsky, where Catherine the Great's company played. It was burnt down in 1805, and twenty years later the Bolshoi (Bolshoy) opened. After the Revolution, the reorganized theatre also took over the Filial Theatre which had been in private hands and was where Chaliapin had enjoyed colossal triumphs in Moscow. The Stanislavsky Opera Theatre gives opera, which is a good moment to note that the great theatre director, writer, actor and reformer, Stanislavsky (1863–1938), was also concerned with opera and considered Chaliapin an ideal actor.

The Bolshoi is best known outside (and inside) Russia for its ballet, but its opera productions, though often aged and over traditional, are also spectacular in the extreme, and travellers may collect rarities such as Rimsky-Korsakov's *Sadko* as well as works known in the West. The chorus is renowned, and recent singers whose names are famous far beyond Russia include Vishnevskaya, Lemshev, Petrov, Pirogov and Reizen. The company has toured outside Russia since 1964, has twice exchanged visits with La Scala, and visited New York in 1975.

Leningrad (St Petersburg). Opera began in the city in the 1730s, Italian opera, now as popular in Russia as everywhere else, being banned by Paul I in 1798. The Bolshoi (which merely means 'big') opened in 1783 and, when rebuilt in 1836, opened with the seminal *A Life for the Tsar* (Glinka). The Teatr Tsirk (1850) was burnt down and then rebuilt as the famous Mary-insky in 1860; it is now the equally famous Kirov. St Peters-burg's many premières have included Verdi's *La Forza del Destino* (1862), Rimsky-Korsakov's *Snow Maiden* (1882),

Tchaikovsky's *The Queen of Spades* (1890) and the second version of *Boris Godunov* (1874). The great impresario, Serge Diaghilev (1872–1929), began his magnificent career in the city, later giving the first full stage *Boris* outside Russia in Paris (1909), with Chaliapin (whose career also began in St. Petersburg). Diaghilev presented the first Russian season in London at Drury Lane in 1913 and, with Beecham, the equally famous one at Covent Garden in 1914. He occasionally turned to opera in the 1920s, including premières of Stravinsky's *Mavra* (1923) and *Oedipus Rex* (1927) in Paris.

SOUTH AFRICA. Touring companies visited South Africa from the 1870s, and occasionally famous singers as well, e.g. Albani in 1902. Johannesburg had seasons of opera between the two world wars, including artists from Europe. Since 1945, the finest performances have been given at Cape Town University under Erik Chisholm, Professor of Music there until 1965 when he died. Opera today is mainly in the hands of the Cape Performing Arts Board Opera, based on Cape Town but also touring.

SPAIN. Barcelona and Madrid are the two operatic centres.
   Barcelona. Opera has been given in the city since 1708. Today the season extends from November until February or March, and a wide range of Italian, German and other works are given, including Spanish operas. Most famous singers down the years have appeared at the Teatro Liceo (1847, rebuilt after fire, 1862), and casts are often still very strong.
   Madrid. The capital is less of an operatic centre than Barcelona, though there was much Italian opera in the 18th century (see Farinelli, page 143). The Teatro del Zarzuela (1856) is named after the Spanish form of *opera buffo* of that name, amusingly and tunefully satirizing a wide range of topics, and with a history of several centuries. Contact with the audience is close and sometimes the dialogue is improvised.

SWEDEN. Though few Swedish operas have travelled abroad, the country is a major nursery of singers and a leading European operatic nation. Stockholm first heard opera in Queen Christina's reign in the 1640s, and, a century later, Italian and French companies were in the capital. Gustavus III started native opera in 1771 by sacking the French companies. Gluck's *Orpheus* was given in Stockholm in 1773, before its Paris première, and Gustav wrote the libretto for a major Swedish work, Naumann's *Gustav Vasa* (1786). Gustav was assassinated in his own opera house, as lovers of Verdi's *Un Ballo in Maschera* know. In the 19th century, Swedish operas long forgotten were given alongside imported ones, and a line of great singers followed Jenny Lind and Christine Nilsson down to Björling and Birgit Nilsson in our own day. The Royal Opera House, Stockholm, opened in 1898, the distinguished tenor, Set Svanholm, being one of its modern directors. The Swedes have a long Wagnerian tradition based on a combination of local love of the music and the singers to perform it. Famous foreign artists sing from time to time with the Opera Company, and foreign companies have included the Deutsche Oper am Rhein (1973), complete with *Moses und Aron*, which created a sensation. Goran Gentele, whose tragic death shortly before opening his first season in command of the Met (1972), was Director of the Royal Opera from 1963 to 1970. His renowned *Ballo in Maschera*, complete with an historically accurate, effeminate Gustav III, was seen in Edinburgh (1959) and London (1960) as well as in Sweden. The Royal Opera paid a very successful visit to the Edinburgh Festival in 1974.

The other main operatic city is Gothenburg (since 1890), where Flagstad sang between the wars. Modern works are given, but the public flock more readily to favourites. Summer seasons are given at the 18th century Drottingholm Castle Theatre.

SWITZERLAND. **Zürich** is the main Swiss operatic centre. The Stadttheater housed the first post-copyright *Parsifal* outside Bayreuth (1913), though Cosima Wagner objected. Since the Hans Zimmermann regime (1937–56), the city's opera has enjoyed a high reputation: premières at its summer festival have included Berg's *Lulu* and Hindemith's *Mathis der Maler*, producers have included Rudolf Hartmann, conductors, Furtwängler and Knappertsbusch, and resident singers, Lisa della Casa. Hans Rosbaud was Music Director, 1955–8. A recent major success was Janáček's *Katya Kabanova* (1973), conducted by Jaroslav Krombholc, with Varnay as Kabanikha and Antigone Sgourda as Katya. The **Berne** Opera is a very enterprising company, smaller than other Swiss houses, but with good young singers and a wide repertoire, including Verdi's *Stiffelio* (1973). Also enterprising is the **Basel** company, which premièred Honegger's *Jeanne d'Arc au Bûcher* in 1938 and gave the first European performance of Menotti's *The Consul* (1951). The Grand Theatre at **Geneva** is a larger organization, attracting famous foreign singers (including, 1973–4, Alva, Dernesch, Craig and McIntyre, and Pears in the English Opera Group's *Turn of the Screw*), and playing a wide repertoire.

TURKEY. Though opera has been given in Turkey since the 18th century, not until the coming of the 'father', of Turkish Opera, Dikran Cuhatsyan (1840–98), did native works make their mark. The new Ankara Opera opened in 1948.

UNITED STATES OF AMERICA. Now that American singers are so thick on the ground in Europe as well as at home, one can only pray that a change of heart overtakes non-operatic Americans, and that they may realize that subsidies are vital and not immoral, un-American, radical, portents of creeping socialism, etc., for America could become an operatic paradise. Like everywhere else, the problem of modern opera has not been solved. Not one American opera appears to have the staying power of the great musicals, with the single exception of *Porgy and Bess*; but then nor does any other country have the magic touch, unless it be England and Britten's works. There follow, in alphabetical order, notes on leading American operatic centres.

Berkshire Festival. See page 317.

Boston. Opera in the city dates back to the 18th century, and many famous singers were heard there from the 1850s when Mario and Grisi appeared. Foreign companies, including Mapleson's, paid visits. The most famous local company was the Boston Opera company which, from 1909 to 1914, gave 516 performances of fifty-one operas, its stars including Bori, Destinn and Garden. Then the money ran out, and there followed two seasons by another company, then regular visits by the Chicago Opera. The Met, which had occasionally appeared, visited regularly from 1934. The New England Opera Theatre gave the American première of *Les Troyens* in 1955. Then, in 1959, a miracle by the name of Sarah Caldwell appeared, a combination of Lilian Baylis, a first-rate conductor, and a Zeffirelli working on a tight budget and never against the music. In other words, and though she does not (?) compose, she is a phenomenon, like Richard Wagner.

Her Opera Company of Boston gives at present four productions a year in the Orpheum Theater, an old cinema and vaudeville house (Boston's Opera House having been a parking lot since 1958), and the total integration of her productions is unique in America. She knows how staggering effects came to be made by simple means—*The Trojans* (the first complete U.S.A. version) being a near miracle—and she can attract the greatest stars (Sutherland, Tebaldi, Sills, etc.) and get them to rehearse for the length of time she demands. Her American firsts include *Moses und Aron* and Sills's first *Norma* and *Lucia di Lammermoor*; also Mussorgsky's orchestration of *Boris Godunov*. 1974 saw a superb *War and Peace* (she is always at her peak when up against it), a highly imaginative *Don Quichotte* (Massenet), set in a Montmartre cabaret theatre, a less fortunate *Butterfly* and a memorable *Il Barbiere* with Sills, Alan Titus (Figaro) and Donald Gramm as a perfect Bartolo. If there is any justice in a wicked world, the State or a millionaire will give Miss Caldwell an opera house and allow Bostonians more of her. She is, so one reads and knows even at a distance, the best thing in American opera.

Chicago. Opera dates back to the 1850s and fans have included Al Capone. The first opera house was destroyed in the great 1871 fire, the Chicago Auditorium being opened in 1889, after which short seasons by touring companies were given. In 1910 came the Chicago Grand Opera Company and Mary Garden (as Mélisande) who was to become the most famous figure in the Windy City's opera. She remained until 1931, having been especially noted for her French roles and for her season as Director (1921–2), a season which saw the world première of Prokofiev's *The Love of Three Oranges* and the girl from Aberdeen amassing a deficit of over $1 million.

Hastily, Samuel Insull became President, solvency was restored, and the company became the Chicago Civic Opera. A new Civic Opera House opened in 1929, but the venture was killed by the Depression. After years of occasional ventures, the Chicago Lyric Theatre (later the Lyric Opera of Chicago) opened with Carol Fox as its head (1954). The first night is a legend, the American début of Callas as Norma, and following Chicago seasons were to be some of the most stellar on earth, Callas's roles including Elvira, Leonora (opposite Björling) and Butterfly. Other stars included Tebaldi, Del Monaco, Gobbi and Nilsson, and more lately Sutherland, Vickers, Caballé, Arroyo and Ludwig, as well as many leading producers and designers. The twentieth season, including a superb *Peter Grimes* and a fine *Götterdämmerung*, played to 99·6% capacity.

Cincinnati. See page 317.

Dallas. Since 1957, the scene of very stellar late autumn seasons, with high artistic standards, the theatre used being the vast State Fair Music Hall. Lawrence Kelly (died 1974), with Nicola Rescigno as Music Director, began with two evenings of Rossini's *L'Italiana*, with Simionato after a gala concert by Callas. La Divina appeared in two of the three operas in 1958, *La Traviata* and *Medea*, with Zeffirelli directing the former and Alexis Minotis the latter. *L'Italiana* was revived with Berganza, also directed by Zeffirelli, and since then singers have included Sutherland, Olivero (as Fedora) and Vickers (as Chenier). Rescigno has done his best work in Dallas, where it is intended to celebrate the 200th anniversary of American independence with John Philip Sousa's *El Capitan*.

Detroit. There has been occasional opera in the city since the mid-19th century. It is now given by the Michigan Opera Theater.

Fort Worth. The oldest continuous opera company in Texas, founded in the mid-1940s, the opera usually gives four productions, two performances each, between December and April. Its budget is small, though it uses a large new theatre. It was here that Lily Pons's career ended in the role of Lucia in 1962, with Domingo making his first major American appearance as Edgardo. Beverly Sills has starred with the company from time to time, including in one double-bill which must be unique: *Pagliacci* and Suppé's *Die schöne Galatea* (1966). The Music Director and general manager is Rudolf Kruger.

Houston. The city's Grand Opera, now 20 years old, has recently become a major company, with the general manager, David Gockley, instituting a fortnight's rehearsals for each opera; guest conductors to share the load with the Music Director, Charles Rosenkrans; borrowed productions (including Caldwell's Boston *La Traviata* with Sills in 1973); and six instead of five operas each season, with performances in the original and in English (with strong American second casts at half price). A stirring *Macbeth* (1973), with Tinsley magnificent in every way, and Mastromei magnificent vocally, began the 1973–4 season, and *Figaro* contained, amongst other delights, the ultimate Cherubino, Frederica von Stade. *Lulu*, complete with sensational publicity and Patricia Brooks stunning in the lead, and Donizetti's *Lucrezia Borgia* (Sutherland in full vocal glory), were among 1975's attractions.

New Orleans. Opera has a long tradition in the city, especially French opera, American premières including *Benvenuto Cellini* and *Samson et Dalila*, both sung at the French Opera House. Built in 1859, it was burned down in 1919. Not until the 1940s did local opera-lovers have their own company again, with Walter Herbert as Music Director. The Municipal Auditorium, sadly wrong for opera, was used until at last a new house was opened in 1973, the Theater of the Performing Arts. Standards have varied down the years in the city, despite many stars and fine up-and-coming artists, but the new *Thaïs* (Massenet) was worthy of the occasion. Carol Neblett, the heroine, had a nude scene, news of which even reached the London papers; Knud Andersson conducted; Bliss Herbert produced.

New York. Opera in the city pre-dates the Revolution, if ballad operas are counted, but the real beginning—a typically starry affair—was the first Italian opera season, at the Park Theater in 1825, with the Garcia family in *Il Barbiere*. So Malibran the incomparable ranks as America's first prima donna—aged 16. The next year the Garcias gave *Don Giovanni* with da Ponte in the audience. The city's pre-Met operatic life was far too rich to chronicle here, except most briefly. Palmo's Opera House (he was a restauranteur), where *I Puritani* was given its local première in 1844, was one notable house; the Astor Place Opera House (1847) had a brief reign; then, in 1854, the important Academy of Music opened with Grisi and Mario in *Norma*. Patti made her début there, Mapleson's seasons were given, and many Verdi operas were staged for the first time; so were Wagner's *Rienzi* and Gounod's *Roméo*. It was used for opera until the end of the 19th century, then became a theatre.

The Metropolitan Opera House, since 1966 at its new home in the Lincoln Center, opened on Broadway in 1883 because some wealthy businessmen could not get boxes at the Academy and decided to start their own opera house. The first season lost a fortune and Leopold Damrosch was called in to replace the manager, Henry Abbey. Damrosch died during his first season, and his son, Walter Damrosch (1862–1950) took over, inheriting his father's policy of works being given in German. From 1885 to 1891, he conducted the American premières of all the *Ring* except *Walküre* (given at the Academy in 1877), *Tristan und Isolde*, *Die Meistersinger*, Cornelius's *Der Barbier von Bagdad*, etc. Later he formed his own company, but was at the Met again, 1900–3. (With his own company he toured Wagner from coast to coast and actually made a profit, but in the end finance finished him.) Meanwhile, Abbey rejoined the Met, which, after he died (1896), was run between 1896 and 1908 by Maurice Grau, Edward Scoeffel and Heinrich Conreid (1903–8), by which time it was established as one of the great houses of the world, firmly believing in superstars and being able to afford them. It was Grau who brought in the De Reszkes, Lilli Lehmann, Maurel, etc. while Conreid hired Caruso, Farrar and also Mahler. Space backstage was totally inadequate and storage space was pitiful, but the Met flourished mightily.

Then came Giulio Gatti-Casazza (1869–1940), who had made his name as Director of La Scala with Toscanini from 1898. He reached the Met in 1908 and left in 1935, staging more than 5,000 performances of 177 works. Toscanini was with him for his first seven seasons, and the many premières included *Boris Godunov*, *Der Rosenkavalier* and *La Fanciulla del West*. As for the casts of the regime, they included most of the world's stars, Americans among them: Ponselle, Johnson, Tibbett, Grace Moore, etc. No conductor comparable to Toscanini joined the Met, but those who worked there included Serafin. American works were given, so were American firsts of Janáček, Strauss, and Puccini (*Il Trittico*). Before he retired, Gatti-Casazza had hired Flagstad, Leider, Lehmann and other rising stars.

The reign of Edward Johnson (1878–1959), a Canadian who had sung Italy's first *Parsifal* at La Scala in 1913 (as Edoardo di Giovanni), was from 1935 to 1950. His chief success (beginning as he did in the Depression period) was to encourage American singers (Traubel, Kirsten, Harshaw, Munsel, Warren, Peerce, Tucker, etc.), and to bring in better conductors (Walter,

Busch, Beecham, Szell, etc.); but, for all the stars, theatrically the Met was in poor repute—especially among theatre people. However, this was a great Wagnerian age, dominated especially by Melchior and Flagstad.

Rudolf Bing (1902–   ), later knighted, of Glyndebourne and Edinburgh Festival fame, followed Johnson from 1950 to 1972, and his controversial reign remains to be evaluated. Faced with lack of rehearsal time (whatever he claims to the contrary in his delightful autobiography, he an old Glyndebourne hand), he brought theatre talent to the Met, including Margaret Webster, Alfred Lunt, Cyril Ritchard, Tyrone Guthrie and Peter Brook, and improved the standard of design. A few modern works crept in, by Britten, Stravinsky, Berg, Barber, etc., to the dismay of many, and the roster of stars, headed by Callas, Tebaldi . . . no, it is impossible even to hint at the composition of the roster. Bing tended to make Americans wait until they had European reputations, but they came in growing numbers, including black singers after Marian Anderson, and the manager undoubtedly had a genius for collecting funds from rich patrons.

He was succeeded by Goran Gentele (1972), who was killed before taking up office, a bitter artistic tragedy, for he could have made the Met the home of music theatre of the first rank. John Dexter now has that responsibility. Rafael Kubelik became Music Director, but was never, despite the first American *Les Troyens*, truly at home at the Met. The great company now has a magnificent theatre, still has a fabulous list of stars, and a catholic, popular repertoire. It has a splendid Musical Director in James Levine. All it needs now is a change of heart by Americans about subsidizing the arts.

The New York City Opera Company, part of the City Center of Music and Drama, has been at Lincoln Center since 1965. It was founded in 1944 and became the perfect complement to the Met, especially after Julius Rudel took over in 1957. Its repertoire is by far the most adventurous in America, ranging from Monteverdi to Henze, Einem, and many modern American works. Recent events have included a masterly production (by Frank Corsaro) of Delius's *A Village Romeo and Juliet*; *La Traviata* conducted by Domingo; and Donizetti's *Anna Bolena* with Sills, the company's home-grown superstar, completing the company's Tudor *Ring* (the others being

Roberto Devereux and *Maria Stuarda*). Labour troubles and inflation have assailed the City Opera. The 1974 season included Sills as Elvira and Lucia, and announced for Spring, 1975 were *I Puritani, Salome* with Maralin Niska, *Idomeneo, Die tote Stadt* (Korngold) and *Turandot*, a typically mixed City Center bill.

Before we leave New York, Oscar Hammerstein (1846–1919), grandfather of (Rodgers and) Hammerstein, should be mentioned for his **Manhattan Opera House** (1906–10) with a company that presented a serious threat to the Met. Melba and Calvé appeared for him, and Mary Garden in the American premières of *Pelléas et Mélisande, Thaïs* and Charpentier's *Louise*, other premières including the first local *Elektra*. He also had Zenatello, Tetrazzini, Nordica, Cavalieri, McCormack and other stars on his books, his company giving 463 performances of forty-nine operas, which included a weekly trip to Philadelphia and visits to Baltimore. Finally, the Met offered him over one million dollars to keep out of New York for a decade and he accepted. When he tried to restart at his Lexington Theater, the Met had him stopped.

Philadelphia. Its operatic history goes back to the 18th century, and America's first grand opera, Fry's *Leonora*, was given there in 1845. The city has seen many American premières, ranging from *Norma* and *Faust* through *Cavalleria Rusticana* to Menotti's *The Consul*, and has had a number of resident companies as well as visits from the Met. Today's companies are the Grand Opera Company and the Philadelphia Lyric Opera, which once were respectively the Philadelphia La Scala Opera Company and the Philadelphia Civic Grand Opera. Both have a number of star visitors. Other opera performances are given at the Curtis Institute (a fine *Rake's Progress* in 1973) and at the Philadelphia Music Theater of the city's musical academy.

San Francisco. The Forty-Niners came in 1849, the opera in 1852. Today, San Francisco ranks second to the Met, being founded in 1923 by Gaetano Merola. On his death, Kurt Adler (1905–   ) took over. Until 1932, the company played in the Civil Auditorium, since then in the War Memorial Opera House. Merola gave a mainly standard Italian repertoire and called on many famous Met artists including Gigli, Muzio, Martinelli and Pinza. Adler, who had assisted Toscanini at

Salzburg, then conducted at Chicago, in keeping with the trend
of the 1930s, gave many German performances, with Melchior,
Flagstad, etc. Many famous singers appeared for him before
they went to the Met, including Baccaloni, Tebaldi, Del
Monaco and Geraint Evans; while his list of American firsts is
most impressive, including *Die Frau ohne Schatten* (1959),
Poulenc's *Les Dialogues des Carmélites* (1957) and Britten's
A Midsummer Night's Dream (1961). The company also appears
in Los Angeles. Recent events include a *Ring*, cut and with a
reduced orchestra, and, more happily, Meyerbeer's *L'Africaine*
with Domingo and Verrett (1972); a superb *Rigoletto*, produced
by Ponelle, with Milnes in the title-role, and conducted by
Kazimierz Kord (1973); and a stunning *Salome* (1974), with a
cast of Rysanek, Varnay as Herodias, Hopf making a success
by not 'doing his thing' as most Herods do, and Siegmund
Nimsgern as a fiery, knowing John. The Spring Opera Theater
presents popularly priced works each year.

Santa Fé. See page 323 (Festival).

Seattle. Seattle Opera has given several productions each
year since the early 1960s, the 1973–4 season including *La
Fille du Régiment*, with Moffo, and *Siegfried*, staged by George
London as part of a projected *Ring* (now completed).

Washington D.C. Not until 1971 did the capital of the world's
richest, most powerful nation have an adequate opera house,
when the Kennedy Center opened that September and at last
ended the hiatus. The first opera heard was Ginastera's *Beatrix
Cenci*, conducted by Rudel. The Opera Society of Washington
has been the mainstay of local opera for many years, and now
has a worthy setting in which to work. The potential audience
must be considerable and sophisticated. Rarer operas, notably
The Coronation of Poppea in 1973, have done and been done
well, while modern opera does not alarm. At least one American
house has seen the audience in flight at the interval of *Billy
Budd*, but *The Turn of the Screw* in Washington (1971) had three
performances sold out.

Many other American cities enjoy short seasons of opera,
including Hartford, Miami, Baltimore, Jackson and Kansas
City, and, at long last, Los Angeles has its own Opera Company, which opened its 1974–5 season with Gencer as Lucrezia
Borgia.

YUGOSLAVIA. Opera in what is now Yugoslavia was heard from the very earliest times, thanks to the nearness of Italy, and a Yugoslav opera, *Atalanta*, was given in Dubrovnik in 1629. Italian influence gave way to German (via Austria–Hungary), but native Slovene and Croatian works were being given some 200 years ago. The nightmare complexity of Balkan politics and boundaries cannot disguise the fact that although many composers of opera flourished from the mid-19th century, some following traditional folk-music, others more external trends, next to none of these musicians are known outside Yugoslavia.

Belgrade, the capital, has had opera since the early 19th century, first run by the Court, then by private companies, and since 1920 as the independent Belgrade Opera. It has toured abroad in recent times and recorded Russian works. **Ljubljana** has a long operatic tradition and, as the capital of Slovenia, remains the centre for performances of Slovene works. There are half a dozen other operatic cities, and there is the Dubrovnik Festival (mentioned on page 318), but the other leading operatic centre is **Zagreb**, in Croatia. Opera there dates back to the 18th century, and the first Croatian national opera, Zajc's *Nikola Subic Zrinski*, was produced in 1902. Today opera is given at the National Theatre. Over the last few decades, it has seen some of its finest artists making careers abroad, most notably Milanov and Jurinac.

A Flourish of Festivals

Festivals are fun, or ought to be, for there should be more to them than Art. Which is why the best and truest festivals tend to be those with a separate identity, not simply those which are the properly rehearsed part of a busy opera season, dubbed 'Festival' to bring in trade and prestige. Of course, for the true opera-lover, every night at the opera is festival night, until proved otherwise, but for the record here are some of the official ones.

AIX-EN-PROVENCE (1948). Founded by Gabriel Dussurget and Roger Bigonnet, most performances are given in the open-air theatre of the Archbishop's Palace. Though Mozart is never absent, many other composers are heard, including Cimarosa, Haydn, Rameau and Rossini. A typically wide-ranging year was 1960: Poulenc's *La Voix Humaine*, Gounod's *Le Médicin Malgré Lui,* Purcell's *Dido and Aeneas* (with Berganza), Vivaldi's *La Senna Festeggiante*, and *Figaro*. The Festival has been a great starmaker: Teresa Stich-Randall, Berganza, Sciutti, Gundula Janowitz, Tatiana Troyanos (her Composer in *Ariadne auf Naxos*, 1966, caused a sensation), and many of the stars have returned. It would seem from the Festival *Opera* (1974) that Aix had a poor season and the theatre has been altered for the worse, but Aix-en-Provence in July casts a very potent spell.

ALDEBURGH FESTIVAL (1948). Founded by Benjamin Britten, Eric Crozier and Peter Pears, it is the most fiercely loved of all British festivals. The atmosphere is informal, other arts are catered for, the area and town have their own special magic, and the whole reflects Britten's taste as well as his genius. Premières have included many of Britten's works, also operas by Berkeley, Walton, Williamson and Birtwistle. The **English Opera Group,** founded by Britten, Crozier and John Piper in 1946, controls the artistic direction of the festival, and its company tour out of season, even as far as Russia. The first opera given was *Albert*

Herring in the tiny Jubilee Hall, the famous Maltings at Snape being opened in 1967, and first used for opera in 1968. Typical of the Aldeburgh spirit is the story of what happened when the Maltings burnt down at the start of the 1969 Festival. *Idomeneo*, about to open, was transferred to Blythburgh Church, a miracle of adjustment and art took place—and a new Maltings was reopened for the 1970 Festival.

BAYREUTH (1876). There are so many references in this book to this first of all European festivals of opera that this will be a short entry. For the events leading up to the first festival, Newman's monumental biography is the ideal authority, and the reader will suffer with Wagner at the overwhelming obstacles he faced, and marvel anew at his monumental luck in meeting Ludwig II of Bavaria. The foundation stone was laid in 1872 and Wagner conducted Beethoven's 9th. On August 13, 1876, the first festival and the first *Ring* cycle were launched in the admirable wood and brick theatre, with its superb acoustics and covered orchestra pit. The audience contained kings and great composers, glory came to Bayreuth, but inevitably money was lost and there was no further festival until 1882, when the first *Parsifal* was given. Cosima Wagner ran the festival from 1883 to 1908, keeping more rigidly to the Master's blueprint than Wagner himself would have done. And Wagner himself, an ultimate man of the theatre, could not match his vision in theatrical terms, for all the musical splendour. Siegfried Wagner ran Bayreuth from 1908 to 1930, Winifred Wagner from 1931 to 1944. The roll call of singers cannot even be hinted at here, but no account can leave out some of the pre-1944 conductors: Richter, Toscanini, Furtwängler and de Sabata. Bayreuth was theatrically transformed by Wagner's grandchildren, Wieland and Wolfgang, from 1951 (see page 264) and became not only an operatic pacesetter, but a theatre with influence far outside opera, so significant were their staging methods and inspired use of lighting, especially Wieland's. Their simplification resulted in Wagner's vision at last being visually achieved on a number of historic occasions. Conductors have included Knappertsbusch, von Karajan, Böhm, Jochum and Kempe; there has never been a lack of major or great artists; and Bayreuth, every July and August, remains an unmatched temple of Art, not so much because of the perfection displayed, which can never be obtained regularly in opera, but because it remains an ideal brought to life.

BERKSHIRE FESTIVAL (1937). Founded by Koussevitsky, it takes place annually at Tanglewood, Mass. The Berkshire Music Center usually gives opera including the American premières of *Peter Grimes*, *Albert Herring* and *Idomeneo*, also world premières of American works.

BREGENZ (1946). This Austrian town has an annual summer festival, with the chief attraction given in the famous 'floating stage' on Lake Constance. The lakeside theatre holds more than 4,000, and the 1974 offering was *Carmen*, with Joann Grillo in the lead. At the small Theater am Kornmarkt, Verdi's *Un Giorno di Regno*, called by its sub-title, *Il Finto Stanislas*, was given, while a Haydn opera was presented in the courtyard of a local castle. Operetta is also an essential part of the festival, 1975's being *Eine Nacht in Venedig*. Until recently, operetta was the star attraction—on the lake—but, in 1973, *Der Fliegende Holländer* was given in a single act. *Carmen*, too, was played without intervals. Many well-known singers have taken part in the festivals.

CAMDEN FESTIVAL (originally St Pancras Festival). This annual event has enabled Londoners to get to know Rossini, Donizetti and, especially, early Verdi well enough to hold forth on the merits of *Un Giorno di Regno, I Masnaderi, Linda di Chamounix*, etc. as well as attend 18th- and 20th-century rarities. Standards have improved down the years since the early 1960s, but the feeling of being an operatic Columbus or Neil Armstrong has not changed. Offenbach's *Robinson Crusoe*, Leoncavallo's *La Bohème* . . . the list is endless.

CINCINNATI (1920). In the zoo each summer open-air opera is given, a season which is known to be 'the cradle of American opera singers' (including Jan Peerce and Dorothy Kirsten). *Boris Godunov*, with Norman Treigle, was the chief attraction in 1974 and was lavishly staged, while Arroyo was a splendid Amelia in *Un Ballo in Maschera*. The month-long season plays fairly safe in its number of operas, and an added attraction, for some at least, is the sound of the animals commenting on the proceedings. Nevertheless, the standard of the season, which attracts fine casts, makes it the 'best warm-weather company in the eastern and mid-western United States', which, at its best, rivals most of the more famous winter companies (Harry Cleaver, *Opera*, 1965).

DUBROVNIK (1946). Spectacular open-air performances are given in this lovely city each July and August.

EDINBURGH FESTIVAL OF MUSIC AND DRAMA (1947). Although it lacks an opera house, opera has always been the centrepiece of the festival, even in years when the standard has slipped, and despite the sheer expense involved. Fortunately, prestige abroad has helped to bring important visiting companies who have put up with conditions at the King's, a fine theatre for drama but woefully short of facilities for large-scale companies. Yet the right company can work marvels, as happened in 1974 when the Royal Opera, Stockholm, gave a stunning *Elektra* with Nilsson and Barbro Ericson as Klytemnestra; a shattering *Jenufa*, produced magnificently by Götz Friedrich and with Söderström giving a great performance in the title role; and a delightful *Il Pastor Fido* (Handel) from Drottningholm.

Glyndebourne's Rudolf Bing and Audrey Mildmay started the Edinburgh Festival, and the Glyndebourne Company gave it five superb years of service: Mozart, Rossini, *The Rake's Progress, La Forza del Destino, Un Ballo in Maschera, Macbeth*, and the original *Ariadne auf Naxos*, conducted by Beecham. After a visit by Hamburg, far less suited to the King's, but with a fine repertoire which included the first British *Mathis der Maler* (Hindemith), Glyndebourne returned until 1955. Since then companies have included Hamburg again; Piccola Scala (with Callas in *La Sonnambula*); Stuttgart; Stockholm; Belgrade; The San Carlo; the National Theatre of Prague; Holland Festival Opera; the Bavarian State in *Intermezzo*; regular seasons by Scottish Opera since 1968, including their famous *Les Troyens*; the Florence Opera; the German Opera; West Berlin; and the Edinburgh Festival Opera, whose *Don Giovanni* (1973/4) was produced and designed by Peter Ustinov, probably the most abused producer (by British critics down the years) of our times. In 1975, Geraint Evans produced a stellar *Figaro*, conducted by Barenboim.

Lord Harewood was Artistic Director from 1961–5, being succeeded by Peter Diamand of Holland Festival fame. Meanwhile there will be an opera house one day, should we be so lucky.

FLORENCE (MAGGIO MUSICALE FIORENTINO) (1933). Founded by Vittorio Gui, this May–June festival began as biennial and became annual in 1938. The Boboli Gardens are used as well as the Teatro Comunale and the Teatro della Pergola, and though a wide range of composers have been represented down the years, including contemporary ones, Verdi and Rossini performances have provided the most successful achievements, including Rossini's *Armida*, with Callas, and *Comte Ory* (Gui's production), Serafin's all-star *Don Carlos* and Kleiber's *I Vespri Siciliani*, with Callas and Christoff. 1974 saw less starry casts than usual and a revival of Spontini's *Agnes von Hohenstaufen*, characterized by William Weaver as a grand, noble, difficult work. A later than usual end to the season saw the 50th anniversary of Puccini's death suitably marked by a splendid *La Fanciulla del West*, with Orianne Santunione triumphing as Minnie; and *Boris Godunov* was also given by the Sofia Opera, with Dimiter Petkov as the Tsar. Visiting companies usually provide Wagner, Mozart, etc. Janáček's fascinating *Excursions of Mr Brouček* being given by the Brno company in 1967.

GLYNDEBOURNE (1934). John Christie (1882–1962), possessor of a beautiful Sussex house, had the good taste to marry a lovely and talented soprano, Audrey Mildmay (see page 173), who suggested he build a theatre, which he did. To stage ideal opera performances, and to run the artistic side, he went to the top, hiring Fritz Busch as conductor, and Carl Ebert as producer. The result was that *Figaro* and *Così fan tutte* on May 28 and 29, 1934, were the most integrated performances of opera ever given in Britain; for, to matchless musical ensemble, was added a standard of production and acting without precedent in British operatic history. Before the war, seating had been raised from 300 to 600 (now 800), and to Mozart had been added

Don Pasquale and Britain's first *Macbeth*, while performances had risen from twelve to thirty-eight. British and foreign artists were used, including Stabile, Baccaloni, Borgioli, Domgraf-Fassbänder, Grandi, Souez, Brownlee and Mildmay; then the voices of evacuees filled the estate. Apart from seasons by the English Opera Group, 1946–8, with the premières of Britten's *The Rape of Lucretia* and *Albert Herring*, and Ferrier in *Orfeo*, there was no true Glyndebourne until, under Rudolf Bing and, happily, Busch and Ebert, Glyndebourne created the Edinburgh Festival (see above), resuming operations in Sussex in 1950. Sadly, Busch died in 1951, having, amongst other triumphs, restored *Idomeneo* from oblivion to popularity.

Vittorio Gui succeeded him and brought in Rossini, including that Glyndebourne treasure, *Comte Ory*. An enormous repertoire was given under Ebert (until 1959), then Rennert, Enriquez and others. Conductors included Pritchard, who became Music Director, and Raymond Leppard, who master-minded the Monteverdi revival and, in the 1970s with Peter Hall and John Bury, the Cavalli revival as well. Designers have included Olive Messel and Osbert Lancaster.

Glyndebourne can no longer (for financial reasons) attract the number of stars it once did, and it never had superstars except in artistry—one thinks especially of Jurinac, Sciutti and Bruscantini, and fine British artists such as Evans and Richard Lewis—but after a period of uncertainty, it has found a new role. It has even more up-and-coming artists than before, an admirable repertoire, the highest possible standards under George Christie, the founder's son, and a goodly share of magnificent artists: Söderström as Christine in the Pritchard/John Cox *Intermezzo*, everyone in Hall's *Figaro* conducted by Pritchard. The 1974 season, with two Mozarts, Strauss, Cavalli and Einem's *The Visit of the Old Lady*, was an admirable one, and the fact that two productions featured in Part IV are from Glyndebourne, Ebert's *Pelléas et Mélisande* and Hall's *Figaro* (page 256), is not horrid chauvinism but sober necessity. The prices are now approaching the prohibitive, for all the joys of a visit, but at least the Glyndebourne Touring Company, with strong casts, plays to large audiences round the country at less alarming prices, while Glyndebourne's regular visits to the Proms are glorious affairs.

HALLE (1951). In the city where Handel was born, an annual festival in his honour is given in the Stadttheater, usually with one work being given for some four performances. A must for the pious Handelian.

HELSINKI. Its festival includes a giant production at the local Ice Hall, Mignon Dunn's *Carmen* shining there in 1971, a year when the Finn, Martti Talvela, gave a magnificent King Philip in *Don Carlos*.

HOLLAND (1947). This important festival was founded by H. J. Reinink, whose secretary, Peter Diamand (1913–) took over from him. Happily, opera has always played a key role and, like the festival as a whole, is given in a number of centres, not just Amsterdam and the Hague. Foreign as well as local companies perform; thus in 1960, the English Opera Group gave Britten's (new) *A Midsummer Night's Dream*; the Bavarian State Opera gave *Capriccio* (with Lila della Casa) and *Wozzeck* (with Pilarczyk); a Dutch and Slavonic team, headed by the glorious Brouwenstijn, gave *Jenufa*; an Italo-Dutch group gave *Don Pasquale*; and a Dutch group gave the world première of Badings's *Martin Korda D.P.* 1974 operas included *Figaro* produced by Götz Friedrich, Cavalli's *L'Erismena*, and also a 1606 piece, Agazzari's *Eumelio*. One of the most remarkable events in recent years was Düsseldorf's production of Zimmermann's *Die Soldaten* (first produced in 1965) which was a rare case of a modern opera, magnificently played by Catherine Gayer and a strong company, achieving a major effect.

MUNICH (1901). From mid-August to early September, the city of Munich (see page 283) becomes a festival city; though, in truth, with opera at full and glorious blast for most of the year in the various houses, and with additional operas being taken into the repertoire at ordinary prices and with virtually the same casts, the word festival can hardly be applied as it can to Edinburgh and Salzburg. Munich's festival was originally essentially Wagnerian; then, from 1919, a Straussian paradise, with the composer on hand. Strauss remains, with Mozart and Verdi especially in strong support. However, the highlight of both the 1973 and 1974 festival was by common consent *Pelléas et Mélisande*, conducted by Reynald Giovaninetti and produced and designed by Jean-Pierre Ponelle, with Wolfgang Brendel as Pelléas both years, and with Edith Mathis one year and Elaine Manchet the other as Mélisande. All three were outstanding.

ORANGE. In the magnificent Roman amphitheatre, opera is given in July, and very starry opera it is in the 1970s. *Tristan und Isolde*, with Böhm, Vickers and Nilsson, was given in 1973; *Norma*, with Caballé, Vickers, and Veasey, in 1974 (though the weather was villainous). Also given in 1974 was *Salome*, conducted by Kempe, with Salome finely interpreted by Rysanek, and Herod portrayed by Vickers, not as the usual rather effete figure, but as a totally lustful, virile man.

OTTAWA (1971). This month-long festival at the National Arts Center (1969) uses the only state-supported orchestra in North America. Mario Bernardi, remembered at the Wells, is Music Director, and the casts are Anglo-American-Canadian, the last predominating. A highlight of 1974 was *Le Comte Ory*, sung sensibly in the original in this bi-lingual city.

SALZBURG (1927). Mozart festivals were held in this venerated, stunning city as early as 1877. The Festspielhaus was conceived by Strauss, Hofmannsthal, Reinhardt and Schalk in 1917 and opened ten years later, though operas were given in the Landestheater in 1921. Salzburg is the real thing (however pricey now), not one of the let-us-label-ourselves-a-festival cities, but, as befits the beautiful birthplace of Mozart, a shrine which sends the visitor's spirits soaring before he has heard a note of music. It began operatically at the top: singers from Vienna and Munich, conducted by Krauss, Walter, Strauss and others, with Mozart and Strauss the main composers. Then, from 1935 to 1937, Toscanini conducted an ultimate *Falstaff*, as well as *Die Zauberflöte*, *Fidelio* and *Die Meistersinger*. The Nazi invasion saw Furtwängler, Gui and Böhm in charge, the legendary event of the period being the public dress rehearsal of Strauss's *Liebe der Danae* (not premièred until 1952). Since 1946, when the Festival reopened, premières have included Einem's *Dantons Tod* (1947) and Barber's *Vanessa* (1958). Herbert von Karajan was Artistic Director 1957–60, resuming the post in 1964, two years after which he inaugurated the Easter Festival. A new Festspielhaus was opened in 1960 alongside the old one, the new stage being the largest in the world.

Recent events have included a magnificent *Die Frau ohne Schatten* in 1973, while, at the time of writing, the Easter Festival, famed for its Wagnerian productions, is due (1975) to present a Karajan/Zeffirelli *La Bohème* and a Karajan/Gunther Schneider–Siemssen/Wakhevitch *Die Meistersinger*, with Karajan producing as well as conducting. As for the roll-call of famous singers who have appeared at Salzburg, it is too vast to begin to list here.

SANTA FÉ (1957). This is one of the truest festivals, founded by the conductor and financial genius, John Crosby (1926–   ). The theatre—the second, the first one having been burnt down in the middle of the 1967 season—is set in the hills, with stage and orchestra covered and half the audience under the stars. Most of the casts are young Americans, though many non-American singers, including Kiri te Kanawa, Catherine Wilson and Stuart Burrows, have appeared, and the repertoire is splendidly catholic without the audience worrying. Being comparatively, even totally, new to opera in the late 1950s, they did not start off with prejudices. At least one American first performance is given every year. The 1973 season was typical: Reimann's *Melusine*, *Madame Butterfly* (with Milla Andrew and George Shirley), *Salome* (Maria Kouba) and Offenbach's *La Grande Duchesse de Gérolstein*. The orchestra, recruited from nearby symphony orchestras, and the chorus, are excellent. The season is in late August and early September.

SPOLETO (1958). In this Umbrian town, Gian-Carlo Menotti founded the Festival of Two Worlds, with performances of opera and other arts in the town's two theatres and elsewhere. Designed to encourage young musicians, it also attracts some very famous names, so persuasive is the combination of Menotti and Spoleto. A typical vintage year was 1973, with a Schippers/Visconti *Manon Lescaut*, and an attractive young cast headed by Nancy Shade and Harry Theyard. Also given was Gagliano's *La Dafne* (1608). In 1974, Menotti's own *Tamu Tamu* was given its European première and *Lulu* was staged by Roman Polanski, with a revival of *Manon Lescaut*. Menotti has made Spoleto as personal as Britten has made Aldeburgh, and, like the latter, it is a marvel.

STRATFORD, ONTARIO (1953). Though primarily a Shakespeare festival, famous throughout the world, opera has played a modest but significant part in it since the early days. 1974's repertoire was Offenbach's *La Vie Parisienne* and a double-bill: *The Medium* (Maureen Forrester) and Charles Wilson's *The Summoning of Everyman*.

VERONA (1913). Founded by the tenor Zenatello in 1913 with a single work, *Aida*, the perfect Verona opera, the festival takes place in the great Roman Arena, which comfortably holds 25,000. Standards are much higher than at other open air festivals, the enjoyable feasts at the Baths of Caracalla in Rome included. Casts are stellar; the orchestral playing and standard of conducting is expected to be high; the productions often rise above the merely sumptuous; and as for the audience, it is a reminder of a time (from Rossini to the death of Puccini and a little beyond) when opera was a national passion with all classes. There may be heard shouts of 'Viva, Verdi!' as if a work was new-minted. The 1974 operas, *Aida* (with Bergonzi as Radamès), *Tosca* (Orianna Santunione, Domingo, Mastromei), and *Samson et Dalila* (Gilbert Py and Cossuto), were the usual arena-fillers, though, unexpectedly, *Samson* was the greatest artistic success (produced by Franco Enriquez, conducted by Peter Maag). Verona is unique, like all the best festivals, its epic scale and quality making it a phenomenon.

WEXFORD (1951). This paradise of *bel canto*, booze and good fellowship was the inspiration of Doctor T. J. Walsh, the sort of genius without whom enterprises of great pith and moment do not get airborne. He was succeeded in 1967 by Brian Dickie and in 1974, Thomson Smillie, a key figure in the Scottish Opera success story (and still with the company), became chief of the glorious festival. The first opera was Balfe's *The Rose of Castile*, and by 1956 two operas were being given, *La Cenerentola* and *Martha* (von Flotow), with casts that included Cantelo, Kern, Shacklock and Rothmüller. By 1970, four operas were given and the range was very wide: Rossini's *L'Inganno Felice*, Donizetti's *Giovedi Grasso*, Delibes' *Lakmé* and Britten's *Albert Herring*; while 1975 saw Cornelius' *Der Barbier von Bagdad*, Mayr's *Medea in Corinto* and Massenet's *Thaïs*. The first was produced splendidly by Wolf Siegfried Wagner, Abul being memorably played by Richard McKee.

Wexford has a reputation for catching stars on the way up, a particular legend being Freni's Elvira in *I Puritani* in 1962. Fiorenza Cossoto, Graziella Sciutti and Janet Baker all appeared in the 1950s, while French opera has been well served. Among many delights of the 1970s has been Christiane Eda-Pierre as Lakmé, Leila in *Les Pêcheurs de Perles*, and Imogene in *Il Pirata* (Bellini). The last was given in 1972 with Weber's *Oberon* and Janáček's *Katya Kabanova*. Space prevents too much coverage of this dream festival, a long account of which may be found in *Opera*, Autumn, 1973. It is an ideal spot to end this festive chapter.

Appendix I

Operatic Terms

ALTO. Except in choirs, the female alto is called a contralto. The alto, whether female or child, has a lower voice than the soprano, though the word in Italian means high. A male alto is normally a bass singing falsetto. See also *Countertenor* and *Castrato*.

APPOGGIATURA. A musical ornament, with an additional note falling (or sometimes rising) to the principal note. In the 18th century, it was unwritten and left to the performer to insert, e.g. in Handel and Mozart. This form of musical grammar has been creeping back into Mozart performances over the last decade or more under certain conductors, usually to the unease of those brought up on the written note and nothing more. But the vocal minority who approve of this revival have history on their side.

ARIA. Stemming from the Italian for 'air', it simply means 'song', however elaborate the song may be. An ARIOSO is best described as half-way between an aria and a recitative. Monteverdi used the form with the utmost flexibility and emotion. See also *da capo*.

BARITONE. The middle male voice between tenor and bass, though sub-divisions exist from country to country, especially bass-baritone (see below).

BASS. The lowest male voice. The many sub-divisions in different countries frequently overlap (and the chief ones can be found in *The Concise Oxford Dictionary of Opera* and elsewhere), but even operagoers of limited experience soon learn the essential differences—with their ears. However, BASS-BARITONE requires some description. It is not simply a high bass between bass and baritone, for roles such as Wotan, Boris and Hans Sachs, which fit into this category, require lyricism and a *basso profondo* (note, not 'profundo'), a voice which can reach the depths. Mention of Boris is a reminder that no mere technical category can describe a Chaliapin or Christoff, for the dark cutting edge of their superbly dramatic voices defy sub-divisions. And the word Slavonic is dangerous: the 'sound' is found in the

West, too, if rarely so spectacularly.

BEL CANTO. Beautiful singing or beautiful song. It is rather a vague phrase, extolling the Italian style: lovely tone, superb phrasing and technique, with drama (unlike the German style) coming a sometimes poor second. But at the height of the most legendary age of *bel canto*, the age of Rossini, Bellini and Donizetti, the most admired performers, notably Pasta and Malibran, were as dramatic vocally as they were physically, and the revival of *bel canto* which Callas did so much to set off in the 1950s has not seen vocal drama neglected. The suspect side of *bel canto* is most apparent when a great Verdian dramatic role is merely an excuse for beautiful singing, and yet Verdi must be beautifully sung. The phrase is at once useful and maddening.

BLEAT. Before the Monteverdi revival, the best-known example of this rapid repetition of a single note with a breath between each repeat was in the last scene of *Die Meistersinger*, performed by the Tailors. Germans call it the Bockstriller (Goat's trill).

BRINDISI. A drinking song, from the Italian *far brindisi* meaning 'to drink one's health'. Verdi provided the most popular one in *La Traviata* and the most remarkable one, musically and dramatically, in *Otello*.

BUFFO. A singer—an actor-singer if the audience is lucky—of comic parts (from the Italian for 'gust' or 'puff'). From this word stem *basso buffo* and *opera buffo*, the latter being another phrase for comic opera.

CABALETTA. There are several meanings of this term, the best known being the brilliant and usually fast final section of an aria. This was its 19th-century meaning, and Verdi above all raised the cabaletta to fiery, often electrifying, heights in duets as well as arias. It also means a short simple aria with repeats, as used by Rossini and others.

CADENZA. Every concertgoer knows what a cadenza is, having experienced (and sometimes endured) the form in concertos, but its origin was in opera, especially in the 18th century, the singer being given carte blanche to indulge in a virtuoso display at the end of an aria. Fortunately, opera survived such self-indulgence which was so much more reprehensible than reasonable ornamentation.

CAMERATA. A group of poets, scholars and musicians who met regularly in Florence in the 1590s to try and recapture the mixture of words and music thought to have been used in Ancient Greek drama. From this, opera was born, the first being Peri's *Dafne* (1597), now lost.

CANTILENA. Smooth, tuneful vocal writing, or the way such a passage should be performed.

CANZONE. Operatically, a song in an opera sung, not as part of the drama, but as a song. The 'Veil Song' in the third scene of *Don Carlos* is a magnificent example.

CASTRATO. A dismal subject, yet historically of great importance, for male sopranos and altos, castrated before puberty, played an enormous part in 17th- and 18th-century opera and were often the superstars of their day. The first entered opera in Venice because of shortage of trained women singers and regular bans (as in England) on female stage performers. The castrati were recruited from choirs and soon spread far outside Italy. At their best, they were technically superb, with trumpetlike voices which even so could be used with the utmost artistry. Monteverdi's *Orfeo* (1607), the first great opera, had a castrato, Gualberto, in the lead. Their talents were utilized until as late as the 1820s, Meyerbeer providing Velluti a role in *Il Crociato in Egitto* (1825). The Vatican continued to use castrati long after opera

abandoned them in preference to the occasional breeches role. As countertenors lack the power of castrati, we can never now know the genuine pleasure and thrill that these often vain, often rich, singers gave.

CAVATINA. A short song as opposed to a full aria, or a short song incorporated into a full-scale dramatic *scena* (see page 336).

CLAQUE. Stern, unbending Anglo-Saxons are usually horrified by the idea of the claque, i.e. individuals hired by artists to support their efforts with suitable shouts of 'Bravo! Encore!' and vigorous applause, but these worthies do more good than harm. Most of them are students and music-lovers, unable to pay high prices, and all they get are their tickets: only the claque leader is paid. The entire proceedings are executed like a military operation, and many a dull audience has been guided into selfimprovement by the carefully timed salvoes of the claque in Milan, Vienna and elsewhere. Anti-claques are less admirable, being mere wreckers, like the ones who were employed to boo Callas in her days of glory at La Scala. She even had to endure organized demonstrations in the middle of arias. Happily, La Divina's supporters won the ensuing punch-up. All claque stories pale before the best of the Parma happenings.

So great is the respect for Art in that toughest of opera houses that on one occasion the claque returned an unfortunate tenor's money to him, then booed all his later performances.

COLORATURA. Elaborate ornamentation of the melodic line, hence a coloratura soprano. From the German 'Koloratur'. See also *Fioritura*.

COMPRIMARIO. The small-part artists in opera. Puccini was particularly kind to them, notably in *Il Trittico*.

CONTRALTO. The lowest female voice, though in fact it is the sound rather than the range (compared with mezzos) which is so distinctive.

COUNTERTENOR. Not as some suppose a male singer using falsetto, but a rare voice, higher than a tenor, and making use of an exceptional amount of head resonance. Britten's Oberon in his *A Midsummer Night's Dream* was written for such a voice. For many, it has singular charm, and its few professional possessors tend to be exceptionally musical. However, there is a lack of power which is exposed in houses the size of Covent Garden. Alfred Deller and Russell Oberlin established the countertenor in the modern opera house, but the most remarkable singer to emerge has been James Bowman, who, apart from his other attributes, has the necessary power.

DA CAPO ARIA. From the 1660s to the late 18th century, arias had three sections, the last being a repeat of the first, e.g. Handel's arias. *Da capo* means 'from the beginning'.

DRAMATURG. German theatrical-operatic term. When the National Theatre was founded in Britain (1963), Kenneth Tynan, the resident dramaturg, became known as the 'literary manager', which is no bad translation. A dramaturg adapts libretti, sometimes provides translations, edits programmes, etc. and, in some houses, acts as press officer as well. The German dramaturg apparently even produces and acts on occasion.

DRAME LYRICE. The French name for serious opera. Debussy used it to describe *Pelléas et Mélisande*.

DRAMMA GIOCOSO. Mozart's description of *Don Giovanni*. This mainly 18th-century term allows for a comic opera with serious or tragic moments.

DRAMMA PER MUSICA. A 17th- and 18th-century term for a libretto and the serious opera which sprang from it.

FIORITURA. The decoration of a melody with either written or ornamental figures, from the

Italian word for 'flowering'. Standard practice from the 17th to the early 19th centuries, it could be mightily abused by singers, to such an extent that a composer could lose all sound of his melody; but, at its best, with great artists or merely good ones, such ornamentation added much. Years of unornamented music have resulted in shocks for audiences suddenly exposed to, say, decorations in the second verse of Mozart's 'Voi, che sapete' in *Figaro*, audiences still recovering from the shock of hearing *appogiaturas*. But the practice, if used with discretion, is historically correct. Sutherland's *fiorituri* in *Lucia* and elsewhere are admirable examples of the art at its finest.

GRAND OPERA. This is widely used in Anglo-Saxon countries as another term for opera, but officially the English term means 'serious opera without spoken dialogue'. However, in France *Grand opéra* is the term for large-scale works in four or five acts, complete with plenty of chorus and a ballet, e.g. the operas of Meyerbeer.

GUERRE DES BOUFFONS. From 1752 to 1754, Paris was divided into supporters of Italian music and those who upheld the native tradition of Rameau, etc. The 'war' was triggered off by an Italian company presenting Pergolesi's *La Serva Padrona*, and the Italian partisans had the notable support of Rousseau and Diderot.

HELDENTENOR. See *Tenor*.

INTERMEZZO. To the average operagoer this means the same as INTERLUDE, a short piece between scenes, as in *Cavalleria Rusticana*; or sometimes a comment on the plot between scenes, as in *Manon Lescaut*. But originally the intermezzo was more important. Before the birth of opera in Italy, it was a small-scale musical and dramatic entertainment, and it remained as a more earthy entertainment grafted on to *opera seria*, becoming the ancestor of *opera buffa*. The most famous of all intermezzi was Pergolesi's *La Serva Padrona*, originally part of the forgotten *Il Prigioniero Superbo*. The intermezzo became more and more remote from its official master, *opera seria*, and helped kill the moribund form.

LEGATO. From the Italian for 'bound together', it means 'smoothly' (as opposed to staccato). For singers and instrumentalists alike, a fine legato is a consummation devoutly to be wished.

LEITMOTIV. Meaning 'leading motive' in German, this form of signature tune goes back much further than Wagner, though it was he who used it incomparably, especially in *The Ring*. The term was actually invented by F. W. Jahns to describe short musical phrases denoting people, ideas and things. Its origins are obscure, but seem to date back to the 18th century. Weber was the first to use the technique regularly (in *Euryanthe*), and it reached its apotheosis in *Götterdämmerung,* though Wagner was never obsessed by the technique as were some of his followers, none of whom possessed his powers of permutating and transfiguring motives.

LIBRETTO. The words of an opera, from the Italian for 'little book'. The first was for Peri's *Dafne* (1600).

MAESTRO. Composers and conductors are so-called in Italy. A KAPPELLMEISTER, once a German choirmaster in a court chapel, is now a term for a conductor in Germany.

MEZZA VOCE. Singing at half-power when required to do so.

MEZZO-SOPRANO. The middle female voice. The word *mezzo* means 'half'.

MUSIC DRAMA. The total integration of music and drama, as realized by Wagner in his greatest works. German opera had aspired to this ideal since Spohr and Weber. It is a slightly irritating phrase, for *Norma*, with its display pieces for singers (an un-Germanic concept in the mid-19th

century), is a music drama too, as are *La Traviata, Rigoletto,* etc.

OPERA BUFFA. As described under INTERMEZZO, the form of comic opera which sprang from amusing scenes about everyday people that were added to the ends of acts in *opera seria*. The characters, like their 18th-century theatrical equivalents, were stock ones, and the melodies were tuneful and simple. *Opera buffa* lived on while *opera seria* died.

OPÉRA COMIQUE. It would be easy to translate the term as comic opera, but wrong, *Faust* (admittedly sometimes comic in performance) and *Carmen* both being *opéras comiques* when given without recitatives. In the 18th century, the genre was comic with spoken dialogue, in striking contrast to loftier, often heroic or mythological pieces. In the 19th century, all operas with spoken dialogue were given the same description in France, including therefore a sublime work such as *Fidelio*.

OPERA SERIA. After the first freedom of Monteverdi and his disciples early in the 17th century, opera became more and more formal, musically and in its plots, until by the mid-18th century, it had lost almost all contact with not so much reality as with life itself. No wonder *opera buffa* (above) made such rapid strides. Operatic dinosaurs of this bleak period were notable for tortuous libretti, heroic or mythological plots, the already mentioned formality, and brilliant singing, by castrati. Even the genius of Handel was held back by the conventions of his day. Ironically, when the genre was almost dead, the young Mozart, as our generation has discovered, proved that *opera seria* could live passionately in his *Idomeneo*. Many admire his later *opera seria, La Clemenza di Tito*, equally.

OPERETTA. Thanks to the American invention of the word 'Musical', neither the theatregoer nor theatre critic need be bemused by terms such as musical play, light opera, operetta and, worst of all, musical-comedy, an ill-defined bunch, all of which could be used to categorize, say, *My Fair Lady*. The opera public cannot opt out so easily, and is hardly helped by the statement 'Carmen is the first great musical', which is reasonable enough, frequently heard, and adds to the confusion. Both the Italian *operetta* and the French *operette* mean 'little play', and remembering that, one might claim that a play complete with overture, singing and dancing, is an operetta. In his *Opera Guide*, Gerhart von Westerman plumps for the phrase, 'classical operetta', a very happy solution, spoiled by

his leaving out Gilbert and Sullivan. He dates the birth of operetta as 1858, the year of Offenbach's *Orphée aux Enfers* (*Orpheus in the Underworld*), claiming the satirical *The Beggar's Opera* (1728) as the ancestor of Offenbach's works. Offenbach, Strauss, Sullivan and Lehár, the four incomparables, are all to be found in Part I of this book. Sullivan is the best known today in Anglo-Saxon countries, the least known elsewhere. Other operetta kings have been Suppé (see page 93), Millöcker, famous for his *Der Bettelstudent* (The Beggar Student, 1882), Genée, Zeller, Fall, Oscar Straus and Kálmán, all of the Viennese school. The other great school has naturally been Parisian, and its leaders, after the glorious (German-Jewish) founding father, have included Messager and Lecocq. *The* operetta remains *Die Fledermaus*, though those preferring a little less sugar might claim that Offenbach's *Orpheus* has never been equalled, let alone surpassed.

OVERTURE. Lully introduced his formal French overtures to opera in the late 17th century, earlier operas having had brief introductions. Alessandro Scarlatti introduced the Italian overture in the 18th century, but it was Gluck, later in the century, who related the overture to the opera that was to follow by using themes from it. The overture reached its peak with *Leonora No. 3* to Beethoven's *Fidelio*, while Weber went a stage further and provided near synopses of what was to follow. In Italy, meanwhile, overtures, many of them now staple concert fare, were for getting the audience seated. Not until Verdi were they truly preparation for glory to come (*La Traviata*'s first prelude is a classic example of this). Wagner, after following Weber's lead (the thrilling and evocative *Holländer* overture), turned to preludes, which are, in fact, overtures, but are more linked to the opera to come, often shorter and infinitely subtler than Weber's *potpourri* methods. Following Verdi's lead, the Italians became more and more flexible, one of the finest *verismo* openings being the Scarpia theme at the start of Puccini's *Tosca*, after which the curtain rises. Strauss, though he gave *Der Rosenkavalier* a prelude, complete with fairly explicit lovemaking, cut preludes out altogether on occasion, as in *Salome* and *Elektra*. Preludes to acts are regular fare in opera, as before the last act of *La Traviata*.

PARLANDO. A direction by the composer to the singer to let his or her voice sound approximately like speech. Marvellous examples occur in the last scene of *La Traviata* when Violetta reads Germont Père's letter, and in the second act of *Tosca* when the heroine has killed Scarpia and half-wonderingly exults: 'E avanti a lui tremava tutta Roma!'—'And all Rome trembled before him!'

PRIMA DONNA, whom we all adore if she is good or we would not be operagoers. She is the leading woman singer in an opera, or the leading soprano in a company, or, more, generally, any famous female singer. Operagoers resent the fact that the term has become a descriptive one used to castigate temperamental footballers, politicians, etc. for, as is well known, butter would not melt in the mouth of the average soprano, so meek and mild is she.

PRODUCER. See *Régisseur*.

PROMPTER/SOUFFLEUR (France and Germany)/MAESTRO SUGGERITORE (Italy). In most opera houses, singers are given the opening words of each phrase a second or two in advance by the prompter from his box downstage centre in the middle of the footlights. There is no reason for straight actors to sneer at this custom, for they can recover as often as not from a 'dry' even if they do not get or take a prompt. Having no music advancing the action, they have time to recover, unlike the singer. Italian prompters repeat the conductor's beat for the singer's benefit, having a small mirror to watch the maestro in action. At the very least, this must aid short-sighted singers without contact lenses. Noisy prompters are a curse, as every operagoer knows, though the job is no sinecure.

RÉGISSEUR. The term for the producer in France. It is frequently used in Germany and elsewhere as well, though the official German term is *Spielleiter*. In Italy, a *Regista* produces opera. Britain uses producer, though the straight theatre has abandoned it finally for the American term, director. In America, General Stage Director is the term, or, more colloquially, director. Within a decade, Britain should have switched to the more logical director, too.

Producers have Part IV to themselves, so this entry is mainly historical. They existed neither in the theatre nor the opera house in the last century. Though *basso buffos* were often in charge of production of *opera buffa*, from the 18th century, and often leading singers—like leading actors of the day—made their own arrangements on stage, composers at least were very much interested in proper staging: Mozart, Weber, Verdi, etc. and especially, Wagner, who was as theatrically minded as any actor of his day. He could not make the first Bayreuth *Ring* as visually effective as he longed to, but he had a marvellous way

with singers, turning many into passable actors. Many critics are so obsessed with scenery and production touches that they underrate the crucial importance of the producer as a teacher of acting. The theatre director can assume a certain standard, the opera producer, unless faced by Callas, Gobbi, etc. cannot. If he cannot— given adequate rehearsal time— get *any* singer to act, relax and look as if he belongs on a stage, he has no place in the opera house. There is a myth, less propagated today, that acting in opera is different from acting in a play. Though opinions vary widely about performances, ultimately there is only good acting and bad acting. Wagner often demands long stretches of immobility until the next lightning flash, and he can be a strain on a singer's leg muscles on modern sets. *Falstaff* demands quicksilver movement much of the time. It is the producer's job to help the singer in every type of opera, as Wagner helped them in his own works at Bayreuth. Did the great musician-producers, Mahler and Toscanini, rank as outstanding producers? One may suspect on the evidence that Mahler certainly did. Producers as such entered opera in the first years of this century, around the time that theatre directors began to emerge. Max Reinhardt was one of the first (see page 262), but it was perhaps Carl Ebert in the 1920s and 1930s (see page 259) who became the first major opera producer. He came from the theatre, and the arguments still rage about recruiting producers, sometimes ones whose knowledge of music is minimal, from the straight theatre. There have been disastrous productions by such recruits, but the opera-goer who wants his favourite art to survive must devoutly hope that the right men of the theatre keep turning to opera. They cannot all be Peter Halls —Hall is a great director who is also exceptionally musical— but, given enough love and practice, and a reasonable ear, their expertise must always be welcome.

RÉPÉTITEUR. A key member of the staff of an opera house whose job it is to coach singers in their roles. He may find himself conducting off-stage bands, choruses, etc. but it is the coaching that counts most. The word is the French for a 'rehearser'. In Italy, he is *maestro collaboratore*; in Germany, the *solo repetiteur*. Many notable conductors have started in this honourable post.

SCENA. A dramatic operatic solo, not so formal or lyrical as an ordinary aria. The classic example is Leonore's 'Abscheulicher' in *Fidelio*. The word comes from the Greek for 'stage'.

SINGSPIEL. This German form—

it means 'song-play'— was not unlike ballad opera and *opéra comique*, being normally funny and always having spoken dialogue. The genre was named towards the end of the 17th century. Only in its transfigured form is it remembered: Mozart's *Die Entführung* and, especially, *Die Zauberflöte*, and Beethoven's *Fidelio*.

SOUBRETTE. This French word means 'cunning', and in opera refers to servant girls such as Susanna and Despina, also to an amusing light soprano role such as Adele in *Die Fledermaus*. Most soubrettes are pretty but inclined to archness unless strictly supervised.

SOPRANO. The highest female voice. The many sub-divisions may be found in The *Concise Oxford Dictionary of Opera* and elsewhere: for reasons of space, only the Italian ones (those most frequently used in reviews) are given. They are: soprano drammatico/Tosca; soprano lirico/Mimi; soprano lirico spinto/Desdemona; soprano leggiero/Norina in *Don Pasquale*. 'Spinto' means 'urged on' or 'pushed', 'leggierto' means 'light' or 'lightly'.

SPRECHGESANG. This 'speech-song' was originated by Schoenberg, and also used by Berg. The singer emits the note without sustaining it, a mixture of speech and song not to be confused with *parlando* (above).

STAGE DESIGN. If the average theatregoer is ten to twenty years behind current theatre designs, operagoers are mostly twenty to fifty years behind. Not that changing styles are automatically right, however brilliantly they are executed. There is no reason to abandon realism in a *verismo* production, and audiences rightly wax enthusiastic over Julia Trevelyan Oman's *La Bohème* sets for Covent Garden (1974). But it must be recognized that *La Bohème* or *Tosca* or *Cavalleria Rusticana* can be done brilliantly with next to no scenery, if the conception is right. What matters is integrity and theatrical know-how; ultra reactionaries and revolutionaries please note...

Before opera's invention in Florence in the 1590s, Renaissance Italy had already seen the birth of changeable perspective scenery (at Vicenza in 1584), and, probably, wings —changeable painted sidepieces—by 1589. And the masques and other entertainments in Italy and elsewhere were often spectacular. Opera does not seem to have been so elaborate until performances in Cardinal Barberini's Roman palace in the 1630s. However, Venice, where the first public opera house opened in 1637, soon led the world in stage spectacle, which has never been excelled since. The diarist John Evelyn's reactions (in Ascension week, 1645) were typical:

'... with variety of scenes painted and contrived with no less art of perspective, and machines for flying in the air, and other wonderful notions ... it is one of the most magnificent and expensive diversions the wit of man can invent.'

The shape of the Italian opera house dominated Europe (until the 20th century), and La Scala (built 1778) was a particular magnet for designers. Pietro Gonzaga even managed to combat poor lighting and a lit auditorium, by brilliant use of colour, and light and shade, to such an extent that he 'brought the sun on to the stage'. Old prints recall the glories of sumptuously pictorial scenery in the 19th century. Rossini and Bellini loved Alessandro Sanquirico's designs, Verdi loved Carlo Ferrario's. Their sets were moved, like their predecessors, sideways in grooves: flying sets from 'towers' did not occur at La Scala until the 1920s.

While the French had gloried in spectacle, German design, when not borrowing from abroad, was notably poor in the 19th century, even Wagner being unable to escape from conventional pictorial realism which did less than justice to his vision. It was that vision which inspired Ellen Terry's son, Gordon Craig, and, particularly, the Swiss, Adolphe Appia (1862–1928), to suggest a symbolic approach, with a minimum of scenery and maximum use of lighting. He was not the first to use actual shadows on the stage, achieved by lighting a three-dimensional set, but he was the first to produce a theory of lighting. In the second of his key books, *La Mise-en-Scène du Drame Wagnérien* (1895), and in *Die Musik und die Inszenierung* (1899), he demanded a theatre not of appearances but of atmosphere, saying that in *Siegfried* 'we need not try to represent a forest; what we must give the spectator is man in the atmosphere of a forest'. The culmination of this was to come at Bayreuth in the 1950s under Wieland and Wolfgang Wagner; but earlier German designers in Germany and Austria had been influenced by Appia and Craig enough to become adventurous, including Alfred Roller in Vienna and Caspar Neher in several German houses. Inevitably, there had been hideous mistakes—especially in German costuming—but Appia's revolution has achieved what really matters: the promotion of Wagner in particular and opera in general.

It would be impossible in a short space to begin to do justice to the designers of today, even more of the last fifty years. Many will be found in the section *Opera round the World* in the various theatre entries. Though American production standards were lower than Europe's between the two world wars, native and refugee designers raised the visual side of opera to occasional notable heights. Donald Oenslager, a disciple of Appia and the American giant, Robert Edmond Jones, designed for the Met as well as Broadway; as did Harry Horner, and Rolf Gérard and Eugen Berman, are other famous names. In Europe, one of the busiest designers after 1945 has been Georges Wakhevitch, who appeals to connoisseur and the public alike. Other leading figures include Josef Svoboda, Gunther Schneider-Siemssen; and Jürgen Rose, and, in the wake of the Wagner brothers reforms, Helmut Jürgens, Ita Maximova, Hein Heckroth, Teo Otto, etc. British designers unmentioned elsewhere include Leslie Hurry, John Piper, Malcolm Pride and Peter Rice.

Because their work lasts longer than producers', and is more obviously apparent to all, it is inevitable that it should provoke such fierce reactions from informed and uninformed alike. In the last resort, opera as music drama— all opera of worth is that— —needs a conductor, orchestra, singers and a producer. The scenery is not essential in the same way, for opera without it can still work. But it would be foolish to deny the enchanted delight, as well as the vital artistic ingredient it brings. Fortunately, the challenges of opera are so great that plenty of designers are always ready to try and surmount them.

STAGIONE. The Italian for 'season', the *stagione lirica* being an opera season. However, the word is used more widely. A stagione house—La Scala and also Covent Garden since the 1960s—presents a number of performances, with few if any cast changes. These may or may not be revived in the following season in the same manner, or are sometimes revived in the same season. Other houses, such as Vienna, use the repertoire system, which, except at festival time, rarely results in such integrated performances. On the other hand, the public can attend more different operas. The stagione system at Covent Garden, where the Royal Ballet shares the house, seriously cuts down the number of different operas, particularly distressing for out-of-town visitors. Yet it has helped to make Covent Garden an international house, and the present author is one of the uncountable many who prefer it.

TENOR. The highest male voice usually heard (see also *Counter-tenor*). The many variations of the voice, though not British Bleating Tenor, may be found in the *Concise Oxford Dictionary of Opera*. Ones often encountered in print include the German Heldentenor (heroic tenor).

Interestingly, Radamès, often sung by heroic tenors, is a *tenore* only, while Otello is naturally a *tenore di forza*. Ernesto in *Don Pasquale* is a typical *tenore di grazia* role. As opera-goers rapidly acquire knowledge of the character of different voices, however much they may argue about the abilities of singers, national divisions are more fascinating than vital knowledge. *Men, Women and Tenors* wrote the soprano, Alda, who should have known. But why should tenors be so singled out? They are usually in short supply, and even the outrageous or outrageous-looking ones are cherished if the voice is there. Besides, some of the rudest and funniest stories are about basses, baritones, mezzos and, especially sopranos.

TESSITURA. A most useful term, it indicates the average range of an aria relative to the voice for which it is composed. For instance, Turandot's 'In questa reggia' has a notably high tessitura. It can be used of a singer's voice as well.

TRANSPOSITION. Only those possessing perfect pitch can be sure of when a singer, often but not always an older one, is having an aria transposed down to avoid very high notes, for instance at the verse endings of Manrico's 'Di quella pira' (*Il Trovatore*). Transposing up may also take place.

TRAVESTI. This is the term to describe such breeches-roles as Octavian, Cherubino, Oscar, etc., the male characters being sung by women. It comes from the French for 'to disguise', though newcomers to opera often regard the whole business as an actual travesty. Happily, they usually succumb by degrees to these mainly ravishing roles, if the singers are vocally and physically worthy of them.

VERISMO. The realistic school of Italian opera which began with Mascagni's *Cavalleria Rusticana* (1890). The other *verismo* composers included Leoncavallo, Giordano, Zandonai and, most notably, Puccini. Allowing that realism is a dangerously imprecise word when applied to the theatre and, especially, opera, it is possible to note the 'real', even earthy plots of many *verismo* operas, notably Puccini's *Il Tabarro*. But just how real and how romantic is *La Bohème*? *Verismo* is artistically tinged realism, one of those useful words to be treated warily.

Appendix II

Some Operatic Roles

An Alphabetical List
(*excluding single title roles*)

Abigaille (sop.) *Nabucco*
Adalgisa (sop.) *Norma*
Adele (sop.) *Die Fledermaus*
Adina (sop.) *L'Elisir d'Amore*
Aeneas (bar.) *Dido and Aeneas*
Aeneas (tenor) *Les Troyens*
Agathe (sop.) *Der Freischütz*
Alberich (bass-bar.) *Ring*
Alfio (bar.) *Cavalleria Rusticana*
Alfonso, Don (bass) *Così fan tutte*
Alfred (ten.)—*Die Fledermaus*
Alfredo (ten.) *La Traviata*
Alice Ford (sop.) *Falstaff*
Almaviva (ten.) *Il Barbiere di Siviglia*
Almaviva (bar.) *Le Nozze di Figaro*
Alvaro (ten.) *La Forza del Destino*
Amelia (sop.) *Un Ballo in Maschera*
Amelia (sop.) *Simon Boccanegra*
Amfortas (bar.) *Parsifal*
Amina (sop.) *La Sonnambula*
Amneris (mezzo) *Aida*
Amonasro (bar.) *Aida*
Angelina (con.) *La Cenerentola*
Antonia (sop.) *Les Contes d'Hoffmann*

Ariadne (sop.) *Ariadne auf Naxos*
Arkel (bass) *Pelléas et Mélisande*
Arnold (ten.) *Guillaume Tell*
Azucena (con.) *Il Trovatore*

Bacchus (ten.) *Ariadne auf Naxos*
Banquo (bass) *Macbeth*
Barbarina (sop.) *Le Nozze di Figaro*
Bardolph (ten.) *Falstaff*
Bartolo, Doctor (bass) *Il Barbiere di Siviglia*
Bartolo, Doctor (bass) *Le Nozze di Figaro*
Beckmesser (bar.) *Die Meistersinger*
Belcore (bar.) *L'Elisir d'Amore*
Belmonte (ten.) *Die Entführung aus dem Serail*
Blondchen or Blonde (sop.) *Die Entführung aus dem Serail*
Brangäne (mezzo) *Tristan und Isolde*
Brünnhilde (sop.) *Ring*

Calaf (ten.) *Turandot*
Canio (ten.) *I Pagliacci*
Cassandra (sop.) *Les Troyens*

Cassio (ten.) *Otello*

Cavaradossi (ten.) *Tosca*

Charlotte (sop.) *Werther*

Cherubino (sop.) *Le Nozze di Figaro*

Chrysothemis (sop.) *Elektra*

Cio-Cio-San (sop.) Japanese name of Madama Butterfly

Colline (bass) *La Bohème*

Composer (sop.) *Ariadne auf Naxos*

Constanze (sop.) *Die Entführung aus dem Serail*

Countess (Almaviva) *Le Nozze di Figaro*

Daland (bass) *Der fliegende Holländer*

Dalila (mezzo) *Samson et Dalila*

Dandini (bar.) *La Cenerentola*

Danilo (ten.) *Die Lustige Witwe*

David (ten.) *Die Meistersinger*

Desdemona (sop.) *Otello*

Des Grieux (ten.) *Manon* and *Manon Lescaut*

Despina (sop.) *Così fan tutte*

Dick Johnson (ten.) *La Fanciulla del West*

Dido (sop.) *Dido and Aeneas*

Dido (sop. or mezzo) *Les Troyens*

Di Luna, Count (bar.) *Il Trovatore*

Dimitri (ten.) *Boris Godunov*

Dodon, King (bass) *The Golden Cockerel*

Don Basilio (bass) *Il Barbiere di Siviglia*

Don Basilio (ten.) *Le Nozze di Figaro*

Don Carlos di Bargas (bar.) *La Forza del Destino*

Don José (ten.) *Carmen*

Don Magnifico (bass) *La Cenerentola*

Don Ottavio (ten.) *Don Giovanni*

Donna Anna (sop.) *Don Giovanni*

Donna Elvira (sop.) *Don Giovanni*

Dorabella (mezzo or sop.) *Così fan tutte*

Dositheus (bass) *Khovanshchina*

Duke of Mantua (ten.) *Rigoletto*

Dulcamara (bass) *L'Elisir d'Amore*

Eboli (mezzo) *Don Carlos*

Edgardo (ten.) *Lucia di Lammermoor*

Eisenstein (ten.) *Die Fledermaus*

Eleazar (ten.) *La Juive*

Elisabeth (sop.) *Tannhäuser*

Elisabeth de Valois (sop.) *Don Carlos*

Ellen Orford (sop.) *Peter Grimes*

Elsa (sop.) *Lohengrin*

Elvino (ten.) *La Sonnambula*

Elvira *see* Donna Elvira

Elvira (sop.) *L'Italiana in Algeri*

Elvira (sop.) *I Puritani*

Elvira (sop.) *Ernani*

Enrico (bar.) *Lucia di Lammermoor*

Enzo (ten.) *La Gioconda*

Erda (con.) *Ring*

Ernesto (ten.) *Don Pasquale*

Escamillo (bar.) *Carmen*

Eva (sop.) *Die Meistersinger*

Fafner (bass) *Ring*

Faninal (bar.) *Der Rosen-kavalier*

Fasolt (bass) *Ring*

Fenton (ten.) *Falstaff*

Ferrando (ten.) *Così fan tutte*

Fidès (mezzo) *Le Prophète*

Fiesco (bass) *Simon Bocca-negra*

Figaro (bar.) *Il Barbiere di Siviglia* and *Le Nozze di Figaro*

Fiordiligi (sop.) *Così fan tutte*

Florestan (ten.) *Fidelio*

Ford (bar.) *Falstaff*

Freia (sop.) *Ring*

Frère Laurent (bass) *Roméo et Juliette*

Fricka (sop.) *Ring*

Froh (ten.) *Ring*

Galitsky, Prince (bass) *Prince Igor*

Gennaro (ten.) *Lucrezia Borgia*

Gérard (bar.) *Andrea Chénier*

Germont (bar.) *La Traviata*

Gilda (sop.) *Rigoletto*

Giorgetta (sop.) *Il Tabarro*

Giuletta (sop. or mezzo) *Les Contes d'Hoffmann*

Golaud (bar). *Pelléas et Mélisande*

Gremin, Prince (bass) *Eugene Onegin*

Guglielmo (bar.) *Così fan tutte*

Gunther (bar.) *Ring*

Gurnemanz (bass) *Parsifal*

Gutrune (sop.) *Ring*

Hagen (bass) *Ring*

Hanna Glawari (sop.) *Die Lustige Witwe*

Hans Sachs (bass-bar.) *Die Meistersinger*

Heinrich (bass) *Lohengrin*

Herod (ten.) *Salome*

Herodias (mezzo) *Salome*

Herzeleide (sop.) *Parsifal*

Hunding (bass) *Ring*

Iago (bar.) *Otello*

Ilia (sop.) *Idomeneo*

Isabella (mezz) *L'Italiana in Algeri*

Isolier (mezzo) *Le Comte Ory*

Isolde (sop.) *Tristan und Isolde*

Jacquino (ten.) *Fidelio*

Jenik (ten.) *The Bartered Bride*

Jochanaan (bar.) *Salome*

Juliette (sop.) *Roméo et Juliette*

Kecal (bass) *The Bartered Bride*

Khan Khonchak (bass) *Prince Igor*

Klingsor (bass) *Parsifal*

Klytemnestra (mezzo) *Elektra*

Kundry (sop.) *Parsifal*

Kurnewal (bar.) *Tristan und Isolde*

Laura (sop.) *La Gioconda*

Lauretta (sop.) *Gianni Schicchi*

Leila (sop.) *Les Pêcheurs des Perles*

Lensky (ten.) *Eugene Onegin*

Leonora (sop.) *Il Trovatore*

Leonora (sop.) *La Forza del Destino*

Leonora (mezzo) *La Favorita*

Leonore (sop.) *Fidelio*

Leporello (bass) *Don Giovanni*

Lescaut (bar.) *Manon* and *Manon Lescaut*

Lionel (ten.) *Martha*

Liù (sop.)   *Turandot*

Loge (ten).   *Ring*

Lola (mezzo)   *Cavalleria Rusticana*

Lucia, Mamma (con.)   *Cavalleria Rusticana*

Ludmilla (sop.)   *Russlan and Ludmilla*

Macbeth, Lady (sop.)   *Macbeth*

Macheath (bar.)   *The Beggar's Opera.*

Maddalena (mezzo)   *Rigoletto*

Madeleine de Coligny (sop.)   *Andrea Chénier*

Magdalene (sop.)   *Die Meistersinger*

Magda Sorel (sop.)   *The Consul*

Malatesta (bar). *Don Pasquale*

Mandryka (bar.)   *Arabella*

Manrico (ten.)   *Il Trovatore*

Marcellina (sop.)   *Fidelio*

Marcellina (con.)   *Le Nozze di Figaro*

Marcello (bar.)   *La Bohème*

Marenka (sop.)   *The Bartered Bride*

Marguerite (sop.)   *Le Damnation de Faust, Faust, Mefistofele*

Marie (sop.)   *La Fille du Régiment*

Marie (sop.)   *Wozzeck*

Marina (mezzo)   *Boris Godunov*

Mark, King (bass)   *Tristan und Isolde*

Marschallin (sop.)   *Der Rosenkavalier*

Masetto (bar.)   *Don Giovanni*

Max (ten.)   *Der Freischütz*

Mélisande (sop.)   *Pelléas et Mélisande*

Melitone (bass)   *La Forza del Destino*

Méphistophélès (bass)   *Faust* and *Le Damnation de Faust*

Mercutio (bar.)   *Roméo et Juliette*

Micaela (sop.)   *Carmen*

Michele (bar.)   *Il Tabarro*

Mimi (sop.)   *La Bohème*

Minnie (sop.)   *La Fanciulla del West*

Monostatos (ten.)   *Die Zauberflöte*

Monterone (bass)   *Rigoletto*

Musetta (sop.)   *La Bohème*

Mustafa (bass)   *L'Italiana in Algeri*

Nadir (ten.)   *Les Pêcheurs des Perles*

Nanetta (sop.)   *Falstaff*

Nedda (sop.)   *I Pagliacci*

Nemorino (ten.)   *L'Elisir d' Amore*

Nicklausse (mezzo)   *Les Contes d'Hoffmann*

Norina (sop.)   *Don Pasquale*

Norns, The Three (con., mezzo, sop.)   *Ring*

Octavian (mezzo)   *Der Rosenkavalier*

Olympia (sop.)   *Les Contes d'Hoffmann*

Orest (bar.)   *Elektra*

Orlofsky (con.)   *Die Fledermaus*

Oroveso (bass)   *Norma*

Ortrud (mezzo)   *Lohengrin*

Oscar (sop.)   *Un Ballo in Maschera*

Osmin (bass)   *Die Entführung aus dem Serail*

Padre Guardiano (bass)   *La Forza del Destino*

Pamina (sop.) *Die Zauberflöte*

Papagena (sop.) *Die Zauber-flöte*

Papageno (bar.) *Die Zauber-flöte*

Pedrillo (ten.) *Die Entführung aus dem Serail*

Pelléas (ten.) *Pelléas et Méli-sande*

Philip II (bass) *Don Carlos*

Pimen (bass) *Boris Godunov*

Pinkerton (ten.) *Madame Butterfly*

Pistol (bass) *Falstaff*

Pizarro (bar.) *Fidelio*

Pogner (bass) *Die Meister-singer*

Pollione (ten.) *Norma*

Preziosilla (mezzo) *La Forza del Destino*

Queen of the Night (sop.) *Die Zauberflöte*

Queen of Shemakhan (sop.) *The Golden Cockerel*

Quickly, Mistress (mezzo) *Falstaff*

Radamès (ten.) *Aida*

Ramfis (bass) *Aida*

Rance, Jack (bar.) *La Fanciulla del West*

Renato (bar.) *Un Ballo in Maschera*

Rezia (sop.) *Oberon*

Rhinemaidens (sop., sop., mezzo) *Ring*

Rocco (bass) *Fidelio*

Rodolfo (ten.) *La Bohème*

Rodrigo (bar.) *Don Carlos*

Roméo (ten.) *Roméo et Juliette*

Rosalinde (sop.) *Die Fleder-maus*

Rosina (mezzo) *Il Barbiere di Siviglia*

Russian (bar.) *Russlan and Ludmilla*

Sachs, Hans *See* Hans Sachs

Samson (ten.) *Samson et Dalila*

Santuzza (sop.) *Cavalleria Rusticana*

Sarastro (bass) *Die Zauber-flöte*

Scarpia (bar.) *Tosca*

Selika (sop.) *L'Africaine*

Senta (sop.) *Der fliegende Holländer*

Sharpless (bar.) *Madama Butterfly*

Shuisky (ten.) *Boris Godunov*

Sieglinde (sop.) *Ring*

Siegmund (ten.) *Ring*

Silva (bass) *Ernani*

Silvio (bar.) *I Pagliacci*

Sophie (sop.) *Der Rosenkava-lier*

Sparafucile (bass) *Rigoletto*

Spoletta (ten.) *Tosca*

Susanna (sop.) *Le Nozze di Figaro*

Suzel (sop.) *L'Amico Fritz*

Suzuki (mezzo) *Madama Butterfly*

Tamino (ten.) *Die Zauberflöte*

Tatiana (sop.) *Eugene Onegin*

Telramund (bar.) *Lohengrin*

Timur (bass) *Turandot*

Tonio (bar.) *I Pagliacci*

Tristan (ten.) *Tristan und Isolde*

Turiddu (ten.) *Cavalleria Rusticana*

Ulrica (mezzo) *Un Ballo in Maschera*

Valentine (bar.)   *Faust*

Valentine (sop.)   *Les Huguenots*

Valzacchi (ten.)   *Der Rosenkavalier*

Varlaam (bass)   *Boris Godunov*

Vasco da Gama (ten.)   *L'
Africaine*

Vasek (ten.)   *The Bartered Bride*

Venus (sop.)   *Tannhäuser*

Viclinda (sop.)   *I Lombardi*

Violetta (sop.)   *La   Traviata*

Walther von Stolzing (ten.)
Die Meistersinger

Waltraute (mezzo)   *Ring*

Wanderer, The (Wotan) (bass-
bar.)   *Ring*

Wolfram (bar.)   *Tannhäuser*

Wotan (bass-bar.)   *Ring*

Zaccaria (bass)   *Nabucco*

Zdenka (sop.)   *Arabella*

Zerbinetta (sop.)   *Ariadne auf
Naxos*

Zerlina (sop.)   *Don Giovanni*

Appendix III

Bibliography

The following have proved useful or invaluable during the writing of this book. *Opera* magazine and the *Concise Oxford Dictionary of Opera* have already been acknowledged at the start of the book.

Arundell, Dennis: *The Story of Sadler's Wells* (Hamish Hamilton, 1965)

Beecham, Sir Thomas: *A Mingled Chime* (Hutchinson, 1944)

Bing, Rudolf: *5,000 Nights at the Opera* (Hamish Hamilton, 1972)

Blom, Eric: *Mozart* (Dent, 1935)

Cairns, David (Editor): *The Memoirs of Hector Berlioz* (Gollancz, 1969)

Carner, Mosco: *Puccini* (Duckworth, 1958)

Hope-Wallace, Philip: *A Picture History of Opera* (Hulton, 1959)

Hughes, Spike: *Glyndebourne* (Methuen, 1965)

Greenfield, Edward: *Puccini: Keeper of the Seal* (Arrow Books, 1957)

Jacobs, Arthur: *A New Dictionary of Music* (Penguin, 1970)

Jacobs, Arthur and Stanley Sadie: *The Opera Guide* (Hamish Hamilton, 1964)

Jelinek, George: *Callas: Portrait of a Prima Donna* (Anthony Gibbs and Phillips, 1961)

Kobbé, Gustave (Edited and revised by Lord Harewood): *Kobbé's Complete Opera Guide* (Putnam, 1958)

Mann, William: *Richard Strauss: A Critical Study of the Operas* (Oxford, 1964)

Newman, Ernest: *The Life of Richard Wagner*, Vols, I–IV (London, 1933–47)

Rosenthal, Harold: *Two Centuries of Opera at Covent Garden* (Putnam, 1958)

Rosenthal, Harold (Editor): *The Mapleson Memoirs* (Putnam, 1966)

Steane, J. B.: *The Grand Tradition* (Duckworth, 1974).

Walker, Frank: *The Man Verdi* (Dent, 1962)

Weinstock, Herbert: *Donizetti* (Methuen, 1964)

Westerman, Gerhart von (Editor: Harold Rosenthal): *Opera Guide* (Thames and Hudson, 1964)

Williams, Stephen: *Come to the Opera* (Hutchinson, 1948).

Selective Index

I People

Abbado, Claudio, 221, 298, 300
Abbott, Emma, 117
Ackermann, Otto, 221
Acté, Aino, 117, 279
Adam, Adolphe, 41
Adam, Theo, 117, 256
Adler, Kurt, 221, 312, 313
Adler, Peter, 221
Albanese, Licia, 117
Albani, Emma, 117
Albert, Eugen d', 41
Alboni, Mariette, 118
Alda, Frances, 118, 339
Alexander, Carlos, 253
Alexander, John, 117
Alfano, Franco, 41
Allen, Thomas, 118
Allin, Norman, 118, 285
Althouse, Paul, 118
Alva, Luigi, 118, 119
Alvary, Max, 119
Anders, Peter, 119
Anderson, Marian, 119
Andrésen, Ivar, 119
Appia, Adolphe, 337, 338
Arié, Raphael, 119
Arlen, Stephen, 292
Armstrong, Richard, 294
Armstrong, Sheila, 119
Arnoldson, Sigrid, 119
Arroyo, Martino, 119, 317
Artôt, Désirée, 119, 120
Arundell, Dennis, 258, 292
Ashbrook, William, 31
Auber, Daniel, 41
Auden, W. H., 269
Austin, Frederick, 120
Austral, Florence, 120

Baccaloni, Salvatore, 120, 320
Bacquier, Gabriel, 120
Bahr-Mildenburg, Anna, 120
Bailey, Norman, 120
Bainbridge, Elizabeth, 121
Baker, Janet, 24, 121, 255, 325
Baklanov, George, 121
Balfe, Michael, 42
Balkwill, Bryan, 292, 294
Balling, Michael, 221
Bampton, Rose, 121
Barber, Samuel, 42, 266
Barbieri, Fedora, 121, 250

Barbieri-Nini, Marianna, 121
Barbirolli, John, 221, 222, 286
Barrientos, Maria, 121, 122
Barsova, Valerija, 122
Barstow, Josephine, 122
Bartók, Béla, 42
Bassi, Amedeo, 122
Bassi, Luigi, 122
Bastianini, Ettore, 122
Battistini, Mattia, 122
Baylis, Lilian, 291
Beecham, Thomas, 117, 141, 153, 175,
    185, 222, 223, 287, 290, 301, 310
Beethoven, Ludwig van, 17, 18, 42,
    255, 256
Begg, Heather, 122
Behrens, Hildegard, 116, 282
Béjart, Maurice, 276
Belcourt, Emile, 122
Bellazza, Vincenzo, 223
Bellini, Vincenzo, 20, 21, 42, 43, 299
Bellinicioni, Gemma, 123
Belloc, Teresa, 123
Bender, Paul, 123
Benedict, Julius, 43
Benelli, Ugo, 123
Benjamin, Arthur, 43
Bennett, Richard Rodney, 43
Benucci, Francesco, 123
Berg, Alban, 37, 38, 43, 336
Berganza, Teresa, 123, 315
Berger, Erna, 123
Berglund, Joel, 123
Bergonzi, Carlo, 123, 124, 324
Berkeley, Lennox, 43, 270, 315
Berlioz, Hector, 23, 24, 43, 44, 269
Berman, Eugen, 338
Bernstein, Leonard, 44, 223, 224, 264
Besanzoni, Gabriella, 124
Besch, Anthony, 249, 254, 255, 258
Betz, Franz, 124
Billington, Elizabeth, 124
Bilt, Peter van der, 255
Bing, Rudolf, 311, 318, 320
Bishop, Henry, 44, 45
Bizet, Georges, 27–29, 45
Bjoner, Ingrid, 256
Björling, Jussi, 124, 305, 308
Björling, Sigurd, 124
Blacher, Boris, 45
Blachut, Beno, 125
Blackham, Joyce, 125

II Operas

This is a selective list, being basically an indication of where the main entry to the opera occurs, plus any extensive references to it elsewhere

362   *Index*

364 *Index*